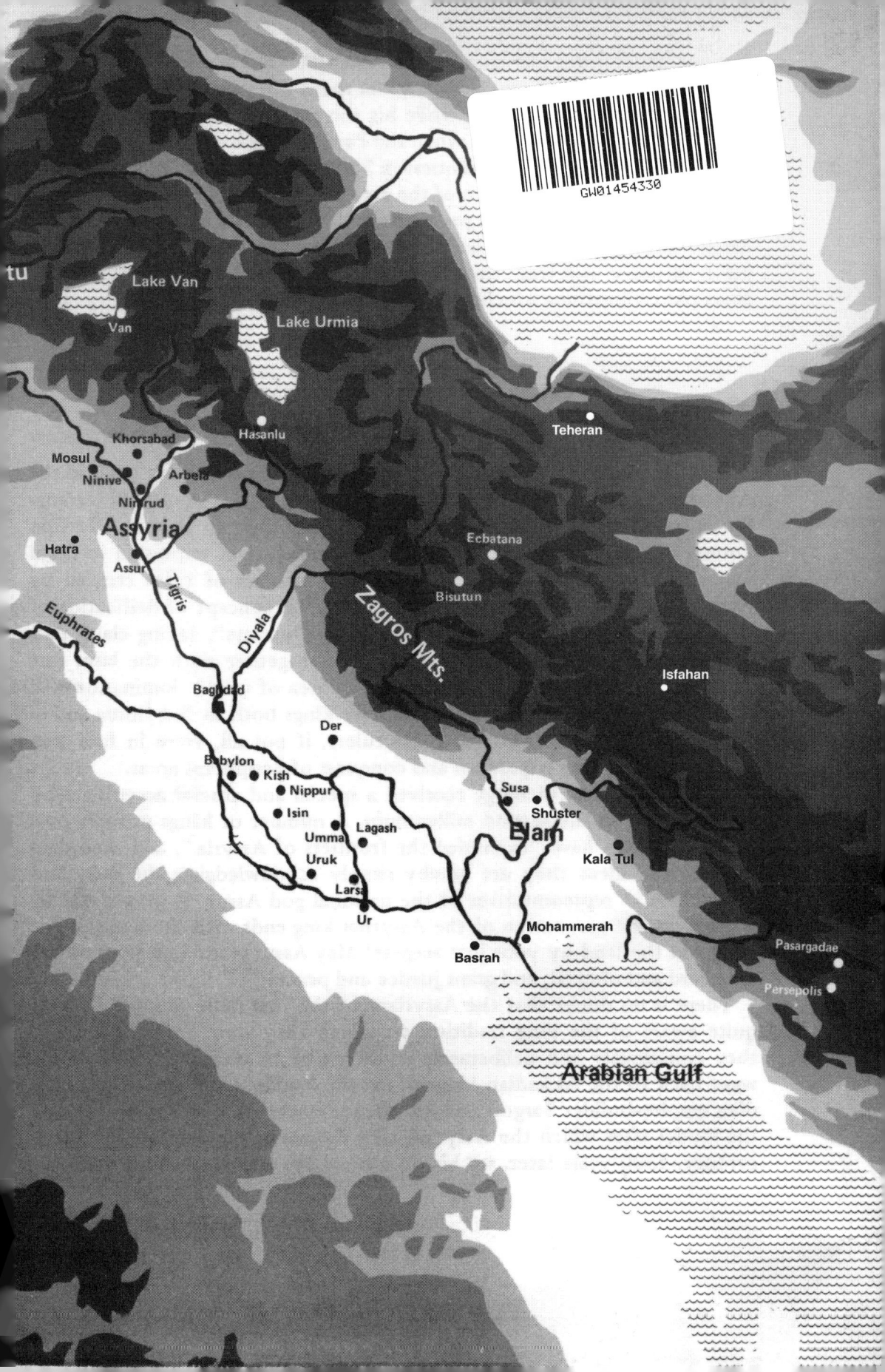

tu

Lake Van

Van

Lake Urmia

Teheran

Hasanlu

Khorsabad

Mosul

Ninive   Arbela

Nimrud

Assyria

Hatra

Assur

Ecbatana

Tigris

Diyala

Zagros Mts.

Bisutun

Euphrates

Isfahan

Baghdad

Der

Babylon   Kish

Nippur

Isin

Susa

Umma   Lagash

Elam

Uruk

Shuster

Larsa

Kala Tul

Ur

Mohammerah

Pasargadae

Basrah

Persepolis

Arabian Gulf

THE CONQUEST OF ASSYRIA

THE CONQUEST
OF ASSYRIA

Excavations in an antique land

1840–1860

Mogens Trolle Larsen

ROUTLEDGE

London and New York

First published 1994
by Gyldendalske Boghandel
Nordisk Forlag A.S. Copenhagen

English edition first published 1996
by Routledge
11 New Fetter Lane, London EC4P 4EE

Simultaneously published in the USA and Canada
by Routledge
29 West 35th Street, New York, NY 10001

Typeset in Garamond by
Florencetype Ltd, Stoodleigh, Devon

Printed and bound in Great Britain by
Butler and Tanner Ltd, London and Frome

British Library Cataloguing in Publication Data
A catalogue record for this book is available from the British Library

Library of Congress Cataloguing in Publication Data
Larsen, Mogens Trolle.
[Sunkne paladser. English]
The conquest of Assyria: excavations in an antique land,
1840–1860 / Mogens Trolle Larsen
Includes bibliographical references and index.
1. Excavations (Archaeology) – Middle East.   2. Assyriologists.
3. Middle East – Antiquities.   I. Title.
DS70L35 1996
939.4–dc20 96–3606

ISBN 0–415–14356–X

CONTENTS

———.•.———

— Contents —

PART II: THE EXCAVATION OF SENNACHERIB'S PALACE

PART III: VICTOR PLACE AND HORMUZD RASSAM

FIGURES

——— •◆• ———

PLATES

——— •◆• ———

The colour plate section appears between pages 98–99

PREFACE AND
ACKNOWLEDGEMENTS

—— •◆• ——

Assyriologists, scholars who have chosen to dedicate their lives to the study of ancient Mesopotamia, are routinely met with a degree of polite scepticism and wonder, feelings which are an expression of the distance felt between our world and ancient Mesopotamia.

The spoken or unspoken question that seems unavoidable now would not have been seen as obvious in the nineteenth century, for the distance separating us from ancient Assyria has in fact expanded since the 1840s and 1850s, the time-frame of this book – paradoxically, since during the same span of time our knowledge about the ancient world has grown explosively. Before the mid-nineteenth century the Mesopotamian past was not only distant and exotic, it was shrouded in myth and legend, and no concrete evidence for its existence could be found in our museums. Yet, the names of kings like Sennacherib and Tiglath-pileser, or of cities such as Babylon and Nineveh, formed part of the intellectual baggage of educated Europeans – although they are now hardly meaningful even to most academics. The reason for their former prominence was their importance in the world of the Old Testament, a book that dominated the world of nineteenth-century Europe. Accordingly, when these cities and kings suddenly became concrete reality, as palaces filled with treasures, reliefs and texts emerged from the mounds of Assyria, it is understandable that public interest was enormous.

Since then, the disciplines of Near Eastern Archaeology and Assyriology which developed on the basis of the continuous stream of new evidence from the ancient cultures in Mesopotamia have to a large extent moved away from their ties to Bible studies. The attempt now is to study and understand Assyria and Babylonia on their own terms, as cultural and historical complexes of interest in their own right, and which should not be seen primarily as providers of comparative and illustrative material for the study of the Bible. This disciplinary emancipation, necessary and obvious though it has been, to some extent removed the broad basis of public interest which these pursuits had enjoyed, and has perhaps lessened their possibilities for establishing a connection with contemporary interests and problems. The pioneers, with whom this book is concerned, had an easier point of departure than we do when they endeavoured to interest their own time in their conclusions concerning the character and meaning of the ancient cultures, and their excitement and absorption in these matters animate and energise their descriptions.

One of the consequences of this feeling of obvious relevance for the new discoveries in a European religious and intellectual framework was the appropriation of the ancient world to form the basis for the history of the West. Here was the 'Cradle of Civilisation', civilisation being of course Europe, and in this way these academic disciplines to some extent may be seen as the 'stepchildren of imperialism' (Stolper 1992: 20)

What gave the Mesopotamian discoveries their peculiar interest was the feeling that the archaeologists were hunting for the very beginning of human history, as perceived in the light of the sacred writings. At the same time, it was stressed repeatedly that the ancient remains meant nothing to the local Arabs, a view formulated, for example, by Alfred William Hunt in the prize poem 'Nineveh', which was recited in the Sheldonian Theatre at Oxford on 3 July 1851:

> . . . oft, when winds in fitful cadence moan
> And pale stars whirl around yon gloomy cone,
> The nomad hears imprisoned spirits' wail
> Inform the sighings of the midnight gale;
> And thinks of demon powers by Allah's doom
> For ever pent within that caverned tomb.
> Or when Orion flames along the sky,
> 'Tis Nimrod's restless shade, careering high
> O'er the weird realms his earthly sceptre swayed
> In star-embroidered robe and glittering belt arrayed.
> And wild fantastic tales of earth's first prime
> Of patriarch virtues and Titanic crime
> Told by the embers' glow of reddening light
> Beguile the starlit watches of the night –
> But aught beyond tradition's oral tale
> Or gleams of truth, like wavering sunlights pale,
> The Arab knows not, though around him rise
> The sepulchres of earth's first monarchies;
> Nor ever dreams, his camel's tinkling tread
> Falls on some silent City of the Dead!
> For know – that circle o'er whose desert ring
> Those shapeless mounds their darkening shadows fling,
> That desolation – far as eye can see
> Forlorn and lifeless – once was NINEVEH.

These cities of the dead had lain hidden in the sand through millennia, unheeded by those who passed them by or pitched their tents on top of them, but

> At last, 'twas thus the Moslem version ran,
> A bright-eyed stranger came from Frangistan:
> Master of mightiest spells – and vaster far

Than wizard aisles of pillared Chilminar
Cities arose – enchanted hall revealed
Treasures untold by primal kings concealed:
It is no dream, though such as dreams alone
Could ever paint – but all is very stone
Calm all and grey. – Before the entranced eyes
The world's primeval palaces arise.

(Hunt 1851)

The magical moment, when the European finally came to the Mesopotamian desert in search of his cultural and historical roots, was described in slightly different words by another poet, Dante Gabriel Rossetti, in a poem written about the great Assyrian bull which was installed in the British Museum in 1852. Here he speculated:

What vows, what rites, what prayers preferr'd,
What songs has the strange image heard?
In what blind vigil stood interr'd
For ages, till an English word
    Broke silence first at Nineveh?

(Rossetti 1974: 14–18)

This book is about the 'bright-eyed stranger from Frangistan' who spoke the English word which broke the Oriental silence, Austen Henry Layard, as well as about the other pioneers, Paolo Emilio Botta, Hormuzd Rassam, Henry Rawlinson and Victor Place, who in Assyria found what was seen as part of Europe's historical heritage, despite its perceived alien and primitive art.

The lives and activities of these men present to us a picture of Europe and the Middle East in the nineteenth century. The basis for their understanding and interpretation of what they unearthed was of course rooted in their time, its perceptions and prejudices. Yet, their discoveries also became part of that great intellectual revolution that swept through Europe in the second half of the nineteenth century, when scientific and scholarly discoveries changed the traditional inherited world view and laid the foundations for our own understanding of the world.

My work on this project began in another world that has now disappeared, the stimulating intellectual community at the Center for Research in the Humanities at Copenhagen University. The debt I owe to my friends and colleagues there is too great to specify, but I want to thank Michael Harbsmeier for his constant, learned and ironic friendship, and Lotte Hedeager for her enthusiasm and support. A year at the Getty Center for the History of Art and the Humanities in Santa Monica provided peace and intellectual stimulation at a time when I most needed it, and in the final writing phase Kirsten Hastrup gave her loving, shrewd and well-informed support.

Over the years I have received help and advice from many colleagues around the world, and I would like to single out Julian Reade and Irving Finkel at the British Museum, Jean Bottéro, Matthew Stolper and Mario Liverani. The staff at my home institute, The Carsten Niebuhr Institute in Copenhagen, have helped and suffered my long absences in good spirit, and the librarian Anne Zeeberg has given me invaluable assistance.

The many weeks I spent in the British Library, the Bodleian, the Bibliothèque Nationale and other archives and libraries have been generously supported by the Carlsberg Foundation, without whose constant aid it would hardly have been possible for me to write this book.

For permission to reproduce figures and illustrations I gratefully acknowledge the following: Annie Searight for colour ill. III; the Louvre for the cover illustration (in a private collection), ill. 2.1 and colour ill. IV; the Trustees of the National Portrait Gallery for ills. 5.1, 8.1, 17.2 and 37.4; Irving Finkel for 37.2; the Trustees of the British Museum for colour ills. I, V and VII; the Trustees of the Victoria & Albert Museum for colour ill. II.

PART I

THE FIRST EXPLORERS

CHAPTER ONE

THE MOUNDS OF NINEVEH

On a sweltering day in June 1842 two riders arrived at the gates of Mosul, a provincial town in the Ottoman empire. They came from Baghdad in the south and had taken the customary road that led them through the fertile country east of the Tigris; they reached Mosul itself by crossing a rickety bridge of boats which connected the town on the western bank with the villages across the Tigris. One of the men was a Turkish post-rider, a 'tatar', who was on his way to Constantinople more than 2,000 km away with official imperial mail. The other was a young man dressed as a Bakhtiyari, a tribe that lived in Khuzistan, the mountainous south-western corner of Iran. A more observant eye would soon decide that he was a European, however, and indeed, after having parted from his travel companion, who entered the local Pasha's palace on the river, he went straight to the British Vice-Consulate where he was received as an old friend. He was the twenty-five-year-old British adventurer Austen Henry Layard.

The same day he was introduced to the new French consul in Mosul, the forty-year-old Paul Émile Botta and the meeting between these two men had a very special significance, for it may be said to mark the beginning of the archaeological exploration of ancient Mesopotamia. Botta and Layard were destined to become the discoverers of ancient Assyria.

Mosul was a somewhat unlikely place to meet. Like most of the Near Eastern towns of the time it was a sleepy and shabby place, and in spite of a glorious past it was now reduced to rubble and decay after decades of neglect and misrule, with large parts of the town in ruins (see Figure 1.1). It was the seat of a Pasha, or provincial governor, appointed by the Turkish government at Constantinople, and he ruled over a mixed population of Muslim and Christian Arabs and the Kurds in the mountains. A contemporary traveller described the town in the following words:

> Mosul is an ill-constructed mud-built town, rising above the banks of the Tigris, and backed by low hills; in the centre is a tall brown ugly minaret, very much out of the perpendicular; the interior of some of the houses is faced with a translucent stone, called Mosul marble. ... Part of the old Saracen walls still remain: they are very massive ... the ground between the

Figure 1.1 The decrepit centre of Mosul, seen from the ruins of Nineveh on the eastern bank of the Tigris. Engraving by E. Flandin, the artist who worked with Botta at Khorsabad. (From Flandin 1853–76: Plate 30)

walls and town is occupied by stagnant pools, ruins and dead bodies of camels and cattle, which is enough to breed a pestilence; the bazaars are mean and dirty.

(Mitford 1884: I, 280)

Not a nice place to spend the summer, or for that matter any other time of the year. The summers here are marked by a heat that quickly becomes unbearable and which scorches the landscape so that all one sees is a bone-dry, brown steppe; the winters, on the other hand, can be very cold, and violent rainstorms turn all roads and streets into slippery, muddy quagmires. Only the brief spring season turns this land into a paradise, where shoulder-high forests of flowers explode in incomparable colours, while clouds of butterflies slowly glide over the fields.

One hundred and fifty years ago most of the Near East was under Turkish control. The countries were governed from Constantinople where the Sultan, the 'Sublime Porte', sat as the sovereign of a realm which was in rapid decay. It was the 'Sick Man of Europe', and the great powers – England, France and Russia – were already in conflict over which attitude to adopt towards the tottering Ottoman Empire. The Russian Czar saw his interest in the collapse of the Turkish state so that he could divide the remains with England, whereas the British government had a somewhat unclear policy, which, however, tended to support the authority of the Sultan and his attempts to keep the vast empire intact.

Not many Europeans found their way to Mosul. A couple of British merchants regularly stayed here trying to conduct some trade in weapons or cloth, knives and scissors. There was an English Vice-Consul here, a local Christian Arab called Christian Rassam who was married to an English lady, Matilda Badger Rassam; her brother was a missionary who had lived in the town earlier and who occasionally passed through. One might also meet a somewhat eccentric English doctor and geologist, Ainsworth, who had settled here after having taken part in a naval exploration of the river Euphrates a few years before (Ainsworth 1888; Chesney 1850). He had been sent out on a new assignment by the Royal Geographical Society and the Society for the Promotion of Christian Knowledge. There were two distinct groups of missionaries: American Presbyterians and a group of Italian Dominican monks led from Baghdad by an intense man called Valerga. These last kept apart from the other Europeans, and especially from the British, who were regarded by them as dangerous heretics (Fletcher 1850). What led Botta and Layard to this God-forsaken place?

Their meeting was accidental, neither of them knew the other before they met in Mosul, but it turned out they had common interests. Layard was on his way to Constantinople carrying official British mail, but since his companion had business to conduct with the Pasha they had to stay in the town a few days. This gave Layard the opportunity to meet Botta, who was the recently appointed French consul at Mosul.

They were not really interested in Mosul but looked with fascination on the mounds that were located across the river on the eastern bank of the Tigris. A series of enormous ramparts or walls encircle a rectangular area of some kilometres' length and breadth, and in this enclosure lay a couple of large mounds.

Local people called the whole area 'Nuniya', and it was believed to be the location of the ancient Assyrian capital city of Nineveh. Today this name probably means little to most people, but in the nineteenth century it would resonate in the mind of any reasonably educated European, who would know the stories about this city from the Old Testament and from a series of legends told by classical authors. Nineveh had been the centre of one of the largest and most important empires in the ancient world, one whose power according to tradition had covered the entire Near East, including Palestine and Egypt. It was also, however, an empire which had left no concrete traces behind at all. Assyria had disappeared, leaving nothing but myths and legends.

Except that there were these vast mounds close to Mosul, which, according to local legend, covered the ruins of the ancient city. This tradition had actually been known by the learned of Europe, those few who had heard of the place, but it had never been information which had been seen as particularly important or interesting.

Layard had already seen the mounds a couple of years previously, when he had been on his way south towards Baghdad, and he had been 'deeply moved by their desolate and solitary grandeur'. In his *Autobiography* he describes this first visit:

The site was covered with grass and flowers, and the enclosure, formed by the long line of mounds which marked the ancient walls of the city, afforded pasture to the flocks of a few poor Arabs who had pitched their black tents within it. There was at that time nothing to indicate the existence of the splendid remains of Assyrian palaces which were covered by the heaps of earth and rubbish. It was believed that the great edifices and monuments which had rendered Nineveh one of the most famous and magnificent cities of the ancient world had perished with her people, and like them had left no wreck behind. But even then, as I wandered over and amongst these vast mounds, I was convinced that they must cover some vestiges of the great capital, and I felt an intense longing to dig into them.

(Layard 1903: 306–7)

He now revisited Nineveh in Botta's company, and he heard with jealous excitement that the Frenchman had been placed in Mosul for the purpose of opening excavations of the ancient city.

The two men wandered about on the great mounds, took measurements and engaged in speculations. What was hiding in the ground under their feet? Was this really the Nineveh mentioned in the Old Testament? There the city appears as the mighty capital of the Assyrians, from which their empire was governed, home to kings like Tiglath-pileser, Shalmaneser, Sennacherib and Esarhaddon. In the Book of Jonah we hear that Nineveh 'even to God' was a large city, covering a distance of three days' journey, and God estimated the population of this metropolis as 'more than twelve times 10,000 people, who are unable to distinguish right from left, and much cattle'.

As the capital of the Assyrians who plagued Judah and Israel, Nineveh was naturally not mentioned in a positive light in the Jewish Bible; the Prophet Nahum sings a glowingly hateful hymn of ecstatic joy over the final destruction of Nineveh:

> Ah! blood-stained city, steeped in deceit,
> full of pillage, never empty of prey!
>   Hark to the crack of the whip,
> the rattle of wheels and stamping of horses,
> bounding chariots, chargers rearing,
>   swords gleaming, flash of spears!
> The dead are past counting, their bodies lie in heaps,
> corpses innumerable, men stumbling over corpses –
>
> (Nahum 3: 1–3)

Many other passages in the Old Testament express the same fathomless hatred of the Assyrians and their enormous capital, for it was from here that the endless campaigns started that eventually crushed Israel and sent the Jews in exile to other provinces in the Assyrian empire. Naturally Assyria, like Babylon, was in the end struck down by God, but only after both countries had inflicted incomprehensible destruction and misery on the Jews and other peoples of the Near East.

Like all reasonably well-educated Europeans, Botta and Layard knew their Bible and the Greek and Roman classics. They were aware that the very first account of the Assyrian ruins was given by the Greek general Xenophon who led 10,000 mercenaries to Babylonia and back in the years 401–400 BCE. His army camped one night on their return journey close by the Tigris on a ruin he calls 'Larissa' – which must be the mound now known as Nimrud, a place that occupies a central role in this book. Xenophon thought that this 'large deserted city' had been built by the Medes, an Iranian people. The following day the army reached another ruin which Xenophon described as 'a large undefended fortification near a city called Mespila'. This name must be a strange version of 'Mosul', and the ruins he described must be the same ones which so occupied Botta and Layard. Xenophon wrote:

> The base of this fortification was made of polished stone in which there were many shells. It was fifty feet broad and fifty feet high. On top of it was built a brick wall fifty feet in breadth and a hundred feet high. The perimeter of the fortification was eighteen miles.
>
> (Xenophon 1979: 162–3)

Xenophon can give this dry, factual description, but he does not even know the name of the site. Yet he was here only two hundred years after the fall of Nineveh, which happened in 612 BCE when a combined force of Medes and Babylonians stormed its walls and destroyed the city; it appears that in the short span of time Nineveh had been forgotten and that, although the ruins themselves could hardly be overlooked, the ancient names of these cities, not to speak of their history, were gone from ordinary memory. That knowledge lived on in the Jewish legends and amongst Greeks who were more learned than Xenophon. Maybe he did not ask carefully, for it is obvious that much later travellers were aware that these ruins were the remains of Nineveh.

A visitor from Europe, the rabbi Benjamin of Tudela, passed by here as early as 1173 and saw Nineveh's ruins – 'now quite decrepit' – and a few more had visited them after him (Pallis 1956). In March 1766, some seventy-five years before Botta and Layard met in Mosul, Carsten Niebuhr had spent a few days here on his way home from the disastrous Danish expedition to Arabia Felix (Hansen 1962; Rasmussen 1990; Niebuhr 1774–8). We know that Botta had read the great account of this journey published by Niebuhr, but it is unclear if Layard had heard of him. Niebuhr gives a map of Mosul (see Figure 1.2) which shows an area he calls Nineveh across the river; he has marked the two large mounds: the smallest to the south is shown as a modern village, which bears the name 'Nuniya', whereas the larger one to the north is called 'Kalla Nuniya', that is, 'the Castle of Nineveh'. Niebuhr says that there was a village located also on this mound and it was called 'Koindsjug'; this is obviously the same name which is now given to the mound as such, 'Kuyunjik', under which it appears in the archaeological literature.

The long lines of fortifications, the vast walls of ancient Nineveh, are not to be found on Niebuhr's map; they run around the entire area and was the only feature noticed by Xenophon, but Niebuhr simply did not see them when he rode through the area on his way to Mosul. He presumably first took them for natural hills, and since he never had an opportunity to measure them carefully he naturally had

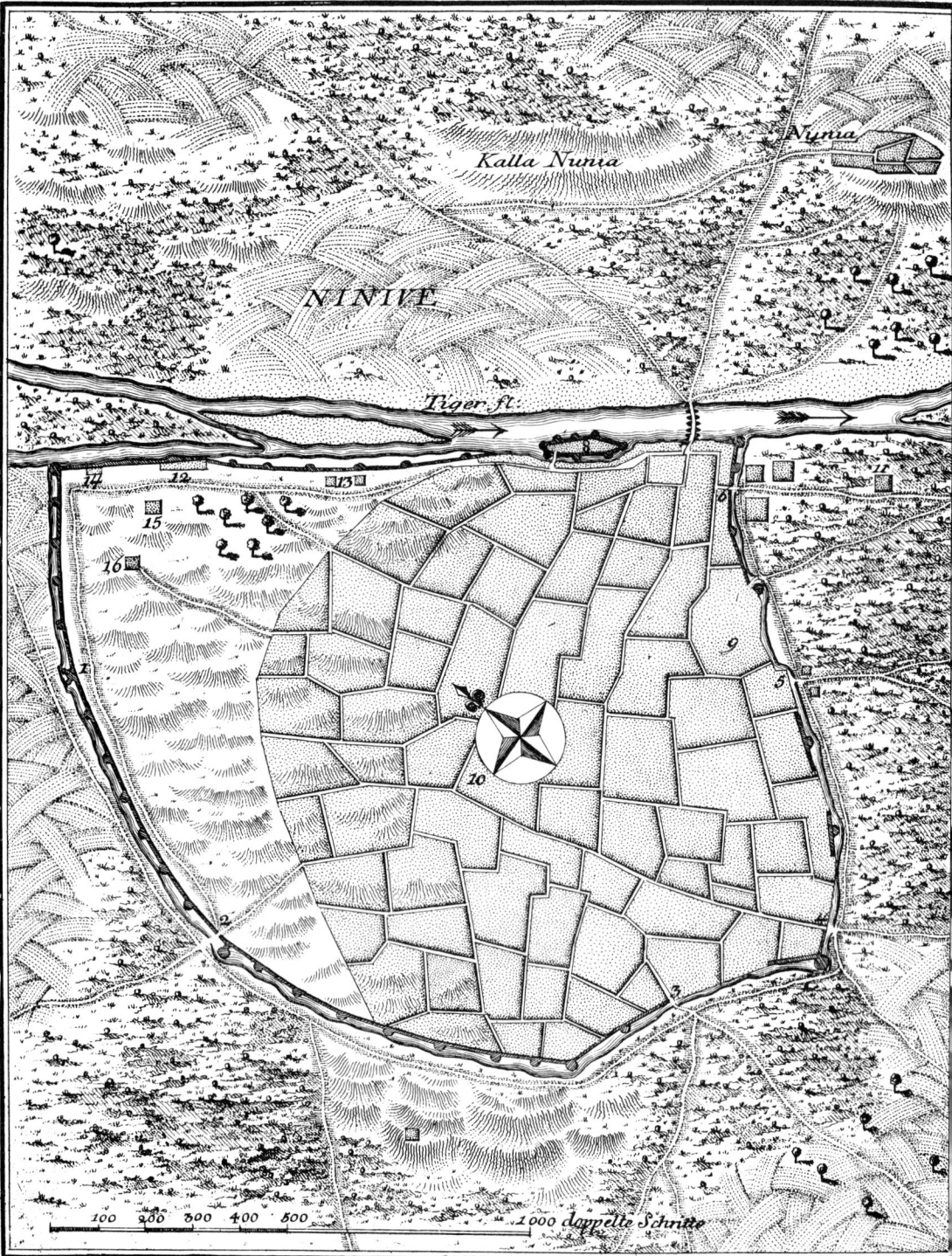

Kalla Nunia

Nunia

NINIVE

Tiger fl.

100 200 300 400 500 1000 *doppelte Schritte*

to ignore them on his map. As a child of the Enlightenment he could not simply invent or guess and draw some lines where they might have been. He does give a special view of the village he calls Nuniya, which he says was built around a mosque that according to Jewish and Muslim tradition contained the grave of the prophet Jonah (Niebuhr 1774–8: II, 360, 392). This is another memory of ancient Nineveh of course, for Jonah – the prophet in the belly of the Whale – was sent by God to Nineveh to warn its inhabitants to abandon their sinful lives.

Niebuhr's drawing and map, although not very correct or aesthetically pleasing, was a major advance, but the real study of the site began with Claudius Rich, who was the 'Resident' in Baghdad, where he represented the interests of the great East India Company in the early nineteenth century (Lloyd 1955). In 1820 he made careful measurements of the whole of Nineveh and produced a remarkably accurate map in the report which was published in 1836, after his death. Here we find both the major mounds and the fortifications, walls which surround an enormous area and which are easily traceable in the landscape. We find the two mounds now called Kuyunjik and Nebbi Yunus, that is, the Arabic name for the southern mound, which means 'the Prophet Jonah'. Rich recounts that he was told that local people had, a few years earlier, found 'an immense bas-relief, representing men and animals, covering a grey stone of the height of two men'. He also says that 'all the town of Mosul went out to see it, and in a few days it was cut up or broken to pieces'. On Nebbi Yunus he saw large blocks of stone with inscriptions in some of the houses, some of them apparently still in their original place.

> One of these, a piece of a slab of alabaster with cuneiform writing on it, was located in the kitchen of a miserable house, and it seemed to be part of the wall in a small passage which is said to continue far into the mound. Some people dug into it last year, but since it passed underneath the houses and they were nervous lest they undermine these, they filled it up again with rubbish and only the part of the passage which was completely opened, and which forms part of the kitchen, can now be seen.
>
> (Rich 1836: 39)

Rich spent many years in Baghdad and visited ruins in all of the country that is now Iraq, making measurements and collecting finds. He had already published a booklet containing his measurements of the ruins of Babylon (Rich 1813; Rich 1818). He had managed to put together a small collection of antiquities from the country, and after his death this was sold to the British Museum by his widow. Here the antiques were displayed in a glass case as one of the extremely few concrete testimonials to the existence of the ancient cultures in Assyria and Babylonia. Layard had seen the collection in the museum, and we know that the publication of Rich's book had played a role in the decision taken by the French authorities to send Botta to Mosul in order to excavate Nineveh.

Figure 1.2 The map of Mosul and Nineveh made by Carsten Niebuhr in March 1766. The city had shrunk within its medieval walls, and across the river, linked with a fragile bridge of boats, is the area of ancient Nineveh with the two mounds. (From Rasmussen 1990: 284)

So, a little was known about ancient Assyria, but the glass case in the British Museum could not prepare anyone for the reality of Mosul. The total desolation of Nineveh, and of the other ancient ruins in all of Mesopotamia, had condemned them to silence, even in the already extensive European literature concerned with the ruins of the Near East. There was quite simply nothing to see here, only grass-covered mounds, and no remains which could evoke memories of past greatness. The mighty ruins of Persepolis – the rows of tall pillars, the delicately carved reliefs and inscriptions which were plainly visible – made it possible for visitors to relate directly to the ancient grandeur; the ruins of Palmyra in the Syrian desert had inspired Count Volney to tearful musings about the fate of human labours (Volney 1822); and, of course, the pyramids and the Egyptian temples could be visited and climbed, and there was a centuries-long scholarly tradition which had tried to find a way to understand them, penetrate to the core of their secrets.

At all of these places the past and its glory was tangible, but in Nineveh the visitor needed a very lively imagination in order to conjure up images of splendour and beauty from the silent and oddly anonymous mounds. 'Où sont-ils, ces remparts de Ninive?' asked Volney, repeating a question which had been asked since the time of the Greek and Roman writers (André-Salvini 1994). Layard wandered among grass-covered hills and cornfields surrounded by long rows of collapsed walls, wondering whether they were really the remains of Nineveh; if they were, what then was hidden underground? Here must be the glorious palaces of the Assyrian king and temples to his gods, and perhaps it would be possible to uncover some of all this, finding concrete evidence of a past which had left so few traces that it appeared to belong to the realm of myth rather than of fact.

The task contemplated by Botta and Layard was much more complicated than they could possibly imagine. Field archaeology was in its most tender infancy in Europe, and it is obviously a much simpler proposition to tackle a Bronze Age barrow than starting on a mound which covers the ruins of an entire city. The difference in size alone is staggering: Kuyunjik is about 15 m high and almost a kilometre long, and Nebbi Yunus is not very much smaller. The entire area encircled by the walls of Nineveh is some 2.5 km wide and *c.* 5 km long. Excavating a mound like Kuyunjik in its entirety using adequate recording and digging techniques is a task that would demand centuries for a substantial workforce. Yet they were envisaging a total uncovering of the ancient city.

In southern Italy a kind of excavation had by then been conducted for a very long time at the sites of Pompeii and Herculaneum, and it is probable that Botta and Layard saw their task as comparable to the work carried out there. However, the two Roman cities had been covered by lava and burning ash which had sealed them in a kind of time-warp; excavating them was simply a matter of removing the cover, revealing the ruins underneath. The Assyrian mounds constituted a quite different kind of challenge, for a site like Kuyunjik is the result of the activity of millennia. People had lived here practically forever, and the mound contains the remains of buildings in a complex pattern, situated on top of each other, ruins of villages, towns, temples and palaces, which followed each other during a span of time which in this particular case covers at least 7,000 years. Sometimes individual houses had been knocked down, the walls pushed over so that a new house could

Figure 1.3 Flandin's engraving of the mound Niebuhr called Nunia, and which was later generally referred to as Nebbi Yunus. The mosque with the grave of the prophet Jonah is the prominent feature, and in the distance one can see the walls of Nineveh. (From Flandin, 1853–76, plate 35)

be constructed on the spot; at other times the entire settlement had been destroyed and resettled after a while. The result of all these individual acts and events is the creation of a kind of insane layered cake constructed by a mad pastry chef. But who can see that, walking around on these grassy mounds?

Actually, there were pointers, for some villages could still be found on top of some of the ancient mounds. In a few cases whole cities were still perched on a mound, giving an indication of how they had been accumulated – while at the same time obviously hindering archaeologists from doing their thing. Yet it is reasonable to maintain that Botta and Layard really could not know what a complex and intricate puzzle was hiding under their feet.

Botta had already begun his archaeological task before Layard's arrival and had become aware of the difficulties of his venture, although the first problems he faced were not really of an archaeological nature. He had placed a few workmen on Nebbi Yunus in order to investigate the old stone foundations which, as Rich had seen, regularly appeared underneath modern houses, but he had to give up this work because of violent opposition from both the Pasha and the local religious leaders, who feared that his activities could violate or destroy the sacred mosque with the grave of the prophet Jonah. This religiously motivated opposition was to develop into a real nightmare for both men in the years that followed.

When he started his archaeological activities Botta had little to go on. The investigations of Rich helped, of course, and his account made it clear that ruins in fact did exist here, so there was reason to trust the traditional view that this was Nineveh. But what exactly was he to look for? There were many stories about stones with images and strange writing, but where were they? When Layard came to Mosul, Botta was unable to show results from his efforts so far.

Having been forced to abandon Nebbi Yunus he seemed hesitant when faced with the challenge of Kuyunjik, so he concentrated for some time on collecting antiquities and gathering information about where finds had been made previously. Even in this field his results were modest, and he was convinced that very few finds had in fact been made in the vicinity of Mosul. He concluded that Rich had collected most of the antiquities which had been discovered here.

On his earlier visit to the area Layard had been especially fascinated by an enormous mound known as Nimrud, which was located close to the Tigris south of Mosul. He had stopped here and dreamt of uncovering the palaces of the past which he was convinced had to be hidden here. Since that visit he had seen many other ruins in Babylonia to the south and in the Iranian mountains, and he had had several opportunities to speak with persons who were deeply interested in the past of the country. He therefore had much to tell Botta and it seems likely that the enthusiasm of the young Englishman helped keep Botta's activities alive.

The brief three-day visit became the beginning of a personal friendship between two men who obviously admired and respected each other. Their relationship was free from both the personal and nationalist–chauvinistic rivalry which otherwise came to mark the work of archaeologists in ancient Mesopotamia during the years that followed.

Layard went on to Constantinople – where he remained as a member of the ambassador's staff, as I shall explain later. While he immersed himself in new adventures in the Turkish capital, Botta continued his fruitless activities and regularly wrote to Layard about his work. He in turn attempted to encourage Botta to go on and suggested that he should try his hand at Nimrud. In December 1842, half a year after Layard's visit, Botta finally placed a group of workers on Kuyunjik where they dug some trenches, but even here he had no luck. We are told that he found nothing, which means that he only found things which meant nothing to him: potsherds, fragments of stone, bricks, sometimes with inscriptions. 'It was impossible to recognise a plan or any construction in the chaotic disturbance of buildings which had once crowned this site', wrote Botta's later assistant (Flandin 1845). Potsherds, the largest single group of finds for the modern archaeologist, could not possibly speak to Botta or his workmen; they had to find something monumental in order simply to become aware that there was anything to find, and to begin with Nineveh did not offer anything useful. He therefore had little to tell in his letters to Layard, and it was not until April of the following year, 1843, that he could write anything truly positive about his activities; then it was on the other hand a sensational message he could send out: he had finally discovered ancient Assyria!

Already when his workmen first began excavating on Kuyunjik he received a visit from a man who came from a village called Khorsabad; he explained that this settlement, some 25 km from Mosul, was built on top of a mound and that stones with images and inscriptions had been discovered here on several occasions. Botta had received many such visits and heard stories which always turned out to be pure imagination, so he did not take the man from Khorsabad seriously. In March, after months of fruitless toil on Kuyunjik, he had become so frustrated that he decided to find out if there was any reality behind the story. He sent a team of workmen to Khorsabad where they were to dig some holes, and three days later he received a message saying that they had found both reliefs and inscriptions. Even then Botta was sceptical and sent one of his servants out to make a drawing of one of these inscriptions, and it was only when he returned with something that looked genuine that Botta finally decided to move his operations to Khorsabad.

On 5 April he could send a letter to Paris in which he announced that he had uncovered 'the ruins of a monument which is remarkable both for the number and the nature of the sculptures which adorn it'. Triumphantly he could conclude:

> I believe I am the first to discover sculptures which may be assumed to belong to the time when Nineveh was still flourishing.
>
> (Mohl 1845: 2, 10)

This message, which Botta sent to Paris through Constantinople, where Layard read it with enthusiasm, became the start of a hectic phase of discovery with excavations in several mounds over the entire country. A civilisation which had disappeared suddenly emerged from the ground.

CHAPTER TWO

PAOLO EMILIO BOTTA

———— •◆• ————

We know surprisingly little about Botta. There are only brief biographical notes available dealing with his life and personality, he appears only in some French biographical lexica, and is usually passed over in the great national encyclopaedias. When he is mentioned, his work is often summed up in a few kind sentences, and he disappeared completely from public life and archaeological activities at a very early stage. He seems almost to have been erased from history. And yet, his accomplishment was quite unique and he created one of the greatest archaeological sensations of all time.

He was born in Turin in 1802, the son of a medical doctor, Carlo Botta, who went on to become one of the leading historians of his age; he wrote on the history of Italy and became especially famous for his large work on the American War of Independence which was published in 1820–1. Carlo Botta became a French citizen, worked for a time as a doctor in Napoleon's armies, and in 1827 was appointed rector of the Academy at Rouen. However, four years later he was forced to resign this post because the authorities found his religious views to be too liberal, so he moved to Paris. Paolo Emilio – or, as he is known in the French version of his name: Paul Émile – also studied medicine, first in Rouen and later on in Paris. We know that in 1824 he was in Salonika in Greece during the Greek war of independence and shortly after the death of Lord Byron, the great hero who helped the Hellenes in their fight against the Turks. There is no explanation of his presence here at this time, but he may of course have been fired by sentiments similar to those which brought Byron to Greece (Bergamini 1994: 70–1). In 1826, before he had completed his medical studies, he joined the crew as ship's doctor on the explorer *Héros*, which was leaving on a scientific journey around the world. He wrote that he was inspired by 'the natural youthful desire to know the world, and also with a view to making some observations of nature' (Botta 1829: 6). The young Botta was a botanist and bird-lover, a 'naturalist', and his journey took him along nearly the same route which was followed fifteen years later by the young Charles Darwin onboard the ship *Beagle*.

The journey went first to Brazil, then to Chile, Peru, Mexico and California where the expedition stopped for a while. California and the areas further north along America's west coast were largely untouched territory at this time, where only Spanish missionaries had established themselves in isolated settlements. Botta wrote a small report on the Indians, plants and birds of California, obviously the topics that interested him. There is nothing in this account which points to his later work as an archaeologist, but one senses a lively intelligence and a frank and genuinely interested personality who looked with sympathy at the Indians and was aware of their problems in the contact with the Europeans (Botta 1952). He was especially fascinated by their musical talents and thought that given real instruments they could become great musicians. He made extensive collections of botanical and zoological specimens which were handed over to the museum (probably the Jardin des Plantes) in Paris on his return.

The journey continued across the Pacific via the Sandwich Islands to China, and from there back to France round the Cape of Good Hope. In the Bancroft Library at Berkeley there is an unpublished notebook from his trip; it primarily contains information about the biological observations he made, but one finds also a small dictionary of the language of the Sandwich Islands (Hawaii) and observations on the life of the native population. In the Chinese city of Canton Botta learned to appreciate the smoking of opium, a habit which followed him throughout the rest of his life. In July 1829, after a journey of thirty-nine months, the *Héros* docked at Le Havre, and Botta resumed his studies in Paris, graduating in 1830. His dissertation written to acquire the final degree as doctor of medicine is a short monograph on the effects of the smoking of opium and some suggestions for a medical use of this practice. Opium was of course being used in medicine, and Botta's contribution consists primarily in the suggestion that patients should smoke rather than eat opium. Still, it is remarkable how clearly and calmly he puts forward his own experience after nearly one year's use of the opium pipe; he does nothing to hide the fact that he still smokes, and he even finds it opportune to complain that it is very difficult to acquire the right quality opium in France – he is dissatisfied with the Near Eastern variety which he finds coarse and too powerful, and he prefers the Indian kind which is smoked in China. It may be significant for an understanding of Botta's special character that the motto to his dissertation is a quote from de Quincy: 'O just, subtle and mighty opium! That to the hearts of poor and rich alike, for the wounds that will never heal, bringest an assuaging balm'. What are the wounds which will never heal for Botta? His mother died when he was small and he grew up together with his busy and famous father; he is said always to have felt awkward and uneasy in the company of women, and his decision to spend his life in Muslim countries where women generally live a secluded life in the harem, may have a connection with his wish to avoid a direct and demanding contact with the opposite sex. At the Louvre there is a single portrait of him as a young man, a serious, gaunt and self-conscious Romantic (see Figure 2.1).

The following passage which begins his dissertation shows with great clarity what a complex and unhappy person he was:

> Man is by nature subjected not only to the physical pains common to all living creatures, but also the moral pain which follows from the intelligence given to him, and he is accordingly forced at all times to find ways of escaping

from his real existence and move into a world of imagination, where he can seek artificial happiness and satisfaction for his insatiable desires. It is therefore necessity which leads him to separate himself, if only for a moment, from the evil which is bound inseparably to his position in the world; it is in order to forget himself that he has developed different drugs, despite the fact that sense and experience unite in making man feel both the shame and the dangers.

(Botta 1829)

It may not be without significance that he stresses that opium dampens the sexual desire and may be used in treatment of diseases like *nymphomania* and *satyriasis*.

After his exam he again went into the world in search of adventure. He took a position as military doctor in Egypt, where the Pasha Mohammed Ali had established his independence from the control of the Sultan in Constantinople and had engaged in a series of wars of conquest. Botta took part in a campaign in Sudan, where he also found time to collect plants and insects which were presented to the museum in Paris (he collected no less than 12,000 insects from Sudan). Many of the military doctors in the Near East were Italians and most of them apparently had no qualifications at all, whereas Botta according to the standards of the time was a well-educated man and presumably a highly valued doctor. According to one account he was in fact the personal physician of the ruler Mohammed Ali (McGovern and McGovern 1986).

We have an interesting sidelight thrown on his person in Cairo, where he was host to the young Benjamin Disraeli (Figure 2.2). The Englishman had gone on a journey round the Near East in 1830–1 to cure a somewhat ill-defined malady, and this had led him to Cairo where he spent some time in Botta's company. Disraeli, a leading London dandy, who had reached a certain literary success a few years earlier with his novel *Vivien Grey*, became deeply fascinated with the French-Italian doctor whose conversation during long nights left a lasting impression on him. In a note in his diary from 1833 he wrote:

All men with great imagination are *indolent*. I have not learnt much through conversation with men. ... But the man from whom I have learnt most through conversation is Botta, son of the Italian historian, who I knew in Egypt where he travelled as a doctor in Syrian dress – the most philosophical intellect with which I have ever come into contact. Hour after hour have passed while we entertained each other, *chibouque* in hand on our divan, in a country where there are no magazines or books. My intellect made a leap in these high conversations. Botta used to say that they formed a special time also in his own intellectual life.

(Blake 1982: 97–100)

How interesting it would be to listen, just for a few minutes, to these nightly exchanges between two young Europeans in Egypt of the 1830s! And, in fact, we do have a unique opportunity to listen in, for Disraeli's fascination with the French man of the world who could talk the night away slung on the pillows has

Figure 2.1   C.-E. Champmartin's painting of Paolo Emilio Botta, from 1840 which shows him shortly before he left for Mosul. As far as I know, this is the only portrait of Botta, and it now hangs in the office of Dr Annie Caubet who is in charge of the department of ancient Near Eastern archaeology at the Louvre. Reproduced by courtesy of the Musée du Louvre, Paris.

left traces in one of his youthful novels, *Contarini Fleming*, which was written in part during his journey in the Near East. Botta appears here in a couple of scenes under the name Marigny. Their first meeting takes place in the Church of the Holy Sepulchre in Jerusalem, an astoundingly prophetic literary device, for Botta's later career was to link his person closely to precisely this church. Disraeli's attention is attracted by a man because of 'his sumptuous dress, his imposing demeanour, self-satisfied air, and the coolness with which, in a Christian temple, he waved in his hand a rosary of Mecca'. He takes him first for an Arab or Turk but is told that this Marigny indeed is a European, although he can hardly be called a Christian. He is described as a prominent scientist.

Having been introduced to Disraeli's alter ego, who is in the company of a Christian monk, Marigny immediately embarks on a discussion on religion and truth, a conversation which shows the Frenchman as a rabid sceptic. He declares that it is impossible to believe in any kind of human revelation, be it Christian or Islamic, 'because it obtrudes the mind of another man into my body, and must destroy morality, which can only be discovered by my own intelligence.' The question of the existence of God is accordingly useless to discuss, because no human can understand it.

A small group joins the three men: Werner, who is described as a German divine and a rationalist, a Jewish merchant called Besso, an Egyptian by the name of Sheriff Effendi and an English missionary called Benson, and the entire party goes to Besso's for a long night of such discussions; further nights follow, with the pipe and 'metaphysical and scientific' debates. Marigny is characterised as 'a sceptic, and an absolute materialist, yet he was influenced by noble views, for he had devoted his life to science, and was now, at his own charge, about to penetrate into the interior of Africa by Sennaar.' His entire personal philosophy is summed up in a single sentence he writes on the wall of Besso's room: 'Knowledge is human' (Disraeli 1832: 353–7).[1]

Botta kept up a correspondence with Disraeli which continued intermittently during the next fifteen years. All was not particularly deep or profound in these letters, however. In the first one written after Disraeli's departure from Cairo he complains that nothing happens any longer in the city; he has been ill with dysentery and fever, but

> now I am in a very good bodily health; but my soul, if I have one, is as sick as ever. I am always tired of myself, disgusted with the world where nothing is certain but misery and longing without any hope after what cannot be obtained, the word of that great secret of Creation and existence. the common comfort of conversation has been almost entirely lost to me, since you left us, for I seldom go out of my room where I spend days in raving and nights in enjoying the delights of opium, that great soother of pains.[2]

Now and then he has returned to the scene of their nightly conversations, which in real life was a house belonging to a certain Mr Galloway, but this is now a desert to him; the host has married and this has changed everything – 'oh shame! they drink european coffee in european cups'.

Botta was, as mentioned in the novel, planning a long trip to Sennaar in the Sudan and his next letter was written from here. He is of course still depressed, but does find a certain pleasure in watching the handsome local people who walk majestically across the sand or ride their enormous dromedaries. The local women ('for we must always come to that') are beautiful:

> but above all they have here an artificial quality which, pour un homme blasé, gives them all the charms of novelty. when young they shut them (don't blush, I shall be as chaste as possible) by a surgical operation and regular cicatrisation which insures their virginity against the most rash attempts. they remain so till the day or rather night of their wedding which to be completed

Figure 2.2 The young dandy Disraeli shortly after his return to England from Egypt. The long pipe is a souvenir from the Orient, and perhaps the letter on the mantelpiece is from Botta. Drawing by Daniel Maclise. (From Blake 1982: plate 2)

requires again the aid of the knife with which a way is made exactly as we cut off a piece of a melon to know if the inside is good. the happy husband ascends then the breach and gets in through blood and shrieks; what do you think of that? is it not worth coming to Sennar?[3]

Even adult women have a tightness which is highly appreciated by the local men, we are told, 'god bless them for the invention'. He is uncertain what effect this description will have on Disraeli, who has now 'breathed the air of England', and therefore perhaps no longer appreciates the free and open discussions which he used to enjoy with his French friend.

If I have been beyond the rules, I pray you, pardon me and remember that if w[e] have so many tedious books of travels it is because the travellers do [not] say things as they are but keep concealed the very things which oug[ht] to be known if we want to have at last a true description of the species.

On top of all this comes an elaborate thanks for the works of Lord Byron which Disraeli sent to him, and which now form his only consolation in the desert where he finds himself.

In 1834 Botta returned to France,[4] and he wrote again to Disraeli from the hospital at Marseilles. His time in Sennaar had been marked by almost constant attacks of disease, which nearly killed him. His fevers remained with him all the way until Cairo, where he had tried to find the Galloways, but in vain. In France he has been met with worries and difficulties, 'fruits amers de notre civilization'. He dreams of returning to the Orient in order to die under the brilliant sun: 'mes os ne pourriront pas dans la fange d'un mesquin cimetière mais blanchiront sur le sable d'un desert si chaud si sec si propre.' This is the first, though certainly not the last reference in the letters to his longing after death, 'cet heureux sort', but in this letter it seems rather casual and stands next to the wish that his friend will find that 'Wine soit still exciting and Women still beautiful'. This is the only letter written in French, by the way.[5]

In Paris his contributions to the collections of the museum were highly appreciated; he was appointed 'travelling naturalist' and sent on an expedition to the Red Sea, where he travelled from Sinai to the Yemen. He wrote a learned book about this expedition and had no less than two plants named after himself.[6] On this journey he visited areas which Carsten Niebuhr's party had traversed seventy-five years earlier and it is interesting to see that Botta's admiration for Niebuhr's meticulous care and precision to some extent is outweighed by his irritation over the absence of more 'stimulating' information. Niebuhr's work is 'an excellent survey of material facts, observed with precision and minutely described. But one searches in vain, it seems to me, after a picture of the soul of the Arabs'. Botta therefore sets himself the task of delivering a description of the 'life, passions and character' of the Arab – rather than a catalogue of concrete observations (Botta 1841: 5).

Also on this journey he suffered constantly from fevers, which forced him to limit his itinerary drastically. After his return to Paris his friends secured access for him to the consular corps, and in August 1841 he was then appointed to the post as Consul at Mosul.

CHAPTER THREE

THE FIRST PALACE
APPEARS

———— •◦• ————

There was nothing accidental about Botta's appointment or his archaeological activities in Mosul. The creation of the post and the choice of Botta to fill it were due to the activities of Jules Mohl, a man who served as secretary for the Asiatic Society and who had a considerable influence in scientific circles in Paris at this time.

Mohl had developed his interest in Nineveh after reading Rich's account of the ruins of Assyria, and he had apparently visited the British Museum and seen the glass case containing the objects Rich had brought back from Mesopotamia. He had become fascinated by this and had seen the possibility of placing France in a central position in the exploration of the great ancient civilisations of the Near East. Placed as he was, Mohl was well aware of the special interest which the collections of the national museums commanded in the public. The British Museum and the Louvre were competitors and their rivalry in acquiring and exhibiting glorious and interesting antiquities reflected national, political interests. Under Napoleon the Louvre had become a kind of treasure-house filled with conquered works of art which could illustrate the national grandeur on the battlefield. According to the prevailing view of the time France's imperial ambition justified the plunder of, for instance, Italy's great works of art: military virtue defeated spiritual decadence (Jenkins 1992: 13). Napoleon's museum policies were rather extreme, since they were built on a systematic art-theft from the countries conquered by his armies (Wescher 1976), but it is characteristic also of England that an enormous prestige was invested in the national museum, and that antiquities from such countries as Egypt, Greece and Mesopotamia were regarded as treasures.

It was also Napoleon who extended France's interests to the Middle East by way of his conquest of Egypt in 1798, a campaign which led to a strong resurgence in the study of the ancient culture of this country. He brought with him not just an army and a navy, but also a large number of scholars, and perhaps the most important result of this military venture was the publication of a majestic work, *Déscription de l'Égypte*, published in thirteen volumes of plates and ten volumes of text between 1809 and 1828, which presented the results of the studies of the many *savants*. Politically and militarily the campaign was a complete failure, for the British of course chased the French out of Egypt again. When Lord Nelson destroyed the French navy in the Battle of the Nile in August 1798, he also laid the basis for the leading position of the British Museum. The many antiquities which had been collected by the French in Egypt were confiscated and sent to London, where they became the backbone of the Egyptian collection. The most famous example is the so-called Rosetta Stone, still one of the greatest treasures of the British Museum; it carries an inscription which contained the key to the understanding of the ancient Egyptian hieroglyphs, and it had been discovered by French troops building fortifications in the Delta.

After Napoleon's final defeat on 8 June 1815 at the Battle of Waterloo, the British saw to it that the large collections of looted art objects from Italy and other European countries, which had accumulated in the Louvre, were shipped back to the places they came from originally. At the same time the British Museum acquired large and very important collections, not least the reliefs from the Parthenon in Athens, the 'Elgin Marbles', which were purchased in 1816, the same year the stolen works returned to Rome from Paris. Obviously, there was a difference: antiquities taken as booty from a civilised European country like Italy or Holland were unacceptable in the eyes of the British, but it was something quite different with respect to Greece (under Turkish control at this time).

Napoleon's defeat did not end French dreams of creating large and prestigious collections of antiquities in Paris, of course. Although Botta's supporter Jules Mohl was of German descent and only became a French citizen in 1844, he was clearly driven by a nationalistic dream of re-establishing French scholarship in a leading position in the study of the Near East. The plan to excavate at Mosul was one part of these designs. Even in his most optimistic moments he can hardly have imagined that this idea would be crowned with such spectacular results. When Mohl chose Botta for the task it was of course because he had many years' experience from Arab countries and spoke the language fluently, but it is difficult to decide whether Botta personally had any particular interest in antiquities or excavations. He refers repeatedly to the fact that his task had been defined for him by Mohl: 'I have only been M. Mohl's tool', he points out in the preface to his final report on the excavations:

> I therefore owe all my discoveries to others, for I have in reality worked on the basis of ideas which were not my own, using resources which were not mine either. The true honour for the discoveries therefore falls to those who delivered these ideas and these resources, and the only praise to which I can aspire is that I have had the luck to be able to make use hereof.
>
> (Botta 1849: 16)

It is true that a friend from his boyhood years at Rouen, a certain M. Levavasseur, has written that both he and young Botta were deeply interested in ruins. Close to Rouen were the ruins of a cloister which Botta's friend had discovered, and he tempted Paolo Emilio to go there one night. He explains how Botta became entranced with the place and its romantic beauty, but we are also told that he promised to go to the Orient in order to discover even more marvellous ruins:

with my courage and God's help I shall find things which are more beautiful and older than these. And then you may come and visit my ruins if you feel strong enough to travel through deserted lands, if you can forget your moist Normandy in order to warm yourself by the burning sun of the Orient. Oh! If I could make another age live again I would, among its ruins, find a corner, a hiding place which no one would envy me.

(Fallue 1851: 98)[7]

Even though the final sentence is in harmony with Botta's own words in his dissertation on opium, we can probably assume that this is not a true quote. The romantic excitement of M. Levavasseur makes it difficult to decide whether he is just a little right in his conclusion that 'the Assyrian gallery would not have enriched the halls of the Louvre, that this discovery which touches the cradle of civilisation would not have been saved for science, had not the young Botta with his burning soul become enraptured by the ruins of Fontaine-Guérard.'

It was in any event a colossal task Botta was given in Mosul, and even the most fervent boyhood dreams could not have prepared him for Kuyunjik. While the *savants* who came to Egypt could begin immediately measuring and drawing the many ruins of temples and graves which were plainly visible, Botta was faced with a far more complex task. He had of course never excavated before. One can hardly say that archaeology had been really invented by 1842, and mounds like Kuyunjik had never before been investigated (Schnapp 1993; Trigger 1989). Nobody could even guess which problems Botta would face when he sent a group of local workers to Kuyunjik with spades and picks in order to find 'something'.

The immediate problem was the immense size of the mound. Despite decades of archaeological activity Kuyunjik itself seems almost untouched today. The mound contains settlements reaching back into prehistory, which means that people have been living here for more than 7,000 years. Precisely this fact ought not, one might think, have concerned Botta, for he was interested in finding Nineveh of the Assyrians, and those ruins were to be expected to lie on top of everything else. However, after the sack and destruction of the city people had lived at various times on top of the mound, although in most cases it had been nothing more than small villages which huddled in a corner – as was in fact still the case. The top had also been under plough for centuries and there were still fields on the mound.

Botta and his workmen could not draw on any previous experience, so they had first to identify the various problems that arose, before they could attempt to do anything about them. The first serious problem was that the top layer of the mound in several places was so disturbed by later activities that only confusing bits and pieces were to be found there. The Assyrian palaces Botta was looking for were hidden so deep in the ground that he simply did not reach them.[8]

It was accordingly not surprising that Botta worked in vain at Kuyunjik. As soon as he moved his activities to Khorsabad his luck changed, for the archaeological conditions were much more favourable here. His workmen ran into the ruins of a gigantic palace complex which lay close to the surface, and it was easy to discover where the rooms had been. Botta had no problem with stratigraphy, for there were no buildings above the Assyrian palace. Since nearly all the walls were decorated with large limestone blocks which carried depictions in low relief of men and animals, gods and monsters, Botta's workers could simply follow the reliefs along the walls and thus get a plan of the building. On top of that, everything was on a large scale, so even if they overlooked details – as, of course, they did – there was plenty to find, many things which could not easily be missed. The problems encountered were caused by the way in which the city had been destroyed: like most of the cities in Assyria it had been conquered and burnt down by the Medes when they attacked the country in 614 BCE; Nineveh with its massive walls had alone withstood the first attack, but even that city was conquered and destroyed two years later, in 612 BCE. Assyria was then completely crushed and the large cities deserted.

Like all later excavators of Assyrian palaces, Botta thus found the ruins of enormous buildings, which had been destroyed by fire, whose walls had collapsed and been slowly covered with earth. Many of the reliefs were severely damaged, partly by the fire, partly by being exposed to the weather, and time and again we read how reliefs just exposed crumbled before the eyes of the excavators. Nevertheless, Khorsabad was a relatively easy site to excavate.

The discovery of this first Assyrian palace was communicated by way of a series of letters addressed to Jules Mohl in Paris, who published them in the *Journal asiatique* (Mohl 1845; English version, Botta 1850). These letters gave the learned world the first glimpse of ancient Assyria and the descriptions and drawings created a sensation. Botta explained in detail about rooms whose walls were covered with reliefs and doorways adorned with large slabs which carried long inscriptions; the carved signs had been filled in with bronze. The finds were sensational and dramatic, but he had in reality no idea of what his workmen were uncovering, so wisely he spoke simply about a 'monument'. The first excavation took place at the very edge of the mound, where there were no modern houses. The problem was that the ancient building had been nearly completely eroded here so that the reliefs were preserved only to a height of about 50 cm. The workmen moved further into the mound, of course, where the finds immediately began to improve, but the villagers complained of the danger to their own houses which might be undermined, so Botta had to proceed with the utmost caution. He was certain, however, that the building of which he had discovered a corner continued all the way underneath the entire mound.

But what had he found? An Assyrian building, perhaps a palace – that was clear, but that was only the starting point for a host of questions to which there were no answers. How old was it? What was the ancient name of the place? What was the meaning and significance of the strange images which appeared on the walls? What was written in the many inscriptions carved into the stones, and which no one could read? Was this Nineveh? Who had built the place?

Botta wrote not only to Mohl in Paris, but also to Layard in Constantinople. It was important for him to provide an opportunity for his young English friend to see and copy the official letters to Mohl before they were sent further on from Turkey, and in the British Library we have Layard's hand-written copies of some of these reports together with several drawings of reliefs and plans of the building. Botta's generosity is quite unique, especially if one compares with other *savants* of his day who found it excruciatingly difficult to share their knowledge and discoveries with their colleagues, who were regarded more as rivals and competitors. Botta appears to have been completely free from such considerations. In fact, he urged Layard to make copies of everything, gave him his full blessing to write about Khorsabad in journals and magazines on the basis of his own information, and he invited him repeatedly to come to Assyria to take part in the excavations. 'I regret very much that you are not now here to take a view of Khorsabad', he wrote. 'I can assure you it is most extraordinary and well worth to be seen'. He offered him board and lodgings and insisted that his presence at the excavation would be most useful:

> I do not know how to draw and therefore I cannot make but bad sketches of the best preserved figures; all the rest will be lost and it is a pity because slight features which I would not notice, as looking quite unimportant to me, could lead others to a certainty as to the age of the monuments, the historical facts depicted and the interpretation of the writing. With my small share of knowledge I am unable to be as useful as you should be. Come then.[9]

The first couple of months Botta was quite uncertain with respect to this 'monument' which was so richly decorated, and which was located in an area where one would expect to find Nineveh. He had no books and no one to talk to in Mosul, and he assured Layard that 'it is quite a treat to receive such letters as yours'. The one letter we possess (in a copy) from Layard was in fact crammed with ideas, questions and suggestions, a very long text which shows how excited the young Englishman was with Botta's news. He praised his friend for his unique discovery which removed any doubt about the existence and importance of ancient Assyria, a discovery which reduced all previous finds to insignificance. He also expressed his satisfaction at knowing that he himself had encouraged Botta to continue his work in spite of the lack of results after the first few months.[10]

In his youthful excitement Layard tended to jump into bold speculations and interpretations, but Botta was considerably more careful and urged him to take it easy. They could readily agree that the ruins had to be Assyrian and not much later, as others suggested. The inscriptions were of exactly the same type as those Botta had found pieces of at Kuyunjik, and the writing was closely related or identical to the one used on texts from Babylonia in southern Mesopotamia. The essential question was, of course, the nature of the ruins and the name of the place. When Botta consistently referred to his discovery as a 'monument', the reason was that he felt unable to exclude the possibility that it might turn out to be a gigantic mausoleum. Layard appears to have been convinced from the start that Khorsabad – about whose location he was somewhat uncertain – had to be part of ancient Nineveh, just like the ruins close to Mosul with the mounds of Kuyunjik and Nebbi Yunus. He referred to classical writers who stated that the city had been enormous, bigger even than Babylon, and it seemed not unlikely that Khorsabad could have been located within the walls of ancient Nineveh. Botta explained that the distance from Mosul to Khorsabad was '4½ caravan hours' (i.e., about 20 km), and he was not really happy to speculate but pointed out that the name and history of the site had to remain unknown as long as the script had not been deciphered.

There were other Europeans in Mosul, and one might have expected them to take a lively interest in Botta's discovery, but his relations with especially the British were very bad. We hear a great deal about the family of the British Vice-Consul Christian Rassam, the missionaries Badger, and it appears that a somewhat strained relationship quickly developed between Botta and them. The Badgers were high Anglicans, 'Puseyites' as Botta called them, and he thought they resented the fact that a Frenchman and a Catholic should have made this find. They did all they could to minimise the importance of Khorsabad, which they suggested had been built sometime after the beginning of the Christian era, and relations became so bad that Botta simply gave up having any contact with them at all. This left him virtually alone in Mosul, without anyone with whom he could discuss his finds, but 'it is not very much to be regretted after all, for the Rd. Badger although an intelligent man decides upon every subject with an air of superiority quite offensive to his interlocutors. there can be no friendly discussion with him, and I leave him undisturbed in his omniscience'.[11]

He was also in correspondence with Colonel Taylor, the English Resident for the East India Company at Baghdad, who directed him to Etruscan sculpture which he found comparable to the finds from Khorsabad; and he sent a letter to a certain Major Rawlinson in the Persian town of Kermanshah, a soldier who had written about ancient inscriptions in the area, hoping that he could persuade him to make a detour through Assyria on his way to Baghdad. Layard could not tear himself away from his duties at Constantinople, even though Botta continued in his pleas:

> as for you my dear Sir you are not a true lover of Semiramis if you do not come here to superintend my work. I cannot remain there and numberless curious things will be lost for want of a constant attendance. I do what I can but it is very little in comparison of what is to be done. ... Come I pray you, and let us have a little archaeological fun at Khorsabad.[12]

The office of Consul took up so much of Botta's energies that he appears to have spent most of his time in Mosul, only now and then visiting the excavations at Khorsabad, which meant that the digging was left to his workers. One cannot entirely discount the idea that he was in fact not completely dedicated to the work as a real field archaeologist and felt more at ease in his house in Mosul. As one can see from the letters to Layard, he was entirely on his own for the first many months, and he was quite aware that he was doing an unsatisfactory job. One shudders at the thought of all the information which was lost due to the lack of supervision and precise recording. A series of reliefs (one cannot even say how many) were simply lost because he did not have the time to draw them. In July he stopped work entirely, because he came down with malaria when he visited the site, which was located close to large swamps; it was also called *kheste abad*, which he translated as 'the abode of sickness'. Work was suspended until September because he knew that the sculptures which might be uncovered by the workmen in the course of the hot summer would be entirely gone when he again had an opportunity to visit Khorsabad.

Obviously our knowledge of Khorsabad would have been far greater if the site had been excavated in accordance with modern, scientific methods and principles, and much later archaeologists from Chicago have since worked here with great success, necessarily revising some of Botta's conclusions (Loud 1936; Loud and Altman 1938). Nevertheless, it is hardly reasonable to blame Botta for neglect or lack of circumspection, for he had to function and act on the basis of the premises of his own time. It would indeed have been an extremely good idea to have had Layard as the daily supervisor at Khorsabad, and Botta's letters indicate clearly his awareness of the unfortunate situation. On the other hand, he knew that seen from Paris his task was primarily the procurement of treasures of various kinds, suitable for public display in the Louvre, and this clearly meant first of all inscriptions and reliefs. He uncovered these, and all he could do was to come to the site now and then to make a plan of the building which was being cleared and to draw the reliefs. He did this to the best of his ability, and his regular letters to Mohl in Paris contained detailed descriptions, drawings and plans.

Jules Mohl presented Botta's accounts to the academy, where they created immediate delight and consternation. It was a hitherto totally unknown world which suddenly emerged, and Botta's drawings of the detailed reliefs opened a window upon a new civilisation. The discovery obviously justified an intensified French effort, and Jules Mohl immediately began shoring up political support for further excavations. In a private letter to an English friend he explained:

> Botta has made great discoveries in Nineveh – the ruins of a palace all covered with sculptures and inscriptions. The sculptures have quite the Persepolitan character. He sent me some raw sketches of some of them, which I showed to Duchâtel (the Minister of the Interior), and got three thousand francs for continuing the *fouilles*. I shall print the letters and lithograph the sketches, bad as they are.
>
> (Simpson 1887: 33)

Botta received not only adequate financial support – an experienced artist, Eugène Flandin, was sent to Mosul in order to secure a proper record of the finds. The French ambassador at Constantinople was asked to procure a permit for further excavations which could be shown to the local authorities at Mosul.

The latter was important, for the Pasha at Mosul had become a severe obstacle for Botta's work. Like all excavators of this period he was faced with the problem that neither the Turkish officials nor the local Arabs were able to grasp the real meaning of the excavations, but were convinced that they must have another, secret goal. It was a widely held opinion that Botta and his later colleagues were really looking for treasures hidden in the ruins, and that the texts were important because they could guide the diggers to the right spots; another theory was that the inscriptions might prove that the Europeans had a prior claim to these lands, where they had perhaps once lived; they might be gathering evidence to support a demand for repossession of the land – an interesting reflection of the impact of European colonialism. There was accordingly considerable opposition also among the inhabitants of the village at Khorsabad, and Botta wrote to Mohl that he hoped more friendly relations could be established once it became clear that he did not have hostile intentions.

The real opponent was however the Pasha in Mosul. He let his own people supervise the excavations in order to discover what Botta was really looking for; all metal objects were immediately taken to the Pasha where they were examined in order to determine whether they were gold. As nothing appeared, the Pasha became convinced that Botta was outsmarting his people, so he began throwing Botta's workmen in jail, threatening them with torture to make them reveal where the treasure was hidden. There were constant negotiations and workmen who felt obliged to quit. This situation continued until October 1843, when the Pasha simply ordered the digging to stop. He wrote a report to the government in Constantinople, in which he pointed out that the house erected by Botta at Khorsabad (with his own permission) was in reality a fortress, from which the territory might be suppressed with force.

Neither Botta nor his successors explain this resistance, for they appear simply to have taken it for granted that most Ottoman officials were deeply reactionary, perversely unqualified and prejudiced. Time and again we hear that archaeologists were hindered in their work by 'religious fanaticism'. But maybe it was not always quite as simple as that, and it is in fact not so difficult to see that a man like the Pasha was in a delicate situation. Being apparently incapable of understanding Botta's task and the reason for his work, he must have suspected that there were hidden motives of which he knew nothing. One can hardly doubt that he felt squeezed in his relationship with the central government at Constantinople, for one must remember that Botta had no permit to excavate, let alone remove any finds from the site in order to send them to France; as an official the Pasha must have worried that orders might suddenly appear from the capital, forbidding Botta's work. His own position could quickly become dangerous if he had helped Botta, or perhaps even if he had simply turned a blind eye on his activities. On top of this there are the less pleasant aspects of the situation: xenophobia and religious intolerance, phenomena which are described in practically every European account from work or travel in the Middle East, and which constituted real, daily problems. On the other hand, such feelings were not necessarily more characteristic of the Arabs or Turks than of the visiting Europeans. Contempt for the local culture radiates from nearly every account we have – with Botta and especially Layard as the honest exceptions – and the Europeans were not exactly diplomatic in their behaviour. They knew deep down that they represented a better, more advanced cultural tradition, and they felt obliged to spread the blessings of this civilisation among the generally ungrateful natives. With few exceptions, they had little respect or understanding for Islam, and in many towns (such as Mosul) the local people had to put up with Christian missionaries, whose activities could be rather disruptive.

It has to be said, though, that Botta appears to have been faced with an unusually unpleasant character, who was deeply hated also by the local population. There was no way he could handle him without help, so on 15 October he wrote to his ambassador in Constantinople to explain the situation, and Mohl recounts how he had to pester the minister in Paris, telling him about the Assyrian Queen Semiramis in order to drum up support for his consul in Mosul. At the same time the Pasha had the local Cadi (the 'judge' and religious leader) go to Khorsabad in order to inspect the 'fortress', and a report with maps and drawings was compiled. Botta's excavations were now described as if they were trenches which formed part of a vast system of fortifications. The Pasha then forced the local inhabitants to sign a complaint addressed to the Sultan. And all the time he pretended to Botta that the villagers were behind it all because of their superstition and stupidity.

There is no reason to doubt Botta's descriptions of the Pasha's manoeuvres, but he himself was perhaps not such an easy man to get along with either. The English merchant Henry Ross, who had settled in Mosul and joined in a partnership with the English Vice-Consul, Christian Rassam, visited Khorsabad in 1844, and he described him in a letter to his sister:

> Last week I visited Paul Botta, son of the famous Italian historian, at Khorsabad, where he is excavating. He is quite a Frenchman, as he was educated at Paris for a doctor, and sent round the world on a botanical mission by the 'Jardin des Plantes'. We are great friends in spite of his violent denunciations of England, which entirely depend on how much opium he has taken. He has once or twice alarmed M. de Bourqueney, the French Ambassador at Constantinople, by wonderful stories about our intrigues at Baghdad; his next despatches by the Tatar fortnightly post were anxiously waited for, and when they arrived there was not a word about 'la perfide Albion', so finally M. de Bourqueney came to the conclusion that Botta must be mad; he is, however, strongly supported by M. Mohl, so that I dare say nothing will be done to him.
>
> (Ross 1902: 23)

Instead the Pasha was deposed, but Botta was now so tired of the constant trouble and chicanery to which he had been exposed, that he decided to wait for the arrival of the artist with safe papers from Constantinople. He was not inactive, however, but used his time in copying the many cuneiform inscriptions and moving reliefs from Khorsabad to Mosul. The artist Flandin was seriously delayed *en route* and did not arrive at Mosul until May 1844. In order to be able to excavate further at Khorsabad Botta now had to buy the entire village on the mound, and then pay for the land on which it was to be moved.

Excavations began again immediately after Flandin's arrival, and they continued until October of that year with enormous success. In August Botta wrote to Layard that the results they were achieving were outstanding, and he praised the skill of the artist; more than half a mile of inscriptions and reliefs had been uncovered and he was convinced that this was less than one-tenth of what was there to be found.

Large parts of the palace were revealed and both Botta and Flandin were fully qualified – according to the standards of the day – to complete the task. Certainly, they could not uncover the entire palace, and the town outside the acropolis was not touched at all; but Botta excavated the northern part of the building with fourteen large halls and some external façades. Here a number of immense bulls were brought to light, more than 5 m in height and weighing many tons, and Flandin's glorious drawings provide a vivid and convincing impression of the grandeur of the Assyrian building (see Figure 3.2). The excavation was an accomplishment which is not materially depreciated by the fact that up to the very end Botta had

Figure 3.1 Flandin's drawing of the Khorsabad mound with the village still placed on its top. In the background the low mountains of Assyria, and in the foreground the swamp which made this a most unhealthy spot during the hot summers. (From Botta 1849: vol. I, Plate 1)

only a vague idea of the nature and extent of the building he was working on. This was the first Assyrian palace to see the light of day for more than 2,500 years, and no one could possibly know what it had looked like and how it had been structured and organised.

The name of the village was Khorsabad, a name that is usually employed for the entire site, but the ruins themselves were also know as Saraoun, and this name contains a faint echo of the original name of the city: Dur-Sharruken or 'Sargonsburg'. Botta had discovered a very special city, a capital which had been built by the Assyrian king Sargon shortly before 700 BCE as a completely new governmental centre; the palace had been deserted by the royal court even before it had been completely finished, because Sargon himself died on one of his military campaigns. His son and successor Sennacherib did not wish to live here and moved to Nineveh (i.e., Kuyunjik), so Sargon's enormous palace served as the royal seat of government for a very short period of time only, although the city continued to function. We now know that the late Assyrian kings used to build a new, personal palace for themselves, which means that more than one such building can be found in, for instance, Kuyunjik and Nebbi Yunus.

These royal residences were all adorned with large blocks of carved limestone or alabaster (so-called Mosul marble, that can be quarried in northern Assyria),

Figure 3.2 One of the colossal bulls from Khorsabad, drawn by Flandin. (From Botta 1849: vol. I, Plate 45)

which functioned as panelling in all the rooms and halls of the palaces. Three different types of scenes were traditionally represented on these reliefs: religious and ceremonial motifs, abundant among the sculptures found by Botta; hunting scenes featuring lions and other animals, some of which are among the masterpieces of Assyrian art; and scenes describing military activities, which often provide detailed information about the numerous campaigns that started from the Assyrian capitals. The very first relief found by Botta's workmen showed a scene where two soldiers armed with bows kneeled in front of an enemy city which was under attack. Many of the most significant gateways in the palaces were decorated with colossal animal figures, mostly bulls with human heads (see Figure 3.2), sometimes also lions. The sculptures, which could be up to 6 m high, made a very strong impression on nineteenth-century Europe, and they emanate a calm and powerful majesty which probably more than anything else created respect for the newly discovered ancient civilisation.

Shortly after Ross's visit, at the end of October 1844, Botta decided that it was time to stop the excavations; he was beginning to discover rooms where there were no reliefs left, or where at best they found only miserable fragments which were so damaged that they seemed worthless. Perhaps part of the reason for Botta's decision was his difficult relations with the artist Flandin. He was still full of praise for the care with which he executed his drawings, where every detail was measured, and he 'made his work with such a care that I was astonished at his patience', as he wrote to Layard.[13] But the two men clearly did not get along, and Botta sent Flandin back to France, apparently against his own wishes, while he remained behind to organise the transportation of some of the most impressive and interesting reliefs and bulls. This meant first that he had to choose which monuments to send away, and which were to stay, presumably to perish. He certainly expected to return in order to finish what he had begun, but he seems to have felt that he had reached a point where he needed to reflect and to communicate what he had discovered. 'It seems to me that Assyria equals Egypt', he wrote to Jules Mohl when he was closing the excavations; 'and it would be good to exploit it completely. I have opened the road' (Fontan 1994b: 12).

Khorsabad is far from any navigable river, so the very heavy and bulky stone blocks had to be transported to Mosul, about 25 km across a landscape without roads. Botta really had to reinvent a method of transportation which had originally been used by the Assyrian architects themselves, and he had to manage this using a workforce which was totally without any tradition for work of this nature. He had to construct gigantic carts on which the reliefs could be placed and dragged to Mosul. Some of the blocks weighed as much as 12 tons, and he had to saw the very largest bulls in pieces in order to make it at all possible to have them transported to Mosul. He had to build a smithy in order to have cramps made for the wheels which were nearly one metre broad. The Pasha let him use some oxen for a while, but suddenly demanded to have them back. Much of the transportation moreover had to take place during the rainy season, and even the very broad wheels sank deep into the mud again and again. Botta in fact had to abandon one of his bulls stranded halfway between Khorsabad and Mosul.

When the carts finally arrived at Mosul, the sculptures had to be placed on large rafts held up by hundreds of inflated sheepskins, and on such vessels they were sailed down to Baghdad, and later to Basrah, the port city on the Persian Gulf. Here they were loaded onto the French ship *Cormoran* which took the boxes to Le Havre. Again they had to be loaded on riverboats in order to reach Paris, where they arrived in February 1847. On 1 May 1847 the Louvre opened the first collection of Assyrian monuments to the public, nearly exactly four years after Botta started digging at Khorsabad.

Figure 3.3 King Sargon in full regalia with crown, staff and sword confronting one of his high officials. The black beards show traces of the original paint. (From Botta 1849: vol. I, Plate 12)

CHAPTER FOUR

AUSTEN HENRY LAYARD

—— •◆• ——

In 1845 Botta had attained an important position among Europe's learned men. The three years which had passed since his meeting in Mosul with Layard had been packed with productive experiences, and he was now on his way back to Paris in order to begin writing a report on his excavations, a work which was to become a magnificent opus. Layard on his part had not exactly been lazy during those three years, and in a short while his fame would eclipse Botta's.

While relatively little is known about Botta, we are extraordinarily well informed about Layard, who was an eager writer and who came to play an important political role in his later career. In the British Library we find a few hundred folio volumes containing his entire collection of letters, diaries and notebooks, reaching back to his early youth. This is an overwhelmingly rich source of information which enables us to paint a far more nuanced picture of the person Layard than is possible in the case of Botta.

Furthermore, we know about his early travels and explorations from the lively and well-written accounts he published immediately after his archaeological adventures, and which appeared in many editions and reached a high popularity. He wrote an autobiography in which he describes his early childhood and youth, and we have a book entitled *Early Adventures* which recounts the incredible experiences he had just before the meeting with Botta in Mosul (Layard 1894).

Layard was a man of little formal schooling, but with a rich and varied adolescence, during which he acquired knowledge and interests which were to characterise his entire life. His father was a sickly man who could not take the British climate, and who therefore spent as much of his time as possible in France and especially in Italy. The family lived for a number of years in Fiesole outside Florence. Layard spent some of his happiest boyhood years here and describes charmingly the free life among peasants and the English eccentrics who had settled here in certain numbers.[14] The father was deeply interested in Italian Renaissance art and the boy was at an early age moved especially by the paintings. He developed a technique for recognising the style of the various artists, and he tells how his father exhibited him during a visit to the Louvre in Paris where, much to the surprise of the other visitors, he was able to identify the painter who had created pictures whose origin was held to be obscure (Layard 1903: 27, 37). The method he describes is very similar to the one developed by his friend Morelli, the art historian who had such a profound influence on the appreciation of art in the nineteenth century (Ginzburg 1988). He was a competent draughtsman and later in life he returned seriously to art history and became the author of a number of articles on Italian Renaissance art as well as a successful collector of paintings; after his death these were all donated to the National Gallery in London. He also took a keen interest in an English translation of Morelli's book on Italian painters (Morelli 1892), for which he wrote a preface.

His parents were not especially rich – according to English upper-middle-class standards – and an uncle by the name of Benjamin Austen, a leading lawyer in London, was the one who because of his wealth had a decisive word to say in the affairs of the family. This deeply conservative man found it unacceptable that Layard and his brothers should live their lives in foreign countries, and especially go to school there; in his opinion they ought to benefit from a proper English education. Accordingly he decided that the family ought to move to England because of the children. This proved to be too much for the father's health, and he died a few years later of his weak chest. Young Layard was of course sent off to boarding school where he had a rough time; speaking both French and Italian fluently, he quickly became unpopular with the other boys. He himself disliked the strong discipline and preferred reading romantic novels, especially those which described the exotic Orient. *The Arabian Nights* was among his favourite books. The lawyer uncle had no heir, and young Henry changed the sequence of his names from Henry Austen to Austen Henry Layard in order to please his uncle. After the awful time at school he was apprenticed to his uncle's firm, and it was assumed that he might rise to a partnership and take over the business in due time. But young Layard, at the tender age of seventeen, was not cut out for this life. He quickly came to detest the completely mindless routine in the office, where he was asked to copy documents and so forth. Life for him therefore soon became what he was able to do outside of office hours, and especially what he could experience on his long holidays.

The Sundays played a special role, for Benjamin Austen, and perhaps especially his lively wife Sara, were important members of the Tory establishment in London, and they held a *salon* in their house in Guildford Street – later the more fashionable Montague Place just behind the British Museum – every Sunday afternoon and evening. Here Layard met some of the well-known figures of the time. One of them was Benjamin Disraeli, who had a particularly close relationship with Sara Austen, in part because she had helped him in the editing of his first novel. During the years when Disraeli travelled in the Middle East he wrote regular letters to the Austens, and these were read out to the guests over dinner. In these Layard heard about the wonders of Constantinople and the splendour of the Turkish army, and it is possible that young Henry heard about Botta for the very first time in these letters. Layard says about Disraeli:

> I constantly met Benjamin Disraeli at my uncle's house. ... He excited my wonder – perhaps my admiration – by his extraordinary and foppish dress. He wore waistcoats of the most gorgeous colours and the most fantastic

patterns, with much gold embroidery, velvet pantaloons, and shoes adorned with red rosettes. I thought him conceited and unkind because he would not answer the questions about his Eastern travels which I had the impertinence to put to him.

(Layard 1903: 49–50)

Another constant guest was Charles Fellows, a man whose occupation was what at the time could be described as 'gentleman traveller' – a wealthy man who went abroad to 'see the world' and perhaps 'discover' new places. In 1827 he had climbed Mont Blanc together with a friend as the thirteenth person to do so, and he wrote a booklet about the achievement. In 1838 he then went to Turkey in order to explore the mountains in south-western Asia Minor, the site of ancient Lycia. This expedition resulted in the discovery of some ancient Lycian towns, among them the capital city of Xanthus. His account of the journey was published the following year in London and created such interest that he went out again in the following five years, and he brought large quantities of sculptures back to the British Museum (Jenkins 1992: 140–53; Slatter 1994).

Fellows' exploits can be said to foreshadow Layard's, and there is little doubt that both Disraeli and Fellows influenced him and helped form his interest both in the Middle East and in archaeology. In contrast to Disraeli, Fellows was always friendly and helpful, 'and the accounts he gave me of his wanderings and explorations inspired me with the strongest desire to follow his example. He very kindly gave me many valuable hints, and urged me to visit parts of that country into which he had not penetrated, and where, he believed, important ruins were yet to be found' (Layard 1903: 104–5).

The young apprentice received another archaeological inspiration in the summer of 1838, when he went on a long trip to Scandinavia and St Petersburg. He stayed a couple of days in Copenhagen where he used the opportunity to see the most important monuments, galleries and museums. He was especially interested in the newly established collection of Danish antiquities, and we find an extensive description of his visit to this museum in his diary. The creator of this collection, Christian Jürgensen Thomsen, who is now remembered as the founder of the Danish National Museum, took the young English visitor on a special guided tour after closing time, so that they could avoid the throng of visitors, and Layard was given a thorough introduction to the new system of classification of ancient artefacts which Thomsen had established. The collection was already at this time known all over Europe because of the new chronological principles which had determined the way in which the objects were displayed, namely the division into Stone, Bronze and Iron Ages. Layard learnt his lesson and explains that the principles were particularly appropriate for the division of weapons:

> They consist chiefly in a series demonstrating the gradual progress from utter ignorance to a state of comparative civilisation – from the rude flint hatchet or arrow heads to the iron sword, in shape somewhat resembling that of modern man. This knowledge of metals and their adoption to the uses of man is singularly traced. ... This gradual improvement is admirably illustrated in this interesting collection.[15]

Layard made careful notes of his experiences for he planned to use these for a travel guide to Scandinavia, and he actually did get involved in such a project with the publisher John Murray. Maybe even more important for the young man was his meeting with Polish immigrants, or, as we would term them now, political refugees. He had been in contact with Polish refugees in London as well, where he took lessons in German from some of them, and it was his own opinion that it was from these men and their descriptions of the cruel Russian suppression and persecution of Poles and other groups in the Russian Empire that he learnt that 'detestation of Russian despotism and of Russian rule that I have retained through life' (Layard 1903: 97).

One of the problems for young Layard in his relationship to the family in London was the radical political and religious views he was developing at the time. The hatred and fear of Russia he shared with many Englishmen, for that country was England's main rival in Asia, and control of India could – according to many – be directly threatened by the Russian expansion especially in Afghanistan.

While his anti-Russian views may have been acceptable, Layard went much further. His childhood in Italy had naturally given him a special relationship to this country, which at the time was on its way towards the national uprising which created the Italy we now know. On a trip to Turin in 1837 he had established contacts to young rebels, and he made no bones about his own sympathies for their cause. He became a friend of the young Cavour, who some twenty-five years later, in 1861, became the first political leader of a united Italy. Layard took part in meetings in secret societies and was even used as a courier with messages for Italian refugees in Lyons in France. In his own evaluation of these young rebels he does not hide his own opinions and sympathies:

> Although these young men were as conspirators odious to, and persecuted by, all Continental Governments, they were, for the most part, honest and sincere patriots in the truest sense of the word – ready to make every sacrifice, even that of life, for the freedom and independence of their country, and for what they believed to be its welfare. . . . If they were irrepressible conspirators, shrinking from no crime, even that of assassination, it was the wickedness and tyranny of Governments that made them so. To their indomitable courage and perseverance, and to their readiness to sacrifice even life for their country, Italy owes her freedom and her regeneration.
>
> (Layard 1903: 91–2)

In our terminology these heroes would be described as nationalist terrorists, and the twenty-year-old Layard would now, as then, be regarded as a political extremist. It is interesting to consider that these words were written by the mature Layard in his autobiography, by a man who had held high posts in the English political system and served as Ambassador to Madrid and Constantinople. He was certainly not in any doubt himself that he was 'what in those days was considered an extreme Radical'.

His views on religion were no less extreme, so young Layard must have felt increasingly ill at ease in his uncle's office, let alone during the Sunday evenings with London's Tories. The religious and social conflicts of the time were deep-rooted and split the country in many different ways. The Anglican Church possessed enormous power, influence and wealth, which were being defended with a massive resistance to change of any kind. At the same time a desperate longing for philosophical and religious reforms spread among intellectuals, who were faced with scientific discoveries and achievements which needed to be addressed, and of course with a social unrest rooted in the economic changes taking place in the country. Layard attached himself closely to Crabb Robinson, one of the leading minds of the day, who introduced him to the great poet Wordsworth. Crabb Robinson had been a friend of Goethe and was one of the best specialists in England on German thought. He was a religious 'non-Conformist', a member of the Unitarian Church, and Layard himself estimated that it was the influence from this man and his special religion which 'rapidly undermined the religious opinions in which I had been brought up, and I soon became as independent in my religious, as I had already become in my political opinions' (Layard 1903: 56).

When this young man had finally finished his apprenticeship in the uncle's firm in 1839, and had passed his exam, it was rather obvious that he did not fit into the career planned for him. With his religious and political views he felt ill at ease in the Austen home, and he could not face the thought of a future in London as a lawyer, a job which in no way suited his temperament. A solution to the dilemma appeared suddenly with the arrival of his uncle Charles from Ceylon. This man had a position in the English colonial administration and recommended that young Henry should seek a future in Ceylon as a lawyer. The Empire placed a whole world at the disposal of the young men of the time, and it seemed certain that possibilities would exist for Layard out there. Even though it meant that he should say goodbye to everybody he knew, first of all his mother, it still appeared to him preferable to a meaningless life as a lawyer in London.

When the decision had been taken, the next question was how to get there, and he had the luck to be introduced to another young man who had similar plans, thirty-two-year-old Edward Ledwich Mitford. He had experiences from travels in Morocco and planned to go to Ceylon to start a coffee farm. Since he had a great fear of the sea, he had already decided to go from England to Ceylon overland, on horseback. This was obviously a very extravagant plan, and Layard became very excited indeed. His family, on the other hand, did not much like the idea, for this journey would lead the young men through some of the most wild and politically unstable areas in the known world. Shortly before this date England had broken off diplomatic ties with Persia, so it would be risky for the two young Englishmen to travel in this country, which of course they had to cross. But Layard's excitement was caused precisely by the fact that he was going to visit those areas of the Orient of which he had been dreaming since boyhood. The Arabian Nights had guided his imagination during long afternoons and nights in boarding school, and he was now faced with the prospect of experiencing the beauty and mystique of the East in real life.

He surprised his family by seriously preparing for the trip. He took courses in surveying, sought the advice of members of the Royal Geographical Society, and visited the famous writer Baillie Fraser who had travelled in Kurdistan and Persia; his romantic novels and accounts had been among the young Layard's favourite books. He also collected pamphlets and articles describing the countries he would pass through, and he took a special interest in a description of the southern Zagros mountains on the border between Iraq and Iran; this had been written by a certain Major Rawlinson who will figure prominently in this account. In the trackless mountains in Khuzistan and Kurdistan a number of rock inscriptions had been discovered, and many learned men in Europe were deeply involved in the study of these; Rawlinson was known as one of the most respected scholars in this field of study.

In this way, almost accidentally, began the journey which would determine the course of Layard's life and which would lead to one of the greatest archaeological sensations of the nineteenth century.

CHAPTER FIVE

THE JOURNEY INTO
THE EAST

——— •◆• ———

Layard took the steamer from London to Ostende on 10 July; after visiting
museums in various Belgian and Dutch towns he met his fellow traveller in
Brussels four days later. Both young men had strictly limited means and were
prepared to travel in as primitive a fashion as possible. They each bought a double-
barrelled gun and Layard moreover acquired two double-barrelled pistols. As they
planned to make surveys *en route* they brought a sextant and a compass as well
as a few other simple instruments. Mitford knew how to stuff birds and carried
the necessary equipment along. The only real luxury was a special bed with netting
to keep out mosquitoes. Layard had deposited £300 on account with a banker in
order to be able to draw money in various places along the route; a publisher
in London had given them £200 as an advance on a proposed travel account to be
written by them.

At this time the Orient began in the Balkans; for the two young Englishmen in
Montenegro. The Ottoman Empire in its heyday had not only ruled most of the
Middle East but had penetrated deep into Europe; as late as 1683 Turkish armies
laid siege to Vienna, and most of the Balkans were for centuries part of the Empire.
The tragic events in Bosnia, where Muslims, Croats and Serbs fight each other, are
the so far latest consequence of these particular historical developments. In the
mid-nineteenth century the Turkish empire was in rapid decay and was often
referred to as the 'Sick Man of Europe'. The two young men were to have plenty
of opportunities to become acquainted with the results of this decay.

As a very young man Layard was portrayed in 'Albanian dress', complete with
rosary (Figure 5.1). He was clearly deeply fascinated with the exotic world that
met him here in the mountains of the Balkans. For some time Layard and Mitford
lived as the guests of the ruler of Montenegro, the Vladika, who as bishop and
political leader governed the last non-Muslim state on the road from Europe to
the Orient. This young man of twenty-eight, Petar Ptrovic Njegosh, who was
destined to become one of the great classic authors in Serbian literature, was
delighted to have the company of the two young Englishmen. Somehow he had
acquired a billiard table and he and Layard amused themselves with that. The situation in this remote corner of Europe was illustrated by an event which interrupted
one of their games: a procession of yelling horsemen rode up to them and dumped

Figure 5.1 Layard in Albanian dress, painted by Henry Phillips.
(Layard 1903, I: frontispiece)

several freshly cut-off human heads, the booty from a raid against the Muslims in Scutari in Albania. The Vladika defended himself, when Layard expressed his disgust, by pointing out that this was an old custom not only of his own people, but also of the Turks they were fighting against. Young Layard eagerly discussed the ruler's plans for turning his people into true, civilised Europeans, which in fact led to the creation of a relatively modern state out of the small mountain society. The young Englishman was full of admiration for the intelligence and liberal political views of the Vladika. Perhaps significantly, his main literary work, *Gorski vijenac* (*The Mountain Garland*), written in 1846, is an epic poem which deals with the killing of the Turks in Montenegro, a historical event which took place in 1707, and which involved the murder of all those Montenegrins who had become Muslims, an early example of the practice of 'ethnic cleansing' (Njegosh 1963; Barac 1955). The billiard table is still in existence and stands in the so-called Billiard House in Cetinje (Spadijer 1980: 130–3).

Mitford and Layard continued through Albania and Macedonia and finally reached Constantinople on 13 September. Along the way, in the rice fields around the town Philippopolis, Layard came down with malaria, and immediately after his arrival at Constantinople he had to take to his bed for several days. The treatment consisted in blood-letting combined with setting leeches on the skin, in accordance with the best knowledge of the time, and this clearly did not speed his recovery. In a letter to his mother he describes this cure:

> Immediately after the first attack the patient is bled copiously; usually as much as 12–14 ounces of blood is taken, and as many as 50 leeches are placed on the stomach. The next day, before the fever can be expected to return, 20–30 grains quinine is taken; after that quinine is given in smaller and smaller doses every day for the next two weeks. One observes a strong diet.

As he notes, it was remarkable that he survived the cure, and the disease never left him as long as he travelled in the Near East; he became seriously ill several times during the following years, with violent fevers that kept him in bed – when he was near such luxuries – for many days. He was strong, active and full of restless energy, but he must have been in mortal danger on several occasions. This first attack forced him to stay in bed for some weeks in Constantinople, and he was unable to continue into Asia Minor until 4 October.

The Anatolian plateau was not particularly well known by European travellers, and even the mountains towards the Aegean Sea, ancient Ionia, were less explored than for instance Syria and Palestine. Layard and Mitford naturally chose a route that took them through some of the less known regions. Layard's account of the trip consists of a long list of ruins and ancient sites which they came across. He must have seen himself as another Fellows, who actually visited Lycia that same year. It is strange to think that the maps of the Anatolian plateau were almost as white as those of central Africa. Layard made careful notes during his trip, took compass measurements and made a map where he marked rivers, villages, mountains and so forth.

In Aleppo in Syria Layard came down with another attack of fever which forced him to stay put for more than a week. At this time Syria and even part of southern Asia Minor was under Egyptian control, since the rebel Pasha in Cairo, Mohammed Ali, Botta's former employer, conducted a largely successful campaign directed against the Sultan in Constantinople. Syria was in very bad shape, suffering not only from the harsh taxation imposed by the Egyptians, but also from a state of general lawlessness outside the towns and the most commonly travelled routes.

When Layard arrived in the region the Egyptian soldiers had received no pay for two years, so it goes without saying that the occupying army found it necessary to take by force what it needed to survive.

After a slow trip through Syria and Palestine, where the two young men constantly had an opportunity to speculate over the misery of the country and the populace, they arrived at Jerusalem on 10 February 1840. Layard estimated that the town then had a population of just 20,000, of which 6–7,000 were Muslims, 5,000 Jews, while the rest (8–9,000) were Christians of various kinds – Greek Orthodox, Roman Catholics, Armenians, Copts, Protestants, Chaldeans and Jacobites. The poverty and suppression was just as noticeable here as in the rest of the country, but the truly embarrassing fact was the constant strife among the Christian sects, who competed with each other over rights to access and special privileges related to the sacred sites in the town. The year before Layard's arrival the Easter service had led to bloody fights in the Church of the Holy Sepulchre between Christian groups, resulting in several deaths. Layard's interest in the artistic and historic monuments in Jerusalem could not outweigh his disgust at the 'degrading superstition nourished by the clergy', or the rivalry which had led to the spilling of blood in the church which was supposed to be the birthplace of Christianity. He was only too happy to get out of Jerusalem again.

Mitford was so upset and enraged by the conditions under which the Jews had to live in Jerusalem – indeed in the Near East as a whole – that he wrote a pamphlet in 1845, after his arrival at Ceylon, in which he argued for the creation of an independent Jewish state in Palestine, 'under the guardianship of Great Britain, during a period to be regulated by their advances towards the present state of knowledge and enlightened civilization'. The one fundamental condition to be defined by the European powers should be in the field of religion; it should be 'an indispensable condition of our assistance, that they should not attempt to restore their obsolete ceremonial' (Mitford 1845).

Layard had heard of the strange and wonderful ruins at Petra in the region south of Jerusalem. In a narrow valley with vertical rock walls are the remains of a city that was the capital for a Nabatean kingdom during the last centuries BCE. A series of monuments have been carved directly out of the rock, with impressive façades. It is one of the most extraordinary ruins in the Middle East, but even today it is far from the beaten tracks. In 1840 the situation here was chaotic. The areas Layard had to get through in order to reach Petra were entirely outside the control of the central authorities and everybody tried to dissuade him from attempting the trip. His travel companion Mitford refused to follow him, considering it a foolhardy and dangerous adventure. The two young men agreed that Mitford would visit less hazardous areas and meet Layard again in Aleppo.

In this situation Layard revealed his youthful stubbornness and determination – nothing could move him from a plan once he had made up his mind, however unrealistic and irresponsible it might appear to others. With enormous trouble he arranged with one of the local sheikhs that against payment he should offer him protection by giving two guides from his tribe to the young Englishman. They could of course help him find his way in the trackless wastes, but more importantly they were supposed to offer defence against attacks and raids; Layard was in this way placed under the guardianship of the sheikh, which in principle meant that any attack on him would be an affront to the tribe and would have to result in a violent reaction. This was in fact the usual system in the Middle East, used many times later by Layard, and normally it functioned reasonably well, but the situation in this region was far from normal and under such lawless conditions it was unclear if the system would work. The best hope for a traveller in his situation was to have enough money to pay off the various potentially threatening tribes *en route*, but Layard did not have that kind of money and had to hope that his guarantor had sufficient prestige to offer a convincing and adequate deterrent.

This turned out to be a miscalculation. On the road to Petra Layard became involved in a dangerous situation as a group of robbers attacked his little company; he only got out of this alive because he had the presence of mind to ride straight up to the leader of the robbers and hold his double-barrelled pistol to his head. In this fashion the two groups continued, watching each other; the robber-chief was quite convinced of Layard's determination and kept his people away, and thus they reached a Bedouin camp where Layard could demand protection as guest from a most unwilling sheikh. When they finally reached Petra Layard was confronted by people from the local tribe who demanded an outrageous sum of money to let him see the ruins. He refused and entered a dramatic confrontation with hundreds of threatening Arabs. On this occasion his protection may have worked, since the local people refrained from an outright physical attack, but his guides were beside themselves with fright.

On the road back through Kerak and Amman Layard was constantly harassed, robbed several times and deserted by his guides, and when he finally reached the gates of Damascus he was dressed only in trousers and a shirt. At the bottom of a saddlebag he found a single coin overlooked by the robbers, and that helped him to avoid the quarantine of forty days which otherwise was imposed on visitors to the town because of plague in the district. The last robbery, which resulted in the loss of his few remaining coins and his clothes, was committed by soldiers who had deserted from the Egyptian army.

In Aleppo Mitford had tired of waiting for Layard and was preparing to go on alone, but Layard's arrival at the last moment saved the situation. On 18 March 1840 they passed through the gates of Aleppo on their way to Mosul. They had then been away from London for more than nine months.

CHAPTER SIX

MESOPOTAMIA – THE FIRST IMPRESSION

———— ·◆· ————

Layard and Mitford spent more than two weeks in Mosul. Of all the ruins they had seen *en route* – and they had seen many – the great mounds of Assyria made the strongest impression on Layard and he insisted on visiting as many of them as he could. 'A deep mystery hangs over Assyria, Babylonia and Chaldaea', he wrote to describe his first impression.

> With these names are linked great nations and great cities dimly shadowed forth in history; mighty ruins in the midst of deserts, defying, by their very desolation and lack of definite form, the description of the traveller; the remnants of the mighty races still roving over the land; the fulfilling and fulfilment of prophecies; the plains to which the Jew and the Gentile alike look as the cradle of their race.
>
> (Layard 1849, vol. I: 2–3)

At this first visit to Mosul Layard met another French explorer, Charles Texier, who was on his way back to France after a protracted journey in Persia. He had examined a number of ancient Persian ruins and brought many detailed plans and drawings. Layard was permitted to study these, and with the plans in hand he could gaze across the river on the ruins of Nineveh and wonder whether similar glorious buildings and monuments might hide there.

The English Vice-Consul Christian Rassam together with the engineer Mr Ainsworth had just been planning a trip to the ruins of the Parthian city Hatra, located far into the desert south-west of Mosul, and Mitford and Layard were invited to join them. This was a trip that could lead to trouble, but Rassam was a respected man in Mosul who knew how to deal with the Bedouins. And Hatra was a tempting goal, for this city from the second century, was extremely well preserved with large wonderful buildings in a style which mixed Iranian and Hellenistic influences. Few had seen and studied the ruins.

They rode out from Mosul and followed the Tigris to the south; the first night they camped right across from the large Assyrian ruin known as Nimrud, and Layard saw for the first time the place where he was going to spend so much time:

As the sun went down, I saw for the first time the great conical mound of Nimrud rising against the clear evening sky. It was on the opposite side of the river and not very distant, and the impression that it made upon me was one never to be forgotten. After my visit to Kuyunjik and Nebbi Yunus, opposite Mosul, and the distant view of Nimrud, my thought ran constantly upon the possibility of thoroughly exploring with the spade those great ruins.

(Layard 1903: 311)

They saw several other ruins on this trip, among them a site called Kalah Shergat, where vast remains are located on top of a rock which juts dramatically into the river. We now know that this was the site of the ancient city Assur, the first real Assyrian city, and it was the place where Rich had discovered a headless statue in black stone, now in the British Museum. Layard's party wandered among the ruins but found nothing.

The desert city Hatra is a magical place, a vast ruin situated in the midst of the emptiness, where one sees the remains of great buildings, now partly restored, in light yellow sandstone. The sacred precinct is surrounded by a high wall and some of the gates with elegant ornamentation are preserved to their full height. Layard made elaborate plans and measurements which became the basis for an article about the site.

The party came through the trip without difficulty, primarily because of Rassam's knowledge of the local people and their customs. Back at Mosul Mitford and Layard regretfully had to take their leave from the friendly hosts, for even though one may get the impression that at least Layard sometimes tended to forget the real purpose of the journey, they were in fact on their way to Ceylon, and excavations in Assyria were entirely impossible to contemplate. So they rented a *kelek*, a raft which was the normal means of transportation for people wanting to go south. A solitary skipper armed with a long pole to keep them away from the banks and out of danger in the rapids took command of the raft which was kept afloat by inflated sheepskins. They soon reached Nimrud where a large underwater hindrance created a kind of weir and rapids; the skipper explained to Layard that this was the remains of a large dam built by King Nimrod, mentioned in Genesis, in order to create a crossing of the river. Layard noted with wonder how the ancient past appeared to be alive and present for the inhabitants of the land. As they glided through Assyria Layard noted the many mounds which could be seen from the raft.

After a week they reached Baghdad where they were received by the English Resident, Colonel Taylor. Mitford and Layard stayed here a couple of months preparing for the trip into Persia; they studied the language and read in the colonel's fine library, but there was of course time also for parties and excursions which took them to other great and tempting ruins.

The most important one went south from Baghdad to Hillah, in the neighbourhood of which were the ruins of ancient Babylon. Here, as in Nineveh, one could clearly trace several kilometres of city walls which appeared as long narrow ridges in the flat landscape, and there were large, isolated mounds as well like Kuyunjik and Nebbi Yunus. At this spot they faced a whole world of legend, reaching all the way back from the beginning of the world to the captivity of the Jews under King Nebuchadnezzar. Who does not know the story of the Tower of Babel, mankind's first attempt to defy God and the order of the world? Travellers were taken to a gigantic ruin some 20 km from the walls of Babylon, a place called Birs Nimrud (see Figure 6.1), where one could see the remains of a colossal tower-like structure; here one could mount what was supposed to be the ruins of the original Tower of Babel! The Greek historian Herodotus had visited Babylon while it was still a great, functioning city, perhaps the largest in the world – and there were very few, one must remember – and his description included a detailed account of the sacred tower. He gives somewhat exaggerated figures for the size of the city, however, and this meant that the distance of Birs Nimrud from the walls of the city, which had to mark the site of the city centre, was not perceived as a problem. Perhaps one should consider also that these men had seen a city like London grow to a similar size in the course of the nineteenth century. The actual temple tower of Babylon, the so-called *ziggurat*, was of course located in the middle of the ruins, but nobody would connect these remains with the ancient myth, for the tower was rapidly being reduced to a hole in the ground. Some of the old ruins of Babylon, and not least the tower, had for centuries been mined for building materials for the inhabitants of Hillah, and there was by then little left of the original

Figure 6.1 Birs Nimrud which at the time was thought to represent the remains of the original Tower of Babel. 'Rising suddenly out of the desert plain, a riven, fragmentary, blasted pile, and standing out against the sky, without another prominent object near to relieve the view, its solitary appearance was strangely impressive. . . . Such was the enchanting power of the vision, that the eye was transfixed, and the spell of history was upon the soul. Before us was the oldest historic monument known to man' (Newman 1876).

construction. Baked bricks are extremely valuable in this country where firewood for ovens is in short supply; houses are therefore ordinarily built of sun-dried bricks; the ancient Babylonian baked bricks were of excellent quality and served their purpose wonderfully after some 2,500 years. Many of them, by the way, had inscriptions stamped into them, commemorating the building for which they were originally used, and these were some of the first antiquities with cuneiform writing to appear in Europe.

Layard was once more caught up in impossible dreams of digging for temples and palaces, but he had to make do with walks on the mounds, looking for fragments of bricks with inscriptions.

In Baghdad he spent many hours in Colonel Taylor's excellent library, looking at Arabic and Persian illuminated manuscripts. A few years earlier Major Rawlinson had been sitting here, engaged in his work on the mysterious cuneiform writing, and Layard could study his papers. This was the same man whose article on the rock inscriptions in southern Zagros Layard had read before he left London.

Of all these monuments the most important was the one on the rock at Bisutun not far from the town Kermanshah, primarily because it had the longest text. Rawlinson was the only person who had copied this, and he had only been able to reach parts of the inscription which is located together with some remarkable reliefs very high up on a vertical rock, a smooth cliff above the plain. The inscription is written with three different kinds of cuneiform writing, in three different languages, and it tells the story of the Persian King Darius's fight for the throne. Rawlinson was at this time 'Political Agent' for the British colonial administration in India in the town Kandahar in Afghanistan, and Layard immersed himself in the study of old Persian and decided to visit Bisutun when they came to Kermanshah.

For they had to move along, even though it appears that Layard was losing interest in Ceylon. The Zagros mountains and Persia were tempting, however, and young Henry presumably decided to take one thing at a time. It was not easy even to enter Persia, for there was trouble and threats of war between the Turkish Pasha in Baghdad and a Persian army which was pushing down from the mountains. Relations between England and Persia were, as already mentioned, very strained. Mitford and Layard now had to put their European clothes in the saddle bags and don the local dress in order to blend in as much as possible. They attached themselves to a caravan of some seventy people, mainly poor Shi'ites on their way back from pilgrimage to the sanctuaries at Kerbala and Nejef south of Baghdad. This proved to be a rather unpleasant travel company, and the two young Englishmen here met for the first time in full force the religious intolerance against 'infidels' which seemed much more common here than in either Asia Minor or Syria.

The day after their arrival at Kermanshah they went to Bisutun (see Figure 6.2) to see the Persian monument, and here they met a man called Flandin, the same French artist who a few years later was to be sent out to assist Botta at Khorsabad. At this time he was attached to the French embassy at Tehran, charged by the government with the task of making drawings and copies of as many monuments and inscriptions as he could find. Again one traces the hand of Jules Mohl. We know that he and other scholars in France were waiting anxiously for the results

Figure 6.2 Flandin's drawing of the Old Persian rock monument at Bisutun. High on the vertical rock one sees the famous relief flanked by the inscriptions. This was as close as Coste and Flandin got to the monument. (From Flandin and Coste 1843–54)

of Flandin's efforts, not least for copies of the inscription at Bisutun. They were
to be disappointed on this point, however, for Flandin and his travelling companion,
the architect Coste, estimated that it would be too dangerous to attempt to repeat
Rawlinson's feat, so they did not even try to make copies at Bisutun. It probably
played a large role that everybody knew that Rawlinson had these copies, so the
learned world expected him to make them available to all others who were interested in working on the decipherment of the cuneiform writing. This did not
happen, however; Rawlinson was deeply engaged in the First Afghan War at
Kandahar, and when he again had the time to immerse himself in the mysteries of
cuneiform he kept his copies to himself until he had finished his work on them,
so they did not appear until 1847. Apart from their failure at Bisutun Flandin and
Coste were very successful, and the results of their work were published in Paris
in a magnificent opus, *Voyage en Perse* (Flandin and Coste 1843–54).

Layard wanted to stay for a long time at Bisutun, but he and Mitford were told
in very clear terms that they should seek out the Persian Shah or his vizier, who
was with the Persian army, in order to secure permission to travel through the
country. Layard had made up his mind that he wanted to take the route which
went through the area called Seistan, which was the southern road through the
towns Yazd and Kerman. He was especially interested in visiting these poorly
known regions where the teachings of Zoroaster were presumed to have originated,
and where many interesting ruins were said to be found. The Persian vizier was
unwilling to permit this, and it became clear that he regarded them as English spies
who had been sent to test the roads leading from India into central Persia. Layard
insisted and declared that he was willing to travel entirely at his own risk, without
any guarantee from the Persian government to protect them *en route*, but the rather
more coolheaded Mitford rejected this. He was certain that their signature on such
an agreement would amount to their death warrant. After long negotiations the
vizier allowed them to continue by the northern route via Mashhad and Herat,
and from there through Afghanistan to India, and Mitford found this entirely satisfactory. But Layard stuck to his decision and repeated that he *must* go through
Seistan – and the consequence was that the two friends separated. Mitford continued
to Ceylon, whereas Layard decided that he wanted to visit some of the ruins
described by Rawlinson in the Bakhtiyari mountains in southern Zagros. His idea
was – he claimed – that next Spring the situation would have changed, so that he
could be permitted to go through Seistan. Mitford was sorry to separate, and
Layard never really explained the break. Many years later he published his own
account of the journey to Ceylon (Mitford 1884).

It seems clear that at this time Layard had lost whatever inclination he may have
had to become a lawyer in Ceylon. The Middle East had captivated him with its
beauty, the exotic experiences and mysterious ruins, and it is characteristic of his
attitude that his desire to go through Seistan was based on the wish to see more
ruins. He may not clearly have realised the consequences of this decision, and he
seems rather to have been driven by his enormous stubbornness, his dreams and
a youthful feeling that things would probably work out somehow. Ceylon was not
officially dropped, he kept referring to this ultimate goal in his letters to the family,
and it is indeed difficult to see what alternatives he had. He could not of course

count on any kind of future in the Middle East. In Baghdad he had lived a life of leisure and some luxury as the house guest of Colonel Taylor, with dinners and hunting expeditions, free as a bird. It must have been extremely attractive, but he surely knew that he had no chance of staying here indefinitely, however charming and entertaining he might be. Similarly, his ideas of making excavations in Assyria were entirely unrealistic, and it seems quite absurd that already during his visit to Bisutun he had suggested to the French architect Coste that they should go back together to Assyria to make plans and drawings of Hatra and Nineveh. It is not hard to understand that Coste found the suggestion uninteresting.

CHAPTER SEVEN

INDIANA JONES
AMONG THE BAKHTIYARIS

— •◆• —

After his separation from Mitford Layard attempted to make his way into the mountains of Luristan and Khuzistan, but he had to give up because of renewed attacks of malaria and the hostility of the local people. So he went east to the city of Isfahan in order to present himself to the local governor, a Georgian eunuch who came to play a decisive role in Layard's life during the coming months. Characteristically travellers of this period fill their accounts with descriptions of the extreme cruelty and brutality which characterised the Persian regime, even compared to the rulers of Ottoman Turkey, who were not exactly delicate when it came to the exercise of power. This governor in Isfahan was notorious and feared for his unique talents. His latest feat just before Layard's arrival had been the construction of a tower of 300 prisoners who were laid on top of each other like bricks with mortar; the tower stood for weeks after the poor creatures had suffered horrible deaths. Another of his prisoners had first had his teeth drawn in order for them to be used as buckshot to shoot him with.

Layard's first meeting with this governor, Manuchar Khan, went peacefully; his demand to be allowed to proceed through Seistan was turned down – and he was perhaps not entirely dissatisfied with that – but he was allowed to travel in the mountains of the Bakhtiyari, and he could accompany a local chief who was just then leaving. This man, Shefi'a Khan, was going to a place called Kala Tul, a forti-fied town in the mountains which was the base for one of the leading Bakhtiyari chiefs, Mehemet Taki Khan. Layard was warned by several people in Isfahan to stay away from this area which was deemed extremely dangerous. The Bakhtiyaris had a reputation as cruel and unreliable people. But Layard was of course enthu-siastic, looking forward to travelling in this country which was nearly entirely unknown by Europeans; he was especially keen to discover whether Rawlinson had been right in some of his observations made when he travelled in these regions in 1836. One of the cities which had to be located in this general area was the Persian capital Susa, which is mentioned so many times in the Bible, for instance in the novella Esther's Book which takes place here. The traditional view was that it was to be found at Shush near the town of Dizful, but Rawlinson claimed to have discovered another likely site, and his report with this suggestion, published by the Royal Geographical Society, had created sensation and confusion among the experts. Layard saw it as an important task to check Rawlinson's observations (Rawlinson 1839; Layard 1846).

In letters to the family he told them about his plans: he was looking forward to the many ruins which were supposed to be located here, and after the visit to Kala Tul he planned a trip to the ruins of Persepolis in south-western Persia. The following year he would then travel through Seistan to Kandahar where he hoped to find Rawlinson. He would like to spend the winter here, making use of the major's great knowledge of 'eastern languages'. He had no reasonable explanation for his separation from Mitford, except that the latter had become so angry because of the unreasonable behaviour of the Persians that he had decided to give up the plan to travel in the country – 'as my funds were still in pretty good condition I persevered in my original plans and we separated', he wrote to his mother;[16] she was, not surprisingly, extremely worried.

On 23 September 1840 he then set out together with a caravan from Isfahan, and after two weeks of difficult travel through a nearly impenetrable landscape, over a series of high mountain passes, they reached Kala Tul. Mehemet Taki Khan was not present, but Layard was received by one of his brothers and taken into the fort to a large reception room where a number of visitors were waiting. Among them were two doctors who had been called to save the Khan's eldest son who was seriously ill with a high fever. Layard had only been in the room a short while before he was called to the boy's mother, the first wife of the chief, who asked him to attend to the sick boy. Layard, who was always deeply affected by female beauty, was completely entranced by her, a tall, dark, graceful and extraordinarily beautiful young woman with long black braids which fell down her back and a scarlet silk scarf around her forehead. She begged him to help and he gave her some quinine for the boy, but the two holy men forbade her to give it to the sick.

They had treated the boy with lemon juice, wine from Shiraz, and water which had first been used to remove quotations from the Koran written in ink on a porcelain cup. His condition worsened none the less, and it was decided to send a messenger after the father. The chieftain arrived at the fort leading his men and riding on a wonderful horse; he too made a strong impression on Layard.

> Mehemet Taki Khan was a man of about fifty years of age, of middle height, somewhat corpulent, and of a very commanding presence. His otherwise handsome countenance was disfigured by a wound received in war from an iron mace, which had broken the bridge of his nose. He had a sympathetic, pleasing voice, a most winning smile, and a merry laugh. He was in the dress which the Bakhtiyari chiefs usually wore on a journey, or when on a raid or warlike expedition – a tight-fitting cloth tunic reaching to about the knees, over a long silk robe, the skirts of which were thrust into capacious trousers, fastened round the ankles by broad embroidered bands. Round his Lur skullcap of felt was twisted the 'lung', or striped shawl. His arms consisted of a gun, with a barrel of the rarest Damascene work, and a stock beautifully inlaid with ivory and gold; a curved sword, or scimitar, of the finest Khorassan steel – its handle and sheath of silver and gold; a jewelled dagger

of great price, and a long, highly ornamented pistol thrust in the 'kesh-kemer', or belt, round his waist, to which were hung his powder-flasks, leather pouches for holding bullets, and various objects used for priming and loading his gun, all of the choicest description. The head and neck of his beautiful Arab mare were adorned with tassels of red silk and silver knobs. His saddle was also richly decorated, and under the girths was passed, on one side, a second sword, and on the other an iron inlaid mace, such as Persian horsemen use in battle. Mehemet Taki Khan was justly proud of his arms, which were renowned throughout Khuzistan. He had a very noble air, and was the very *beau-idéal* of a great feudal chief.

(Layard 1894: 149)

Layard was immediately called to the sickbed where he found the father who had broken down in tears, having been told by the two doctors that his son would die. He begged the young Englishman to help and promised him all kinds of rewards if he could save his son's life. Somewhat nervous Layard accepted responsibility for the boy's cure; if the patient were to die in his hands, he would undoubtedly face a charge of poisoning and his own life might not be worth much. On the other hand, if the cure were to succeed, he would have won a most influential friend who could help him with his further plans to travel in the mountains. He gave the boy Dover's Powder, an opiate which calls forth sweat, and he stayed at his bedside all night; when morning came the boy began to sweat violently and then improved so much that Layard could give him a dose of quinine. The next day he was out of danger.

This success secured the Khan's friendship and sympathy, and Layard reciprocated with his unbounded admiration for these two people. Khatun-jan, 'The Lady of my soul', as the wife of the Khan was called, asked Layard to stay as a member of the family, and he says that she became like a loving mother to him. She took charge of his money and advised him on everything; her younger sister lived in the fortress too and she was generally acknowledged to be the most beautiful woman in all of Khuzistan, lively, gay and intelligent. Mehemet Taki Khan several times suggested that Layard should become a Muslim and marry her; 'the inducement was great, but the temptation was resisted'. Time was passed with hunts for boar, lions and wild goats, expeditions into the mountains and riding exercises with the warriors of the fortress. Layard also visited the place where Rawlinson had claimed that the ruins of ancient Susa were to be found, but he concluded that the major could not have seen the site with his own eyes, for the ruins were small and much too late.

The trip was Layard's first real experience of conditions in these wild and lawless mountains. Despite letters from the Khan at Kala Tul he was robbed, beaten and threatened on several occasions. The very people who were supposed to take him to the ruins were convinced that he came looking for treasure – why else take an interest in old ruins? – and they proved quite unwilling to let him get away with it without leaving all the gold to them. His watch and compass were taken, but on his return to Kala Tul he complained to the chief and new letters quickly led to the restoration of the stolen items.

Layard's daring and his enormous stubbornness constantly placed him in situations where he was in mortal danger, but those same qualities also appear to have impressed the people who time and again challenged him. It is characteristic that his descriptions of these dramatic and unpleasant confrontations are completely free from the violent, generalising condemnation which so easily attains racist overtones with many of his contemporaries. He evaluated the people he met as individuals, not as representatives of a 'race' (using one of the favourite words of the time, employed very differently in the nineteenth as compared to the twentieth century), and he very rarely offers general characterisations of 'the Persians' or 'the Arabs' or 'the Turks'.[17] He met unbelievably many people who really and truly wished him ill, and he was attacked and plundered so many times that it is difficult to keep track of, but this twenty-three-year-old appears to have been completely capable of taking each person on his or her own terms, admiring and loving or detesting and despising in consequence of the treatment he himself received from them.

Things were not going really well at Kala Tul, however, for the governor at Isfahan had been ordered to break Mehemet Taki Khan's power, which was getting too great for the liking of the central Persian authorities. The Bakhtiyari chief was practically outside the influence of the government in Tehran, and it seems that he was dreaming of creating an independent state of his own. Layard joined in these dreams and speculated that the English government might take an interest in his friend at Kala Tul. The Georgian governor in Isfahan started a regular campaign against him and began by issuing an order for the payment of tax. Emissaries came from the governor, demanding a large sum of money. The Khan's authority among the tribes in the mountains would evaporate if he started demanding taxes from them, so he was quite unable to raise the sum demanded, and instead he tried to stall and hoped to reach a settlement with the governor.

It was general knowledge that England had broken off diplomatic ties with Persia, and Mehemet Taki Khan developed a plan which involved an alliance and military assistance from the English troops stationed on the island Karak in the Persian Gulf. It seems that the chief was still somewhat uncertain about Layard himself, not quite sure whether he was in fact an agent for the English military, so he might be the ideal man to send to Karak. All this fitted well with Layard's own intention to visit the island, where he had directed his mail from London. He therefore left in the company of one of Mehemet Taki Khan's trusted men and they reached the coast after several days' ride. Layard boarded a boat, a large leaking rowing boat which was to take him to Karak. Of course, a storm broke and the trip took a couple of days instead of one night, but at least he made it. His first priority was a bath, a luxury he had not enjoyed in a long time. After that he came down with an attack of fever, but the military doctor cured him and gave him medicine which he looked forward to bringing back to Kala Tul. The English commanding officer then explained to him the utter futility of his dreams of military support, so Layard decided to get back to Kala Tul as soon as possible with the depressing news. He had just time to write a few letters to the family and explain about his experiences in the wild mountains.

The Khan's man had not waited for him, though, convinced that Layard would stay with his countrymen, so he was left without a guide, even without a horse. He was furthermore told that the Persian governor had sent his army into the mountains in order to force a confrontation with the Bakhtiyari chief. Layard borrowed a donkey and rushed off as quickly as he could.

In his conflict with the governor Mehemet Taki Khan had met his master with respect to tactical finesse, and he was slowly driven into a corner. He felt forced to give his eldest son, the same one Layard had saved from fever, as a hostage against a guarantee from the governor, who promised that then everything would be in order. We hear how this ten-year-old, who was sent to the tent of the Persian governor accompanied by Layard, proudly challenged the slimy eunuch, who had no intention of honouring his promise; he simply regarded the boy as his prisoner so the father's gesture had no effect. At last Mehemet Taki Khan decided to flee from the mountains with his family in order to avoid capture. They went down onto the Mesopotamian plain and sought refuge in the extensive marshes with an old Arab ally, and here they sat down to await the arrival of the governor's army. The Persian army tried in vain to penetrate the marshes but had to strike camp outside; instead the governor sent a message to Mehemet Taki Khan promising free passage, reappointment as Bakhtiyari chief, even the post as governor of Khuzistan. Despite the violent protests of his entire family the chief decided to trust the governor's word; together with some of his men, who refused to abandon him, and in the company of Layard, he went to the Persian camp and entered the sumptuous tent of the governor. Here he was thrown into chains on the spot. Layard stayed in the background and had not been noticed by the governor or his men, so he got away in a small boat and found his way back to the others in the swamps late into the night. The next morning a new message came from the governor, demanding that the marsh Arabs should pay a large sum in taxes. A war council was summoned and the meeting took all night, with Layard as an active participant of course, and the tribe decided to agree to the payment of a smaller sum in return for a promise that the governor would withdraw his army. The moment he had received the money he sent out a new messenger with an order for the surrender of the entire family and company of Mehemet Taki Khan. This was too much for the Arab sense of honour and hospitality. A unanimous decision was reached that a nightly raid should be attempted on the Persian camp in order to liberate the prisoners. Layard enthusiastically joined in this expedition.

> The camp of an Eastern army has rarely any proper outposts, and we were almost in the midst of the Persian tents before our approach was perceived. A scene of indescribable tumult and confusion ensued. The matchlock-men kept up a continuous but random fire in the dark. The Arabs who were not armed with guns were cutting down with their swords indiscriminately all whom they met. Bakhtiyari and Arab horsemen dashed into the encampment yelling their war-cries. The horses of the Persians, alarmed by the firing and the shouts, broke from their tethers and galloped wildly about, adding to the general disorder. I kept close to Au Baba Khan, who made his way to the park of artillery, near which, he had learnt, were the tents in which his brothers

were confined. I was so near the guns that I could see and hear Suleiman Khan giving his orders, and was almost in front of them when the gunners were commanded to fire grape into a seething crowd which appeared to be advancing on the Matamet's pavilion. It consisted mainly of a Persian regiment, which, having failed to form, was falling back in disorder. It was afterwards found to have lost a number of men from this volley.

(Layard 1894: 261–2)

In the end the attack was unsuccessful and they had to withdraw with heavy losses. One of the brothers of Mehemet Taki Khan, Au Kerim, had been liberated however, and the Persian army had suffered so badly that the governor had to withdraw after this event.

The violent heat in the marshes and the constant attacks of malaria from which all of the mountain people suffered – as well as Layard – made Khatun-jan decide to try to reach a friendly relative in the mountains and seek his protection, and Layard went with her. The first tribe they came into contact with immediately sent a message to the governor, promising the handing over of the party. They succeeded in getting away from the camp, even though they were pursued by a large group of horsemen. A couple of days later they reached a mountain stronghold which belonged to the brother of one of Mehemet Taki Khan's wives, therefore a probable ally. He turned out to be just as faithless as the others and threw Layard and Au Kerim in jail. Layard was now convinced that his last hour had come:

I was labouring under too much anxiety, and overwhelmed by too many thoughts to be able to sleep. To be murdered in cold blood by a barbarian, far away from all help or sympathy, the place and cause of one's death to be probably forever unknown, and the author of it to escape with impunity, was a fate which could not be contemplated with indifference.

(Layard 1894: 272)

Khalyl Khan, the treacherous brother-in-law, feasted all evening long while Layard was lying on the floor pondering his destiny. He could hear the shouting and the drunken songs. As all became quiet some time after midnight, he suddenly heard the bolt being drawn from the lock and he and Au Kerim jumped up, ready to defend themselves. It turned out to be Khalyl Khan's wife who cursed her husband for his faithlessness and asked them to get away as quickly as possible. They found their horses in the courtyard and slipped away in the dark.

They were immediately pursued by a large group of riders, and in a narrow gully Au Kerim's horse stumbled and threw him to the ground where he hurt himself badly. Layard turned round to help, but Au Kerim insisted that he must go on since there was nothing he could do for him. Some time later Layard found a spring where he drank some water and fell asleep. The next morning he made up his mind that there was nothing more he could do for Mehemet Taki Khan and his family, and the safest course to follow seemed to be to proceed to the town of Shuster, where the governor now resided. Layard felt certain that he would not dare to harm him, but that he would send him away to Baghdad or Basrah.

He reached Shuster after several days' ride through the mountains, where he was lucky enough to avoid human contact of any kind. He was told that Au Kerim had been captured and that Khalyl Khan had handed him over to the new Bakhtiyari chief, who had been appointed by the governor. He had executed Au Kerim on the spot.

The governor was in the middle of his morning meeting but received Layard immediately. Not surprisingly he was angry: 'You Englishmen are always meddling in matters which do not concern you, and intervene in the affairs of other countries!' But he then sent him to Suleiman Khan, the Persian general who Layard had confronted during the nightly battle, and he became a forced house guest here, ordered not to leave Shuster. After a month in this house arrest Layard decided to run away together with a group of Arab horsemen. Characteristically he says that this would enable him to survey the areas around the river Kerkhah, where many ancient ruins had been reported. After a trip of several weeks in the month of August, the hottest time when the country is completely bare, he succeeded in reaching the Tigris in the neighbourhood of Basrah; here he found an English ship.

> After my long wanderings, no ordinary hardships, and constant perils, I found myself once more amongst English comforts and in English society. I sat up to a late hour in the night, talking with my host and learning from him the many important political events which had occurred since I had received a letter or seen a newspaper. For the first time in many months I could undress, and enjoy the pleasant sensation of sleeping between clean sheets. My bed had hitherto been my carpet or the bare ground.
>
> (Layard 1894: 296–7)

Layard spent three days in Basrah. He then decided to go north to Baghdad together with a post-rider in English service, and they reached the area around Hillah before things went really wrong. They were stopped by Bedouins who took their horses, packs and most of their clothes, including Layard's shoes. The robbers clearly intended to kill Layard, but he escaped by a miracle because one of the Arabs thought he was the English doctor, Ross, who lived in Baghdad and who had special relations to the important Shammar tribe in the desert. But the two had to continue barefoot in the sand in the burning sun and a temperature of 45°. Layard's feet quickly began to swell and bleed, but things became even worse, for at night they were stopped by two Arabs who were on foot, armed with clubs. They stole their last pieces of clothing, but agreed kindly to let them have their own dirty rags in exchange. In this way Layard arrived at Baghdad before sunrise and found the gates closed. He sat down outside and fell asleep.

> A crowd of men and women bringing the produce of their gardens, laden on donkeys, to the bazaars, were waiting for the moment when they were to be admitted. At length the sun rose and the gate was thrown open. Two cawasses of the British Residency, in their gold-embroidered uniforms, came out, driving before them with their courbashes the Arabs who were outside,

to make way for a party of mounted European ladies and gentlemen. It was the same party that, on my previous visit to Baghdad, I had almost daily accompanied on their morning rides. They passed close to me, but did not recognise me in the dirty Arab in rags crouched near the entrance, nor, clothed as I was, could I venture to make myself known to them. But at a little distance behind them came Dr. Ross. I called to him, and he turned towards me in the utmost surprise, scarcely believing his senses when he saw me without cover to my bare head, with naked feet, and in my tattered 'abba'.

(Layard 1894: 312)

Dr Ross put Layard to bed for three or four days, but it took considerably longer before he could walk normally again. The things stolen from him were sent to Baghdad after Ross had written to the sheikh of the Shammar tribe and complained. But Layard could not stay put. He writes that 'there were still some questions connected with the course and navigation of the Karun that I was desirous of settling, and some important ruins in Susiana which I wished to explore'.

He went with one of the English river boats which were based in Basrah on a trip along the Persian coast towards the Gulf, and again visited many ruins. Hardly had he returned to Basrah before he went on a new expedition to Khuzistan with the double purpose of finding ruins and seeking information about the fate of his friends from Kala Tul. In the city of Shuster he found them all; Mehemet Taki Khan in chains in a small dark room, but still reasonably well; and the women led by Khatun-jan in a ruined house where they spent their days lamenting their misfortune. He stayed a couple of days in the town, but he could of course do nothing for his formerly so powerful friends. In a characteristic passage he writes:

I spent some hours daily with Khatun-jan Khanum and her companions in misfortune, who treated me as if I were one of Mehemet Taki Khan's family. I learnt much from them relating to female life and customs among Shi'a Musulmans. Their affectionate gratitude to me in return for my sympathy, which was all I could give them, was most affecting. I found in these poor sufferers qualities and sentiments which would have ennobled Christian women in a civilised country.

(Layard 1894: 348)

In the midst of all these touching scenes and moving farewells the curiosity of young Layard was still fully active, and he observed not only the loving emotions of these women, but also their interesting customs. It is precisely this openness which makes Layard's travel accounts so alive and so captivating – he lived on several levels at the same time, so even if he became a Bakhtiyari and risked his life for his beloved chief, he was also always the observing Englishman. There was no conflict between these personalities.

Layard actually returned to Shuster some weeks later in the company of English officers and Dr Ross, and they found Mehemet Taki Khan still in chains and the women in their miserable hovel. Shortly afterwards the entire family was transferred to Tehran; Khatun-jan's once so beautiful sister had fallen seriously ill, but had begun to recover under Dr Ross's treatment; despite Layard's entreaties she was removed from the doctor's care and sent away with the others. She died on the trip.

Mehemet Taki Khan died in Tehran in 1851 after having been held there as the unwilling guest of the shah. He was able to live tolerably well, however, as can be seen from the anecdote about his success on the race track in Tehran, where his favourite horse won an important race in the Spring of 1843. He then presented the horse to the shah, who refused to accept it but instead expressed the wish that he would fight against the enemies of the shah on that horse. He was not given an opportunity to show such loyalty, however, but was forced to spend the rest of his life in Tehran. His beloved son died shortly after him. Khatun-jan was then allowed to settle with her family in a village close to Isfahan. Layard continued to hear about them now and then in letters from English friends who visited Tehran, but he never saw his friends from Kala Tul again.

CHAPTER EIGHT

MOSUL AND CONSTANTINOPLE

———— •◆• ————

In Baghdad Layard collected many letters from his family in England and he wrote a series of replies in which he recounted his adventures and told about the many ruins he had seen. He had to address the question of his plans for the future, of course, but his letters were unclear and the only obvious conclusion was that he had given up the idea of going to Ceylon. That left only one option: returning to England, even though it was not obvious how he was to support himself there. So many changes had taken place in his family's affairs since he left London that he saw the situation as radically different. The uncle in Ceylon had been declared bankrupt, so there was not as expected a good basis for him to start from out there anyway; also his other paternal uncle, Nathaniel, had been in difficulties and uncle Benjamin had been forced to assist. All this had resulted in a new and closer relationship between Layard's mother and Benjamin and Sara Austen, which he felt made it possible for her to move to London and live close to them. In a letter to his mother he developed his own interpretation of the situation:

> Should you be once settled in London and a right understanding exist between yourself and my uncle and aunt, which I trust is now the case, the great, in fact the *only* reason for my having left England and forfeited what those who knew me considered most excellent prospects, is at an end. You must know and those who were acquainted with my feelings whilst in England well knew my reasons for quitting my country; my uncle was probably ignorant of them and I studiously endeavoured to conceal the true reason not wishing to render him uncomfortable. ... Whilst in London, you may remember, that I was far from happy. Indeed I had my books which were to me always the best of friends but I had no home and after nearly six years residence alone and in lodgings without the society I longed for and without a circle in which I found myself truly welcome I resolved to leave England and seek a home in some other country.[18]

His mother answered that uncle Benjamin was unwilling to commit himself to any promises, including the idea of taking him back into the firm, but he also did not wish to dissuade Layard from returning to London:

in fact – *all depends upon yourself, after your return*, & if you *really* apply, *in good will* to the business of law, I have *no doubt* but that ultimately all may go well. Many persuade him of it but after all that has passed you cannot but see there is reason, & justice in his hesitation to believe. He says your opinions in politics, religion, & morals were so opposed to his that you never could have got on *cordially* together.[19]

It is sometimes easy to forget that Layard was only twenty-five. He was faced with a new, drastic decision concerning his own life, and that in a situation where he had to convince those very people on whom he depended about his sincerity. The letters from Baghdad reveal the young man's insecurity and despair at finding himself in an almost impossible personal situation. He wrote a long letter to the uncle in which he deplored the fact that his mother still had to live outside London because of complications with the Austens, whose acceptance clearly was necessary for her to be able to move. Uncle Benjamin was the unquestioned head of the family, the one who was supposed to evaluate all the dispositions of the family's members, obviously including young Henry's. But what was he supposed to do as long as he could get no clear messages or even a little trust and goodwill? As he wrote to his uncle: 'The fact is I scarcely know which way to turn – and I feel so miserable I would willingly return and live among the wild tribes of the mountains – cursing the very name of England and an Englishman'.[20] Shortly afterwards he did receive a letter from uncle Benjamin in which he was invited back to England, even though it contained no promises with respect to future prospects.

While in Baghdad he worked hard on a long report on his observations in Khuzistan, meant to be published by the Royal Geographical Society, and he convinced Colonel Taylor that there were many possibilities for developing commercial ties with this region. A special report was written and Taylor declared his willingness to send it to the Foreign Secretary in London together with a suggestion that Layard should be made Vice-Consul at Shuster. All this came to nothing, however.

Layard's chance came from a quite different direction. The campaign of the Persian governor against Mehemet Taki Khan had become part of a wider conflict between Persia and Turkey because he had attacked the Marsh Arabs who were protecting the Bakhtiyaris. The Persians had conquered the town Mohammerah, which according to the Turks belonged to them, and a steadily more tense situation between the two countries developed because of these happenings, threatening to escalate into open war. In this situation Layard's unique knowledge of the local conditions and of Persian politics was of vital interest to the English, and especially to the ambassador at Constantinople. Colonel Taylor was very keen to have England intervene to put an end to the conflict, and he asked Layard to bring fresh reports about the developments to Constantinople. He joined a *tatar*, an official Ottoman post-rider, and left Baghdad in June 1842. Their first stop was Mosul, where Layard met the newly appointed French Consul Botta – the meeting with which this account began.

The further trip to Constantinople took place without incidents and by 9 July Layard was back in the Turkish capital. He had ridden the entire journey in Bakhtiyari dress, but in Samsun he borrowed a set of European clothes from the

English consul, in order that he might be more presentable. His expectations to the meeting with the ambassador were very high, and he certainly hoped that his special expertise would secure him a position at the embassy.

> I disembarked from the steamer in the Golden Horn. Having secured a room, and deposited my scant luggage, I engaged a caïque to take me to Buyukdereh, where Sir Stratford Canning, the British Ambassador, was then residing. On arriving there I presented myself at the Embassy and delivered my letter for the Ambassador to a servant. I was told to wait, which I did for a considerable time. At length a fashionably-dressed young gentleman appeared, asked me roughly for the despatches of which I was the bearer, informed me that the Ambassador was too much occupied to see any one, and turning on his heel left the room without deigning to listen to what I had to say.
>
> (Layard 1894: 387)

Layard saw his own dreams crash to the ground and left enraged and hurt to go back to his hotel. Here he sat down to write an angry letter to the ambassador, in which he complained of the treatment he had received. He secured a passport from the British Consul-General and prepared to leave Constantinople, but a few hours after he had handed in his letter to the embassy he received a friendly reply from the ambassador who asked him back to Buyukdereh in order to tell him about the conflict in southern Mesopotamia. The following morning he had a long interview with Canning, who seemed to imply that a man with his special knowledge would be of great use at Constantinople, and a hint of a connection with the embassy was enough to satisfy Layard. He returned to his hotel and waited for a new invitation from the embassy, but before that came he ran out of money and felt constrained to purchase a ticket for a boat leaving Constantinople. He wrote to Canning and explained that he had to leave, and sat down to wait for an answer which did not come. In frustration he packed his few belongings on 10 August and was on his way down the narrow and steep streets in Pera which lead to the harbour, when he was hailed by a messenger from the embassy who brought him a letter from Canning. It was marked 'Confidential' and ran:

> Dear Sir,
>
> I think I can see my way to making use of your proffered services. Instead of going away, come & dine with me *tomorrow*, & I will try to arrange a plan with you.
>
> Sincerely Yrs.
>
> S.C.[21]

Plans were being made for a joint Anglo-Russian mediatory commission in the conflict between Turkey and Persia; in view of Layard's personal involvement in the affair it was only natural for the ambassador to make use of his special expertise and have him placed as a member of the commission.

Canning decided first to try the young man's abilities before placing him in a truly trusted position, so he was sent on a mission to Serbia in order to untangle the chaotic politics of this region. Characteristically Layard recommended that England should support a popular uprising which had just led to the deposing of the Serbian king. His recommendation created difficulties in the longer run, however, for the struggle in Serbia was part of a much wider conflict involving English and Russian interests. The deposed Serbian king was supported by Russia, who put pressure upon the English foreign secretary, Lord Aberdeen, who in turn ordered Canning to support the Russian views. The ambassador agreed with his own envoy, however, and opposed the British policy, and this episode which resulted in a loss of prestige for Aberdeen, formed the basis for a very tense relationship between Canning and the British government. As the protégé of the ambassador Layard could not stay out of this strife. Like Canning he was a determined opponent of Russian expansion at the expense of the Turkish Empire, but this was not so clearly England's policy under Aberdeen. One of the consequences was that the government denied Canning permission to hire Layard for a job at the embassy, so he came to function in an unofficial position as Canning's personal advisor, paid by the ambassador's own money.

In the beginning his position was extremely difficult. He wrote to his uncle that it had even been necessary for the ambassador to distance himself from Layard, or at least make it appear so:

> I have most powerful enemies but I think that I shall succeed in overthrowing them. ... So jealous is everyone here of an intruder – all take the alarm – each fancies that he is the person who is to be displaced to make room for the newcomer. ... The persecutions that I have undergone during the last three weeks are perfectly ridiculous. Sir Stratford Canning is, at the same time, very suspicious and it requires the most straightforward and open conduct to remove doubts from his mind – he sifts evidence more minutely than an Old Bailey lawyer – and it would be difficult for anyone to deceive him. He is a man of great penetration and judgement and very candid.[22]

Canning asked Layard to make a draft for a settlement of the border conflict in southern Mesopotamia which involved Turkey and Persia. The problems were basically the same as those which one hundred and fifty years later gave rise to the war between Iraq and Iran, namely the question of the control of the waterways leading to the Persian Gulf. The rivers Euphrates and Tigris merge into a single channel, called Shatt al-Arab, before they reach the sea; the country that controls the banks of this river consequently also controls all river traffic linking Baghdad and Basrah with the Persian Gulf. England again bowed to Russian pressure and Turkey was forced to accept a solution which was far from the one proposed by Layard in his report to which Canning had agreed. This defeat had serious consequences for the internal politics at Constantinople, where a new and considerably more conservative government was installed.

Like Layard the ambassador felt that England should support the reform movement in Turkey in order that a renewed empire could form a counterbalance against Russian penetration in Asia. Canning was in contact with leading reformers in the Turkish power elite, but his cool and condescending personal style was a

Figure 8.1 Sir Stratford Canning, the dynamic and powerful Ambassador at Constantinople, Layard's benefactor and employer. Painting by George Richmond. Reproduced by courtesy of the National Portrait Gallery, London.

serious problem. He managed to alienate people who were really his allies, and it seems clear that at bottom he had very little respect for the Turks and their traditions.

Most contemporaries describe him as a cold man with very little patience and a temper he only controlled with difficulty (see Figure 8.1). His fundamental attitude towards the Turks appears to have been a slightly annoyed irritation, the classic imperialist resentment over the fact that the 'natives' are incapable of understanding what is good for themselves. In a letter to his friend Lord Wellesley he wrote that 'to reason with persons so totally regardless of justice, so insensible to the honour and interests of their sovereign, so ignorant of the law of nations, or rather so utterly indifferent to the consequences of their misconduct, was but a hopeless labour'. He concluded that the empire would collapse by itself, not because of the threat from the north but because 'it is rotten at the heart; the seat of corruption is in the government itself. (Searight 1979: 104–5).

In the biography published after his death, which to a large extent draws upon a sketch of his life and achievements which he wrote himself, his policy towards Turkey is described in the following manner:

> He used his power, not for power's sake, but to attain a definite end. He entered upon his dominion at Constantinople with a fixed purpose – to make the continuance of the Ottoman Empire possible by making it European. His policy was open, avowed, straightforward. Private motives he had none. He would save Turkey in spite of herself if she could be saved at all.
>
> (Lane-Poole 1888: 2, 70)

Like a father who must attempt to guide a naughty and complaining child along the path of reason and good behaviour he directed England's policy towards Turkey during a span of years, and his influence was enormous.

Layard admired Canning for his diplomatic mastery and his unbounded energy, which quite matched the young man's capacity for hard work, but the great ambassador was not a particularly pleasant employer. One of Layard's later fellow excavators, Dr Sandwith, recounts in his autobiography his first meeting with the great man in the embassy; Sandwith was a young, inexperienced doctor who was trying to carve out a living for himself in Constantinople, and he had asked for an audience with Canning. A lackey took him into the ambassador's study:

> I found myself standing in the presence of a remarkably handsome, refined-looking man, an unmistakable English gentleman, of about sixty, hale and vigorous as a man could be. He was standing with his back to the fire, posed with the obvious intention of producing an effect and overawing the young doctor. . . . I took my cue, gravely bowed in answer to his very cold and stately nod, and remained standing. After a very decided pause, his Excellency deigned to seat himself, bidding me to take a chair. . . . I afterwards saw a great deal of Sir Stratford Canning, but my impression of him, gained at this interview, never changed. I thought him then proud, cold, and self-absorbed; and my further experience of him showed him in precisely the same character.
>
> (Ward 1884: 26–7)

Neither Canning's difficult temper nor Layard's rather delicate position in Constantinople prevented the young man from enjoying life to the full. He struck up friendships with a group of wealthy young Turks, all of them eager for a reform which would turn the Ottoman Empire into a European state. As Canning's agent he lived a sometimes dangerous night life with meetings in obscure places where he consulted with the reform Turks who had been forced out of power as a consequence of Turkey's defeat in the conflict with Persia. Twice every week he spent the night at the house of a young friend, Ahmed Vefik Effendi, who spoke fluent French and was a great lover of European literature. At this time non-Turks were not permitted to spend the night in Constantinople's Turkish quarter, but they did not care.

In the middle of this exciting and dramatic life Botta's letters began to arrive. The repeated invitations to come to Khorsabad were extremely tempting but Layard had no possibility of escaping from Canning at this time. Instead he used Botta's letters and especially Flandin's marvellous drawings as the basis for a series of articles which were published in *The Malta Times* in January 1845, even before Botta's own reports had been printed. Flandin stopped in Constantinople on his way to Paris after Botta had closed the excavations in October 1844, and he showed Layard his drawings and plans. The articles created considerable interest and became the basis for much debate in several English papers and magazines (Layard 1845).

They also induced Rawlinson to write to Layard and tell him about his own renewed efforts to find the key to unlock the secret of the cuneiform writing system. He had become the Resident in Baghdad at the end of 1843, succeeding Colonel Taylor, and in the latter's library he had seen the notes left by Layard. He said in his letter to Layard that he had long wished to establish contact, and he was particularly interested in getting copies of the inscriptions Layard had seen and copied during his time with the Bakhtiyaris.

Layard attempted to convince Canning to support an excavation at Nimrud, and he could refer to a letter from Rawlinson who had urged Layard to arouse the ambassador's interest:

> I should be exceedingly glad indeed if the Ambassador and through him the Govt could be induced to take an interest in the antiquities of this country. It pains me grievously to see the French monopolise the field, for the fruits of Botta's labors ... are not things to pass away in a day but will constitute a national glory in future ages, when perhaps the Turkish Empire that we are now struggling so hard to preserve, shall be but a matter of history.
>
> (Brackman 1980: 121)

Canning was at first more interested in another archaeological project, which eventually secured him great personal honour. Layard had suggested that he should attempt to gain access to the old crusader castle in the town Bodrum on the Aegean coast of Asia Minor. It had long been known that the crusaders had used a number of reliefs from the ancient town of Halicarnassus in the construction of the inner walls, but the castle had been closed to foreigners. The reliefs presumably came from the famous funerary monument of King Mausolos, 'The Mausoleum', which in the ancient world was counted as one of the seven wonders of the world. One of Canning's friends, Lord Eastnor, was allowed to see the reliefs, but it took a couple of years more before Canning could secure permission from the Sultan to remove them and send them to England. He gave them to the British Museum where they became known as 'Canning's Marbles'; they were regarded as nearly on the same level of artistic perfection as the sculptures from the Parthenon, the 'Elgin Marbles'.

One can hardly doubt that it was the enormous interest created by Botta's discoveries which persuaded Canning to support Layard's plans for excavations in Assyria in the autumn of 1845. It could now be said with a degree of certainty that the Assyrian mounds actually contained things worth finding, and there was a great expectation of discovering both more reliefs and new inscriptions which would soon be readable. Botta's special enemy, the missionary Percy Badger, had visited Nimrud in March 1844 and found a block of marble with an inscription. It had been sent to Rawlinson in Baghdad, and Badger wrote a report to Canning in October of the same year, supporting Layard's ideas about excavations at this particular spot. The purpose of course was to get reliefs back to England where they could be exhibited together with the rapidly growing collection of Egyptian and Greek sculpture.

The understanding of Assyrian monuments which formed at least part of the motivation for further excavations, was based on two main considerations: the idea that Assyria was of direct relevance for a better elucidation of the Old Testament; and the notion of a kind of evolution of the arts, which postulated that a line could be drawn which linked the most primitive attempts in the earliest human civilisations to Greek art, the absolute pinnacle which was represented by the sculptures from the Parthenon. In this way the collection of sculptures in the British Museum could appear as a pedagogic tool showing what was called 'The Chain of Art', the long sequence of works of art which constituted concrete evidence of the progress of human civilisation (Jenkins 1992: 56–74). The national ambition to fill the British Museum with the most prestigious and glorious accumulation of works of art from the history of mankind fitted perfectly with Canning's own personal ambition. He understood very well the significance of Rawlinson's remarks that it was essential to prevent France from establishing a kind of monopoly in Assyria, and he knew that his private political plans could only benefit from having his name associated with new and sensational finds.

Canning's personal interest in the excavations was evident in the letters he wrote to his family once the excavations had started (Lane-Poole 1888: 2, 145). When they had already proven to live up to the highest expectations, Canning wrote to his wife, who was clearly worried about his economic involvement in this effort, whose relevance she did not understand. He tried to calm her fears:

> I am quite proud of my public spirit in the cause of antiquity and fine art. But I must not ruin either you or the children; and I propose to call in the aid of the Government – whether Whig or Tory – to accomplish what may easily prove beyond my reach. Now you must be tired, dead tired of all this, and perhaps you think me crazy for caring so much about such trifles, but

they are trifles for which colleges universities and nations would take each other by the ears, and as Major Rawlinson tells me, the inscriptions are likely to throw much light upon Scripture history, particularly on our old friend *Tiglath-pileser*.

(Lane-Poole 1888: 2, 148–9)

CHAPTER NINE

NIMRUD

—— .◆. ——

Layard went back to Mosul in October 1845. In a small informal note to the ambassador from 30 September he estimated the expenses as follows: £30 for the journey, 4–5 piastres per day per worker, 3–400 piastres a month for a guard, plus expenses for a small tent and a horse; in all he thought that it would cost some 15,000 piastres, corresponding to £138 – 'say £150'.

Canning agreed to support an expedition for two months. He wrote a set of instructions, whose main points were as follows:

I rely upon Mr Layard's obliging attention to the following points:

1 To keep me informed of his operations, and of any objects of sufficient interest and curiosity which he may see or discover.
2 To keep clear of political and religious questions, and as much as possible of Missionaries, or native chiefs and tribes regarded with enmity or jealousy by the Turkish authorities.
3 To cultivate the goodwill of the Pashas and others of the Sultan's functionaries by all becoming means.
4 To bear in mind that his professed occupation will be that of a traveller, fond of antiquities, of picturesque scenery, and of the manners peculiar to Asia.
5 Not to start on his return without a previous communication with me subsequent to his first inquiries and attempts at discovery.
6 In case of success to give me early and exact information as to the nature of the objects discovered, & the best means of removal &c with an estimate of cost, doing what he can to obtain the necessary help on the spot.[23]

Extremely detailed instructions concerning money follow, and it appears that Layard's pay of £200 per annum as embassy functionary was part of the budget together with Canning's own contribution. The ambassador added that if Layard after two months of work concluded that it would be reasonable to continue his activities, he could do so on his own initiative for a further ten or fourteen days.

Canning's instructions reveal a certain degree of worry over Layard's youthful unpredictability, and one may suspect that Layard on his side was slightly irritated

Figure 9.1 Henry James Ross, the merchant who lived at Mosul and who became Layard's
close friend. (From Waterfield 1963: 150)

at being admonished in this somewhat supercilious manner. After all, he had shown
himself to be capable of handling far greater and more dangerous difficulties than
any he was likely to face in his role as archaeologist.

The English merchant Henry Ross (see Figure 9.1) and the Vice-Consul Christian
Rassam received Layard in Mosul. As a 'gentleman traveller' interested in ruins

and beautiful landscapes he obviously did not carry any kind of permission for excavations, and the local Pasha was known as a very difficult man who would be unlikely to view such activities with sympathy. Accordingly, there could be no question of excavating at Kuyunjik across the river, for the people of Mosul would of course immediately become aware of his work there. Nimrud, the large ruin some 25 km further downstream, was a much better option.

In his first letter to Canning from Mosul Layard explained that the Pasha seemed disposed to be civil and he felt he had no reason to anticipate any difficulties from that quarter. Nevertheless, he kept up his cover and planned for his expedition to Nimrud in secrecy. Rassam was building a house in Mosul, and this gave them an opportunity to acquire tools needed for the digging. Ross tells us that in order to fool the Pasha he sent his greyhounds and horses down to Nimrud, announcing that he and Layard were planning an extended hunting expedition. They followed on board a *kelek*, a raft which carried their tools and some food.

They left Mosul early in the afternoon on 8 November 1845, and after five hours on the river they stopped at a small deserted village called Naifa, where they found a single Arab family living in a miserable hut. The leader of the group was a certain Awad, who was also, it turned out, the sheikh of the Jerash tribe. The Pasha had crushed this tribe, and the cruel behaviour of his agents and tax collectors had led to a situation where most of the villages in the area were deserted. On his trip to Mosul Layard had already noticed that the brutal rule of the Pasha had nearly depopulated the agricultural lands, making it necessary to travel with an armed escort.

Ross and Layard were received cordially, however, and they spent the night in the hut. Layard explained to Awad that he planned excavations on the great mound in the neighbourhood and that he needed men for the work, and the sheikh went off in the middle of the night to the nearby village of Selamiyah and to Bedouin camps in the area in order to collect a crew for the excavations. The promise of a little extra income was bound to induce people to come.

The two Europeans lay down on their blankets on the floor of the hut together with Awad's family; the women withdrew to another room. But Layard could not sleep. He was finally close to his goal. Five years earlier he had seen Nimrud as a large conical silhouette against the night sky, and now he was on the brink of realising the dream he had carried ever since.

To Layard Nimrud was the great mound only. It is some 650 by 350 m in extent, and the most prominent feature is the great 'pyramid', about 200 m in diameter, which rises from the northwestern corner of the mound. Like Nineveh the ancient city at Nimrud had been considerably larger – which could be seen from the city walls which encircled an area of some square kilometres – and the mound which interested Layard was in fact the acropolis of the city, where palaces and the main temples were located; the living quarters of the population were spread around it in the landscape.

Botta's work at Khorsabad had proven that it was possible to find both great buildings and exciting works of art, and Layard was certain that something similar to Khorsabad had to lie hidden in the mound at Nimrud. He tossed and turned on his blanket and sleep would not come. In a dream, half-awake, he fantasised:

Visions of palaces underground, of gigantic monsters, of sculptured figures, and endless inscriptions, floated before me. After forming plan after plan for removing the earth, and extricating these treasures, I fancied myself wandering in a maze of chambers from which I could find no outlet. Then again, all was reburied, and I was standing on the grass-covered mound. Exhausted, I was at length sinking into sleep, when hearing the voice of Awad, I rose from my carpet, and joined him outside the hovel. The day already dawned; he had returned with six Arabs, who agreed for a small sum to work under my direction.

(Layard 1849, vol. I: 25)

There was a twenty-minute walk from the village to the mound and on his way there in the cool morning air Layard in his tense excitement noticed every detail. The mound itself rose like a small mountain against the morning sky; the landscape around it was bare and dry at this time of year, without the lush cover of flowers which had hidden everything on his first visit; his eye wandered over the flat, deserted landscape and followed a small tornado which moved on the horizon and dragged a cloud of dust towards the sky.

The small group of men climbed up on the mound which was entirely bare of vegetation. Layard could immediately see bits of pots and bricks with broken inscriptions lying in the dust. Like all later archaeologists he first went around the top of the mound with bowed head, letting the eye scan the dusty ground. The Arabs watched with surprise while he picked up bits and pieces, but they soon understood what he was after and started looking themselves. After a short time one man brought Layard a piece of a marble relief, and this caused great excitement: there really were the same possibilities here as on Botta's Khorsabad! The piece was clearly marked by fire, and Layard was immediately convinced that it was of exactly the same nature as those which had been discovered by the French.

Awad then found a bit of a marble block, but it would not budge. When they cleaned the earth away it turned out to be the top corner of a block which continued down into the mound. Layard ordered his men to remove the earth around it and several other blocks appeared; they formed a rectangle with a gap in one corner, and Layard at once realised that they stood above a room with a door. The palace had been found!

As they dug down into the chamber they were disappointed to see that there were no reliefs carved into the blocks, but only a long band of inscriptions which ran across the middle of the slabs.

Layard had noticed a concentration of marble fragments in the southwestern corner of the mound, and he now took his men to this spot in order to dig. Shortly after they discovered a wall here too, but again covered with inscriptions and without reliefs. Moreover, these stones had been so damaged by fire that they crumbled before their eyes as soon as they were exposed to the effects of the open air.

It was now getting dark and they had to stop working. On this the very first day Layard had discovered two palaces, one in the northwestern and another in the southwestern corner of the mound, and even though no reliefs had appeared there were so many fragments spread on the surface of the mound that he was convinced that it was only a matter of time before he would find them *in situ*.

Layard's excavation can be followed in detail, not only through his own account which was published a few years later, but also in his correspondence which is kept at the British Library in London. He sent a letter to Canning every two weeks when there was a post-*tatar* from Mosul to Constantinople, and in the same way he corresponded with Major Rawlinson in Baghdad. One of his old close friends from his time in Constantinople, an embassy functionary called Alison,[24] also wrote regularly – usually witty, caustic comments on life in the capital, and Layard finally had an extensive correspondence with his family and friends in England. This entire material remains unpublished but as will appear this account relies heavily on the letters.

A few days after his arrival at Nimrud Layard received a letter from Rawlinson who expressed his pleasure at hearing that Layard was in Mosul in order to excavate. He expected Nimrud to be too far away from the mountains for it to contain 'marble palaces' like Khorsabad, 'but you can hardly fail to find inscriptions and other relics that will repay your labor'. In his view Nebbi Yunus had to be 'one of the most promising sites in the vicinity of Mosul, but its sanctity I fear is not to be invaded.'[25]

After a week's work Layard decided to go back to Mosul in order to confront the Pasha who had been informed of his activities at Nimrud. Ross tells us that one day he was taking a break, smoking a cigarette, as a group of horsemen hunting a gazelle suddenly became aware of the presence of a European in this godforsaken spot. They halted and asked him in surprise what he was doing here, and it was clear that they intended to rush back to Mosul with the news of Layard's diggings at Nimrud. So, a difficult interview with the Pasha was to be expected.

In his description of this man, Mohammed Keritli Oglu, Layard does not mince his words: 'He had only one eye and one ear; he was short and fat, pockmarked, coarse in his movements and with a shrill voice'. Already before his arrival at Mosul he had been notorious for his cruelty, and *en route* from Constantinople he had, for example, reintroduced a tax on the villages where he stayed, *dish parassi*, meant to compensate him for the wear on his teeth caused by eating the food the villagers were forced to serve him. The local leaders of Mosul had run from the town before his arrival, but he seduced them back with promises of a fair treatment, after which he had them beheaded. He had also made use of a trick which involved spreading the rumour that he had died; the poor people who were so unlucky that their relief at this was noted by the Pasha's agents promptly lost their possessions.

In fact, Layard arrived the day after the one-eyed Pasha had pulled this stunt, so when he was ushered into the audience room Layard began by congratulating the Pasha on his speedy recovery, a remark which was met with laughter. The meeting went fairly peacefully, but Layard realised that he was going to be bitterly opposed from another direction, the religious authorities in Mosul. Botta already had his difficulties with the Cadi, the 'judge' and religious leader in the town, for instance in connection with a plan to expand the Dominican convent in Mosul and build a church; just now it was Christian Rassam, the British Vice-Consul, who had run into trouble. He had purchased an old building, planning to use it to store his goods, but this was perceived by the Cadi as the beginning of a process which would end with the British buying the entire town. He was busy stirring up the populace to do something about the matter, and Mosul was in a condition of excitement and tension. Shortly after Layard's departure for Nimrud the Cadi actually succeeded in arousing the passions of his followers to such an extent that they attacked the British consulate and destroyed the offending building. Also Layard's activities were viewed with suspicion. Reports that he had found tremendous treasures had reached the town, and Layard more than hinted that even the French consulate in Mosul, now directed by Botta's successor M. Rouet, actively helped to build up a feeling of resentment directed against Layard's excavations.

Consequently, he hurried back to Nimrud, having first hired some Nestorian Arabs and sent them on ahead; others he instructed to find mounds in the vicinity of Mosul and make trial excavations to determine whether they contained Assyrian remains.

Back at Nimrud he learnt that the workmen in his absence had continued digging along the wall they had found, and they had reached a doorway, but still without finding reliefs. Rawlinson wrote and explained that inscriptions at any rate were of very much greater interest than reliefs:

> For my own part I regard Inscriptions as of infinitely greater value than sculptures – the latter may please virtuosi – they have no doubt a certain degree of intrinsic interest, but the tablets are bona fide histories and very shortly I feel perfectly certain they will be completely intelligible. The building at Nimrood probably will hardly be worth a transport en masse to London, but your copies of the Inscriptions will be of the very highest interest.[26]

Of course, that was nice to know, and Layard wrote to Canning that the inscriptions already found were quite enough to justify the entire exercise. But nothing could hide the fact that the situation was disappointing, and he must have been truly worried that his palace might continue like this.

Layard now expanded his workforce to thirty men; the Nestorians, hardy men from the mountains, were the only ones who had the strength to loosen the hard surface with their large pick-axes, for the bone-dry earth was as impenetrable as concrete. The local Arabs were mainly employed as carriers of the excavated earth in reed baskets. Botta too had used Christian Arabs as workmen at Khorsabad. During 1843 large groups of Nestorians had been chased from their traditional mountain villages by the Kurds who pushed them down onto the plains around Mosul. This tragic development resulted in a serious refugee problem, but it also gave the excavators access to a willing and religiously unproblematic workforce.

Layard stuck to the burnt palace in the southwestern corner, and on 28 November 1845, after a further nine days of work, his men encountered a wall which finally bore relief slabs. He had no idea where in the building he was, he did not even know when he saw the top of the marble slab which side was the front, so first he had one side completely cleaned – it was quite bare – and then the other, where a badly damaged but very clear relief immediately appeared:

The Arabs were no less excited than myself by the discovery; and notwith-standing a violent shower of rain, working until dark, they completely exposed to view two slabs.

On each slab were two bas-reliefs, separated from one another by a band of inscriptions. The subject on the upper part of No. 1. was a battle scene. Two chariots, drawn by horses richly caparisoned, were each occupied by a group of three warriors; the principal person in both groups was beardless, and evidently a eunuch. He was clothed in a complete suit of mail, and wore a pointed helmet on his head, from the sides of which fell lappets covering the ears, the lower part of the face, and the neck. The left hand, the arm being extended, grasped a bow at full stretch; whilst the right, drawing the string to the ear, held an arrow ready to be discharged. A second warrior urged, with the reins and whip, to the utmost of their speed three horses, which were galloping over the plain. A third, without helmet, and with flowing hair and beard, held a shield for the defence of the principal figure. Under the horses' feet, and scattered about the relief, were the conquered, wounded by the arrows of the conquerors.

Unfortunately the stone was so fragile because of the fire which had destroyed the palace that it was hopeless to think of removing it. Layard made drawings as best he could, and he noted with surprise 'the elegance and richness in the ornaments, the careful and fine rendering of bodies and muscles, both for the horses and the humans, and the artistic ability which revealed itself in the placing of the figures and the composition as a whole' (Layard 1849, vol. I: 40–1). He felt that these reliefs in a number of ways were superior to those found by Botta at Khorsabad.

The other slab also showed scenes of war, and in the bottom panel there was a picture of a castle with walls and towers. On one of the towers stood a woman who tore her hair in grief, while at the foot of the castle there was a scene with a man who was fishing in a small river. This slab was placed upside down, however, and it was partially destroyed, so Layard could immediately conclude that these reliefs did not originally belong in this building but had been brought here in order to be reused in a palace which appeared never to have been finished.

In the evening, as Layard sat in his hut writing about his discoveries, he received a visit from Daoud Agha, the leader of a small group of irregular soldiers who were stationed in the village Selamiyah some 5 km from Nimrud. Layard had befriended this man, whom he describes as an intelligent and straightforward person; after his return from his visit to the Pasha at Mosul Layard had moved to Selamiyah where he lived in a small hovel he had rented, so he was in daily contact with Daoud.

As I was meditating in the evening over my discovery, Daoud Agha entered, and seating himself near me, delivered a long speech, to the effect that he was the servant of the Pasha, who was again the slave of the Sultan; and that servants were bound to obey the commands of their master, however disagree-able and unjust they might be.

(Layard 1849, vol. I: 43–4)

Layard immediately understood the situation: Daoud had received orders from the Pasha to stop the excavation. Next morning, when he rode to Mosul and went to the palace, the Pasha expressed his complete surprise and promised to write a letter to Daoud, ordering him to let Layard continue. With this he went back to Nimrud, but later that day he received a new visit from Daoud who told him that he had just received a new letter, which contained even stronger orders that he must at all cost prevent Layard from digging.

Back to Mosul and a new audience with the Pasha, who now explained that he had just been informed that the mound at Nimrud was a traditional Islamic burial ground, and he could not of course allow Layard to destroy graves. The Cadi had visited him, he explained, and he had emphasised this point. Layard then sat down to write a letter to Canning, asking him to apply to the Sultan for an official permit which would allow him to excavate and remove sculptures.

> I trust your Excellency will deem my present discovery of sufficient impor-
> tance to warrant an application to the Porte for a firman not only for
> excavating, but for removing sculptures when found. Unless such an order
> be procured I fear there will be considerable difficulty in carrying on the
> work to any extent.

He added that he had been extremely polite in his dealings with the Pasha, despite his feeling of deep resentment. M. Rouet, the new French consul, had travelled around the country and found interesting rock sculptures, and Layard attempted to play on Canning's vanity by emphasising that his 'most liberal advance will not be made in vain, but that a most valuable addition will be made to our national Museum and to our knowledge of the history and language of one of the most ancient and remarkable nations of the earth'.

He felt certain that the French consul through his 'dragoman' or interpreter was directly responsible for many of the difficulties thrown in his way by the Pasha; however, there might be a possibility for a sweet revenge, for he had been informed by Rawlinson that Botta's sculptures were still at Basrah waiting for a ship to carry them to France. With a little luck 'I think we might manage to transmit some sculpture to Europe as soon if not sooner than the French. This would be very important for our reputation'.[27]

But Canning was not minded to make an appeal to the Sultan at this time, while he had still not secured permission to bring the Mausolos reliefs from the Bodrum castle to London. That project clearly took precedence over Layard's excavations, which meant that these now necessarily became strictly limited in scope. He did not stop entirely but kept a group of men on the mound to guard the slabs that had been uncovered in order that they could be drawn. When he was alone with his men on the mound he let them continue the excavations. Daoud Agha was willing to overlook quite a lot, for he was furious with the Pasha, having been ordered to establish a completely new burial ground on top of the mound; in the course of the night he and his men had removed grave-stones from many real cemeteries in the neighbourhood and dragged them to the mound.

'We have destroyed more real tombs of the true Believers', said he, 'in making sham ones than you could have defiled between the Zab and Selamiyah. We have killed our horses and ourselves in carrying those accursed stones'.

(Layard 1849, vol. I: 46)

The excavations progressed both in the southwestern and the northwestern corner, but Layard still had no clear idea of what type of building – or how many – he was engaged in excavating. His workers discovered fragmentary bull statues, gate lions and badly damaged reliefs, enough to make it clear that Nimrud contained richly decorated buildings, but he could not make head or tail of his finds.

In Baghdad Rawlinson had followed Layard's work with joy, and in a letter written on 10 December he explained that his studies of the Classical authors had convinced him that Nimrud had to be the original Nineveh. The best-known story connected with that city in Greek literature is about Sardanapal, the last king of Nineveh who perished in a fire together with his riches and his harem when the city was conquered; Layard could confirm that the palace at Nimrud had been destroyed in a colossal conflagration. The Sardanapal story was widely known and had been depicted in a famous painting by Delacroix, exhibited in the Paris *salon* in 1828, a picture which shows the European view of the Assyrian king as the archetypal Oriental despot, while at the same time revealing how little concrete knowledge existed about vanished Assyria.

Layard decided to take a break from the excavations at the end of December, and when he arrived at Mosul he found the whole town in a state of jubilant joy. The day before a message from Constantinople had arrived with the *tatar* which deposed the Pasha, Mohammed Keritli Oglu, replacing him with a popular official by the name of Ismail, who was known to favour reforms. Layard explains that the interpreter of the consulate found the deposed Pasha the following day sitting in a miserable, roofless hovel in streaming rain. 'Thus it is', said he, 'with God's creatures. Yesterday all those dogs were kissing my feet; to-day every one, and every thing, falls upon me, even the rain!'

Nobody felt sorry for him, however, and Layard now expected to be able to count on the full goodwill of the authorities in Mosul, so that he could continue his work at Nimrud. After a few days in Mosul he left together with an English visitor on a raft bound for Baghdad, and they arrived here on Christmas eve. Layard wanted finally to meet his penfriend Major Rawlinson face to face and discuss Assyrian antiquities with him.

CHAPTER TEN

THE IDEAL
ENGLISH SOLDIER

———— •◆• ————

Henry Creswicke Rawlinson, who was then thirty-five-years old, had been Political Resident in Baghdad for two years. In the British colonial administration he had early become known as a specialist in Persian affairs and a great scholar with respect to its languages and literature; his articles about travels in the country had been among the most important things the young Layard had read to prepare himself for his journey.

In many ways Rawlinson was the ideal English soldier. His brother, who wrote a very extensive biographical presentation of his life and career, described him as 'six feet tall, with broad shoulders, strong limbs and excellent muscles and sinews', and he was known as an excellent sportsman, which meant horseman and hunter. In 1827 he had been sent to India at the age of seventeen as a young cadet, and he soon distinguished himself as a fine officer, and especially as a sportsman; he won several wagers based on his abilities as a rider, for instance a trip from Poonah to Panwell, a distance of 72 miles which was covered in three hours and seven minutes on 11 horses, a feat which was mentioned prominently in *The Sporting Magazine* in 1832 (Rawlinson 1898: 27–34). However, he also quickly became a specialist in several languages, and from his very first time in India he interested himself in linguistic studies and won the status of official interpreter in several dialects. As a lieutenant he was sent to Tabriz in Persia in 1833, where, together with a group of young English officers, he was supposed to reorganise the Persian army, which did not do well in the constant conflicts with Russia. From 1835 he was stationed in the provincial town of Kermanshah.

It was here that his interest in cuneiform studies was awakened, and during the winter of 1836–7 he spent a great deal of time in this pursuit. Some 30 km east of the town is one of the most famous ancient monuments in the Middle East, the Bisutun Rock, which became a favourite spot for the young Rawlinson when he had time to spare. High on a dramatic cliff one sees a very large Persian relief carved directly into the rock, flanked by a very long inscription which is written in three different varieties of cuneiform. The details of the relief can hardly be discerned with the naked eye from the ground, and the inscription is of course entirely illegible. Like most royal inscriptions from the ancient civilisations in the Middle East, the entire monument is directed towards the gods, not to men.

Figure 10.1 The Old Persian text at Bisutun was just one of several rock inscriptions, although the most impressive. Flandin and Coste are here seen engaged in copying two others in the mountains close to Hamadan. (From Flandin and Coste 1843–54)

For instance, inscriptions on Egyptian temples are often located in places where no one can read them, and Assyrian memorial inscriptions were often buried underground. The fact is, of course, that very few people would have been able to read any inscription in the ancient past.

Rawlinson could not read the text either, of course, but he immediately realised the importance of this monument. This was clearly the longest Persian inscription known, and that in itself gave the hope that it would be possible to offer decisive clues to the correct decipherment of the script. If it were possible to read the first column in Old Persian, then such a reading would offer a good basis for anyone who wished to tackle the other two types of script on the monument (see Figure 10.1).

He knew that it was such a 'trilingual' text, an inscription with three different versions of the same text, in different languages and/or scripts, which had made it possible to decipher the Egyptian hieroglyphs. However, one cannot really compare the Bisutun inscription with the Rosetta Stone, for the latter contained a Greek translation of the Egyptian text, that is, it could be read because both script and language was known. We now know that Bisutun gives the same text in Old Persian with a mixed alphabetic and syllabic cuneiform script, in Elamite using a special version of the cuneiform script, and in Babylonian using the 'standard'

Mesopotamian cuneiform system of writing. Therefore, none of these versions could be read, all had to be deciphered. The reason why there was some ground for optimism was the expectation that the first version, which used the simplest script, had to be in Old Persian, the official language of the Achaemenid empire. It is true that one did not have any directly readable Old Persian texts, but the language was known from later, Medieval documents in the Zend-Avesta texts, and it is Indo-European in type and related to Sanskrit. This would, it was felt, form a sufficiently strong basis for a decipherment, and that expectation proved correct.

The effort to unravel the mysteries of the cuneiform script had been going on for some time, and much had already been accomplished with respect to the first, Old Persian column. Carsten Niebuhr returning home from his tragic expedition to Arabia Felix had brought with him the first truly reliable copies of a fairly large collection of inscriptions from Persepolis, and he had contributed to the correct understanding of them in his book. Another Dane, the Bishop of Zealand, F.C.C. Münter, furthered the understanding a little by pointing out that a certain oblique wedge had to function as a word divider; he also suggested that the inscriptions had to have been written by the Achaemenid kings; consequently they should be close to the language of the Avestan texts. He guessed correctly that the three versions gave the same text, but incorrectly that it was only the scripts, not the language which was different from one version to the next; he even suggested that certain repeated combinations of signs contained the words 'king' and 'king of kings' (Münter 1802).

It was a German high school teacher, G.F. Grotefend, who really set things moving. Like Münter he assumed that the inscriptions were royal ones and that they must contain a specific royal formula which was known from later texts: this included such phrases as 'the great king' and 'king of kings'. His decisive achievement was that he succeeded in isolating the words in these titles and he could then concentrate on the personal names which were associated with them. The names of the Persian kings were known from Greek writers, and by inserting reconstructed readings of these names into the inscriptions Grotefend was able to make very good suggestions about the reading of a number of signs; twelve of these suggestions proved to be correct. His ideas were published in 1802 and were soon known to the learned world in Europe. The Danish linguist Rasmus Rask was inspired by Grotefend's successes to press on with the work, and on the basis of his intimate knowledge of the Zend-Avesta texts he could provide very valuable corrections. After him came a series of minor successes achieved by a number of scholars, and these had led to a situation where more than half of the signs could be read.

So, Rawlinson did not really have to start from scratch, but at the very beginning he had no access to the results achieved by other scholars, so in effect he had to begin on virgin soil without the help of other scholars' results. However, as can be seen from the letters to his sister, he was soon in contact with Colonel Taylor, who was the Resident for the British East India Company at Baghdad, a man he described as 'the best scholar living probably in the ancient languages of the East', and he was able to consult his extensive library in Baghdad already in late 1835 (Borger 1975–8a).

He realised that the Bisutun text could furnish the key to the decipherment, simply because of its length, and he did all he could to get it copied. He visited the site many times while he lived at Kermanshah, and he succeeded in copying the first two columns by climbing around on the cliff with the help of ropes and ladders. The third column, the Babylonian one, was located in such a way that it was inaccessible without special mountaineering equipment.

In a letter dated Tehran, 1 January 1838, Rawlinson made his first announcement of his discoveries to the Secretary of the Royal Asiatic Society. The following year he then submitted a sixteen-page scholarly report to the society in which he presented his readings, a work which represented a quite substantial scholarly achievement. He was well aware of this as appears from a letter he wrote to his sister in which he triumphantly reminded her that she had earlier laughed at him and expressed her disdain with respect to his chances of making real progress where so many illustrious scholars had failed before him: 'Let him laugh who wishes. Depend on it I shall only be a short way in hind of Champollion and De Sacy some day' (Borger 1975–8a: 5).

Since that time he had worked hard on his copies and studied the learned literature on the subject, and when Layard visited him in Baghdad he was just finishing the very large paper he wrote on the Bisutun text. Part of the manuscript had already been sent to London to be published in the *Journal of the Royal Asiatic Society*, and while he sat in Constantinople Layard had helped in getting the manuscript sent on from there by diplomatic mail. The two men had corresponded regularly for more than a year, mainly on the subject of cuneiform decipherment, and this had continued after Layard had moved to Mosul.

Rawlinson had not lived a quiet scholarly life, and it had taken him a long time to conclude his manuscript. In 1839 he returned to India, and the following year he was sent to Afghanistan, now with the rank of major, where he was to function as 'Political Agent' in the westernmost part of the country. He was very effective during the siege of Kandahar, a lengthy episode in the 'Great Afghan War' of 1841–3. This war was related to the conflict with Russia which appeared steadily more threatening for English interests in India. It began with an unprovoked British occupation of the country which was caused by fear that the Russians were preparing for military action, but it all went wrong very quickly. The capital Kabul was besieged and conquered by so-called Afghan 'rebels' who carried out a massacre of the British colony in the city. Rawlinson was the politically responsible person in the second largest town in the country, and he succeeded with great diplomatic and military skill in saving it from the fate of Kabul; this allowed the British soldiers to beat an orderly retreat to India (Hopkirk 1994).

After the end of the Afghan War Rawlinson again returned to India, and he now had to find a new role for himself. He was offered various posts in the colonial administration, of such importance as to reflect positively on the high reputation he had built up; he could have become Resident in Nepal or Agent for central India. However, the brother writes that

> he was somewhat weary of governing half-civilised Orientals, and longed to
> get back to those linguistic and archæological investigations which had

engaged his attention and fascinated his imagination when he was in Persia during the years 1833–39. It happened that the 'Political Agency in Turkish Arabia' was also among the posts vacant.

(Rawlinson 1898: 139–40)

This was the post in Baghdad, where Colonel Taylor was about to resign. Rawlinson got the job and in December 1843 he landed in Baghdad and was received by a salute from thirteen cannons.

His position here was marked by pomp and circumstance which was designed to make a suitable impression on the local people. The Residency itself was a large and impressive building, certainly after Baghdad standards, and he had an enormous staff of servants, cooks, stable boys, valets, guards, coffee-grinders, pipe fillers and so on. When he moved out of the Residency in a formal capacity he was accompanied by a guard of honour consisting of Indian soldiers.

It is not easy to gain a precise impression of Rawlinson the man. His letters are pervaded by a formal politeness which only very rarely gives one a glimpse of the man behind the façade; when that happens he often expresses a direct and frank rudeness. The brother quotes a set of rules to live by which were formulated by the young Lieutenant Rawlinson in India, and which appear to have remained valid throughout his life:

> Create business for yourself. Lose no opportunity of making yourself useful, whatever may be the affair which may happen to present the chance. Grasp at everything, and never yield an inch. Above all, never stand upon trifles. Be careful of outward observances. Maintain a good establishment; keep good horses and showy ones; dress well; have good and handsome arms; in your conversation and intercourse with the natives, be sure to observe the customary etiquette.

(Rawlinson 1898: 57)

Layard's friend at Mosul, the astute merchant Henry Ross, visited Rawlinson a year before Layard, and in a letter to his sister he has given a description of the special British way of life in the East which Major Rawlinson was eager to keep up. The food in the Residency was prepared by a cook from Bombay and it was according to Ross 'very good'; everything was done in accordance with Indian custom: after cheese and beer had been served following the dessert, 'in came the major-domo and said *Sahib, tchai hadr* (Master, tea is ready), and we left for the tea-room, where we were served with tea and "kalians" (Persian water-pipes)'. Having smoked for half an hour the party was again summoned into the dining room. Here 'we found the table cleared of fruit and wine and in their place a tureen full of smoking punch; scattered about the table were devilled herrings and turkey's legs'. That was the end of the more formal part of the dinner party and the rest of the night was spent with speeches, singing and constant drinking, so it was a very gay group of gentlemen who finally tumbled into bed. The following day Ross again met Rawlinson, who to his surprise was very polite and forthcoming, 'for I should say he is rather haughty and keeps all around him at a certain distance. He is excessively clever and bears a high reputation amongst the diplomatists both at home and in India' (Ross 1902: letter dated 26 January 1845).

The brother's biography is not much use in providing us with a nuanced picture of Rawlinson's character – he is described as invariably upright, hardworking, fair and sportsmanlike. There is a small anecdote, however, which may tell us something about the man behind the façade. He had bought a very small lion cub whose mother had been shot, and he took it to live at the Residency:

> To tame it, and attach it to himself, he gave his household strict orders that no one but himself should ever feed it; and sometimes, when he was feeding it, he would make a servant approach and make a show of taking the food away, when he would rise to his feet, scold the servant loudly, and knock him down, or chase him out of the room. He would then bring the beast back his food, make him eat it out of his hand, pat his head, and find him a cool place to lie down in. The lion would follow him about, all over his house and garden, like a dog, and was never altogether happy unless he could be with him. But the poor creature had not a long life. In one very hot season he became manifestly unwell, moped, and rejected his food. As a matter of course he was in his master's room, where he paced wearily about, or lay down and groaned. His master, who was very busy writing despatches for the evening's post, finding himself disturbed by the sounds and movements, summoned a couple of servants and said, 'Take the lion away!' They tried their best; but the lion would not go. He retreated nearer and nearer to his master's chair, and at last sat down under it with his head between his master's knees. When the servants pulled at him to drag him out, he growled at them and showed his teeth. 'Oh!' said my brother, 'if he won't go, let him bide'. The attendants departed; Major Rawlinson was absorbed in his despatches; the lion by degrees sank from a sitting position into that of a 'lion couchant'; all was quiet for some hours, save the scratching of a pen; then, his work over, Major Rawlinson put down his hand to pat his favourite; but his hand fell on a stiff form – the lion was dead.

The composed, cool, gifted Rawlinson had perhaps here found the one creature to which he could relate emotionally, and even though the story appears first of all to be a kind of parable of the relationship between the colonial master and his subjects, the anecdote also has a nearly tragic dimension; this may perhaps explain why the brother chose to elaborate so much. In the entire book of some 400 pages, this is the only place where Major Rawlinson actually speaks, where his own words are quoted.

The brother also tells about the meeting between the Major and Layard in Baghdad (even though he gives a completely wrong date for it), and he takes the opportunity to characterise the two men and compare them. Layard, he says, was eminently suited for the task he had set for himself, 'strong, robust, determined, able to exert a powerful influence over Orientals, and calculated to compel obedience from them; active, energetic, and inured to hardship by his previous travels in wild regions.' It is accepted that he had some Arabic and was quick to pick up foreign languages, but 'he was not a scholar, or a man of any great culture, or of any wide reading'. It would perhaps have been impossible to find a man better suited for the rough work which was needed at this point, and it was a happy chance which brought together two such men as him and Major Rawlinson as labourers at the same time and in the same field, but with each his own special task – each strongest where the other was weakest – Layard, the excavator, the effective task-master, the hard-working and judicious gatherer together of materials; and Rawlinson, the classical scholar, the linguist, the diligent student of history, the man at once of wide reading and keen insight, the cool, dispassionate investigator and weigher of evidence.

(Rawlinson 1898: 149–50)

Layard was hardly as lacking in culture or learning as Rawlinson's brother describes, and there are sides of Rawlinson's character which are not touched upon. His youthful letters to his sister reveal him as a man whose character, as he said himself, was 'one of restless, insatiable ambition – in whatever sphere I am thrown my whole spirit is absorbed in an eager struggle for the first place . . .' (Borger 1975–8a: 1; letter dated 15 July 1835). Accordingly, while he was a recognised expert with respect to the decipherment of cuneiform in its different varieties, he was also known to be a man who was apt to withhold his aces until the very last moment, avoiding any real competition from the people he perceived to be his 'rivals'. When he began his correspondence with Layard the intention was very clear: he wished to have access to the inscriptions he knew Layard had copied in the mountains of Khuzistan, but he gave very little in return.

Rawlinson was in fact severely criticised by a number of scholars for his unwillingness to make his texts available to the scholarly community, and he was accused of having hindered the speedy decipherment. According to the famous German-British historian of religion Max Müller this went so far that the impatience of the learned public in all of Europe to have new materials and new insights became so strong 'that the small kingdom of Denmark sent Westergaard to Persia in order to copy cuneiform inscriptions and study the ancient language of Zend-Avesta' (Mohl 1879: xxiv). Westergaard was Professor of Indian and Oriental Philology at Copenhagen University (Asmussen 1992: 684–8), and Max Müller was probably not right in his somewhat audacious interpretation of the motives behind his trip – which, by the way, he paid for out of his own pocket. Nevertheless, his remarks are revealing in showing that Rawlinson was not entirely popular because of his stinginess with the special knowledge he possessed.

Perhaps it was not entirely fair to blame him in this way, for he was after all not a professor like Max Müller with ample time for studies and research. That work was in the nature of a hobby which had to be fitted in whenever he had some spare time from his many official duties. Since he was also a perfectionist, it can hardly surprise that it took a while for him to complete his work. The ten years that passed are by the way nothing compared with the tardiness of many later scholars with respect to publication projects. Quite a few archaeologists and philologists have died without ever having been able to communicate to their colleagues what they had discovered. It is certain, however, that Rawlinson was loath to share the knowledge he had acquired, which can be seen for instance from the scores of letters written to Layard, for they contain practically no concrete information concerning his achievements. Time and again he writes that he is now able to read this or that type of text with 'passing certainty', but he never tells Layard what the texts then said.

However, at this time Layard had all the reason in the world to look forward to an intense collaboration while he was enjoying the hospitality of his friend during the Christmas festivities in Baghdad in 1845. After all, in his letters Rawlinson had expressed great interest and a willingness to be helpful. In a letter to his mother Layard wrote:

> I had long wished to make the personal acquaintance of Major Rawlinson, with whom I had long kept up a constant & regular correspondence and I received no disappointment on meeting him. You may suppose that we are already deep in discussion & researches on Assyrian, Persian & Babylonian antiquities, languages, geography &c &c – for on these subjects, you know, the Major is probably the first living authority. The result of our delibera-tions lead me to hope that before two or three years have expired we shall be able to get at the mysterious contents of the Assyrian cuneiform inscrip-tions – and then Nimroud will give us a rich historical collection.[28]

In the course of the two months he had worked at Nimrud, Layard had uncov-ered a lot of inscriptions, so there was plenty of new material to tackle for the two men. It was immediately obvious that one particular inscription had been cut into the reliefs and other slabs over and over again; they called it the 'Standard text' and could note that even though it was nearly identical from one example to the next, there were small variants. Layard felt that these variant writings were of decisive importance for an analysis of the script, and he had attempted to estab-lish a complete list of them.

There were many fundamental problems which had to be cleared away before the texts could be read, and several gaps of understanding blocked the way, not only for the two men in Baghdad, but for all those engaged in the attempt to resolve the mysteries of cuneiform. Botta was now sitting in Paris preparing a major study of the script, and Rawlinson corresponded with him; scholars in Ireland, Britain, France, Germany and Denmark were at the same time deeply immersed in the same task, but none had the advantage enjoyed by Rawlinson: access to the most complete textual material. Botta did have his texts from Khorsabad, of course, but a considerable part of those had been published in his letters to Mohl in the *Journal asiatique*, so scholars like Rawlinson knew about at least a representative sample of these texts. Everybody was in effect waiting for Rawlinson.

The meeting of the two men was a great success, and Layard anticipated a kind of division of labour between them, which would inevitably lead to a clearing up of the riddles. He would have to concentrate primarily on the manual work at Nimrud, while Rawlinson with his large library in the Residency would be able to tackle the script. From now on Rawlinson's letters no longer start with the formal 'My dear Sir', but with the more confidential 'My dear Layard'. Undoubtedly, it was a jolly Christmas in Baghdad that year, and young Layard's intense interest in the opposite sex appears to have manifested itself on this occasion, as we read from a remark with which Rawlinson's first letter of the new year ends:

> There are various stories afloat about Madame having come over to bid you adieu. She is said to have been closeted with you for at least ten minutes and there has been the devil's own work to patch up Jones's broken zeal.[29]

CHAPTER ELEVEN

THE RETURN OF
NIMROD

—— ·◆· ——

The new Pasha in Mosul, Ismail, was known as a liberal man, eager for reforms, and he expressed his interest in Layard's excavations when they first met after his return in the beginning of January 1846. There was accordingly reason for optimism, but certainly also major problems. The contract with Canning stipulated that Layard was to dig for two months, and that time had now passed without a new agreement being set up. It was first of all a matter of money, for Layard had to operate under such a limited budget that he was quite unable to make use of the opportunities which were so plain to see. Already before Christmas he had written to Canning to make him aware of the need for a resolution of the situation:

> Indeed I hope that should your Excellency determine upon carrying on the excavation or induce the Government to do so, we shall be able to make such a collection of Assyrian antiquities as can never be equalled in Europe.[30]

His friend Alison had written at the same time to tell him that Canning was 'vastly pleased with you', and assured him that he could be certain the ambassador was doing what he could. At the same time he advised Layard to prepare 'something for the public enlightenment, and – hide neither your talents nor your labors under a bushel, but import unto us a full understanding of every dodge, scheme & idea'.[31]

That was all very good, but it did not give him any more money. And even though the new Pasha was friendly, it was clear to Layard that new difficulties could easily arise, and they could only be dealt with effectively with the help of a regular permit from the Sultan in Constantinople, a so-called *firman*.

In the event there was nothing he could do, other than restart his work at Nimrud where at least the false graves had been removed again. His primary interest was to find reliefs which could be shipped to England, so he let his men work in different places. They found the sad remains of a badly damaged bull colossus, without head and wings. He let his workers concentrate their efforts mainly in the southwestern corner, the only place where reliefs had been discovered; here was a damaged building which appeared never to have been completed before the fire raged through it. So he found reliefs, but nearly all of them were so severely marked by fire that they were impossible to remove.

After a couple of weeks he received a summons from the Pasha, who explained that the Cadi, the religious leader in Mosul, was preparing a campaign directed against Layard's excavations. Therefore it would be best if he – as a gesture of friendship towards the Pasha – would stop his activities for a while until the threatening storm had passed. Reluctantly Layard agreed to limit his work, but perhaps it actually suited him fairly well to take a little pause until Canning saw fit to obtain some money and a *firman*. The rainy season was also about to start in earnest, so it would have been difficult under all circumstances to keep up the full-scale activities.

So he took a little holiday and made use of the opportunity to establish friendly relations with some of the local Bedouin tribes, especially the Abu Salman tribe who lived in the region around Nimrud, and who at an earlier occasion had created some difficulties for him. One morning he therefore rode to the main camp of the tribe where he was met by sheikh Abd-ur-rahman, a man who was to be very important for him in the following months. He stood at the entrance to his large, black, goat-hair tent, in which Layard found a group of Arabs, relatives of the sheikh, tribesmen and visitors who enjoyed the traditional hospitality of the tribe. Layard was impressed with Abd-ur-rahman:

> He was one of the handsomest Arabs I ever saw; tall, robust, and well-made, with a countenance in which intelligence was no less marked than courage and resolution. On his head he wore a turban of dark linen, from under which a many-coloured handkerchief fell over his shoulders; his dress was a simple white shirt, descending to the ankles, and an Arab cloak thrown loosely over it. Unlike Arabs in general, he had shaved his beard; and although he could scarcely be much beyond forty, I observed that the little hair which could be distinguished from under his turban was grey. He received me with every demonstration of hospitality, and led me to the upper place, divided by a goat-hair curtain from the harem. The tent was capacious; half was appropriated for the women, the rest formed the place of reception, and was at the same time occupied by two favourite mares and a colt. A few camels were kneeling on the grass around, and the horses of the strangers were tied by the halter to the tent-pins. From the carpets and cushions, which were spread for me, stretched on both sides a long line of men of the most motley appearance, seated on the bare ground. The Sheikh himself, as is the custom in some of the tribes, to show his respect for the guest, placed himself at the furthest end; and could only be prevailed upon, after many excuses and protestations, to share the carpet with me. In the centre of the group, near a small fire of camel's dung, crouched a half-naked Arab, engaged alternately in blowing up the expiring embers, and in pounding the roasted coffee in a copper mortar, ready to replenish the huge pots which stood near him.
>
> (Layard 1849, vol. I: 56–7)

Layard had brought gifts which he handed over to the sheikh. At the same time he expressed the wish that they were now friends, and he reminded him of the previous troubles. Abd-ur-rahman accepted the friendship, but at the same time he explained his tribe's situation as it looked from his perspective: like true Arabs they would serve the Sultan, but if that was not possible they had to take from others, just as others would take from themselves. His tribe had been treated with the utmost hostility by the former Pasha, and they had been forced to resort to robberies as their only possibility for saving their own lives. He had personally been caught by the Pasha and tortured for weeks, which explained his white hair.

Layard spent the entire day in Abd-ur-rahman's camp and was happy to have secured his friendship.

At this time he received a letter from Botta in Paris, in which he said that he expected to return to Assyria soon with ample funds from the French state, and that he planned to tackle Kuyunjik again. However, it soon appeared that there were difficulties getting the act through the parliament, so instead a certain M. Guillois was appointed the new French Vice-Consul at Mosul. Layard was annoyed to hear that he had applied for a *firman* to excavate Kuyunjik, and he immediately wrote to Canning to make him aware that this would be a French gain which the British should not simply allow. Apparently, had it been Botta who applied, the situation would have been perceived differently by Layard.[32]

Despite his promise to the Pasha to stop work at Nimrud Layard actually continued the excavations, albeit on a smaller scale, and he made new finds. The southwestern palace turned out to be a curious building. He found many reliefs here, but most of them turned the carved side towards the wall and some were upside down, so it was obvious these reliefs did not originally belong here; they had to have been taken from another building and brought here in order to be reused, having new reliefs carved on their backs, in a new palace. This had clearly never been finished. But where did the reliefs originally come from? He knew there was a large building in the northwestern corner, but so far Layard had discovered nothing but inscriptions here. There was a steep ravine just north of the place where he had been excavating, carved by rain water deep into the mound, and he decided to let his men try this place. It would be possible here to enter the building horizontally from the ravine.

There was almost instant success. First they began to find well-preserved reliefs, and a few days later his workmen made a decisive discovery. Layard had been visiting with Abd-ur-rahman and on his way back to Nimrud he was met by a couple of very excited Arabs who rushed towards him at full gallop shouting 'Hurry Bey, for they have found Nimrod himself!'

When he got to the mound he saw that the men had uncovered an enormous head, between 1 and 1.5 m in height, perfectly preserved without a scratch. This was what he had been dreaming about. He immediately realised that it had to be the head of one of the large bulls which guarded the main gateways, a figure which was still hidden in the earth underneath the feet of the workers. He knew from Botta's palace that such figures stood in pairs so he could expect to find another similar figure next to the one that had appeared, marking the other side of the entrance.

The Arabs were extremely agitated and considerably nervous, and he too was deeply affected:

Figure 11.1 Nimrod returns! This illustration from Layard's book captures the moment when Abd-ur-rahman with great caution inspected the colossal head which had appeared in one of Layard's trenches. This image of Arab superstition may be compared with the pictures from *Illustrated London News* which show the coolly observant gaze of the visitors to the British Museum (see p. 221); clearly, the Europeans are related to this ancient past, not the Arabs. (From Layard 1849, vol. I: 66)

I was not surprised that the Arabs had been amazed and terrified at this apparition. It required no stretch of imagination to conjure up the most strange fancies. This gigantic head, blanched with age, thus rising from the bowels of the earth, might well have belonged to one of those fearful beings which are pictured in the traditions of the country, as appearing to mortals slowly ascending from the regions below.

While Layard started removing dirt from the head Abd-ur-rahman arrived with half his tribe. 'There is no God other than God, and Mohammed is his prophet!' was the conjuration from the top of the trench, and no one seemed quite sure whether this head was really of stone. After some hesitation Abd-ur-rahman was persuaded to crawl into the trench to inspect the head more closely (see Figure 11.1), and he determined that this was not the work of human beings. It was made by 'those infidel giants of whom the Prophet – peace be with him! – has said that they were higher than the tallest date tree; this is one of the idols which Noah – peace be with him! – cursed before the flood! (Layard 1849, vol. I: 66–7).

All present agreed with this analysis, which was not exactly apt to create a calm and relaxed atmosphere. Layard had sufficient control over his men, nevertheless, to get them to continue digging in order to find the other figure which he knew had to be there. Before nightfall they found it, and he then got two of his trusted men to spend the night next to the head in order to prevent anyone from sneaking up to it in order to try to destroy it and make sure it was dead. He withdrew to the village where he slaughtered a sheep and held a party. Some wandering musicians who were in the neighbourhood were called to play and the dancing continued through most of the night.

Layard realised that the matter was now settled. He sat down to write Canning a letter, in which he informed him that Nimrud had now finally begun to reveal its treasures. He told him about his financial problems and explained that he had been forced to use his own slender means to buy the necessary presents for Abd-ur-rahman, and he suggested again that the British government should be asked to take over the responsibility for the excavations. He asked for money to pay a personal guard, a *cawass*, and a few other necessities.

> I did not trouble Your Excellency with these particulars before as I was not quite satisfied with the results of the experiment and could not confidently recommend Your Excellency to urge upon the Government to enter seriously into the work. I have now, however, no doubt whatsoever, as to the riches of Nimroud, and may reasonably predict that we shall far exceed the French at Khorsabad.[33]

He then suggested that a public statement or announcement of his discoveries should be made quickly, pointing out that 'a strong public interest in the undertaking would always be very useful', and noting that Botta's success with the French government was based largely on 'the notice taken by the public of his discoveries'.

He was no doubt right in his expectation that the public in Europe would be deeply interested in his finds, but a more immediate problem was what the Arabs in Mosul thought about the matter. Layard knew that one of the workers had been so terrified at finding himself face to face with what he thought was the ancient giant Nimrod himself, that he had run all the way from Nimrud to Mosul in order to broadcast the incredible news. He could imagine that the town was in an uproar at receiving this information, and his worry was soon justified.

> He had scarcely checked his speed before reaching the bridge. Entering breathless into the bazars, he announced to every one he met that Nimrod had appeared. The news soon got to the ears of the Cadi, who, anxious for a fresh opportunity to annoy me, called the Mufti and the Ulema together, to consult upon this unexpected occurrence. Their deliberations ended in a procession to the Governor, and a formal protest, on the part of the Mussulmans of the town, against proceedings so directly contrary to the laws of the Koran. The Cadi had no distinct idea whether the bones of the mighty hunter had been uncovered, or only his image; nor did Ismail Pasha very clearly remember whether Nimrod was a true-believing prophet, or an Infidel. I consequently received a somewhat unintelligible message from his Excellency, to the effect that the remains should be treated with respect, and be by no means further disturbed; that he wished the excavations to be stopped at once, and desired to confer with me on the subject.
>
> (Layard 1849, vol. I: 67–8)

Layard now had to close his excavations, waiting for more money and for a *firman*. This frustrating situation had its less sombre sides, however, for he now had an opportunity to relax and do some sight-seeing. The reputation of this young Englishman had travelled far and wide, and he was subjected to a regular invasion of visitors who were eager to discover what kind of a man he was, and not least what marvellous treasures he had discovered. The old Arab maxim 'My house is your house' became something of a burden to him, and things went all wrong when a high-ranking Kurdish chief from the mountains north of Mosul visited him with a large following. He brought some gifts and clearly expected substantial honours and large gifts in return for his visit. As a matter of course he settled down with his large number of followers, and he annoyed Layard by demonstrating his disgust with the way of life of his infidel host. He refused to eat together with Layard and any physical touch led to immediate and violent ablutions. The greyhounds who ran free in the camp bothered him especially, and he never let an opportunity pass to vent his deep irritation. Layard finally got rid of him by making it crystal clear to his trusted advisor that he had no intention of offering any of the gifts which were politely but insistently being demanded.

Hardly had this man gone before Layard then invited all the Arabs in the district, men and women, to a large party where also the Christian population of Mosul was to come. It could seem rather crazy to spend so much money on a party, and Alison in Constantinople had a fit when he heard of it, but Layard considered the money well spent. It was a deliberate decision, and the primary goal of the party was to enhance his own standing and reputation among the Arabs. At the same time it gave him an opportunity to invite some of the leading families from Mosul to come and see what he had found; finally, there is no doubt that he enjoyed being the lavish, generous host at a really gay party. Most of the Christian women had never set foot beyond the walls of Mosul, so for them it was a unique experience simply to get away for a short time. The French consul and his wife came together with Mr and Mrs Rassam.

Layard had borrowed some white pavilions from the Pasha and these were set up together with many black Bedouin tents in a circle around a large space where the entertainment was to be. Fourteen sheep had been cooked for the party. In the morning Abd-ur-rahman with his tribe arrived first, all dressed in their finest clothes. Layard rode out to meet them accompanied by a group of Kurdish musicians whose drums and flutes drowned out all other sounds, even the most energetic war-cries of the Abu Salman. Then followed other sheikhs and at last Abd-ur-rahman's wife and daughter. The women were taken to a special tent where a lavish meal consisting of the traditional Arab specialities awaited them.

In the evening the feast began. First the men got what they could eat, then the food was sent to the women's tent, and at last the poor Arabs were given the leftovers. The entertainment began with the Arab chain dance, the Dibke, which starts in a slow and solemn rhythm but ends with very energetic and violent shouts and jumps. Layard was sorry to note that the women were dressed in their dark capes so that 'their forms, which the simple Arab shirt so finely displays' became quite impossible to discern. A sword dance followed, and this quickly developed to such a frenzy that it became necessary to intervene and disarm the dancers, who had to make do with sticks. Kurdish musicians and clowns entertained and the dance continued until daybreak.

The following day Abd-ur-rahman invited Layard and all his guests from Mosul to his own camp, where they were entertained with dances and displays of weapons. Layard and Abd-ur-rahman took the lead in a Dibke together with 500 warriors and women. The sheikh was completely entranced by Madame Guillois, the wife of the French consul, and his eyes never left her. Layard did not get along well with this gentleman so he probably relished the situation with the sheikh's open, uninhibited admiration. 'Wallah', he whispered to me, 'she is the sister of the Sun! what would you have more beautiful than that? Had I a thousand purses, I would give them all for such a wife. See! – her eyes are like the eyes of my mare, her hair is bitumen, and her complexion resembles the finest Busrah dates. Anyone would die for a Houri like that'. Layard found his admiration 'almost justified' (Layard 1849, vol. I: 121).

With just a couple of workmen Layard continued with very limited work, simply clearing debris, and by the beginning of April it became clear that 'Nimrod's head' belonged to a colossal winged lion rather than a bull. 'I believe the great winged lions to be finer than anything found at Khorsabad', he wrote proudly to Canning. The Pasha visited the excavation and left clearly impressed with what he had found. Layard felt that it would now be rather easy to get permission to begin digging again, but 'I prefer waiting for instructions from Your Excellency'.[34] He had still neither money nor a *firman*.

A new Pasha had been installed in Mosul, a fine elderly gentleman of the old school called Tahyar, courteous and well educated. This appointment would surely help. There was also good news from Rawlinson who suggested that they should attempt to get the river steamer sent north to Nimrud in order to fetch some of the sculptures, and the major could inform Layard that this was also Canning's strong wish. It did not happen, however, for the steamer could not manoeuvre on the river so far north because of rapids.

So, here he sat on his ruin, without funds to do anything about it. Rawlinson declared himself completely at a loss to understand the lack of financial support on the part of the ambassador.

> I would myself willingly place a sum at your disposal, if I were to get a share of the marbles – but Sir Stratford would certainly think this an improper interference – he writes to me – 'I am working on my own account, though with a view to national benefit and Govt support in due season' – and if I were therefore to come forward he would evidently think me an interloper.[35]

One week later Layard sat down to write a long letter to Canning in which he tried to describe in detail his own view of the situation.

> Excavating in Assyria appears to me to be a work of a peculiar nature. It is one of those undertakings which, like a scientific expedition into Egypt or any other country containing antiquities of a highly interesting nature, belongs exclusively to the Government.

He had clearly realised that Canning was not willing or able to provide the necessary funding for an extensive excavation out of his own pocket, so he attempted to provide a convincing case for government involvement. One of the main reasons given for this is somewhat surprising, since he maintained that

> the objects to be discovered cannot have any intrinsic value for their beauty, and altho the sculptures of Assyria show a wonderful *comparative* knowledge of the arts, when the time and country of their execution are taken into consideration, they are undoubtedly inferior to the most secondary works of Greece or Rome.

On the other hand, 'the field is full of interest to literature, philology and history'. He reminded Canning that despite the great discoveries made by Botta at Khorsabad, Assyrian history was still 'a blank in the history of the world, and yet its connection with that of the Jews, the continual mention of the Assyrian Kings in the inspired writings, and the prominent part they played in the remotest periods, render it of the highest interest'.

He again referred to the interest created throughout Europe by Botta's discoveries, and his final point was the nationalistic argument:

> The national honour is also concerned in competing with the French in deciphering the cuneiform inscriptions. To accomplish this task materials are necessary. The French have theirs in their Khorsabad inscriptions. We must seek for them at Nimroud. I think with the results which my communications with Major Rawlinson will probably lead to, we shall have a better chance than our neighbours. ... The sculptures, which may be discovered at

Nimroud, are really of a secondary consideration, alltho there cannot be a doubt that specimens would be a most valuable addition to a Museum which contains relics of all other nations of antiquity.[36]

Layard could not know that Canning was in fact planning to leave the responsibility for the excavations to the government; in fact, he had already written a letter to the Prime Minister, Sir Robert Peel, in which he explained that the success achieved by Botta had persuaded him to

> adventure in the same lottery, and my ticket has turned up a prize. On the banks of the Tigris not far from Mosil there is a gigantic mound called *Nimrud*. My agent has succeeded in opening it here and there, and his labours have been rewarded by the discovery of many interesting sculptures, and a world of inscriptions. If the excavation keeps its promise to the end there is much reason to hope that Montagu House [the British Museum] will beat the Louvre hollow.

He expressed the wish that the government would at some point consider stepping in to 'carry off the prize on behalf of the Museum'. He suggested that 'the expense would be small in comparison with the object, which promises results of the highest historical interest' (Lane-Poole 1888: 2, 149–50).

The reasoning used by Layard in his letter to Canning was not truly his own opinion of the Assyrian finds but echoed what Rawlinson had expressed, and he apparently expected Canning to have the same view. The same day he wrote to Canning he also sent off a long letter to his mother, in which he described the discovery of the two gigantic lions which he was sure were of a higher artistic quality than anything Botta had found at Khorsabad. He wondered what they could possibly mean and was struck by the descriptions he had read in the prophet Ezekiel, who had lived in captivity in Babylon in the early sixth century BCE. He describes pictures on the walls of a palace: 'men pourtrayed upon the wall, the images of the Chaldeans pourtrayed with vermilion, girded with girdles upon their loins, exceeding in dyed attire upon their heads, all of them princes to look to, after the manner of the Babylonians of Chaldea, the land of their nativity ...' (Ezekiel 23: 14–15). Layard looked at his reliefs and felt sure that these were the very images described by the Hebrew prophet (see Figure 11.2). Maybe he had seen them before they had been conquered and destroyed in 614–612 BCE. Looking at the ruins still left it was not hard to understand the strong impression Assyria's magnificence and wealth had made. 'The inhabitants of Assyria must at that time have exceeded all the nations of the earth in power, riches and luxury. Their knowledge of the arts is surprising and greatly superior to that of any contemporary nation'. Here, in a letter to his mother, he can freely express his enthusiasm for Assyrian art, even though it necessarily had to be a conditional admiration. 'There is as much difference between their sculptures and those of Egypt as there exists between those of Assyria & Greece and they hold relative positions in point of knowledge of the arts', he wrote. He was deeply impressed with the lions in particular, noting that they 'are admirably drawn – the muscles, bones, veins quite true to nature and

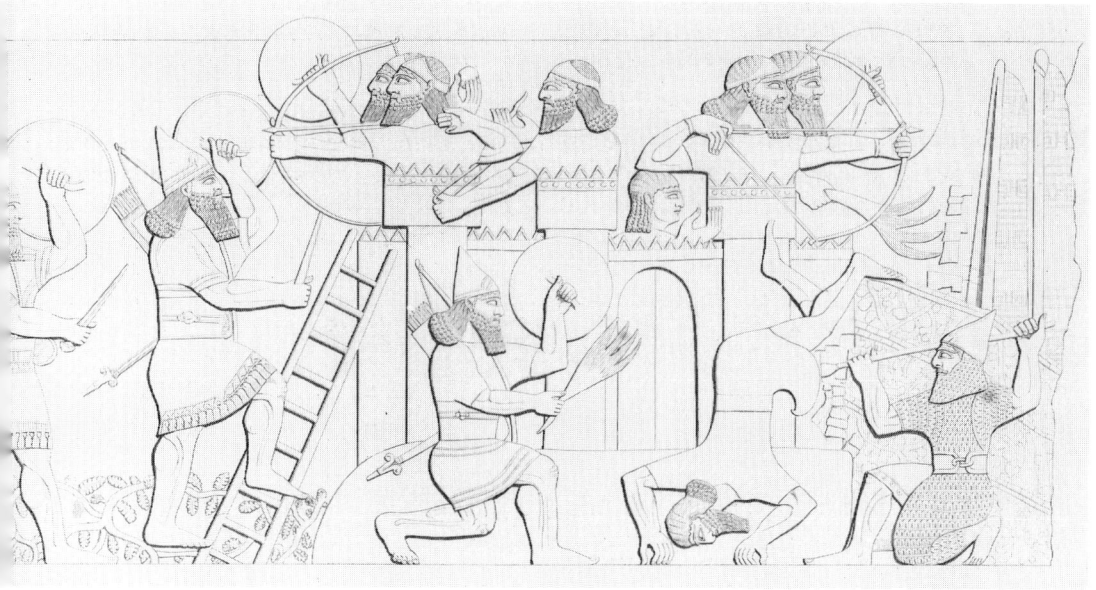

Figure 11.2 Battle scene from the Northwest palace. Assyrian soldiers attack a fortress, some with ladders, a soldier attempts to burn down the gate, while a third is busy trying to undermine the wall. (From Layard 1849–53: I, 29)

pourtrayed with great spirit – there is also a great "*mouvement*" (as the French well term it) and the attitude of the animal and "sa pose est parfaite" ...'[37]

His feeling that Nimrud was surpassing Khorsabad was shared by Botta, who in several letters expressed his delight in Layard's discoveries, which appeared to him to be of such importance that his own contribution was quickly being reduced to being the one who led the way. He was not at all surprised that such finds could be made at Nimrud, 'since Khorsabad could not have been alone and I am sure that many similar monuments remain concealed all around. time and money will dig them out'.[38] When he wrote in his next letter that Layard's success made him happy, 'although of course it lessens mine', he received a quick answer which expressed concern that he was suffering from jealousy; this was entirely unjust, and Botta had patiently to explain to his impetuous young friend that he was misunderstanding his intentions. He was quite certain that Layard's discoveries were destined to surpass his own, but the modest Botta could honestly enjoy the success achieved by his rival.[39]

For the time being Layard was sitting here without money, on top of archaeological treasures whose richness could only be guessed at. His working day was hard and intense,

> up by daylight, after a cup of coffee ride to the mound. There I am occupied until sunset, directing & overlooking the workmen, drawing and copying

inscriptions. The stupidity of the men drives me wild and I fear I have lost much of my good temper. .... On returning home in the evening I am glad to get a bath, snatch a hasty dinner and turn into bed heartily tired-out by my day's work.[40]

He knew that in his relation to Canning impatience or too sharp words would hurt rather than help, but it was not easy to stay cool in the situation he found himself in. In fact, coolness was a distinct rarity, for summer had arrived with a suddenness that overwhelmed him. In no time the lush, flowering landscape was transformed into a barren desert. His tent was no longer a possible place to sleep, nor the huts in the village – hot and full of insects. For a while he set up his bed in the river, in a spot where it was only a foot deep, because this was the coolest, most pleasant place available at night, but it did not work in the long run.

In this dilemma I ordered a recess to be cut into the bank of the river, where it rose perpendicularly from the water's edge. By screening the front with reeds and boughs of trees, and covering the whole with similar materials, a small room was formed. I was much troubled, however, with scorpions and other reptiles, which issued from the earth forming the walls of my apartment; and later in the summer by the gnats and sandflies, which hovered on a calm night over the river.

(Layard 1849, vol. I: 123)

Plate I Watercolour made in Constantinople in 1843 of young Layard in Bakhtiyari dress. The Kala Tul fortress in the background.

Plate II A *kelek* glides down the river loaded with one of the bulls from Nimrud. Watercolour by F. C. Cooper.

Plate III Excavation at the Ninurta temple, Nimrud. Watercolour by F. C. Cooper.

Plate IV The great French painter Delacroix created a sensation at the *salon* in Paris in 1828 with this enormous canvas entitled *The Death of Sardanapal*. It builds on the classical stories about the Assyrian king whose palace went up in flames, and being painted before anything at all was known about Assyria its main interest (apart from its artistic qualities) is that it shows how the ancient Assyrian world was imagined by European minds; it reflects the western fascination at the sensual, erotic world of the Orient, which embodied the repressed dreams of the Europeans.

Plate V Cooper made a series of watercolours from the excavations at Nimrud and Kuyunjik. This one shows the entrance to one of the tunnels which ran underneath Kuyunjik. One may dimly see reliefs along the back wall.

Plate VI Nimrud as Fergusson imagined it. The picture shows the acropolis, with the *ziggurat* in the north, followed by the Northwest palace, the high building after that, and at the southwestern corner the palace of Esarhaddon.

Plate VII At Bavian was a large installation which included rock reliefs and inscriptions from the time of Sennacherib. Much later rock-cut graves have partially destroyed the Assyrian reliefs. Layard is here seen in an acrobatic manoeuvre examining the monument. It included a tunnel and a dam and was part of a large scheme designed to bring water to Nineveh.

ESSAI DE RESTAURATION

Plate VIII One of Thomas' reconstruction drawings from Khorsabad, one which gives an excellent impression of the power of the Assyrian architecture.

CHAPTER TWELVE

BUT IS IT ART?

—— •◆• ——

On its way to Constantinople Layard's last letter crossed a long letter from
Canning which finally contained the long expected *firman*. It was in the form
of a message from the Grand Vizier to the Pasha in Mosul, in which a broadly
defined permission was granted for further activities. Characteristically, Canning's
letter was filled with cautionary warnings.

> The permission is indeed so complete that I am tempted to remind you of
> the *discretion*, and *moderation* which we have both felt from the beginning
> ought to accompany your proceedings, and never so much so as when the
> generosity and confidence of the Turkish Government appeal so strongly to
> our gratitude.[41]

How did these words sound in Layard's ears that morning when he received this
message? He was visiting with Abd-ur-rahman and they were planning a gazelle
hunt when the letter arrived; he read it in the light from a small fire of camel
dung, 'the document which secured the antiquities of Nimrud for the British
nation', as he wrote with some pathos.

The permission was really very extensive. The Grand Vizier began his letter in
the following way:

> There are, as Your Excellency knows, quantities of stones and remains of
> antiquities in the environs of Mosul. Further, a British gentleman who has
> placed himself on these places in order to discover stones of this nature, has
> found on the banks of the Tigris, in certain uninhabited spots, antique stones
> on which there are figures and inscriptions.[42]

The Pasha was informed that the British embassy had asked that this gentleman
should be permitted to continue his researches and be allowed to send his discoveries back to England. 'The sincere friendship which exists firmly between the two
governments obliges that such demands be granted', wrote the Grand Vizier. It
was accordingly clear that Layard could excavate not only at Nimrud, but wherever he pleased, albeit only 'in deserted places', and that he was free to send his
finds to London.

The problem was that no money accompanied the permit. Canning had written to the British Museum in order to interest them in the matter, but no funds had been set aside by the government, and Layard's own resources were nearly entirely exhausted. It could not even be taken for granted that the ministers in London would come up with funds that could ensure the completion of his project. On that background it seemed somewhat strange that Canning felt the need to caution his young agent against being 'too greedy' in his choice of further ruins to excavate.

His worry was the relationship to the French who had already staked out their interests in Assyria, and in fact it soon became clear that the letter from the Grand Vizier led to open conflict with the French Vice-Consul Guillois. There had been a strained atmosphere for some time and it could not be covered up any longer. Guillois insisted on personally inspecting Layard's *firman*, and then he declared that France had the right to Kuyunjik since Botta had excavated here. Layard politely but firmly rejected this and maintained that the mound had to be big enough for both to work there. Since Guillois had no official permit from Constantinople, Layard felt secure in his position, and he decided to open some trenches on the mound at once in order to make his intentions clear.

The most serious problems did not arise from the conflict with Guillois, however. Layard had hardly started working at Kuyunjik before things went wrong. One evening as he was going back to Mosul from the mound he happened to share the boat with his old enemy, the Cadi, the reactionary religious leader who had already caused so much trouble for Botta. Layard and his party had reached the last boat to cross the river before the gates were closed, and it was already filled up when they discovered a group of men who hastened towards the riverbank. He asked for the boat to wait, but then saw to his irritation that it was the Cadi and a group of holy men who had been to the grave of the prophet Jonah to pray. They were all taken aboard and Layard placed himself at the back next to the steersman. The Cadi stood in the bottom of the boat close to Layard and when they were in the middle of the river he shouted in a loud voice: 'Must the dogs have the highest places while the true believers stand below?' Exhausted by the sun and on the edge of an attack of fever, Layard lost his temper, grabbed his stick and hit the Cadi a blow on the turban. He struck him so forcefully that the blood, despite the rather voluminous headgear, began to trickle down over his face. His followers immediately pulled out their weapons in order to kill Layard, but a couple of soldiers who happened to be in the boat stopped them. Layard himself grabbed hold of the Cadi and threatened to throw him into the river. The rest of the crossing was tense, and as soon as they had landed the old man in a rage rushed through the streets of Mosul, exhibiting his bleeding head and shouting for revenge against all Europeans and Layard in particular (Brackman 1980: 143–5).

He immediately realised the danger he had created for the Europeans in the town and hurried to the Pasha's palace in order to ask for protection from the authorities. The new governor was no admirer of the Cadi and promised his full support. Layard was asked to seek refuge in his palace until the crisis had blown over, but that was unacceptable to the hot-headed young man. He was convinced that it was of paramount importance for his reputation among the Arabs that he should show his complete disregard for the Cadi by continuing his daily routine, as if nothing had happened. He could not prevent Rassam from issuing a public apology though.

A few days later he received a strongly disapproving letter from Rawlinson, who suspected the incident would make his further activities in the country impossible. 'The insult was certainly gross, but no provocation justifies personal violence and viewing the case as I do at present I am inclined to think Rassam was right in apologising'. The problem in his eyes was that Layard not only had chastised the Cadi on the spot, but that he had then complained to the authorities. He felt certain that he himself would have responded verbally, only to pursue the matter to the utmost later on, but he was willing to consider the possibility that he might be wrong. 'We are all fallible & I make no pretensions to any clearer view than my neighbours'. The matter had created a sensation in Baghdad where the clergy was discussing it intensely, and Rawlinson felt sure that it would be taken up and used by the conservative group at the court in Constantinople.[43]

Because of the Pasha's support for Layard the crisis ebbed out with surprising speed, and he was able to continue his excavations – though still without funds. The heat was now so intense that work at Nimrud was becoming unbearable, where temperatures of 50° in the shade and violent dust storms in the middle of the day became a daily routine; however, he felt obliged to have as many reliefs sent back to England as possible, and as fast as he could manage. Botta's discoveries from Khorsabad had finally been picked up at Basrah by a French frigate in May, so the chance of getting ahead of the French had passed, but it was essential to ride on the wave of interest which was bound to come in Europe. Since he had no more money he was forced to borrow £100 from his mother to pay for the packing and shipment.[44] In July he had packed twelve cases which were sent down the river on big rafts to Rawlinson in Baghdad.

Down here in the south the weather was no more comfortable, and Rawlinson suffered intensely from the heat. In letter after letter he complained at being totally unable to do anything meaningful. In the Residency he had a room which was hanging out over the river, and which was doused with water from a large water-wheel in order to create a tolerable temperature inside, but even that did not really help. It is clear that he felt that his time in the East was coming to an end, fearing that his health would be seriously damaged unless he could arrange for himself to get out of the terrible heat. He did have the energy to try in various ways to secure passage on a ship for Layard's cases, and every day he looked anxiously up the river for them to arrive.

Finally they came, and in a letter dated 5 August he tells Layard about his first impression. It is easy to imagine how eagerly Layard was looking forward to this letter, how he waited in tense excitement to hear what the expert in Baghdad had to say, for this would be the first evaluation of his results after many, many months of determined effort. Apart from the few Europeans in Mosul, nobody whose opinions counted for Layard had seen what he had discovered.

It was a very brief letter Rawlinson wrote, and it started with the usual complaints about the weather: 'I have been ailing so much all this last fortnight that I have had serious thoughts of taking shelter somewhere in the mountains. I think the heat has affected my liver but Ross says it is merely my stomach and I am accordingly trying what castor oil & soda water and constitutional rides in the desert will do for me'. Rawlinson clearly had no idea how important it was for the young man in Mosul to hear his opinion, or that it might not be his first priority in this situation to be entertained with tales of the major's stomach trouble. The letter continued:

> Your cases arrived all right and we have been regaling our antiquarian appetites on the contents ever since. The dying lion and the two Gods (winged and Eagle headed) are my favorites. The battle pieces, Seiges(sic) etc. are curious, but I do not think they rank very highly as art. Ross is altogether disappointed with the specimens and I must confess I think the general style crude & cramped but still the curiosity of the thing is very great, if not a full compensation.[45]

'Curious'! That is what Rawlinson can see, his highest praise! And this is all – he then passes on to local gossip, possible passage on a ship, and politics; the missionaries are driving him to desperation, but the biggest problem is that he understands that Canning is leaving the post at Constantinople to be replaced by a certain Wellesley, about whom Rawlinson knows nothing.

It is not difficult to understand that Layard fell into deep despair when he received this letter. It is true that some months earlier he had maintained in his letter to Canning that the Assyrian reliefs as works of art were inferior to even secondary Greek and Roman works, but that was as part of a special pleading, and he had since found reliefs which had made him modify his opinion. More importantly, these were *his discoveries*, the result of a stubborn effort which had been carried on through sickness, lack of money and nearly constant challenges from the authorities in Mosul. So this rejection was almost more than he could bear.

Unfortunately we do not possess Layard's response to Rawlinson's sour letter, but from the major's next we can understand that it must have been exceptionally agitated. Layard even convinced himself that Rawlinson would withdraw his support for the excavations, perhaps even wanted them stopped, but of course their disagreement was not at all on that level. On the other hand, the letters reveal how the two men had embarked on a discussion which mirrors central aesthetic and artistic concerns in Victorian England, and Rawlinson's explanations are worth quoting:

> My dear Layard
> I am sorry you have taken such desperate alarms at my criticisms. I never pretended to depreciate the *value* of the marbles. I merely objected to their style & execution, which in my opinion have nothing whatever to do with value. You ask by what standard I compare them. Why of course, in any abstract matter we adopt the highest standard available – and I say therefore the Elgin marbles, or better sculpture even if it could be found. And I still think the Nineveh marbles are not valuable as works of art. The test is – can modern science learn anything from them? – Can a mere admirer of the

beautiful view them with pleasure? – certainly not and in this respect they are in the same category with the paintings and sculptures of Egypt and India – but far be it from me to say that either one or the other be of no *value*. I look upon the Nimrud slabs as *invaluable* and my opinion of them would be the same were they ten times inferior to what they are. Their value consists in unfolding both the history, theology, language, arts, manners, military skill, political relations to (sic) of one of the most illustrious nations of antiquity, and in thus filling up an enormous blank in our knowledge of the early history of the world. Compared with this true & Catholic view of value I look upon artistical skill as altogether a secondary consideration.

Why quarrel with the Assyrians because they were not as far advanced in the arts of design & execution as the Greeks in the time of Pericles? We have them as they were and that is what we want. I admit a certain degree of excellence in the conception & execution of some of the sculptures – but when we come to value, *a certain degree*, won't do. We have specimens of the very highest art – and anything short of that is, as a work of art & a work of art merely, valueless, for it can neither instruct nor enrapture us.

I hope you understand the distinction & when I criticize design and execution will understand I do so merely because your winged god is not the Apollo Belvedere. Heaven forefend that I should do anything to impede the excavations. I look upon them as of more value than Pompeii or Herculaneum and view every new Inscription as equal to gaining one of the lost decades of Livy.[46]

For Rawlinson it is a question of saving new land from 'the Ocean of Time', and this is what Layard is doing with every new inscription and every new relief. He is occupied by the perspective of history, not the history of art, and his criteria are typical for his time, even though a new set of ideas were developing. Classical Greek art was the standard which had to be used in the evaluation of all art, a summit which all had to strive to reconquer – however impossible the task. Other artistic traditions with entirely different aesthetic notions obviously had to fall through in such a comparison. This is the Eurocentric, classically academic view of art which had been defined by great writers like Winckelmann in the eighteenth century. Anyone who has stood in front of the imposing entrance to the British Museum in Great Russell Street in London will realise the power of this ideology, for here we have a magnificent building designed to contain the treasures of the nation, which is shaped like a gigantic Doric temple. The friezes above the pillared entrance were executed by Professor Westmacott, one of the leading sculptors of the time in the classicist tradition, and a man who later was to repeat the same evaluations which we find in Rawlinson's letter, once the Assyrian reliefs had arrived at London and were installed in the great house (see Figure 24.3). He declared to a parliamentary commission that the Assyrian reliefs were entirely devoid of artistic qualities, and therefore did not really belong under the same roof as the Parthenon sculptures, those same Greek masterpieces which Rawlinson had defined as the highest artistic standard. Westmacott took the view that artists could even be hurt in their aesthetic soul by studying the

Figure 12.1 Lion-hunt relief from Nimrud, probably one of the very first slabs Rawlinson saw. (From Layard 1849–53: I, 31)

Assyrian reliefs too closely: 'The less people, in their capacity as artists, view objects of this kind, the better' (Bohrer 1989: 20).

As a child Layard had learnt to appreciate Italian Renaissance art, for instance, which was not really accepted in learned art-historical circles, and he had the beginnings of an understanding of the potential wealth in a broader view of art. In this he was in agreement with the dawning anti-classicist movement, which in England was known as the 'Pre-Raphaelites', and whose most famous member, the painter and poet Dante Gabriel Rossetti, later wrote a great poem about the bull colossus from Nineveh.

As we know from Layard's letters to his aunt Sara Austen he was aware of the unique character of Assyrian art and its special qualities. He had noticed that the reliefs displayed not only an ability to depict events, but that they showed a highly developed sense of composition:

> Of this essential feature of what may properly be termed the fine Arts, the Egyptians appear to have been entirely ignorant. The Greeks were acquainted with it only at a comparatively recent period ... I compare the Assyrian sculpture with painting, as they comprised both branches, and it appears

highly probable that the sculptured reliefs were merely subservient to the color laid upon them. I think the Nimroud basreliefs will furnish new ideas on the history of the Arts, and throw great light upon that interesting subject.[47]

His eye could now evaluate the reliefs as an expression of an independent artistic tradition, but Rawlinson could not see that. Nevertheless, Rawlinson's letter did somewhat satisfy him; he quoted long passages from it in a letter to his mother and says: 'This is very encouraging and I only hope people at home will take the same view of the subject'.[48] At any rate, these fascinating concerns had to be pushed aside because Layard's failing health began to block further work both at Mosul and at Nimrud. For a time he lived in Mosul itself, whose better built houses had a special basement, a *sardaub*, which was used as living quarters during the hottest weeks of the summer. He went back to Nimrud briefly in August, where he uncovered the reliefs in three additional rooms, but his fever began to return so he had to go back to Mosul.

Instead, he decided to take a long trip into the mountains northeast of Mosul, the Tiyari district from where most of his Christian Nestorian workmen came. Christianity had been entrenched here for centuries, far longer than Islam of course, and the Nestorian or 'Chaldean' Christians lived according to traditions which were severely threatened at this time. The Chaldean Church supported the view of the Greek theologian Nestorios, who interpreted the figure of Christ as consisting of two entirely separate elements, the divine and the human. His teachings had been condemned at the Church meeting in Ephesos in Asia Minor in 431, but they remained the basis for large Christian groups in the Middle East. Christian missionaries, especially Catholic, were engaged in a concerted effort to eradicate the Nestorian 'heresy' by way of mass conversions. At the same time, Kurdish mountain tribes were carrying out a religiously motivated campaign of destruction and conquest directed against the Christians in the mountains.

Layard's sympathies were entirely with the Chaldeans, and his description of the conditions in the mountain valleys reveal clearly his limitless contempt for the Kurdish chieftains who were waging a merciless war on peaceful village communities. Their leader, a certain Beder Khan-bey, had started his attack on the Tiyari district in 1843, and more than 10,000 people were supposed to have been killed; most of the survivors were taken away as slaves. A considerable number of these had since been released, partly because of an energetic intervention by Canning. His representations had also led to the dispatch of a special commissar to the area, and the ambassador paid for the release of hundreds of prisoners out of his own pocket.

When Layard travelled through the area three years later he encountered a completely destroyed environment and a society that was dissolving – burnt-down villages, fruit orchards cut down and churches razed to the ground. The few survivors who had dared return lived in constant fear of new attacks, and their religious life had been reduced to a pathetic reflection of their normal practices. The churches were destroyed and the holy books were gone, hidden away by those priests who were the first to fall victims to the atrocities, and therefore impossible to find. He also reached the mountain valleys which had not been attacked in 1843, but which were faced with the threat of a new campaign. He took part in a meeting in the Tokhma valley, where the men devised a strategy for its defence, apparently in the full awareness that it was going to be in vain under all circumstances. This turned out to be correct. After Layard's departure Beder Khan-bey returned and reduced the valley to smoking ruin heaps.

But this was warfare directed against Christians, and the international pressure became so strong that in the end the Sultan felt obliged to intervene. The Western powers in collaboration with Russia expressed their anger at what they saw as religious persecution of large Christian minority groups in the Sultan's empire. The threat of military intervention, unless the Turks themselves proved able to deal effectively with the situation, was felt as very real and taken most seriously. The Kurdish chieftain was finally forced into a fairly civilised exile on a Greek island, but only after having nearly completely destroyed the Chaldean societies in the mountains.

Rawlinson reacted with considerable scepticism to Layard's enthusiasm for the Nestorians, and he rejected his criticism of the Kurds:

> I cannot go the whole way with you on the subject of Kurdistan. I prefer the Kurds, I must say, as a body, either to the Turks or Persians and I should be sorry to see the vices and spurious civilisation of the plains introduced generally into the mountains. I look further indeed. Persia in the course of the next ten years at latest must be a Russian province & I doubt if the political existence of the Porte is destined to a much longer duration. When the great crash arrives then we must look to Kurdistan as a point d'appui of some value and in this view, I should see I confess with regret an entire extinction of the feeling of independence among the tribes.[49]

On his way back from the mountains Layard stopped in the village Alkosh, nearly on the Mosul plain itself, which had recently been converted to Catholicism. His follower, the strongly orthodox Muslim Ibrahim Agha, expressed his feelings in no uncertain terms:

> Wallah! O Bey! The entire village is intoxicated. It is always like that with the infidel. Now they have a good Pasha who takes neither *jerum* nor extra *salian* (special taxes) or forces them to accept expenses for soldiers. And then what is the rubbish they eat? Instead of repairing their houses and sow their fields they spend every penny on *raki* and sit and eat and drink, like hogs, day and night!
>
> (Layard 1849, vol. I: 237–8).

Another religious group in which Layard took a close interest were the so-called 'Devil-worshippers', the Yezidis. Their religion, whose origins are cloaked in obscurity, mixes Christian and Muslim elements, adding some unique and rather strange fundamental features. They are convinced that evil, represented by Satan honoured in the form of a peacock, has a major influence on everything going on in this world, and their cult is therefore in large measure designed to adore him as the emissary of God. Their religious practices were not well known, however, and

Layard was one of the few outsiders who had been invited to see their rituals at the grave of their saint Sheikh Adi in the mountains north of Mosul. He became deeply impressed by their seriousness and their friendly attitude which was in glaring contrast to their reputation. It is not hard to imagine how people who are said to worship the Devil could be seen as the incarnation of evil, sin and perversity, but their religion was in actual fact based on peaceful and humane principles.

This did not prevent them from being exceedingly tough and bellicose people, and during the years with bad Pashas in Mosul they had good reason to be suspicious of the intentions of the Turkish authorities. In reality, the government had lost all control of some of the regions inhabited by the Yezidis, such as the Sinjar area west of Mosul, for instance. The new Pasha decided to go there in order to re-establish connections and Layard was allowed to follow him on the way. An enormous caravan of soldiers and officials left with waving banners, and after a few days they arrived at the main Yezidi settlement, Mirkan; the population had become so suspicious of the Turks that they simply refused to enter into negotiations with the Pasha. He sent a group of riders to the village to discuss with them, but they were met by a salvo of guns which killed two. Tahyar Pasha was now compelled to ask his troops to conquer the place, but it turned out that the town had already been deserted; the soldiers found only a few old people who could be killed and beheaded. The remainder of the inhabitants had taken up position in a gully which proved very difficult to attack; the Turkish soldiers were beaten back several times with heavy losses. Layard stayed in the background, for this was not his fight. In fact, he brought letters to the Yezidis of Mirkan from their highest religious leader, and his sympathies were not really with the Turks. Notwithstanding, he became involved the following day as the guest of the Pasha, when a new attack was ordered.

> To encourage his men he advanced himself into the gorge, and directed his carpet to be spread on a rock. Here he sat, with the greatest apathy, smoking his pipe, and carrying on a frivolous conversation with me, although he was the object of the aim of the Yezidis; several persons within a few feet of us falling dead, and the balls frequently throwing up the dirt into our faces. Coffee was brought to him occasionally as usual, and his pipe was filled when the tobacco was exhausted; yet he was not a soldier, but what is termed 'a man of the pen'.
>
> (Layard 1849, vol. I: 319)

In spite of this demonstration of bravery the soldiers were still unable to take the gorge, and Layard felt that he had more important matters to attend to, so he returned to Mosul. On his arrival he found letters from London informing him that he was now an agent of the British Museum, which had taken over responsibility for the excavations and its funding.

CHAPTER THIRTEEN

CHOLERA AND
SMALL-MINDEDNESS

—— •◆• ——

In September 1846 the Persian cholera epidemic reached Baghdad, and Rawlinson felt obliged to move his entire household south of the city to Ctesiphon, where a town of tents was set up in the shadow of the colossal ruins of the ancient Sasanian palace on the Tigris. In the opinion of the major the epidemic was not severe, since two-thirds, perhaps more, of the people infected recovered, but the situation could quickly change for the worse. In Tehran at least 12,000 had died from the disease, and Rawlinson's staff had in fact been touched before he moved out of the city. By the end of October the situation was again getting under control in Baghdad, with now only fifteen deaths a day as compared to one hundred and sixty or one hundred and seventy when the epidemic was at its peak. However, the cholera was now on its way to Mosul and Dr Ross sent Layard detailed instructions on how to avoid getting infected. Rawlinson's advice was 'stimulants of all kinds internally & warm applications externally'.

We have a number of accounts of life in European cities stricken by cholera which give an impression of the terror and disruption it caused. To take an example: the epidemic reached Copenhagen in July 1853 and raged for about three months creating chaos; 7,219 persons were infected and 66 per cent of these died, 4,737. Even though this was no more than a few per cent of the entire population, it sufficed to create a panic, and the only known safeguard was to flee. People moved out of the city, which was compressed behind the city walls, and they spent the summer in camps in the military areas outside. No one knew what caused the disease, but the prevailing view was that it was 'miasmic', caused by unknown agents or vapours floating in the air which arose from damp soil, swamps or decaying organisms. It was this epidemic which finally persuaded the authorities in Copenhagen that the walls should be razed so that the city could spread over the surrounding countryside. The contemporary descriptions of the horrors of the situation in Copenhagen can give an impression of what it must have been like in cities like Baghdad and Mosul, where sanitary and hygienic conditions were even worse.

In the middle of all this misery came the official statement that the British Museum had taken responsibility for the excavations in Assyria and appointed Layard to be its agent. Triumph, finally, but it turned out to be a victory mixed with difficulty and combined with unsatisfactory conditions. Canning was in London and had negotiated an agreement with the leaders of the Museum, 'the Trustees', and he had got what he wanted. He seems to have realised that the arrangement was not likely to please Layard in all respects, however, for he cautioned him in his letters. 'I am sure you will not find it worth your while to complain of details', he wrote. Layard did not see the problems as details.

It turned out that the Museum had raised £2,000 for the completion of the excavations at Nimrud. This did not sound impossible, even though it did not compare with what the French government had given to Botta, but the sum was drastically reduced by further arrangements: first, Canning's personal expenses had been repaid out of this amount; next, £500 was to be regarded as salary for Layard personally; and finally, a further £100 was deducted to pay for his travel back to England. He was left with £1,000 which had to cover expenses connected with the excavation and with the transportation of the reliefs and other objects back to London. Anyone could see that this was simply unrealistic, and Layard was deeply offended by this small-mindedness, which he very naturally interpreted as an expression that his work was not truly valued. Seen from our contemporary perspective it is perhaps not such a simple matter to evaluate the meaningfulness of the size of such a grant, which, compared to the sums set aside for a modern excavation, does not appear unreasonable (Saggs 1970: 54). Layard compared his conditions with Botta, however, and felt that the British authorities were intolerably stingy; it should also be kept in mind that his ambition was to conduct a complete excavation of several sites, a task which he would have been unable to accomplish under all circumstances.

It became even worse when a seven-page document signed by J. Forshall, the secretary to the Trustees, arrived at Mosul; it was a contract which stipulated Layard's working conditions in his role as agent for the Museum. If Canning's letters had sometimes been hard to swallow, they were like nothing compared to this sermon. One may imagine his irritation at being told that 'the first object of the Museum is the preservation of objects of Antiquity. Mr. Layard will therefore be extremely careful not to injure any Sculptures, Inscriptions or other objects which he may not remove with the intention of shipping them for England.' What did they imagine in London? What was the basis for the lack of confidence which he felt pervaded the entire document? The instructions were not simply supercilious in tone, they entered into details which he felt quite unnecessary, and on some points they were brutally direct. On behalf of the Trustees Mr Forshall found it in order and

> right towards Mr. Layard to state plainly, that when the now contemplated operations in Kurdistan are brought to a close, it will be impossible for them to provide in any way for Mr. Layard's further employment, or to assist him in any objects he may then have in view. In tendering him the pecuniary remuneration which they have named, they do all which they have or can have in their power to do.

Some of the instructions that caused most irritation were, seen from the point of view of posterity, quite reasonable, such as the duty to fill in the excavated trenches again when he left the site. Even though his first reaction was annoyance at what he regarded as needless extra expense in a budget already stretched to the limit, Layard must have realised that this rule was sensible, at least after he had visited Botta's old trenches at Khorsabad where the unprotected reliefs had perished. This order exasperated Rawlinson in Baghdad; he had never found the time to come up to Nimrud to see the palaces, so he had only seen the chosen reliefs that had been sent down-river on their way to England. He now had to face the realisation that he would never have the opportunity to see the exposed ruins. Layard was also ordered to make two copies of all inscriptions – as if it was not hard enough simply to keep up and produce one! Again, seen from London this was a reasonable precaution on which to insist, but Layard had to compare with the conditions offered to Botta, who had been given a professional draughtsman to take care of such matters. Completely alone – and of course without access to a photocopier – he realised that he had just been given a colossal task. The very last paragraph in the contract was not suited to make him any happier either:

> The Trustees wish that every cause of offence should be avoided as well to the authorities as to the population, and particularly that proper respect should be paid to the religious feeling and habitual prejudices of all, whether Mohammedans or Christians. It will be very gratifying to the Trustees to find, when the operations on which Mr. Layard is engaged are concluded, that his prudence and good feeling have enabled him to leave in Kurdistan an impression entirely favourable to the English character.

Layard had himself partly to blame for this last haughty admonishment, for it must have been based on his collision with the Cadi. One can understand that the Trustees, a group of distinguished gentlemen from the British aristocracy, must have felt uncertain about the unknown young man in Mosul. It seems that Canning did not make things any better, for he was clearly interested mainly in securing recognition for his own central part in the operation – as he saw it. Layard felt treated 'like a master bricklayer', he wrote in a letter to his uncle, 'but I suppose this is what is styled "making a man feel his position"'.[50]

The contract expressed the fear that he might 'meet with competition from the Agents of other European powers', if he extended his activities beyond Nimrud; Forshall found it in order to stress that he should behave properly and 'maintain a spirit and bearing of honorable liberality'. In other words, he was not to enter into any kind of conflict with the French consul at Mosul and let him have whatever mounds he laid claim to. Is this an example of Canning's influence? The reasons given for avoiding such competitive behaviour were expressed in a condescending passage which stated that the only goal was to save 'the Monuments of the distant past in ancient Assyria from destruction and bringing them out of their present concealment to the illustration which European knowledge may be able to throw upon their meaning and history.' It did not matter who found what – an extraordinary statement on the part of the leaders of the British Museum.

But the contract continued with an even more bizarre mixture of platitudes and condescension towards not only Layard, but especially the Turks and Arabs:

Nor can any thing have a more direct tendency to teach the natives some respect for the remains of the great works of art executed by the early occupiers of their country than the leading them to believe, that Europeans desire to possess these remains, not because of any pecuniary value attaching to them, but because of their connexion with ancient nations and languages, and of the hope which the study of these affords of contributing to the more extended cultivation of learning and taste, and the prevalence of those principles of justice and benevolence, by which only, if by any means the general concord and prosperity of the human race is to be attained.[51]

It may be that Layard felt a certain satisfaction at seeing his efforts placed in these lofty regions where it was a matter of securing peace on earth and goodwill in mankind, but he must have experienced the crass contrast between these grand phrases and the stinginess of the Museum in financing the operations. He tried as politely as possible to point out to Forshall that the means placed at his disposal were too small, and he was especially bothered by the £500 which the Trustees had set aside for him personally. This amount reduced the money available for the excavations by one-third. He stressed that he had under no circumstances worked for his own gain and suggested that the money be used for excavation and transportation instead. Also, Rawlinson found the letter from Forshall completely unacceptable and told Layard that he would have been tempted simply to return it to the sender unanswered. 'Those lousy English Commissioners', as he called the fine gentlemen in London.[52]

They finally answered Layard's complaints in a letter from the end of January 1847, in which they specified seven points which they saw as having created misunderstandings. They thanked Layard for his reports and expressed their great satisfaction with his work, but they then made it clear that they would not budge in the matter of the £500, his personal pay for the work done, since they could not accept his services *gratis*. Also, his personal expenses in Assyria had to be paid out of the main grant, not taken from the £500. On the other hand, the transportation of his discoveries and his own travel expenses back to Europe would be covered separately. He must, however, send them a special budget for the cost of moving and transporting the very large objects, bulls and lions, for their approval before anything was taken away. Finally, he was told in very clear terms that it was his duty to send regular reports to London, which must contain detailed accounts.

What was it all about? It seems clear that there was a certain degree of uncertainty and ignorance at the Museum with respect to Layard's finds. There was obviously no understanding of the immense effort which had gone into the discovery of the palaces of Nimrud, and young Layard remained a nebulous entity. The fact that he had made discoveries which in reality represented a completely new and hitherto unsuspected cultural and artistic tradition was slow to be realised in London. Botta's finds had not yet been seen by the public, and Layard stood with results which were in fact much more extensive, in a considerably better state of preservation, and in reality much more varied in nature, and for that reason alone of greater interest. Botta had an extremely effective spokesman in Jules Mohl, whose untiring political lobbying secured considerable sums from the French government. Canning in London could not be nearly as effective; his personal motives were mixed, for he was primarily interested in securing that his own name became attached to the finds, and his relationship with Layard was complicated by the diametrically opposed personalities of the two men.

There was certainly also a degree of uneasiness with respect to Layard's social position. His friend Sir Charles Fellows, who had found and excavated the Lycian tombs at Xanthus, had been a 'gentleman traveller'. Layard was a young man of somewhat uncertain background, without money, and he found it difficult to accept a position as a salaried agent for the Museum, a subordinate position which might impede his progress into a socially satisfactory status once he returned home. The contrast with Canning was stark: he had been refunded his personal expenses, Layard was not; the money Layard had contributed to the excavation, both his salary as Canning's personal assistant and the money he had borrowed from his mother, had apparently not been mentioned by Canning. This may be another reflection of the ambassador's wish to put himself forward as the one who had taken the initiative and carried the full responsibility for the project. Layard, on the contrary, was seen as a hired hand who was expected to work on the basis of a set of instructions which did not reflect much confidence in him or his judgement. That this was in fact acknowledged by the Museum authorities comes out from the very first sentence in the contract where it is said that 'Sir Stratford Canning has very liberally offered to the Trustees of the British Museum the results of the researches and excavations made by Mr. Layard under His Excellency's directions in Kurdistan'.

While bitter letters were exchanged between Mosul and the British Museum, Layard's reputation was in fact spreading in London. In October a friend of his, a young architect called George Mair, presented Layard's description of the Parthian ruins at Hatra, located in the desert west of Mosul and visited by Layard a couple of times. His drawings and plans were displayed at a meeting of the Royal Institute of British Architects and created a great deal of interest. Mair was also able to show Layard's drawing of the great human-headed gate lion from Nimrud, and the gathering had unanimously moved that sufficient means should be allocated to these so obviously important excavations.

Mair had been especially happy that Layard's uncle, Benjamin Austen, had been present and had heard his nephew's work praised. An extensive report from the meeting was brought into several newspapers and in the professional journal 'Builder', and Mair had seen to it that Layard's mother was given these articles.[53] One of the leading British magazines, the *Athenæum*, carried no less than five articles about the excavations in the course of 1846. The first one, published in February, was a rather confused and largely incorrect report about 'interesting discoveries' made under the supervision of 'colonel' Rawlinson; in June Canning was given the honour for 'the splendid discoveries which are now being made by Mr. Austen Layard at Nimroud'. In October we find a very long and careful report which told about Nimrud in some detail, and gave a summary of Layard's and Rawlinson's efforts to decipher the cuneiform writing. It also contained a passage about the conditions under which Layard was working:

Enough, I trust, has been written to show the value of these discoveries as connected with Art, History, and Biblical Illustration. I will add a word with respect to Mr. Layard himself. It is but due to him to mention that the existence of these remains had been pointed out by him before M. Botta commenced his excavations at Khorsabad. The reason why the French were the first in the field is simply because they have a king and government who are prompt to appreciate and promote any enterprise which can reflect honour on the national reputation for taste and intelligence ... the money spent by the French is said to amount to nearly 30,000 £.

This, at least, will prove the importance which they attach to these discoveries. It is painful, after witnessing this munificent patronage of science by the French Government, to think that, up to this moment, nothing whatever has been done to assist Mr. Layard in his researches by our own. It is true that Sir Stratford Canning, at his personal risk and expense, has very liberally contributed. ... But in an undertaking of this nature private munificence can scarcely be expected to keep pace with national; and you can imagine how mortifying it must be to Mr. Layard to find, after a year's indefatigable exertions – crowned too with such brilliant results – that nothing has been done by the British Government to mark its interest in his labours. For anything he can know to the contrary, his civilised countrymen sympathise with his pursuits just as little as the Turks themselves. Such neglect is discreditable to the English ministry.[54]

For Layard himself it was now becoming a question of his future. He could not, of course, become an Archaeologist, for that profession had not yet been invented, and any dreams he may have entertained of a more permanent attachment to the British Museum seemed quite ruled out on the basis of the letter from Mr Forshall. Canning wrote from London to Alison in Constantinople that he 'had every wish to help him in matters more important than Archaeology' (Waterfield 1963: 159). It might not be entirely clear in which direction this would lead, but a diplomatic career seemed a logical proposition. Benjamin and Sara Austen, who had now finally become convinced that their wandering nephew was getting onto more solid ground, tried as best they could to work for his cause in London, talking to Canning and to the people at the British Museum, their next door neighbours. They wrote a number of letters to Layard filled with advice admonishing him to be careful in this situation, 'the crisis of your career'. The aunt summed up the young man's personality in a single phrase: 'The freedom of thought and action which your strong intellect and bold heart demand can in reality not fit with the conditions set for a human existence' (Waterfield 1963: 160). If that were true, there really were grounds for deep worry.

Canning stressed several times that both Layard and Rawlinson ought to recognise that he was the one who had started the excavations, and that he wished to secure his own place in history; young Layard's growing fame obviously made him worry that he might be pushed entirely into the background. It went so far that Forshall warned the Austens that their nephew was in danger of losing the loyalty of the mighty ambassador. Sara had several conversations with Canning, and Layard could not hide his irritation over this contact, fearing that it might tie him in an even closer dependence. He was quite aware that it was his exertion which alone had led to the discovery of these incredible treasures, and he found it difficult to see that Canning deserved any significant part of the honour. The fact that the entire venture had been made possible by Canning, and that he had clearly been the ambassador's personal agent, appeared less significant now after many months of hard personal work and sacrifice. Undoubtedly he found it irritating, in fact, deeply depressing that the ambassador – despite Layard's loyal reporting of all of his activities and discoveries – apparently had no real idea of the importance of what he had found. He of all people ought to be able to realise that Layard's toil had been quite extraordinary, and that it would have been impossible to find anyone else who could have carried through the excavations under the conditions which he had been forced to accept.

CHAPTER FOURTEEN

MONUMENTS AND INSCRIPTIONS

—— •◆• ——

Given the limited means at his disposal, Layard had to take some drastic deci-sions concerning the continuation of the excavations. It was obvious that he was not in a position to conduct a real uncovering of the large palaces, systemat-ically moving from room to room, and he instead felt constrained to simply follow the walls where the reliefs were. This was a procedure also adopted by Botta at Khorsabad, as can be seen from his plans, which show the rooms themselves as unexcavated, and it was naturally based on the fact that the sculptures were seen by all as the most important finds. It was obvious that he had to take a special interest in them, but he was painfully aware that there was a major risk that impor-tant antiquities were hidden in those parts of the rooms which were not touched. The method meant that the excavations took place in narrow trenches which followed the walls of the palace, turning at corners and doorways and creating a veritable labyrinth. It was of course an effective way of securing the finds he was most interested in, and when used on the Northwest palace at Nimrud it was not so damaging, for this building had been largely empty before it was abandoned and became an open ruin. Nevertheless, British archaeologists working here since the Second World War have indeed made unique finds in rooms which Layard felt forced to leave untouched.

The Northwest palace at Nimrud quickly yielded enormous treasures in the form of well-preserved reliefs, and in spite of the excavation method he managed to make other types of finds as well, first of all a complete coat of mail and several helmets. They fell apart as soon as they were exposed to the air, however, but he also discovered several vases of alabaster and glass, and these he found of partic-ular interest.

The most important find was the monument known as the Black Obelisk (see Figure 14.1). It was discovered in a trench which Layard took in towards the centre of the mound, where another palace with very badly damaged reliefs and bulls had

Figure 14.1 The black obelisk, one of the most important finds from the first campaign at Nimrud. It may well have stood together with other similar monuments, from which we have only fragments, in a small square between the main palaces at Nimrud. The text and pictures give an account of King Shalmaneser III's campaigns and shows in one of the panel's the submission of the Jewish king Jehu. (From Layard 1849, I: 347)

appeared. At first this trench did not seem to lead to anything, but when it had been taken some 20 m into the mound and Layard was considering stopping it, the workers suddenly came across a black stone pillar, more than 2 m tall and covered with both pictures and inscriptions. It was lying on its side in a secondary position, but it was completely preserved without a scratch and as sharp in the contours of both images and signs as if it had been carved the day before.

Layard immediately realised that this was a uniquely important find, and he had it shipped to Baghdad as quickly as possible. In a long letter from New Year's Day 1847 he gave his first impression of the monument which was immediately known as 'The Black Obelisk'. It had clearly been free-standing and not a direct part of any architectural construction. It had a flat top and three steps above the friezes. There were five panels on each side, giving a total of twenty, and nearly the entire rest of the stone was covered with a long cuneiform inscription, more than 200 lines. He wrote:

> It appears to have been erected to celebrate the conquest of some remote country, for amongst the animals represented as brought to the King are the elephant, rhinocerus, lion, Bactrian camel, wild mule, ibex, stag, several species of Baboon & monkey &c – you will observe that the basreliefs are in many instances repetitions of the larger sculptures in the earlier building of Nimroud, with which it was evidently contemporary.[55]

One of the stories about the Assyrians which had been handed down by the Greeks concerned the legendary Queen Semiramis, about whom it was told that she had conducted a successful campaign against India. Was he confronted with a pictorial description of that event? The elephant and the other exotic animals appeared to point in that direction, but other panels showed an Assyrian king, rather than a queen; in two different situations he confronted a vanquished foe who was kissing the ground before his feet. It was clear for anyone to see that the cuneiform inscriptions over these panels must contain the names of the main participants, and it is easy to understand with what desperate impatience Layard gazed upon the impenetrable signs.

Had he known that it was Jehu, King of Israel, lying at the feet of the Assyrian king, his delight would have known no limits. When the inscriptions could finally begin to be deciphered, this monument came to have an enormous importance for the understanding of the connections between the Assyrian finds and the events referred to in the Old Testament.

But he could not know this, and when Rawlinson began his study of the obelisk in Baghdad shortly afterwards he was equally confused. He was in no doubt about the importance of the obelisk, however, and he wrote to Layard in great excitement that it 'is I conceive the most noble trophy in the world and would alone have been well worth the whole expense of excavating Nimrud'.[56]

It was probably the long inscription which was the main reason for his delight, for he attached much greater importance to texts than to images, as already pointed out. The special character of the Obelisk was, on the other hand, precisely the marriage between text and picture, and this gave it such an obvious appeal that he decided to throw away all other work for a fortnight in order to concentrate exclusively on it, copying the text and attempting to find a clue to its understanding. Since he was still unable to grasp the precise nature of cuneiform writing, he was obviously not in a position to reach the language which was hiding behind the signs.

The point of departure for Rawlinson was the group of Persian monumental inscriptions, and at this time he had in effect concluded his decipherment of the first, Old Persian, column. His great monograph on the Bisutun inscription was complete and had been sent to the printers in London. The next step was logically to make use of the information which the Persian text gave, and especially to use names in an effort to get through the opaque wall of the Babylonian column, which was evidently closely related to the inscriptions known from both Khorsabad and Nimrud. This was, however, a much tougher task than reading the Persian version, and Rawlinson's letters show us how frustrating it was to come to a complete halt before this wall again and again.

One might think that being able to read the Old Persian version meant that he also would be in a position to recognise names of persons and places in the Babylonian version, and that in itself should have been enough to give him the values for a number of signs. There were problems, however, for the version he had of the Babylonian column at Bisutun was very unsatisfactory; as already mentioned, it was located in such a spot that it would demand special mountaineering skills and equipment to get to it. Consequently, he did not have a very secure text with which to compare, where he could look for the personal names which he knew had to be there. From Tehran he had received a notebook containing a copy made by Professor Westergaard of another great Persian inscription at Naksh i-Rustam; the problem with that was that it was so full of lacunae that it did not really help.

The script used in the Babylonian column was obviously much more complicated than the Persian one; where the latter could be understood as an alphabet, it was obvious that the Babylonian script with its more than one hundred signs had to have another character, for no spoken language could need so many letters to represent it. One of Rawlinson's problems was that he was unable to tear himself loose from the idea of an alphabetic script, so that he found it difficult to account for the many signs. He felt that the Persian phonetic system was complex, but the Babylonian one was on a completely different level of complexity. In May he wrote that more than one hundred signs now were 'pretty well defined', but what exactly that meant is not very clear.[57] A month later he wrote that

> I can *read* pretty well to my satisfaction all the Inscriptions Median as well
> as Babylonian given by Westergaard – but this does not enable me by any
> means to *understand* a Babylonian Inscription, of which I have not a trans-
> lation. The language as I have often told you has to be reconstructed
> 'ab origine'. It is in my opinion utterly unrelated – correspondents do not
> exist in any available speech, Semitic, Arian or Scythic – so how we are ever
> to interpret it with any thing like certainty I am at a loss to divine.[58]

On such a basis he would of course have to run into constant difficulties, for it stands to reason that if one is faced with both an unknown script and a language which is unrelated to any known tongue, then there really is no way one can penetrate the fog. It is nearly as if one found inscriptions after a non-human civilisation on Mars. But of course it was not nearly as bad as that with the Babylonian script, for there was a great deal one could glean from the Persian versions of the texts; moreover, Rawlinson was wrong in his pessimistic evaluation of the nature of the language, for it was certainly not unrelated to other languages but was a Semitic tongue, which both structurally and semantically was relatively close to Arabic and Hebrew. One may, perhaps, think that Rawlinson should have had good chances of reaching a meaningful result, given the fairly extensive material at his disposal, but he was unable to find the key that would open the treasure chest.

Layard had spent much time poring over the inscriptions while he was engaged in copying them, and he had sent his various ideas and observations to Rawlinson. He had for instance made a very long list of sign forms which he felt had to be variants, that is signs with the same or nearly the same phonetic value, and Rawlinson had written appreciatively that this list was the basis for his own efforts.

Some elementary observations appeared to be certain: names of persons were normally marked by a single vertical wedge which stood before the name, a so-called determinative sign; similarly, another sign seemed to stand before names of countries and a third marked names of cities. As early as May 1846 Rawlinson expressed an optimistic hope of finding texts which contained lists of names of lands or persons, but the inscriptions which had appeared – albeit not of this type – did actually contain a great deal of the necessary information. These same determinatives, marking names of persons, lands and cities, occurred again and again in the texts Layard found at Nimrud; this meant for instance that in a number of cases it was known which combination of signs covered the names of the kings who had built the palaces – despite the fact that no one could so far read these signs.

A comparison with the Persian text enabled him to make a further observation: a certain sign had to denote 'son', and this again made it possible to reconstruct parts of a genealogical chain; the kings would normally introduce themselves as 'King A, son of B', so the text should be expected to give the sequence: [personal name 1] SON OF [personal name 2]. This led to the problem of which names to insert as being represented by these so far unreadable signs – which of the available king lists from secondary sources should be utilised? Here Rawlinson engaged in a mistaken and quite futile search through the Greek authors who wrote about Assyrian history. His learning was immense and the reasoning extremely sophisticated, but the results were utterly wrong.

One can perhaps say that even if he had introduced the correct names it is doubtful whether it would have helped, for there were special, unrealised difficulties with respect to the way in which precisely personal names were written in the cuneiform script. It seemed logical to attempt to make use of the names in the effort to break the code, and it was of course an analysis of this nature which had laid the ground for the decipherment of the Old Persian script – not to mention the Egyptian hieroglyphs. However, this procedure turned out to be unproductive when applied to the Babylonian-Assyrian script. As will be described in detail later, names were often written by way of ideograms, signs which stand for a complete word, and therefore not using signs which were to be read phonetically, representing syllables. We are in fact quite used to ideograms, for our own writing system makes use of them as well, for instance when rendering the names of currencies: $ for the word 'dollar', £ for the word 'pound sterling', ¥ for 'yen;' or consider signs like § for 'paragraph' or © for 'copyright'.

Ideograms were much more common in cuneiform than they are in our system of writing, however, and precisely such words as royal names were usually not spelled out as other 'normal' words would be, but were written in a learned, complex way, using many ideograms. Divine names nearly always formed part of royal names, for instance, and they were practically never spelled syllabically. The result of this was that Rawlinson found it enormously difficult to combine his readings of signs from ordinary running text with the same signs as they were used in the writing of royal names. In a simple consecutive text the signs might be used with syllabic values, whereas they would be used as ideograms in personal names. He consequently felt that the system was nearly entirely devoid of clear rules, and that practically all signs could be read in all kinds of ways.

Therefore, even though Rawlinson and Layard could establish sequences of royal names, they were unable to read a single one of them. Actually, Rawlinson chose a totally erroneous path in his studies of the Greek historians, and he ended up with the sequence Ninus, son of Arkelus, grandson of Anebus, as the name for the man who had built the great northwestern palace at Nimrud.[59] He took these names from Abydenus, and they had no relationship to actual Assyrian history. According to Abydenus, Ninus was the very first king of Assyria, a figure belonging to mankind's primeval period. Layard was somewhat sceptical with respect to these ideas and he wrote to his mother about it: 'this, I fear, is rather too good a joke, & one may as well go back to the "mighty hunter" himself to explain the hunting scenes which are so frequent among the sculptures'.[60] The mythical founder of Assyria according to the Greek traditions seemed as improbable as the 'mighty hunter before God', King Nimrod from the Hebrew Bible.

None the less, Rawlinson felt that he was close to the final breakthrough and he asked in a very long letter that Layard should send him all the genealogies, sequences of names, which occurred at Nimrud. It is characteristic of his erratic course through the enquiry and constantly changing views that he now felt that the vertical arrow, which stands as a determinative in front of personal names, was in fact an unsafe guide; he now saw it as the definite article, which accordingly may mark not just names but nouns of any kind. On the other hand, he had hit upon the very sound idea that the best key to an understanding of the names was to be found in the many inscriptions on bricks, which had appeared especially in the south, in Babylonia. The texts on these objects are necessarily very brief, and it seemed a safe bet that they would contain the name of the king who had built the structure for which the brick had been used, whether a palace or a temple. In such inscriptions the vertical wedge would accordingly stand in front of names only. He did not expect that such new readings would enable him to get to the language used in the texts, but he felt certain that the names in themselves would contain sensational revelations. He therefore asked for Layard's permission to announce his identifications of the names of the Assyrian kings together with a limited list of signs. He regarded translations of the texts as such to be an unrealisable goal.

Before he could present such a list of names he must however have all the material in Layard's hands, and he attached a pencil sketch with copies of

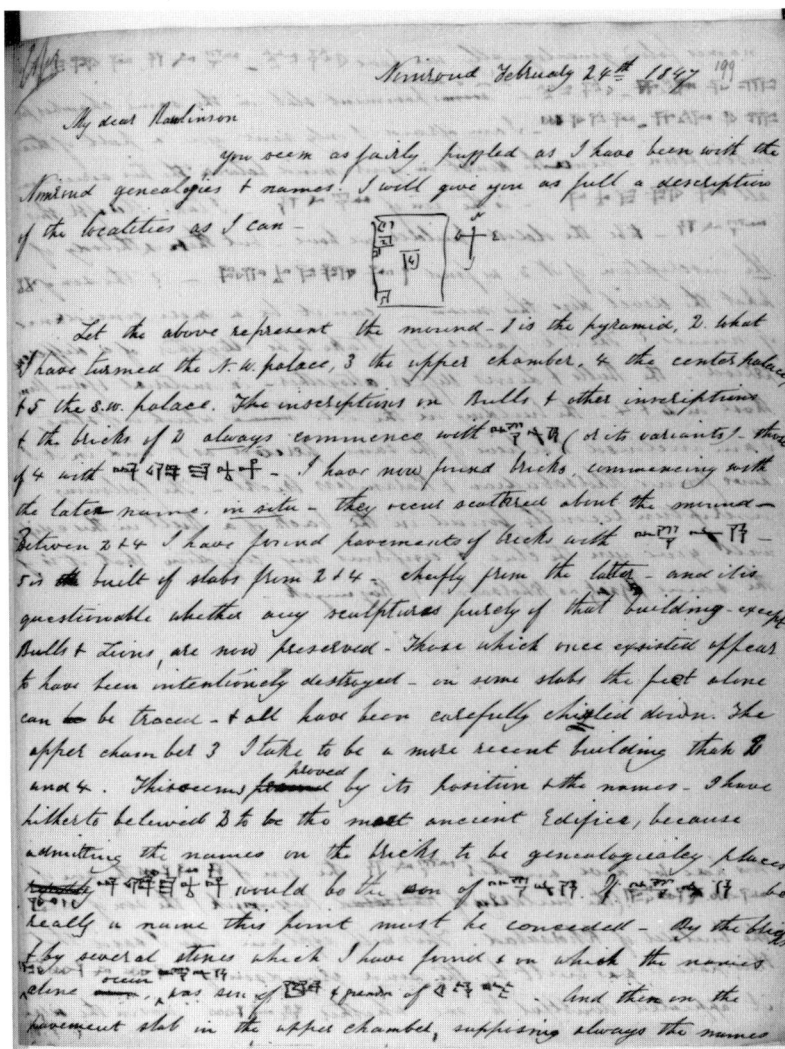

Figure 14.2 The first page of Layard's letter to Rawlinson, dated 24 February 1847, with his sketch of Nimrud. Reproduced by courtesy of the Trustees of the British Library.

the cuneiform writing for the names he wanted to know more about.[61] Layard answered in a very long letter, of which we have a draft in the British Library (see Figure 14.2).

This is of interest by showing us both how much he had understood, and perhaps especially how little was certain with respect to the history of the site. He began by giving a description of Nimrud, explaining which buildings he had uncovered parts of and appending a plan:

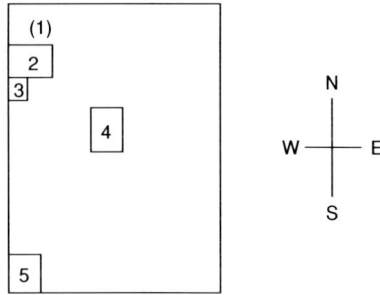

The figure '1' marks the large 'pyramid' which sat on top of the mound; '2' is the Northwest palace, '3' a group of rooms which were on higher ground than the palace, '4' is the so-called 'Central palace' from where the Black Obelisk came, and '5' is the Southwest palace. He had observed that all inscriptions from '2' begin with a name written by way of four signs – the one Rawlinson wanted to read 'Ninus' and which we now know should be read Ashur-nasir-pal (which means 'the god Ashur is the protector of the heir'); this same name appears as the designation for the father of the king who built '4', the central palace, a man whose name we now read Shulmanu-ashared – normally rendered Shalmaneser because that is the form given in the Bible, and which means 'the god Shulmanu is the leader'. Layard had further noticed that the palace marked as '5' had been constructed in part with material taken from the two other buildings, and that the central palace in this way in fact had been robbed of its sculptures. Later excavations have taught us that the central area in fact contained more than one building: a palace built by Ashurnasirpal II, later repaired by his son Shalmaneser III; in association with this a pair of colossal bulls from the time of the latter king, probably belonging to a palace which was later destroyed to make room for the central palace of Tiglath-pileser III in the eighth century (Postgate and Reade 1976–80; Barnett and Falkner 1962).

Layard had constructed an internal chronology for the palaces on Nimrud on the basis of his observations: the well-preserved Northwest palace was the oldest; it had decayed in antiquity, someone had repaired it, but later again others had removed a number of reliefs from here to be used in the Southwest palace. When Nimrud was finally destroyed, it was probably a ruin, and for that reason it had not been burnt down. The central palace was a generation younger, but it was so destroyed that little could be said about it. Finally, the palace in the southwestern corner was the youngest of the three and had not been finished when Nimrud was sacked.

Layard could thus refer to two different Assyrian dynasties, and he felt they had to be separated by a span of centuries. The first dynasty had constructed the two palaces in the northwest and in the centre of the mound, and the later dynasty could be connected with the king who had begun the palace in the southwest. In Layard's opinion this was contemporary with the palace at Khorsabad which Botta had discovered, a conclusion he drew on the basis of a stylistic observation of the reliefs; a similar analysis led him to conclude that the palaces which had to be hidden in Kuyunjik likewise belonged to the time of the later dynasty.[62]

There was a great deal of good sense in Layard's observations, and it is particularly interesting to see how he felt capable of distinguishing between different stylistic phases of Assyrian art.

Several weeks passed before he received an answer from Baghdad, for Rawlinson was ill again and unable to work seriously. He was planning another stay in a camp of tents outside the city, and after that a trip into the mountains of Kurdistan where he wished to spend the summer – 'otherwise I fear I must go home, for twenty years in the East with the knocking about I have had is no joke – and although I should be loath to forfeit the Baghdad post, I should be still more loath seriously to endanger my health'.

He had in fact been doing some work on the basis of the new information provided by Layard, and once again he appears to be on the brink of a major breakthrough. He had realised that his basic view of the character of cuneiform writing, which had so far governed his thought, was erroneous. Where he had seen it as a kind of alphabet, where the various consonants like /s/ or /d/ could be combined with any vowel, an idea which was inspired by his knowledge of later Semitic writing systems like Arabic and Hebrew, he now realised that it was in fact predominantly a syllabic system.

> One of the most important discoveries I have made in the alphabet is that it is far more syllabic than I had formerly supposed. I now suspect there are 1 or more characters for every phonetic power with every species of syllabic complement, whereas I used only to take the initial sound and to suppose the complement I found in the Persian names, had been dropped in Median & Babylonian.[63]

Any single sign therefore represented both a consonant and a vowel, which meant there were special signs for /sa/, /si/ and /su/, and others again for /as/, /is/ and /us/. This was an important step forward, but unfortunately it was not one to which he would stick with any tenacity in the following period; many things indicate that he continued to think of the Babylonian-Assyrian script as fundamentally alphabetic in nature. There was still a long way to go, and, in fact, the new realisation meant that he had to go through his material again, trying to implement the theory. He was quite incapable of such a task.

At the same time it was obvious that he alone had command of material so varied and extensive that it could sustain an effort to establish a decipherment; consequently his rivals had very small chances of overtaking him. Botta sat in Paris working on his inscriptions from Khorsabad, but he wrote to Layard saying that he did not feel that he was making any progress whatever. As already mentioned, the French state had financed a journey for Coste and Flandin, who were supposed to copy all the Persian inscriptions, but as Botta wrote:

> M.M. Coste and Flandin took great care in Persia not to copy the important inscriptions which had been left uncopied by the precedent (sic) travellers and you know how easy should be the work if we had the sixty or seventy proper names recorded at Persepolis or Bisitun. Major Rawlinson will do it.[64]

In an earlier letter he considered the possibility of asking Rawlinson for a copy of one of the missing texts, 'but I dare not ask it because it would be too much'.[65] It does not appear likely that he would have received a positive reply to such a request; instead he exchanged inscriptions with Layard, but they did not provide the necessary key.

Layard was now working intensely in order to get as much as possible done before his impending departure for England. He uncovered more than twenty rooms in the Northwest palace, all of them with reliefs or inscriptions, and he observed that the building continued towards the south with rooms whose walls were decorated with frescos rather than reliefs. The subject matter was the same, he says, but he was unable to preserve any of them; they disappeared so quickly after being exposed to the air that he rarely had the time to make adequate draw-ings of them. By way of trial trenches he observed that such frescos were the norm in the southern parts of the building, but he felt constrained to stop the excava-tions for lack of money. Frescos were found by later excavators at Nimrud, occasionally in the Northwest palace as well, and designs very similar to the ones described by Layard were discovered in other palaces; in most cases they found only what were described as 'faint traces' however (Oates 1959: 117–19, and plate XXIX; Mallowan 1966: 467; Nunn 1988: 123–30).

The excavations were also slowed by the discovery of many small finds. He found a large number of ivory objects, often gilded and inlaid with blue paste. They formed part of the ornamentation on the furniture of the Assyrian king, and later British excavations have discovered many more of these marvellous works of art (Orchard 1967; Mallowan and Davies 1970; Mallowan and Herrmann 1974; Herrmann 1986; Herrmann 1992). They are particularly fascinating in the way in which they combine different stylistic traditions and motifs, Egyptian, Levantine and Assyrian. The majority of them must have been produced outside of Assyria, presumably in the Levant, in Phoenicia or Palestine. Layard was delighted with their fragile beauty and spent hours lying on the ground, separating them from the earth with a pen-knife.

The Southwest palace was problematic, since it had been burnt down before it was completed. Reliefs and bulls were almost completely destroyed by the flames. In one of the rooms he discovered relief blocks laid out in a row before the wall they were supposed to decorate, ready to be raised and put into position. In another room he found miserable remains of strange, free-standing sphinxes, but they proved impossible to move.

CHAPTER FIFTEEN

PACKING BULLS AND OTHER LUGGAGE

———— •◆• ————

One of the last tasks Layard had to complete as he neared the end of the excavations at Nimrud in late Spring was to organise the shipment of as many of his finds as he could manage to send down the river to Baghdad. This demanded a great deal of sturdy rope and mats to protect the reliefs, and these had to be brought all the way from Aleppo in Syria. The theft of a shipment of these essential goods gave rise to one of Layard's more bizarre exploits. Having first turned to the Pasha in Mosul in order to have the thieves found and punished, he learnt that since they were Bedouin from the steppe there was no hope that they would be caught. He could not accept that. Instead, he activated his own intelligence system and after a couple of days learned which tribe was responsible. Together with two Turkish soldiers he rode into the desert and after a few hours' ride found the camp, which however was considerably larger than he had anticipated. He rode directly up to the tent of the sheikh and sat down.

'Peace be with you', he said to the sheikh, who was clearly aware of the reason for Layard's visit. The tent they sat in was raised with new ropes which undoubtedly came from the robbery.

> Your health and spirits are, please 'God, good. We have long been friends, although it has never yet been my good fortune to see you. I know the laws of friendship; that which is my property is your property, and the contrary. But there are a few things, such as mats, felts, and ropes, which come from afar, and are very necessary to me, whilst they can be of little use to you; otherwise God forbid that I should ask for them. You will greatly oblige me by giving these things to me.

The sheikh denied that he was in possession of such things, and all his warriors confirmed his words. Layard answered that he would like to look more closely at this, and at a sign his trusted servant ran up to the sheikh and handcuffed him; jumping into his saddle he quickly dragged the amazed sheikh away from the tent. 'Now, my sons', Layard said to the surprised warriors, 'I have found a part of that which I wanted; you must search for the rest'. The heavily armed Arabs were simply too astonished by this daring manoeuvre to react, so Layard and his men were already far from the camp before they recovered and could do anything. The

Figure 15.1 The first great bull is taken down. The transportation of these enormous sculptures presented Layard with a complex problem. Botta had sawed his in four pieces to make their handling easier, but Layard refused to do this. (From Layard 1849, I: frontispiece)

sheikh was taken to Mosul and handed over to the Pasha, and the following morning a donkey loaded with Layard's ropes, felts and mats was found at the camp in Nimrud together with a lamb and a kid as a peace offering (Layard 1849: 366–8).

In March he then made his attempt to move one of the great bulls, a block of stone weighing more than 10 tons (see Figure 15.1). The bulls stood in pairs guarding the most important doors and gates in the palace, and in order to move one of them he first had to remove the wall behind it, in order that it might be lowered to a horizontal position and placed on heavy wooden rollers. These in turn were placed on top of less thick branches covered in grease. Layard's ropes were far from solid and he had no cranes or other technical aids – everything had to be done with the aid of strong human arms. The ropes were anchored in the facing wall above the bull that was not supposed to be moved, and Layard ordered the colossus to be lowered slowly onto the rollers.

> The men being ready, and all my preparations complete, I stationed myself on top of the high bank of earth over the second bull, and ordered the wedges to be struck out from under the sculpture to be moved. Still, however, it remained firmly in its place. A rope having been passed around it, six or

seven men easily tilted it over. The thick, ill-made cable stretched with the strain, and almost buried itself in the earth round which it was coiled. The ropes held well. The mass descended gradually, the Chaldæans propping it up with the beams. It was a moment of great anxiety. The drums and shrill pipes of the Kurdish musicians increased the din and confusion caused by the war-cry of the Arabs, who were half frantic with excitement. They had thrown off nearly all their garments; their long hair floated in the wind; and they indulged in the wildest postures and gesticulations as they clung to the ropes. The women had congregated on the sides of the trenches, and by their incessant screams, and by the ear-piercing tahlehl, added to the enthusiasm of the men. The bull once in motion, it was no longer possible to obtain a hearing. The loudest cries I could produce were lost in the crash of discordant sounds. Neither the hippopotamus-hide whips of the Cawasses, nor the bricks and clods of earth with which I endeavoured to draw attention from some of the most noisy of the group, were of any avail. Away went the bull, steady enough as long as supported by the props behind; but as it came nearer to the rollers, the beams could no longer be used. The cable and ropes stretched more and more. Dry from the climate, as they felt the strain, they creaked and threw out dust. Water was thrown over them, but in vain, for they all broke together when the sculpture was within four or five feet of the rollers. The bull was precipitated to the ground. Those who held the ropes, thus suddenly released, followed its example, and were rolling, one over the other, in the dust. A sudden silence succeeded to the clamour. I rushed into the trenches, prepared to find the bull in many pieces. It would be difficult to describe my satisfaction, when I saw it lying precisely where I had wished to place it, and uninjured! The Arabs no sooner got on their legs again, than, seeing the result of the accident, they darted out of the trenches, and, seizing by the hands the women who were looking on, formed a large circle, and, yelling their war-cry with redoubled energy, commenced a most mad dance. The musicians exerted themselves to the utmost; but their music was drowned by the cries of the dancers. Even Abd-ur-rahman shared in the excitement, and, throwing his cloak to one of his attendants, insisted upon leading off the debkhé.

(Layard 1849, vol. I: 81–5)

When the excitement had died down somewhat, the men had to drag the bull out of the palace, to the edge of the mound. Everything went well, without further mishap, and the following morning it could be rolled down off the mound and on to a large cart which was to bring it all the way to the river. This cart had been built in Mosul, and some of the enormous iron parts originated in the one Botta had built for his bulls (see Figure 15.2). Later the same procedure was used to remove a great lion, and both were eventually floated down to Baghdad.

On the way back to the village after the first day's toil Layard rode with his friend Abd-ur-rahman. His enthusiasm had slowly turned to wonder and he made a little speech, which eloquently and with great clarity expresses the feelings he and his men had towards the work of the young Englishman.

Figure 15.2 On the background of the silhouette of the Nimrud acropolis one sees the further transportation to the river bank. Kurdish musicians walk at the front, Arabs pull the ropes, the hardy Nestorians drag the cart, and Abd-ur-rahman stands with his men in the foreground, wondering about the meaning of all this. (From Layard 1849, II: frontispiece)

'Wonderful! Wonderful! There is surely no God but God, and Mohammed is his Prophet', exclaimed he, after a long pause. 'In the name of the Most High, tell me, O Bey, what you are going to do with those stones. So many thousands of purses spent upon such things! Can it be, as you say, that your people learn wisdom from them; or is it, as his reverence the Cadi declares, that they are going to go to the palace of your Queen, who, with the rest of the unbelievers, worships these idols? As for wisdom, these figures will not teach you to make any better knives, or scissors, or chintzes; and it is in the making of those things that the English show their wisdom. But God is great! God is great! Here are stones which have been buried ever since the time of the holy Noah, – peace be with him! Perhaps they were under ground before the deluge. I have lived on these lands for years. My father, and the father of my father, pitched their tents here before me; but they never heard of these figures. For twelve hundred years have the true believers (and, praise be to God! all true wisdom is with them alone) been settled in this country, and none of them ever heard of a palace under ground. Neither did they who went before them. But lo! here comes a Frank from many days' journey off, and he walks up to the very place, and he takes a stick (illustrating the

Figure 15.3 Layard's activities were followed with great interest in the pages of the popular magazine *Illustrated London News*, where one could find pictures of the stages in the transportation of the bull to London. This shows the delicate manoeuvre at Basrah, when the bull was loaded on the ship 'The Apprentice'; the British river-steamer led by captain Felix Jones in the background. (From *Illustrated London News* 27 July 1850: 72)

description at the same time with the point of his spear), and makes a line here, and makes a line there. Here, says he, is the palace; there, says he, is the gate; and he shows us what has been all our lives beneath our feet, without our having known about it. Wonderful! Wonderful! Is it by books, is it by magic, is it by your prophets, that you have learnt these things? Speak, O Bey; tell me the secret of wisdom'.

(Layard 1849, vol. 1: 81–5)

Layard writes how he had been musing somewhat along the same lines, in wonder that the civilisation and knowledge which the West had now reached had apparently already existed here at an unimaginably early time. His own work was in some sense a kind of recognition of the debt owed by the West to the East.

As he turned to Abd-ur-rahman to answer him he did not choose to express these thoughts, however. Instead he used the opportunity to impress upon the sheikh how immensely superior western culture was, explaining the strength which European civilisation had reached, and he saw with satisfaction that his words made an impression on Abd-ur-rahman. Layard's idea was that such notions would help secure his personal status among the Arabs, making him immune to feelings of hostility. Perhaps it was not possible for these two men to engage in a true exchange of ideas about these matters, which had so deeply touched the sheikh. One can hardly claim that this dialogue has in fact ever started.

Another, no less emotional, consideration was brought into the open by the removal of the bull and the lion. When the bull was installed some years later in the British Museum (see Figure 15.4), the great poet Dante Gabriel Rossetti wrote a poem about it, in which he said:

> Now, thou poor god, within this hall
> Where the blank windows blind the wall
> From pedestal to pedestal,
> The kind of light shall on thee fall
> Which London takes the day to be:
> While school-foundations in the act
> Of holiday, three files compact,
> Shall learn to view thee as a fact
> Connected with that zealous tract:
> 'Rome, – Babylon and Nineveh'.
> (Rossetti 1974)

Layard describes how he sat one night, watching with mixed emotions the two giant lions in the moonlight, while shadows slowly flowed over the torsos of stone, which seemed to become alive in the dark. 'I shall never forget that night, or the emotions which these venerable figures caused within me', he wrote. In a few hours they would be taken from their calm resting-place, turned over and transported to a distant world, where they would be 'a mere wonder-stock to the busy crowd of a new world'. But they belonged here, brooding over the secrets, the forgotten ideas which had been thought in the rooms and corridors of the palace. In the British Museum they were going to be, as Rossetti said, exhibited as examples of

Figure 15.4 Finally arrived at London, the bull is on its way into the British Museum through the hall of Doric pillars. (From *Illustrated London News* 28 February 1852: 184)

the passage of history, a link in a chain of argument about the roots and origin of western civilisation. Torn from their own world, which had never considered Rome or London but which had been concerned with entirely different problems. As Layard sat here in the darkness watching them, they were still real, if only for a short while; they were meaningful in spite of the death of their own world. Or precisely because of it. As they had guarded the palace in its grandeur, they ought to guard it in its destruction (Layard 1853: 201–2).

When the finds had been packed and sent to Baghdad, he could look back upon more than eighteen months' work at Nimrud, a place which had become a part of himself. He could be satisfied with his achievements, and no doubt satisfaction was a dominant emotion for him, but at the same time he was painfully aware of the limitations and inadequacy of his work. 'The ruins were, of course, very inadequately explored; but with the small sum at my disposal I was unable to pursue my researches to the extent that I could have wished', he complained. He felt that it had been impossible to gain a clear impression of what was there to be found in the rest of the large mound itself. Using search trenches outside of the palace areas he had tried to make sure that no large buildings with new treasures were to be found anywhere else, but it goes without saying that this method did not reveal what was there. Later excavations have discovered not only other palaces, but large temple complexes, whose existence remained unknown to Layard. He entertained the naive dream of being able to excavate the mound in its entirety, but that was (and remains) quite simply an impossible task. What he had discovered was quite enough to make any archaeologist proud and satisfied (Layard 1849: 2, 42–3).

He also managed to open excavations on the Kuyunjik mound, and here he found the remains of a gigantic palace whose reliefs had, unfortunately, been very severely damaged by fire. He had also attempted to dig at other sites, first of all at Kalah Shergat, where the city called Assur, the oldest Assyrian city, is located. He did not really find anything here, apart from a headless statue of a king which had been seen already by Rich. It was now sent to London.

He was convinced that the palace at Kuyunjik had belonged to one of the great Assyrian kings who appear in the historical books of the Old Testament, either Sennacherib, Esarhaddon or Tiglath-pileser; he was entirely right in this, for the building was later revealed to have been the palace of Sennacherib. He was of course clear in his mind that this building was later in time than the Northwest palace which had yielded such treasures at Nimrud.

With more than 300 drawings in his baggage he left Mosul in June 1847 after a tearful farewell to all those men and women who had become close friends and associates. The Arab women of the district moaned his departure, for he had been a staunch supporter of their rights in the many disputes which had been brought before him for decision.

He took his young friend Hormuzd Rassam with him on the trip; he was a younger brother of Christian Rassam, the British Vice-Consul at Mosul, and only eighteen years old. For months he had been Layard's most trusted man in the excavation, handling all connections with the Arab workmen and paying all salaries. Layard had become his great hero and the warm feelings were reciprocated. Mrs Badger Rassam was keen to have him placed with some parson in England for a couple of years, and Layard had written to his own mother asking her to find a suitable position. 'Of course latin and french are not wanted, a good English education would be most important, & most important of all the inculcation of English principles & feelings', he explains.[66] He further explained that Hormuzd was very well behaved, an amiable and incredibly amusing man. Escorted by fifty horsemen the two left for Constantinople.

Shortly before the departure Forshall in London sent off a letter, which arrived too late to reach Layard in Mosul, however; he announced the arrival of the first twelve cases with reliefs from Nimrud to the British Museum. 'They have created great interest, and all who have examined appear to be much gratified', wrote Forshall.[67]

CHAPTER SIXTEEN

TRIUMPH AND REVOLUTION

————— •◆• —————

A letter was waiting for Layard in Constantinople informing him that he could expect to receive an official appointment from the Foreign Office. Canning had spoken to Lord Palmerston in London and had written immediately to explain to his young protégé that things were looking better. He asked him to stay in Constantinople, waiting for his own arrival, so Layard sat here waiting with growing impatience for the ambassador or at least a message authorising him to continue to London. Canning, however, was involved in delicate diplomatic manoeuvres which took him first to Switzerland where he was supposed to mediate in a civil war which had broken out between Catholics and Protestants. He had personally been heavily involved in the creation of the cantonal state in 1815. He returned to London in February 1848, leaving finally for Turkey on 17 March. Along the way he was supposed to sound out the political situation in various European capitals. Berlin, where he was to go first, was the scene of massacre and anarchy; Vienna had students storming the council chamber, forcing Metternich to flee. While Canning was in Vienna there were strong student protests. So he was busy and Layard in Constantinople could not claim his full attention.

While he was waiting he received letters from friends and family telling him that the reliefs were now arriving at the British Museum, and his mother wrote in great agitation and excitement:

> all the learned and really intellectual people seem delighted with them ... they are in very low relief I find, but the beauty of execution exceeded my expectations, in every way! ... you will understand with what gratification I regarded them! I felt myself a little bit of a Lion as belonging to you!! I long for the remainder to arrive. These do not attract the common herd of sight-seers, but they are of the highest order of interest ... they are much talked of in the high quarters, & they speak of building another wing on purpose for the Assyrian antiquities, if those expected equal those already arrived![68]

It was intolerable to have to sit idle in Constantinople waiting for Canning, who did not show up. Hormuzd was placed in the household of a Turkish Pasha Layard knew in order to learn some more Turkish, and he enjoyed himself – dressed as a Turk he amused himself with all kinds of pranks, entering the mosques, speaking openly to Turkish ladies and so forth. Layard suffered from malaria, and in October he had a series of attacks that were so violent that the embassy's doctor recommended that he should leave for England as quickly as possible. He took a steamer to Italy where he met old friends. The country was in turmoil, and the idea of a united, independent Italy was finally beginning to be realised. But Layard was uncharacteristically sceptical, as can be seen from a letter he wrote to his aunt: 'all this may lead to a great deal of good or a great deal of mischief – as a sincere lover of Italy I hope for the good – but I confess that the issue appears to me very doubtful. There is something wanting in the Italian character, as formed by the present system of education and of course, by a long period of misgovernment'.

He also visited the excavations at Pompeii and was particularly enthusiastic about the major find which had been made only a few years previously, the Roman mosaic copy of a Greek painting of the great Battle of Arbela, where Alexander the Great crushed the Persian armies. 'It gave me a completely new idea as to the state of arts amongst the ancients', he wrote.[69]

He met the Dominican monk Valerga who had just been appointed to the post of Latin Patriarch in Jerusalem, and who was expected to become the official ambassador for the Vatican at the court of the Sultan in Constantinople. Valerga had been the head of the Catholic mission in Mesopotamia and had visited Mosul while Botta was the consul there; he had become the central figure in a row over the building of a new church in Mosul, an affair which ended in a violent uprising started by the Cadi. Valerga had been wounded, and only Botta's resolute interference had saved him from a worse fate.

From Italy he continued on to Paris, where he was received with open arms by Botta. A meeting was arranged in the prestigious *Académie des Inscriptions et Belles Lettres*, where Layard was to present the results of the many months of work at Nimrud. There was great interest in Assyria in Paris after Botta's finds had been displayed in the Louvre, and the meeting was attended by much of the academic elite in the city. The members of the Academy were aware of Layard's work, since Botta had presented information from his letters to the learned body on several occasions. It is not possible to improve upon Layard's own account – in a letter to his aunt – of this important occasion:

> The meeting was opened by an old lawyer, too well known, it appears, to the Institute; hair white, ears well stuffed with cotton, too toothless to be intelligible. He had written, and was to read, a paper on the origin of Parliaments and 'États Généraux' (perhaps something on their use would have been more helpful to his countrymen), but when, after an hour's preliminary discussion, he proceeded to divide his subject into five parts, with each of which the Académie was to be entertained in detail, the patience of that learned body became exhausted, and there was so strong a demonstration in favour of the opposition – the Nimroud antiquities – that the President was obliged to bring up the indignant lawyer in the middle of his course. I was still suffering from my attack of fever, and those who have had the

advantage of experience in these matters know that one of the results of fever is a considerable excitement of the brain, consequent audacity, and no small additional loquacity, only controlled by physical debility. Consequently, when placed in the middle of this rather formidable assembly, I contrived to make them, without nervousness, a moderately lengthy speech, probably in very bad French, but to all appearances perfectly intelligible. The drawings, of which I took only a small selection, created general surprise; particularly those which have reference to the mythology of the Assyrians – a subject untouched by the Khorsabad monuments. On one side, M. Lagard, in ecstasies, convinced me by frequent, as I thought at the time very unnecessary, digs in the ribs, that I had established fully to his satisfaction theories which, in spite of the sneers of the learned, he had been building up for nearly half a century. On the other, M. Raoul Rochette looked serious and perplexed, and was apparently not much gratified by the look of triumph with which M. Lagard asked him what had now become of his speculations on the origin of Greek Art. From all sides poured questions and compliments, from MM. Letronne, Mohl, Lenormand, etc. From opposite, old Humboldt, with all the quiet blandness of a German philosopher, endeavoured, but in vain, to put a question. What German could be heard amongst fifty Frenchmen? It was equally in vain that I endeavoured to isolate myself in imagination from the mass to catch the words, real golden words, of M. Burnouf, who never says anything not worth hearing. Equally in vain the President agitated himself and his small bell to restore order, but his indignation fell harmlessly on the backs, for he could see nothing else, of the learned. All this was very gratifying, and, had I not remembered that I was on the banks of the Seine, I might have left the Académie very well satisfied with myself, and fully convinced that I had bestowed upon some fifty most intelligent Frenchmen the happiest day of their lives! ...

I had fully expected that the mythological part of the drawings would be a subject of astonishment here, as this subject is so new, gives rise to so many new ideas, destroys so many old ones, and resolves so many long-disputed questions. M. Lenormand remarked to the Académie that hereafter no one could venture to enter upon the subject of Greek Art or Mythology without being thoroughly acquainted with the details of Nimroud.

(Layard 1903: 184–7)

This was indeed extremely gratifying and the young man must have been beside himself with happy pride. Not many people experience such an unconditional success, and even fewer have had the honour of being invited to become a corresponding member of the French *Institut*, an honour he was promised as soon as a vacancy should arise. He never did get this appointment, but at the time, in wintry Paris, he had every reason to expect it. Another meeting with members of the Academy was held the following day, and some of the scholars wanted to arrange an audience with the king, Louis-Philippe, but it turned out that he was on a tour in the provinces. As it happened, it was only a matter of months before the king was to sit in London as a political refugee, and Layard was in no doubt

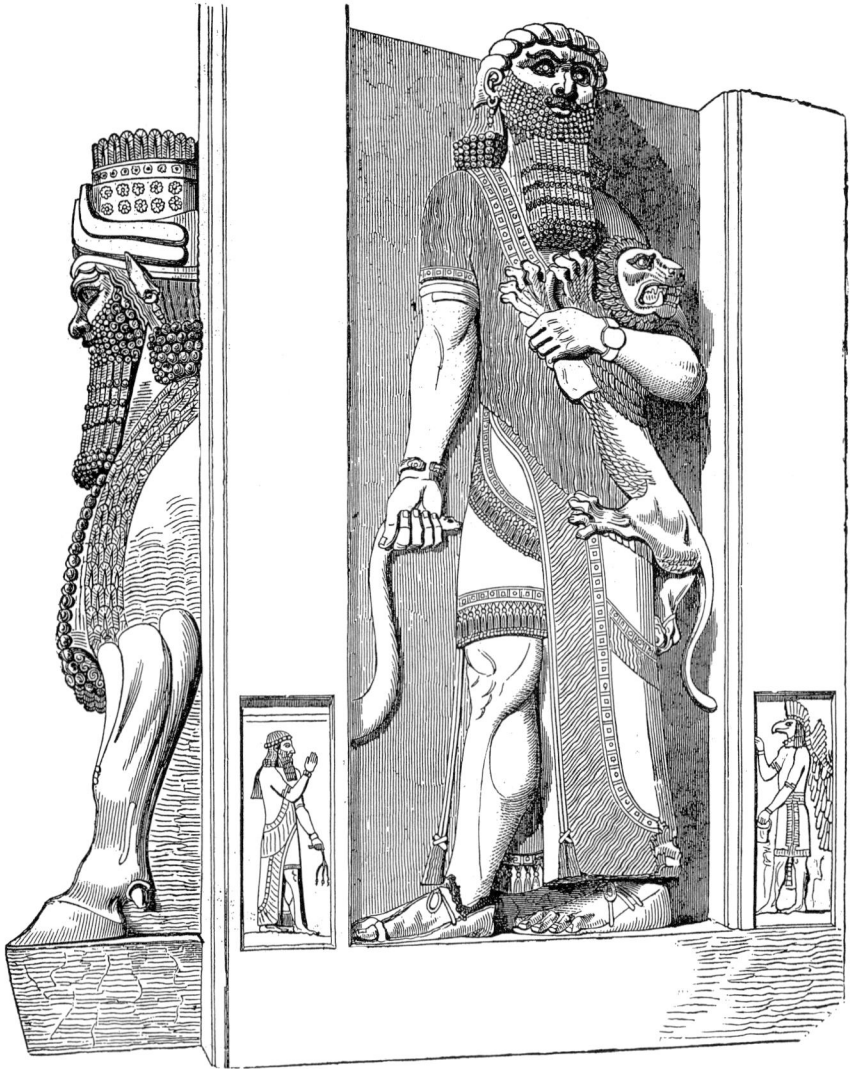

Figure 16.1 Botta's discoveries at Khorsabad were quickly installed in a special hall at the Louvre, and the *Illustrated London News* sent a reporter and an artist to Paris to take a closer look at the sensation. (From *Illustrated London News* 8 February 1851: 120)

that France was in a deep crisis. He had an interview with Tocqueville, the great politician and historian, whose influential book from 1835–40 about democracy in America had put forward a political programme for the future of Europe. When the revolution broke out in Paris two months after Layard's departure, in February 1848, Tocqueville became the Minister of Foreign Affairs in the new republican government.

Layard also saw the 'Nineveh Room' at the Louvre (see Figure 16.1), and it disappointed him. In his view there were no more than four important pieces in the collection, but he had to admit that the giant bulls were much larger than the ones he had found at Nimrud. He felt certain that he had been able to convince the learned French gentlemen that the sculptures from Khorsabad had to be much younger than his own from Nimrud, and he wrote to his aunt that if Nimrud would be just half as successful in London as Khorsabad had been in Paris, it would surely be easy to have his finds published.

The amiable Botta, who saw his own fame quite eclipsed by Layard's success, seems to have expressed nothing but pleasure and appears genuinely free from envy.

Botta's presence in Paris at this time was not really of his own choosing. In letters from 1847 he had repeatedly told Layard of his intention to return to Mosul to take up his dual duties as consul and archaeologist, and had he been in Assyria when the revolution broke out in Paris, he would undoubtedly have continued as excavator; however, he had been held back, first because of problems with the passage of the bill to pay for the publication, and after that because of a conflict with Flandin, the artist who had worked with him at Khorsabad. In fact, matters developed to a point where a committee was set up to evaluate the rival claims of the two men, and this had in the end supported Botta. Flandin had been accommodating, according to Botta because he expected that a new excavation was bound to make further, sensational finds, and he wanted to become involved. 'I know him too well not to do all that I can for preventing his success in case the occasion should present itself'.[70] The fight broke out again, and according to Botta it finished with his complete victory, since Flandin revealed such bad faith that he even lost an otherwise promised position at the Louvre.[71]

Botta was preparing the publication of the magnificent work on the Khorsabad excavations, but he found time as well to take part in the political life of the city. He invited Layard to a dinner at one of the finest restaurants in Paris, and introduced him to a number of his friends, all young men involved in politics and government. After dinner they walked in the Palais-Royal and described to Layard the crisis which was ravaging the country. They were certain that the ruling dynasty, which was increasingly unpopular, would fall very soon, and that after a period of anarchy and bloodshed a new republic would emerge.

The political climate in France had been very tense for months, and there was a number of groups and individuals in exile who were waiting for the right moment to strike; one of these was the pretender to the throne Louis Bonaparte, who lived in London. When some of Layard's letters had been lost in 1847 on their way to Botta in Paris, he suggested jokingly that they must have ended with the secret police:

> I suppose the letter has been opened and the inscription in such strange characters may have been taken for a new kind of ciphered letter, lettre chiffrée. the supposition is plausible enough when we have so many pretendents abroad; if true it would be capital. Fancy all the employés at the post and police office poring over an inscription from Nimroud and trying to find the

key of arrow headed character in hope of getting a clue to a deep laid con-
spiration in favour of Henry the fifth or Louis Bonaparte. would it not be
capital![72]

If the police succeeded in deciphering the cuneiform writing, they kept the secret
to themselves, and when the revolution came in February 1848 it stopped being
funny. Botta appears to have been badly squeezed by the events.

Layard left Paris on 19 December and said goodbye to Botta. This was the last
time the two men met. The friendship that had begun one summer's day five-and-
a-half years earlier in Mosul was not destined to develop further, for they were
heading in quite different directions. At this time Botta was expecting to go back
to Assyria to try his hand on Kuyunjik, but that was not to be, for he fell foul
of the violent political events which shortly afterwards overwhelmed France. It is
not entirely clear what happened to Botta during the revolutions in February and
June of 1848. The descriptions we have of his life take it for granted that he fell
into disgrace as a result of his political involvement, and that as a consequence he
was banished to an insignificant post as consul at Jerusalem, but it really is not
very clear what was the background for this change in his position. He was obviously a royalist, and his letters to both Layard and Disraeli make it clear that he
most definitely did not appreciate the republican revolution.

It is interesting to observe that while he was writing his scholarly letters to
Layard during 1846 and 1847, letters which are quite sober in tone, even though
they repeatedly refer to his constant bad health which prevented him from working,
he was also writing to Disraeli, letters which were quite different – desperate and
obsessed with death. The first of these dates from January 1846; his English friend
had visited Paris and Botta sadly excuses himself for not having seen as much of
Disraeli as he had wished, but 'various circumstances which preyed very much
upon my mind, broken hopes, family quarrels' have made it impossible for him
to enjoy human contact.

> When things dont go as I wish them to do the best for me is to shut myself
> in my shell. what we call in French *distraction* is of no use for me because
> I cannot conceal the state I am in and I hate nothing so much as being asked
> why I am melancholy when I dont like to tell the reason. Solitude in those
> cases is better for me; when alone I can argue with myself till I am perfectly
> convinced that every thing is vanity and vexation of spirit, and that it is
> useless to fret since there is a very certain and never failing end to all sorrows,
> death.
>
> I think much about death and although I am not a believer I cannot help
> thinking that it is only the beginning of another life and I hope a better one.
> what it shall be, god knows but I cannot believe that every thing ends for
> us with this miserable life of ours. I can afford no reason for my belief, but
> I like it because it comforts me and lightens the darkness around me with a
> ray of hope.[73]

Some nine months later he wrote to Disraeli again, this time from London where
he was to take a personal look at Layard's sculptures from Nimrud. He does not

write about that, however. Instead, the visit to London, a city he has not seen for twenty-five years, caused him to compare it with Paris, which at this time was entering a phase of rapid development and change. He felt that France was in fact about to overtake England with respect to technological and economic development, and this provokes the question:

> but is that for the better? no, my dear sir, I dont think so; it is for us the last show of a dying people; we were something when we fought for an idea; but now, alas, we think about our material comforts. we do, what you do, because we are all men and have the same wants but what is there at the bottom of that racing for comfort? death, my dear sir, and a shameful death; France is gone; it was a country formerly and it was a necessary and useful *contrepoids* to your tendencies. but now we imitate you as apes and the result is clear to me, although few people can see it or dare tell it; we lost our strength when we set aside our spiritual tendencies and now we are but the tender behind the moving engine; I think we shall see it, although we are no more young men.

He fears that France is about to suffer the same fate as Poland: becoming dismembered by the conquering neighbours, England, Prussia and Austria. The governing political class, which is ruled entirely by egotism, will not care at all, 'provided they save their own cash and nobody interferes in their own concerns. let the english and prussians and austrians take our country provided we dine and drink and the bawdy houses are left open. that is all what they care for'. This political analysis, this desperate and shrill criticism of modernity, leads him back to his own personal crisis:

> that is the reason, my dear sir, why I grow every day more religious and I intend to get into holy orders and [spend] my life in a convent; I am convinced we are not born for this life only because it would be to [sic] stupid if it would end there; I hope for a better one where there shall be neither rail roads nor steamers; damn them! they take the poetry of life.[74]

Disraeli added a comment on top of the first page of this letter: 'Mr Botta – most interesting'. This is the same man who appeared under the pseudonym Marigny in the novel *Contarini Fleming* as a rabid sceptic who ridicules the Christian faith! It is not hard to understand that Botta could get into trouble in revolutionary Paris with such views.

Layard wrote to Ross in Mosul in late March 1848 and expressed concern for Botta: 'I have heard nothing of Botta since the late wonderful occurrences in France. I fear he will be amongst the sufferers – as everyone else is. All Europe is at this moment in a state of convulsion & no one can guess how it will all end. I do not dread anything from Germany, as the public are sufficiently sober minded to avoid extremes – but as for those d—d Frenchmen there is no seeing how matters will go'.[75] Shortly afterwards he received a letter from Botta in which he compared the Parisians with the savage Maoris of New Zealand: 'every body must be ready to fight for his life and property and we think of nothing else but guns, cartridges, swords etc. that is what they call fraternity; if it lasts a little longer we shall be

perfect barbarians'. He is still working on his excavation report, but the seriousness of the situation appears from his account of how he and the prominent
orientalist Saulcy, armed to the teeth, confronted a mass of people who tried to
storm the Parliament building. *En passant* he writes: 'I am no more consul at Mosul
where they have sent an ass but I have been appointed at Jerusalem. I wish I might
die there. death is better than the life we lead'.[76]

It seems clear that Botta was disappointed at not being sent to Mosul, but the
letters to Disraeli show that his despair had more deep-rooted causes in his personal
life. He returns to the matter of his interrupted archaeological work in a letter
from Jerusalem some nine months later, where he writes to Layard:

> I am just now very busy finishing my work, and a tedious business it is. it
> shall be a mere description because I consider that such work must be
> material for others, and therefore one must not mingle his own theories
> and opinions with real facts which alone can serve as sure ground for
> other people's researches. besides I am disgusted with the thing; since our
> blessed revolution I have no more taste for archaeological studies. who
> can take any interest in them when there is no rest, no certainty for the
> persons no hope for the future. I wish I lie as deep under ground as Nimrod
> is now.[77]

His letter shows that in spite of all he did retain an interest in cuneiform studies,
and he repeats the constant question of the French scholars: why does Rawlinson
not publish his texts? Botta says that he had planned to visit Bisutun himself in
order to make a copy of the inscription, in order to force Rawlinson to bring out
his material, but he of course never got the chance to get near the place again.

However, it is legitimate to ask whether his appointment to Jerusalem was really
meant to be a demotion, or whether the diplomatic system did not regard this post
as an advancement. It has recently been claimed that the posting to Jerusalem was
to be seen as 'une sérieuse disgrâce' (Beyer 1994: 54.) He was certainly described
as a most unhappy man by Gustave Flaubert who visited him in Jerusalem in 1850;
he had supper with him and wrote as follows in his diary:

> Dîner chez Botta, homme en ruine, homme de ruines, dans la ville des ruines;
> nie tout, et m'a l'air de tout haïr si ce n'est pas les morts; rappelle le moyen
> âge de tous ses vœux, admire M. de Maistre. Il apprend maintenant le piano
> et avoue qu'il n'est pas un creuseur. C'est une phase de la vie de cet homme:
> fatigué de tentatives (sa vie en est un tissu, médecin, naturaliste, archéologue,
> consul), il a essayé de celle-là, il n'en veut pas d'autre, c'est assez. 'Que l'hu-
> manité soit comme moi', disent tous ceux qui ne peuvent soit la dominer,
> soit la comprendre.

> (Flaubert 1910: 296)

Yet Jerusalem was not quite as provincial as Mosul after all, even though Botta
found it to be nearly as boring; he did have a slightly more interesting circle of
acquaintances, and he notes that the English consul here at least is an Englishman,
and not 'a nasty *pigo* as M. Rassam was'; this word is one he has learnt from an

English officer from India who has explained that it referred to 'the lowest kind of Negro we have in India'. Botta is also pleased with the Anglican bishop in Jerusalem, even though he wonders why he is there since there are no other Anglicans in the city.

Jerusalem was a hotbed of religious rivalries. It is not entirely clear whether France was already at this time preparing for the strong emphasis on Catholic interests which was going to develop into a major diplomatic crisis in the years ahead. One of the central figures in this was the Dominican Valerga, with whom Botta had been involved in Mosul, and who was now the Latin Patriarch of Jerusalem. In all events, this was to have a strong impact on Botta's life and his position as consul in Jerusalem soon proved to be both politically important and very influential.

The two men never met again, but their destinies were to some extent related during the violent crises which lay ahead. However, blissfully unaware of all this Layard returned with Hormuzd to London, arriving in time for the Christmas festivities after eight-and-a-half years' absence. In the Austen home on Montague Square, right next to the British Museum, he celebrated Christmas with roast beef and Yorkshire pudding, and he was of course the sensation, the young hero who regaled everyone with stories about his travels and the incredible discoveries he had made. The Austens accepted him with pride.

On New Year's Eve he wrote to his friend Ross in Mosul, who had been asked to carry on the excavations at Kuyunjik in order to mark the continued English interest in the site; he explained that he had had his very first contact with the people at the British Museum, who saw their famous agent for the first time. The first finds from Nimrud had already arrived and been put on display, but he complained that they were placed in such an awkward spot that they could hardly be seen by the public.

On 8 January the grand Trustees finally had the opportunity to meet the young hero in person, hear his account and see some of the many drawings and plans. The meeting was chaired by the Duke of Cambridge, Queen Victoria's cousin, and a gathering which included some of the leading men in the country listened with open satisfaction and interest to Layard's report. The Duke closed the meeting by expressing the gratitude of the Museum for Layard's

> zealous, successful and in every respect satisfactory services, by which the discoveries commenced under the instructions of Sir Stratford Canning and continued under the direction of the Trustees, had been pursued and accomplished in a manner to fulfil their most sanguine hope.[78]

Layard requested that the Trustees should aid in securing the speedy transportation to London of the last boxes which were still awaiting a ship on the quay in Basrah; he also asked that money should be found for the publication of the many drawings he had brought home. In Paris he had seen the advanced plans for the publication of Botta's report and Flandin's drawings, an extremely grand and costly edition, but he stressed his own wish that the Museum should make his results available to the public in an inexpensive format; he wished as many people as possible to be able to acquire them. A committee was in fact set up to consider this proposal, and Layard left the meeting with his head swimming with excitement and new ideas.

However, the French revolution a month later put an end to all such plans, for the Exchequer was not in the least interested in spending £4,000 (twice what had been allocated to the excavations themselves) on such matters in a time of international crisis. The revolutionary fever spread all over Europe, from Naples to Copenhagen, so the bulls from Nimrud receded into the background.

PART II

THE EXCAVATION OF SENNACHERIB'S PALACE

CHAPTER SEVENTEEN

HOME AGAIN

—— •◆• ——

When Christmas and the New Year had passed, the uncertainties of real daily life announced themselves to our young hero, together with the need for decisions and some hard work. His personal position was far from clear. He was in England to recuperate after the many attacks of malaria that had plagued him during his eight years in the Middle East. But the Foreign Office had appointed him to be a member of a special international commission set up by Russia and England in order to establish once and for all a fair and practical border between Turkey and Persia.[79] The creation of this body was one of the results of the peace which had been imposed on the Turks, and it seemed logical to think of Layard as a member. It was not unproblematic, however, for his exact role in the commission had not been spelled out, whether he was to lead it together with Colonel Fenwick Williams, or whether he was in fact to act as a kind of secretary to the commission. Alison in Constantinople warned him against this assignment, which he felt would be impossible to carry through to a satisfactory conclusion because of the countless ethnic and religious conflicts which characterised life in the region where the commission was supposed to work.

In any event it cannot have been his ardent desire to return to the Middle East right away. There was the natural wish to enjoy the fame he had achieved, appearing as the guest of honour at parties organised by the family or on various estates, and he also wished to have the time to work in peace on the report on his excavations that he was planning to write. The British Museum had of course made it crystal clear in the contract he had received that it did not wish to accept any kind of responsibility for his future, but it seemed reasonable to expect that his brilliant results might lead them to support him in some way. Edward Hawkins, the keeper of the Department of Antiquities, had put forward a plan for the various publication projects to be considered. He thought it would be possible to produce an economically viable edition of drawings and copies of texts; only this task was to be taken in hand by the Museum, and he suggested that it be left to Layard himself to 'draw up a popular work upon his proceedings' (Bohrer 1992: 88–9). This plan had clearly been agreed with Layard who wished to write a personal account which could be widely distributed. Two weeks after the 8 January meeting the Trustees decided to apply to the Admiralty to send a ship to Basrah to fetch

145

the reliefs lying there, and to the Exchequer for £4,000 for the publication of Layard's drawings.

In his first letter to Ross in December 1847 he expressed his conviction that the Trustees would be unwilling to continue the work in Assyria; Ross had otherwise been given £50 to be spent on a very limited activity at Kuyunjik, but Layard asked him to wind this up.[80] But after his meetings with the Trustees he was encouraged to believe that means would be found, not only for the publication of his finds, but also for a much more intensive English effort in Assyria in the wake of the interest which was bound to be generated by his discoveries. He therefore sat down to write a detailed and comprehensive report to the Trustees, in which he sketched a grandiose plan for careful archaeological investigations in Assyria and Babylonia, including a series of expeditions to ruins in a vast area from the Taurus Mountains to the Persian Gulf. It was all to last at least three years, and the expenses for just the first year alone were estimated at £4–5,000. The plan also comprised an extensive programme of publications.

This was his proposal after the first successful meeting with the Trustees and the Duke of Cambridge, and it shows to what an extent he misread the situation. Apart from the *naiveté* in the project as seen with the advantage of historical hindsight, it was also politically unrealistic. There was no will to embark on a scheme of this nature, and the Exchequer declined to offer its support already on 19 February. No doubt there was a general satisfaction with Layard's results, to the extent that they were known at the time, but Assyria was clearly not at the top of the list of priorities in the British Museum. There were plans to build a new wing for the Assyrian reliefs, but so far only a few of them had reached further than Basrah, and the sculptures which had arrived in London were displayed in a quite unsatisfactory way. It seemed incomprehensible to him that the largest naval power in the world could not arrange for the transportation from Basrah to London, and it is unclear whether he sensed the cool lack of commitment behind the polite surface. In fact, the public had only a very limited understanding of his discoveries, even the Trustees who had seen his plans and drawings.

Accordingly, there was a certain room for doubt concerning the importance of his discoveries. Moreover, after an absence of eight years Layard was a rather unclear figure for London's society and for the leaders of the British Museum, all of them men from the highest layers of British society. They expressed their consent to the plan for a personal account of the excavation, and he was welcome to publish the reliefs, but it would all be his own, private affair. No money would be forthcoming from public funds for this purpose. In the end the Museum agreed to take responsibility only for the publication of the cuneiform inscriptions, a matter which alone was felt by the Trustees to be of such an antiquarian interest that the institution could feel obliged to contribute both money and expertise.

This set of priorities was totally in accordance with the normal evaluation of the academic disciplines: philological and literary studies were well-established as a most respectable pursuit, a central part of the academic tradition, and in fact through the classical education one of the cornerstones of the self-definition of the upper classes. A gentleman was characterised among other things by being able to relate to Herodotus and Homer with a carefree obviousness. The effort to decipher the cuneiform script was always referred to under the rubric 'Literary studies', and as such it was surrounded with great prestige. In contrast, Archaeology was a new interest, poor in traditions, and its prestige was tied first of all to the discoveries themselves, great works of art or strange and interesting objects. It was therefore characteristically a popular interest which related to the reliefs and bulls in the halls of the British Museum, and it was a publication like *The Illustrated London News*, rather than the more academically oriented magazines and journals, which kept this interest in the public mind. In England archaeological societies were almost exclusively concerned with local, provincial history. There were no professional archaeologists, and the discipline had as yet developed no theoretical or methodological structure. Accordingly, there was no tradition for writing real excavation reports, for it was the find itself, the objects themselves, rather than the circumstances under which they had been discovered or their archaeologically defined context which were deemed relevant. The Trustees undoubtedly felt that the only essential matter was to have the objects in the Museum where they could be inspected by the public.

Layard's employers at the British Foreign Office were naturally even less under-standing and could hardly appreciate the need for a publication of his results; they did acknowledge, however, that he was not fit to be sent back to Turkey right away. Clearly, he had a strictly limited time for the task he had set for himself.

Disappointments of a different nature awaited him. He had returned to a funda-mentally changed England, and the years since his departure for Ceylon had been marked by both powerful economic and industrial growth and by deep and recur-rent social and economic crises. Shortly before he sat down to write his grand plan to the Trustees, Karl Marx and Friedrich Engels had taken part in the second conference of the revolutionary organisation 'Bund der Kommunisten', which was held in London, and they had been occupied by the task of making the draft for the *Communist Manifesto*, a document which was deeply inspired by the social and economic conditions in England and Ireland.

In 1846 Layard's old acquaintance Benjamin Disraeli had published a novel enti-tled *Sybil. Or the Two Nations*, a book which proved to be shocking reading for the ruling class in the country. This deeply romantic and rather sticky novel was seen by contemporary England as a ruthless revelation of the colossal social inequal-ities which now had resulted in a situation where the Queen of England ruled not one, but two nations: the rich and the poor. It described some of the effects of the industrialisation which had developed with explosive speed. The production of textiles was now entirely dependent on the steam engine, a vast network of rail-ways stretching across the face of the entire country was being created at just this time, and the cities had experienced a violent growth (the number of city-dwellers had now reached 30 per cent of the total population, a figure which was quite unique for the European nations); this entire development had resulted in the creation of an underprivileged working class, whose hopeless and degrading life in the horribly polluted cities was being described by a group of writers and novel-ists. In 1845 Engels had delivered an indignant analysis in *The Condition of the Working Class in England*, and Charles Dickens had provided a searing depiction of British class society in a series of novels, although the darkest and most bitter books such as *Bleak House* and *Hard Times* had not yet appeared.

The 1840s was a decade ravaged by crisis, where structural problems in the industrial sector, caused to some extent by a completely uncontrolled and unregulated growth, created serious difficulties for the workers and prevented them from successfully bettering their conditions and achieving higher pay. The period was particularly destructive – indeed catastrophic is a more adequate term – for Ireland, at this time still a British colony. The traditional diet of the Irish population was the potato, and disease in this crop over a number of years from 1845 onwards resulted in a catastrophic famine. During the years until 1850 it is suggested that about one million persons died of starvation and a similar number emigrated, so that about a quarter of the total population was thus directly affected. Emigration was primarily directed towards the United States, but poor Irish workers also became a common feature of English cities. The year 1848 was another year of failing crops (Harrison 1989; Morgan 1984; Thomson 1978; Hobsbawm 1988, 1989).

It was, moreover, a revolutionary year. The February revolt in Paris was followed by disorders and revolutions in many other European countries, and even in England there seemed to be a real threat that revolutionary fever was about to spread across the broad population. The political development during the preceding decade had been marked by a reform movement, 'Chartism', named after the 'People's Charter' which had been created by leaders of the workers' movement in 1838; Disraeli's novel had described the background for this movement. The Charter was basically a recipe for a kind of democratic reform of the political system in England, including demands for universal voting rights for all men, a secret ballot, new electoral districts which reflected the real distribution of the population after the growth of the cities, a salary for members of Parliament, and similar constitutional reforms. This document became the foundation for a popular movement which could muster enormous numbers of participants in demonstrations across the country. The potato disease in Ireland and the revolutionary fever from the Continent led to one last resurgence of Chartism in April 1848, when a colossal sea of people gathered on Kennington Common in London, just south of the Thames. The newspapers were still full of the bloody news from the Continent and it is not surprising that panic spread in London faced with the prospect of a popular uprising. Ten thousand extra constables – including the staff of the British Museum – were hurriedly sworn in and given weapons. The Museum was fortified with sandbags and armed guards patrolled the grounds, some of them veterans called in from the military hospital in Chelsea, and everybody waited anxiously to see what the sea of people at Kennington Common was going to do. It all ended quite peacefully, however, with yet another petition to Parliament about reforms, which was promptly rejected and forgotten.

It was this crisis-ridden England Layard had returned to, and he came to experience personal disappointments which sprang from his own insecure social position. He enjoyed a certain notoriety as 'Mr Nineveh', but it was only too obvious that his archaeological reputation was too fragile a platform for a real career. He had a degree of success in the buoyant life of the learned societies in

London; on 11 January he was present at a meeting in the Syro-Egyptian Society where a certain Mr Landseer lectured on some of the figures in the Assyrian reliefs, and Layard was given the opportunity to 'communicate to the Society many interesting particulars in connection with his explorations at Nimrud'.[81] On 29 January he gave a lecture to the Institute of British Architects, in which he spoke about Assyrian architecture, especially the use of arches and vaults.[82] He presented a paper to the Royal Asiatic Society on 15 April, displaying his plans and drawings; this meeting concluded with a discussion of matters of chronology and Layard here maintained his view that the Assyrian discoveries had to predate the Greeks by several centuries.[83]

These meetings, the invitations to dinners and luncheons, and the often very flattering reports in the newspapers could not hide the fact that official London remained reluctant to bestow honour and recognition on this young adventurer; he was still largely an unknown entity, an intense and impulsive man who probably frightened a number of people in the better circles. He did have a close and confidential relationship with Hawkins, the new Keeper at the Museum, but many must have felt it tempting to shrug him off – after all, what kind of a person was he? Not a scholar, a truly learned man who knew his Classics; he had never studied at a university, and he even had a somewhat dubious circle of friends.

Layard was deeply disappointed and felt that his work was not valued as it deserved to be, and in a long letter to Rawlinson written at the end of February he let some of these emotions out.

> I believe some of the venerable heads of the National Museum fancy that I have been making a handsome thing in the way of business with those sculptures. I don't leave England much the richer for my Assyrian labors. The fact is between you & I, I am somewhat disgusted at such things ... I think those who ought, for the sake of the principle involved, to have taken the matter up in a proper manner, might have done more for me.[84]

He describes his own situation as marked by a narrow, ugly jealousy, and there can be no doubt that he is referring to Canning. Precisely this word, 'jealousy', reappears time and again in the correspondence with respect to Canning's attitude towards Layard, and this was noticed by both Alison and Rawlinson. Apparently, Canning could not persuade himself to really promote the young man, who, as he felt, was about to claim the honour for the discoveries the ambassador himself had given to the country. And Layard needed the support of Canning who had a secure, entrenched position.

In this strongly class-ridden society, where nepotism and privilege defined most people's careers, Layard had of course expected that his loyal work for the influential ambassador would lead him to fulfil his promises and start the young man on a career. In his letter to Rawlinson he expresses his feeling that the four years spent as the ambassador's assistant at a salary of £250 a year have led to nothing. At the same time he observes how others are being promoted, in spite of what he feels to be a total lack of claims, service or even common abilities. 'One cannot but regret the system', he says. A young man he knows has just been helped to a job which pays £1,000 a year, 'I believe because he has a pretty sister'. Maybe one sees here the first glimmerings of that political fight for a reform of the system of privileges which came to distinguish Layard's parliamentary activities a few years later.

He experienced himself some of the unfairness to which this system led, but the letter to Rawlinson is first of all an expression of his deep disappointment and feeling of having been let down by the man he otherwise had to see as his benefactor. 'One can't begin life once again – if I could I should certainly go to the United States'.

We have to realise, of course, that Layard could not really be compared to a poor worker from Lancaster or Ireland. His salary of £250 a year corresponded more or less to a normal middle-class income; £300 was usually seen as the absolute minimum necessary for the start of a family life, but lower-middle-class earnings were about £150–200, and a school teacher could not reckon with more than *c.* £60 a year; a factory worker earned no more than ten or fifteen shillings a week, some £25–40 a year (Harrison 1989: 39–53, 106–7).

So Layard could maintain a reasonable standard of life, but his worries were primarily due to an apparent lack of future opportunities. Where was he going to end up? He had no real and meaningful career ahead of him. He had the immediate support of many people, of course, but how was he to create a future of promise and hope?

Among the many friends and family members who helped him, one was of particular importance: his cousin Charlotte, who appears to have arranged for his contact with the publisher John Murray, and who threw herself with energy and zest into the task of furthering the prospects of her cousin in any way she could.

She became a central person in his life during the year 1848. As Lady Charlotte Guest (see Figure 17.1) she presided over the social life at the family's country house Canford Manor, near Bournemouth, in southern England, and Layard spent much of his first months in England here, where he began writing his book about Nimrud. Lady Charlotte was a beautiful, lively and intelligent woman with many artistic and intellectual interests. At the age of twenty-one she had been introduced to London society where she had met and briefly become wildly taken with the young Disraeli; they had seen each other one evening at the theatre and she found him 'wild, enthusiastic, and very poetic'. Soon afterwards she met Josiah John Guest who was twenty-eight years older than herself, the founder and part-owner of a large ironworks in the village of Dowlais, near Cardiff, in Wales. They were married after a brief engagement.

Charlotte's marriage was regarded as a terrible *mésalliance* by her family and friends, not so much because of the discrepancy in age, but because Guest was 'in trade', an entrepreneur with genuine dirt on his hands. He represented the new class of bourgeois industrial magnates who were creating the flourishing economic development, men who rose in status and importance during these years. His ironworks at Dowlais employed more than 7,000 men and was often referred to as the greatest industrial concern in the world, but all his money helped little when it came to his social reputation, and it took years for Charlotte and her husband to become accepted by London's society (Bessborough 1950: 4–5).

Figure 17.1   Lady Charlotte Guest, drawn by G.F. Watts.

In her fifteen years of marriage to Sir John, Charlotte gave birth to no less than ten children, five daughters and five sons. This did not prevent her from developing several rather extraordinary interests; she acquired some competence in Greek, Arabic, Persian and Welsh. As a kind of private secretary for her husband she took a lively interest in the affairs of the ironworks, even to the point of writing a manual of iron industry. In Dowlais she helped create several schools for workers' children, and she ran their affairs in detail and with great energy. Her interest in Welsh led her into extensive research, which resulted in an edition of the classic Welsh text *Mabinogion*, a work which appeared in three volumes and which for decades remained the standard edition. She naturally had social contacts with many of the leading intellectuals of the age, and the great poet Tennyson was inspired by her Welsh myths to write some of his finest poetry. Her translation was published in 1846, and it is said to have been the first book Tennyson bought after his marriage.

Layard became 'Uncle Henry' for her children and entered wholeheartedly into the role as playmate and the teller of tall tales and exotic adventures. He spent so much time at Canford Manor with his beautiful cousin that it necessarily led to a good deal of talk. He was thirty-one, she was thirty-six, and her husband was sixty-four, so it cannot surprise that the relationship gave rise to some lifted eyebrows. No doubt the two cousins were very close, and it is hard to avoid the suspicion that they did fall in love with each other. It is not easy to know now, some century- and-a-half later, what happened at Canford Manor, and it should be noted that Layard was always extremely discreet in his affairs with women. It is through letters from Ross in Mosul, not from Layard's own writings, that we gain glimpses of his erotic adventures. At the same time it appears from his correspondence with his aunt that at this time he had a kind of affair with a certain 'Miss A.', a young lady who misunderstood his intentions to such a degree that to his chagrin she felt engaged to him. His relationship to cousin Charlotte must remain obscure, not least because in his enormous correspondence in the British Library one finds not a single letter exchanged between the two. This fact alone tends to rouse one's suspicions, however.

We have portraits of both Charlotte and Henry from this period. In contrast to her placid and calm gaze, his strangely fleshy face expresses the kind of nervous energy which characterised his entire life and which we know made him very attractive to many women, at times leading to some complex and tense romantic experiences. But he also looks ill at ease, like a man suspended in uncertainty and conflicting emotions. The future is viewed with some apprehension by this young man (see Figure 17.2).

Lady Charlotte was engaged in a substantial rebuilding of Canford Manor, and what was more natural than that Layard should offer her some genuine Assyrian reliefs to decorate her home. He wrote to his friend, the merchant Henry Ross in Mosul, who was still continuing the excavations at Kuyunjik and asked him to send a series of reliefs from Nimrud, and the letter even contained a small sketch of the precise spot where Ross was to take a certain slab.[85] This was the basis for the creation of the 'Nineveh Porch' at Canford Manor, where the reliefs sat for nearly a century before they were taken down and moved to the British Museum. In fact, the last slab, which had received so many coats of plaster during the decades since it had been installed that everyone had taken it for a cast, was only realised for what it was a couple of years ago; it was sold at auction in London for the largest sum of money ever paid for an antique monument to a Japanese sect which venerates great works of art from the past.

Figure 17.2 Layard, drawn by G.F. Watts.
Reproduced by courtesy of the National Portrait Gallery, London.

It was in this circle, helped, prodded and supported by a group of friends and his family, that he sat down to write his book. It appears from his letter to Rawlinson from the end of February that Layard was plagued by his illness: 'Here I am dividing my time between fever and my book – shaking one day, writing the next'. Lady Charlotte wrote in her diary that when he showed his drawings to a private party in March, he appeared so ill that he was hardly able to provide any explanation of them (Waterfield 1963: 183). He had to settle in Cheltenham, where there was a spa, and had to drink the water from the local spring in accordance with a doctor's prescription. He was clearly in no condition to leave as early as May, as had been planned by the Foreign Office.

Nevertheless, he worked with great energy. The publisher John Murray visited Canford Manor and was very interested in a collaboration with Layard on a book describing his adventures as well as the results of his excavation. He had long thought about such a project, encouraged, for instance, by Alison in Constantinople who already two years earlier had suggested that he should prepare 'something for the public enlightenment, and – hide neither your talents nor your labors under a bushel, but import unto us a full understanding of every dodge, scheme & idea'.[86] In a letter to his American painter friend Miner Kellogg, Layard wrote in January about his plans for such an account that it should contain a report on his work, a simple sketch of the history of Nineveh, a brief investigation of Assyrian religion and ancient customs, his own adventures, and some mention of the languages and of cuneiform writing, including a report on the decipherment efforts. He expected such a book to have a special impact in America, 'where there are so many who read the Bible' (Waterfield 1963: 182).

Layard and his friends were in no doubt that this book represented his best opportunity to profit personally from all his exertions in Nimrud. From the very beginning it was accordingly clear that he neither could, nor wished, to follow in Botta's footsteps, creating a grand, magnificent opus which aimed to reflect the honour and glory of the French state. A tradition existed in France for such editions, and the best example is the colossal work *Déscription de l'Égypte*, which presented the results of the investigations into Egypt's past and present resulting from Napoleon's failed campaign in 1798. Twenty-four volumes appeared in the format which is called 'elephant folio' where each volume in opened state fills more than a square meter and weighs several kilos. Botta's five volumes about Khorsabad were published in the same format and with just as lavish a use of paper and ink. It was published in 1849–50 under the title *Monument de Ninive*, and it contained a description of Khorsabad, an account of Botta's excavations, a careful analysis of the discoveries accompanied by many glorious plates of Flandin's illustrations and reconstructions, Botta's copies of the cuneiform texts and his study of the cuneiform writing; it was in other words a truly excellent publication which set standards which would be extremely difficult to follow (Botta 1849).

Layard had to find a publisher who had faith in the project and felt that a book on Nineveh would become a commercial success. While the French tomes appeared in a few hundred copies and cost so much that neither Layard nor Rawlinson could afford to buy them – the two men in the world who most needed the books – Layard had to aim at a popular account which could be enjoyed by all who took an interest. Botta had attempted to secure that the volume with inscriptions could be purchased separately so that the scholars could find the money to buy it, for, as he pointed out: 'who could buy a book which will cost about two thousand francs?'[87]

At the same time it was essential for Layard to publish his drawings of sculptures and other finds, simply because such an edition would have the more serious (in the sense of academic, scholarly) character which could place him securely in the learned world. The friends led by Charlotte succeeded in persuading Murray to publish Layard's drawings after a deal had already been struck with respect to what was referred to as his 'journal with illustrations' (Bohrer 1992: 91). This was to become the two-volume work entitled *Nineveh and Its Remains*, published early in 1849 in normal octavo format and containing many, relatively modest engravings. The first volume with drawings appeared about a year later.

Layard's book is closely modelled after the popular travel accounts of the time. The first part contains a lively and entertaining description of his experiences and his main discoveries, and it includes long sections on such exotic topics as the Yezidis and Nestorians and the daily life and customs of the country. The excavations are treated as part of these adventures and the weight is on the excitement involved in discoveries and finds. The second part contains an extensive analysis of the ancient Assyrian world and its history, as revealed by the discoveries. The main emphasis is clearly upon the personal experiences. He seems to have felt a little apologetic about this scheme, for he wrote to Rawlinson:

> I fear I am collecting together about as much rubbish as could well be put into a heap – however, my friends say that it is just what the public want & the public must, therefore, make the most of it. I think I shall give all the genealogies I have and they must serve as a bonnebouche to make the rest go down with those, who expect more than they are likely to get.[88]

He is of course worried because of the expectations of the public with its strong interest in and knowledge of the Bible, since he is aware that it will be impossible to satisfy their desire for secure connections between his discoveries and the stories in the Old Testament. As long as it remained impossible to read a single word in the cuneiform inscriptions such links simply could not be established with certainty. He was probably also worried about the reaction from the learned major in Baghdad, for Rawlinson's own writings were extremely academic in style, full of references to classical and more exotic sources.

Despite the obvious differences in their publication projects, Botta and Layard faced a similar, complex analytic task, which involved creating a meaningful framework for their discoveries. This is a task every archaeologist has had to face, and such work is in many ways of a unique character which puts special demands on the writer's analytical faculties and perhaps especially on his ability to carry out his work with great care and precision. In the field one is engrossed in the innumerable practical decisions which demand to be addressed: where to dig, how, whether to follow this wall or not, how deep to go and so on. The daily routine and the quite enormous effort involved in the registration and immediate description of finds and circumstances overshadows most other concerns, so that it is not until one is back home in the study that it is possible to attempt to analyse what one has found. It is at this moment that one has to establish precisely what was found and what it means. Rarely, if ever, is the archaeologist given a second chance, should he or she become aware that some essential detail was lost or not recorded, for excavation always entails the destruction of the evidence, monuments and buildings, which are being uncovered. The real examination and scrutiny is therefore entirely dependent upon what was observed, registered and noted down while the excavation was going on. Not a few archaeologists have had to re-evaluate in drastic fashion those ideas and theories which governed the practical work in the field, for at home, faced with the plans and notes, one is often able to see quite new connections and combinations.

Neither Layard nor Botta was in possession of a material which would be even moderately satisfactory in the eyes of a modern archaeologist. Much of the work in the palaces had been carried out while they were absent, so they obviously had limited scope for any close evaluation of the evidence. Botta was in a slightly more favourable position than Layard, however, for he could rely on the plans and drawings made by Flandin. The artist had apparently spent most of his time at Khorsabad while Botta moved back and forth between the mound and the consulate in Mosul. Layard, on the other hand, had only his own sketches and notebooks, and the practical work had quite often been left to his trusted Arabic and Nestorian foremen.

There was of course no firm tradition for what an excavation report should contain and attempt to offer, no pre-existing pattern to which they could refer. Botta's work took a long time to write and produce, and it only appeared after Layard's, so there was no possibility to find inspiration here either. Layard was quite aware that his task was not only very large, but exceptionally difficult, and he began his preface with an apology which went far beyond the customary expression of humility:

> It is with considerable diffidence that I venture to submit the following narrative to the reader. The opinions of friends, and a desire on my part to communicate the little information that opportunities may have enabled me to acquire, with regard to a country and city so little known as Assyria and Nineveh, have alone induced me to undertake a work of this nature under the united disadvantages of incapacity, literary inexperience, ill-health, and a very short residence in England.
>
> (Layard 1849, vol. I: vii)

He points out that he has furthermore had the responsibility for the publication of the drawings of his discoveries and the supervision of the edition of the cuneiform texts, so he feels entitled to appeal to 'the kind indulgence of my readers'. It appears that he was particularly nervous with regard to the analytic description of Assyrian culture and history because this might lead to criticism from orthodox religious circles.

CHAPTER EIGHTEEN

DEPTHS OF TIME

——— •◆• ———

We can only truly appreciate Layard's work when we place it against the background of his own intellectual and religious world, the contemporary England to whom he addressed his book. Great changes had taken place since he left the country in 1839. England in the high Victorian age now appears to most people as marked by a smug, self-righteous bourgeois respectability that was characterised by a placid acceptance of narrow moral norms and rules, but just below the tasselled surface lurked strong conflicts. Uncertainty and change was not only characteristic of social and political life; the cultural and religious debates reflected a deep convulsion in the traditional patterns. The intensity involved in these controversies was partly due to the fact that orthodox religious circles had a very solid and determined grip on the power in the country.

Religious matters were among the most widely and hotly debated subjects in the magazines and books of the time, and strong tensions existed between new ideas and the enormously well-established and strongly traditional clergy. One of the clearest examples of this strain concerns the matter of time and chronology. In 1650 Archbishop James Ussher published a thesis establishing a precise chronology for all events mentioned in the Bible, which for the scholars of the time meant the entire history of the world, from Creation to the present day. This learned calculation gained an enormous prestige and became the foundation for the common understanding of all history, and it was still being maintained in the England of the mid-nineteenth century. One of Ussher's most important conclusions was that the world was created in the year 4004 BCE, so that the entire history of the globe had to be contained within a time-frame of some 6,000 years. He could also reveal that Assyria was founded in 1770 BCE, one-hundred-and-fourteen years after the great Flood.

It is not easy to accept that intelligent, well-informed people could be satisfied with this scheme, even in 1848, and there were of course many who privately – and some publicly – questioned this orthodoxy. Most books and articles which came into contact with the problem simply avoided a head-on confrontation and skirted open argumentation. On the other hand, in order to understand the debates of the time one must realise that many of the ideas and much of the understanding which eventually caused the old paradigm to collapse were relatively new. One cannot but be amazed when confronted with intelligent people of the twentieth century who maintain a biblical fundamentalism, claiming that every word in the Book derives directly from God and is unconditionally true; but the situation was different in the nineteenth century and the challenges to the naive literalism were just beginning to gain strength in England around 1850.

These challenges came from different directions, from various scientific disciplines and in fact primarily from Germany and France. England was a deeply conservative country where the Anglican church retained a dominant influence. Only members of the church could study at the universities of Cambridge or Oxford, and only after having signed the famous '39 Articles', a document which set out the central dogmas of the Anglican faith. University College in London was created in 1826 as a 'non-conformist' alternative to these old universities, and until that date Edinburgh University had been the only place where one could study without having to accept the dogmas of the Anglican church.

Even an apparently innocuous and peaceful field of learning such as prehistoric archaeology contained intellectual explosives. Human bones found in France and other places in deep layers together with extremely primitive flint tools and animal remains, which clearly belonged to now extinct races, needed explanation. In some caves bones were discovered sealed under thick layers of sediments, that had clearly been formed by water seeping through the soil and dripping from the cave ceiling – obviously through extremely long periods of time. Such discoveries appeared to indicate that man had existed during much longer spans of time than could be allowed by the traditional scheme of chronology. The orthodox explanation, maintained by a large number of British scholars, consisted of a combination of Bible interpretation and a lack of faith in the results and observations of the excavators. In awkward cases one could speak of types of animals which had been wiped out by the Flood, for some reason not having been saved by the Ark; and of the remains of human victims of that cataclysmic event washed up into these caves (Grayson 1983).

Geology had an even greater impact on many of the intellectuals of the time, and there are of course close connections between these disciplines. Geologists could point to more and more observations which showed that the planet had lived through a long and complex history. Seashells discovered high up in the Andes in Latin America – as seen by Darwin on his trip around the world – showed that this land had been created by enormous forces, that had raised ancient seabeds thousands of meters to become mountain peaks. Such observations could not be explained by or accommodated to Bishop Ussher's scheme, there was simply not enough time. Darwin's friend, the famous geologist Charles Lyell, had provided his famous 'actuality theory' which postulated that the geological processes which can now be observed in the world have to form the basis for our understanding of the history of the Earth, that the same geological processes and forces have been active throughout its existence. Lyell showed that the planet we see has been created by millions of years of geological activity, not on a single day by a divine act of creation, but it did not necessarily mean that human history had to be seen in the same way. It seemed possible to some to accept the literal truth of the biblical account beginning with the creation of Adam and Eve. In fact, Lyell did not accept the discoveries of the prehistorians until 1863, when he finally, and with some hesitation, acknowledged that also mankind had a much longer history than postulated by the Bible. Darwin never succeeded in persuading him that his own theories about biological development were correct (Desmond and Moore 1992).

The essayist and art historian John Ruskin is a good example of the dilemma felt by many of the intellectuals of the time. When he had his 'unconversion' experience in Turin in 1858, which led him to discard his evangelical beliefs, this was in his own words the conclusion to 'courses of thought which had been leading me to such end through many years' (Kemp 1990: 261–2). The traditional foundation inherited from his parents gave way, and he complained of the 'flimsiness' of his own religious faith, blaming the new sciences: 'If only the Geologists would let me alone, I could do very well, but those dreadful hammers! I hear the clink of them at the end of every cadence of the Bible verses' (Abrams 1986: 924). Despite such personal pain felt in England, many on the Continent felt that the British debate was characterised by an exasperating conservatism; in 1834 a French geologist wrote this devastating critique of his British colleagues:

> Certain English theologians ridiculously persist in their mania of wanting to make the results of geology agree with Genesis. England is so pervaded with the spirit of sect that everyone is obliged, by force or by will, to enroll under a religious banner; in such a way that in the midst of the marvels of industry and an advanced civilization, the most elevated minds are too often mired in theological disputes that recall the middle ages, and of which continental Europe offers no more than rare examples.
>
> (Grayson 1983: 112)

The German poet Heinrich Heine visited London in 1830 and noted with his usual acerbic wit that whereas even the most stupid Englishman could find something sensible to say about politics, nothing but stupidities came from even the most intelligent one when the talk was of religious matters (Holthof 1899: 452).

In this climate of entrenched orthodoxy it was Biology and the theory of evolution which in the end had a decisive influence on the intellectual debate, leading in the final instance to a release from the restricting dogmatism. However, it is an indication of the power of conservatism that Darwin, who in no way wished to be equated by his social peers with the rabid radical non-conformists, did not dare publish his ideas until 1859 in the book *The Origin of Species*, and then strongly prompted by the danger that he might be overtaken by a rival scholar with similar ideas (Desmond and Moore 1992). The social pressures were immense, and there was a clear tendency to regard scientific and political radicalism as two sides of the same coin. The new ideas challenged the religious orthodoxy, which in turn was seen as the foundation for the social order as a whole, so it was with a very real danger of losing social respectability and status that anyone defended new and radical scholarly theories.

By laying the foundation for a new understanding of the world, sciences like Geology, Astronomy and Biology created, or at least exacerbated, a moral and intellectual crisis. To many the basic message of the natural sciences appeared to consist in a loss for humanity of its central place in the order of the world, in fact its purpose and dignity. With the collapse of the traditional Christian explanation of the physical world, the clear and simple framework for man's history and the explanation of his role disappeared. All this was replaced with laws of nature and abstractions, the children's tales gave way to statistics and calm treatises of description and analysis. For a poet like Tennyson these new sciences were the 'Terrible Muses' of literature, and the stars in the heavens had become

> Innumerable, pitiless, passionless eyes,
> Cold fires, yet with power to burn and brand
> His nothingness into man.
> (Abrams 1986, 1181; from *Maud*)

Another leading intellectual of the age, Matthew Arnold, expressed his personal situation as marked by genuine despair:

> Wandering between two worlds, one dead,
> The other powerless to be born,
> With nowhere yet to rest my head.
> (Arnold 1890, 321; from *Stanzas from the Grande Chartreuse*)

Even the very foundation for Christianity, the Holy Bible itself, became the subject of scholarly research, and the discipline which developed from such studies, Higher Criticism, was by its very nature a 'dangerous' branch of scholarship whose results and theories were viewed by many with great consternation and indignant rejection. This research tradition of literary criticism, which on the basis of a detailed textual analysis reached conclusions concerning the complex, composite and often quite disconnected and incoherent nature of the biblical text, had first developed in Germany. From here it spread slowly to England where it gained real importance in the 1850s, and it reached the United States in the 1880s.

Literary analysis of this kind had been applied with great success on other, almost holy, texts like the *Odyssey* and the *Iliad*, the most important epics from ancient Greece. The results indicated that these long poems could not have been composed by one man, but that they represented a combination of many independent traditions, which could not even stem from exactly the same time. In other words, at some point a compiler had composed a new text on the basis of several poetic tales, an epic which came to form a new, complex whole; and it was particularly exciting that it was still possible for the modern scholar to disentangle the many threads, take apart the new composite work of art into its original elements.

For classically trained scholars in England it was painful to have to accept the results of such investigations, for Homer had a status as one of the giants of world literature. He might not even have existed. These ideas had first been presented by the German scholar Friedrich August Wolf, as early as 1795, and he had recommended to his pupils that they should study precisely the Old Testament as a clear case where these literary methods could be applied with interesting results (Hoffmann 1988: 39, n. 102).

It was obvious to many in England that this German influence was dangerous, not only to those who wished to maintain the purity of the classical heritage, but also to Christianity. 'Those who believe in a great poem', wrote the classical philologist John Stuart Blackie, 'cannot avoid thinking that the Wolfians are engaged in a perverse attempt, closely analogous to the meagre method of explaining the world without a God, in which certain incomplete intellects have in all ages found an unnatural delight' (Blackie 1866, vol. I: 245, n.; Turner 1981). In other words: if you abolish Homer, the next inevitable step is to abolish God.

Higher Criticism involved a series of drastic conclusions and reinterpretations which were very difficult to accept for the Church, not least with respect to the proper understanding of the first five books in the Old Testament, the 'Pentateuch'. These so-called 'Mosaic' books could not have been written by Moses, it was concluded, because a textual analysis showed them to be composed of several individual texts which could be taken apart from each other. This one point was enough to shake the classic theory of Verbal Inspiration which postulated the sacred nature of the text as directly inspired from God. Instead the Bible had to be regarded as an extremely complex composition which encompassed texts that represented quite separate, often mutually contradictory traditions.

The orthodox doctrine which came under attack in this way was defined in 1873 by an American Professor, Charles Hodge of the Princeton Seminary, in his influential book *Systematic Theology*; this doctrine claimed

> that the Scriptures of the Old and New Testaments are the Word of God, written under the inspiration of the Holy Spirit, and therefore infallible, and of divine authority in all things pertaining to faith and practice, and consequently free from all error, whether of doctrines, fact or precept.
>
> (Brown 1960: 193–4)

This was not all, however, for a number of other conclusions or observations flowed from this, for instance the Mosaic authorship of the Pentateuch and the chronology of some 6,000 years. Undoubtedly, these views were maintained by most ordinary parishioners and many clergymen, but intellectuals like Arnold saw the issue in a different light. For him the results of Higher Criticism were beyond doubt, but the only meaningful question which resulted from this realisation was:

> *What then?* What follows from all this? What change is it, if true, to produce in the relations of mankind to the Christian religion? If the old theory of Scripture Inspiration is to be abandoned, what place is the Bible henceforth to hold among books? What is the new Christianity to be like? How are Governments to deal with national churches founded to maintain a very different conception of Christianity?
>
> (Arnold 1973 [1863]: 49)

The one German work which had the most profound influence on the debate in England was concerned with the New Testament; it was a biography of Jesus written by David Friedrich Strauss and translated to English in 1846 by the famous novelist George Eliot. Strauss explains the Jesus-story as a myth, it is not a factually true historical account, but it contains a fundamental spiritual truth, which can be separated from the outer form of the myth as told in the Gospels. In the church this means in practice that it must be the task of the individual priest to make his congregation grasp this spiritual truth. Since the hypocrisy in this attitude constantly risks being made plain, the final and only truthful solution appears to be a renunciation of his priesthood. Not surprisingly the theme of the parson who has lost his faith is a recurrent one in the novels of the time.

The following year the poet Arthur Henry Clough wrote a poem which, as can be seen from its strange title: 'Epi-strauss-ium', was directly inspired by Strauss' book:

> Matthew and Mark and Luke and holy John
> Evanished all and gone!
> . . .
> However,
> The place of worship the meantime with light
> Is, if less richly, more sincerely bright,
> And in blue skies the Orb is manifest to sight.

The sun takes the place of God, and it is truth and sincerity which triumphs in the end (Abrams 1986: 1355).

All these ideas and scientific developments necessarily led to insecurity and confusion, and these feelings were in England combined in a sometimes bizarre fashion with the fear of being overrun by foreign influences: the French Revolution which led to the temporary breakdown of the Catholic Church and the learned German professors with their Higher Criticism merged in a weird image of the enemy. The British historian Owen Chadwick described the attitude:

> It must not happen here. Then haste to educate the children, haste to build churches for the poor, haste to practice the self-sacrifice which alone could bring Christian doctrine into real life, revere tradition, guard every precious drop of the orthodox stream. The haste was a sign of inner insecurity. . . . Confident of Christian truth, they wanted to be more confident. Grateful for their treasure, they felt nervous enough to want it locked from prying hands. You will end a sceptic unless you believe all the doctrines of the ancient church. You will end a sceptic unless you become a Roman Catholic. You will end a sceptic unless you believe that the Holy Spirit penned every comma of Leviticus – the dire refrains were chanted too often to be preaching tricks.
>
> (Chadwick 1966: 528)

A special term was invented to describe lax doctrines of inspiration and revelation: *neologies*. Liberal theologians were suspected of introducing 'Germanisms' into English thought and, as pointed out by Chadwick, 'Germanism consisted in anything from Straussian myth theories to lax attitudes towards Jonah's whale. It was at least held to include recognition of legend in the Old Testament, and willingness to torture scriptural truth into the ill-fitting jacket of idealist philosophy' (Chadwick 1966: 551). The result was a defensive attitude among those who adhered to a critical point of view, for they found it necessary to distance themselves from German philosophy, while still acknowledging their debt to the German scholars. They maintained with force that

we are by no means likely to be mystified by their philosophical speculations, nor to be carried away by an inclination to force all facts within the
sweep of some preconceived comprehensive theory. If the German biblical
critics have gathered together much evidence, the verdict will have to be
pronounced by the sober English judgment.

(Wilson 1860: 157)

There were other forces involved in this religious crisis, however. Chadwick
points out that a perhaps more fundamental cause was the widespread feeling that
the Yahweh of the Old Testament was a morally unacceptable god. 'Natural science
shattered assumptions about Genesis and about miracles. Criticism questioned
whether all history in the Bible was true. Moral feeling found the love of God
hard to reconcile with hellfire or scapegoat-atonement' (Chadwick 1966: 551).
Layard's friend Charles Dickens was one of those who reacted with 'a moral revul-
sion against the God of Israel or the doctrine of avenging wrath, and attributed
half the misery and hypocrisy of the Christian world to forcing the Old Testament
into unnatural alliance with the New Testament' (Chadwick 1966: 528).

The young Layard had been deeply touched by these questions even before his
departure and had been attracted to the Unitarian church, one of the many
movements which helped spread biblical criticism. He now returned to an England
which appeared even more bogged down in religious controversy, and his
work on the discoveries from Nimrud necessarily had to become influenced by
this. His excavations were potentially extremely important for the understanding
of the Old Testament as an historical source. Nineveh is mentioned some twenty
times in the Bible and there are more than one-hundred-and-thirty references to
Assyria. Direct contemporary evidence from this ancient country might in other
words throw a sharp – perhaps revealing – light on the holy text. References to
events and persons already known from the Bible were to be expected, and for
the one who regarded the Bible as God's word it was complicated to entertain the
notion that this might be commented upon or cast into doubt by humans, especially contemporary eyewitnesses. Some certainly maintained that no such conflict
could possibly arise, and that on the contrary the texts from Assyria were bound
to give us a wider and deeper understanding of events known from the Bible –
without in any way taking away from the veracity of the holy text. As late as 1876
the American divine J.P. Newman expressed his hopes in endearingly naive and
rosy terms:

who can tell how much more remote such records may carry us into the
past? The day may not be far distant when Nimrod's Biography, Noah's
History of the Flood, and Adam's Autobiography, shall become standard
works among the civilized nations of the earth.

(Newman 1876: 360)

Nevertheless, the dread of a clash between two textual traditions dominated the
first comments, although there was another, perhaps deeper fear that the Bible
might turn out to be seen as in some way 'polluted' by a too close contact with
a pagan, Mesopotamian tradition. After all, the Jews were a part of the cultural

continuum of a dimly visible ancient world; characteristically, Strauss in his Jesus biography pointed out that the Bible originated in a 'spiritual condition' which belonged to the ancient Oriental world, and it was logical, and tempting, to search for close ties, also with respect to religious traditions, between the Hebrew Bible and this early world. Strauss could express such convictions at a time when as yet nothing at all was really known about ancient Mesopotamia, a fact which underscores the potential vehemence of the controversy.

In fact, as early as 1847 Layard had been given the first hint of the difficulties which could arise, for Rawlinson could inform him of the views held by members of the Anglican church on his activities at Nimrud:

> They write me from England that Assyrian antiquities were exciting great interest and that the Clergy had got perfectly alarmed at the idea of there being contemporary annals whereby to test the credibility of Jewish history. A brother indeed of mine, a Fellow of Exeter College & joint Editor of the 'Oxford Magazine' protests most vehemently against the further prosecution of the enquiry. Did you ever hear such downright *rot*?[89]

Even before that Layard had heard from his friend Miner Kellogg who was ecstatic with respect to Nimrud's potential importance for the proper understanding of the Bible:

> You can scarcely *dream* of the importance which your solitary labors may have upon the right understanding of the Historical & Prophetical parts of the Holy Word. Every image which you uncover, may add a link in that chain of interpretation which is now being unfolded in regard to the signification of those hitherto inexplicable and I may say, apparently *absurd* passages which abound in the words of the Old Testament.[90]

Faced with these expectations and fears, and fully aware of the violence and bitterness of the religious conflicts of his time, Layard had to step with great care in his interpretation of the significance of his discoveries, not least with respect to the matter of chronology. He was clearly no orthodox Anglican, but he also had no desire to be very provocative or to exhibit his own religious doubts.

The reliefs which had been uncovered before his eyes had of course led him to speculate about their connection with the biblical accounts of Assyria, and he had been particularly struck by some passages in Ezekiel which appeared to describe the Assyrian reliefs in detail. The historical connection was therefore obvious, but he did not feel tempted to go beyond such observations and a kind of vague religiosity. Indeed, he was mainly interested in the Bible in so far as it could throw light on his discoveries – where others placed the emphasis on the opposite direction.

As long as the texts remained unreadable it was impossible to say which historical events and personages were depicted on the reliefs anyway, which meant that no firm linkages between Assyria and the Hebrew Bible could be established. It is clear from his letter to Rawlinson, in which he wrote about throwing titbits to the knowledgeable, that he found it impossible to locate his finds in time and therefore in their relationship to Jewish history. The dating of the palaces and their builders remained an insurmountable barrier.

Even so, his readers and listeners clearly realised that his discoveries could add centuries or millennia to mankind's recorded history. An anonymous commentator noted in 1852 that Geology had shown us the 'Pre-adamite' earth inhabited with some peculiar organised beings; Astronomy had resolved the flickering lights in the night sky into a system of suns and galaxies and shown these to be incomprehensibly ancient. 'All science is thus carrying us into the past', he wrote, and pointed out that in the same way Layard's discoveries made available to modern man a world which had long since perished. Yet, the streets of these ancient cities could be walked again, the mighty palaces could be entered and examined, as could the temples where the ancient kings worshipped and the tombs where they had been laid to rest.

CHAPTER NINETEEN

EUSEBIUS OR MOSES?

——— .•. ———

It is sometimes surprising to see how learned and intelligent people become bogged down in misunderstandings which render them incapable of resolving the problems facing them – to which we, of course, have the solution. Precisely that makes it difficult for us to appreciate fully the obstacles they faced, the universe of understanding in which they lived and which was determined by authoritative pronouncements, prejudices and fixed ideas, all of which necessarily limited their possibilities. By the same token it is fascinating to follow the process which eventually led to the flash of insight, the lucid and self-evident realisation that must have been felt as an enormous relief, a head-shaking happy experience of the simplicity of the problem! Men like Rawlinson, Layard and Botta faced a whole series of questions in 1848, riddles which they felt were capable of solution, but without any true understanding of which of their opinions and views they would have to discard and replace because they would turn out to be fundamentally flawed and unproductive.

A decisive question was of course how to understand the strange writing which was found on monuments, on walls and floor slabs, on bricks and on cylinders and other objects of clay. But before we tackle this matter we must attempt to grasp what Layard could make of his discoveries without any help from the texts, for it was this task that he faced in 1848.

The excavations at Nimrud and Khorsabad had resulted in the uncovering of portions of gigantic palaces, and it quickly became clear to Layard that they were not contemporary but reflected different historical periods. In his interpretation he had found the remains of three palaces on Nimrud: the relatively well-preserved building in the northwestern corner, from where most of his reliefs came; a palace in the centre of the mound which had been almost entirely destroyed; and finally the ruined and never completed palace in the southwestern corner. His study of the style of the reliefs had convinced him that the Northwest palace had to be the oldest Assyrian building so far discovered; then came the Central palace, which on the basis of the texts could be dated to the time of the following king, who was the son of the builder of the Northwest palace. A chronological gap followed between these two buildings and the palaces at Khorsabad and Kuyunjik and the Southwest palace at Nimrud, and he could not establish any connection between these two phases. On the other hand, the texts showed that the king at Khorsabad was the father of the one who built at Kuyunjik, and he in turn was the father of the man who began the Southwest palace at Nimrud. He thus had two separate groups, but it was impossible to say how much time separated them or how they might be connected with each other. And it was of course utterly unclear who these kings had been, which names should be given to them.

How could he make sense of these observations, was it possible to combine the evidence from the buildings with the other types of knowledge which existed about Assyrian history? What kind of information was in fact available, and could one estimate the value of the different traditions in relation to each other? Since one of the historical sources was the Bible, whose words were claimed to represent unqualified truth, the conditions under which scholars could work were neither simple nor easy, but there appeared nevertheless to be certain possibilities for a result which was both reasonably satisfactory to the intellect and which did not clash too violently with religious sensibilities. In fact, it might not be a great problem that there appeared to be two Assyrian dynasties, for both the Bible and the Greek authors spoke of the country in two quite distinct contexts (André-Salvini 1994).

In Genesis Chapter 10 we are told that Noah's sons became the ancestors of the succeeding population groups on earth, and it is said that one of them, Shem, had a son called Ashur. Even though nothing further is said about him it seemed logical to assume that this Ashur became the founder of Assyria, which must be 'Ashur's land'. One generation later we find Nimrod, son of Cush, son of Cham, who in turn was the son of Noah, and this Nimrod is given a surprisingly extensive treatment:

> And Cush begat Nimrod: he began to be a mighty one in the earth. He was a mighty hunter before the Lord: wherefore it is said: Even as Nimrod the mighty hunter before the Lord. And the beginning of his kingdom was Babel, and Erech, and Accad and Chalneh in the land of Shinar. Out of that land went forth Asshur, and builded Nineveh, and the city Rehoboth, and Calah, and Resen between Nineveh and Calah: the same is a great city.

This is the translation in the *King James Bible*, but modern renderings disagree with it in a number of places; the most significant difference for our purposes is that it was Nimrod who went to Assyria where he built the cities mentioned, rather than the king named 'Asshur'. In any event, we are here at the very beginning of mankind's history after the nearly complete destruction under the Flood, so this section deals not only with the origin of Assyria, but with the primeval state created by Nimrod, the first political leader in the world. In the biblical universe this is obviously one of the determining events in history, even though nothing more is said about it in the text. In fact, Assyria is not heard of again until we have come much further down into recorded time, after an interval which according to the computations of Bishop Ussher lasted no less than 1,500 years. It was only with Jonah and the so-called 'historical' books in the Old Testament that Assyria reappeared, and now it was in the role as the enemy of the Jews, the enormous empire ruled from Nineveh. These events should, it was generally agreed, be dated to the first millennium BCE, a few centuries prior to the appearance of the Greeks.

Now we hear of King Pul who forced Menachem, the king of Israel, to pay a tribute of 1,000 talents of silver; of Tiglath-Pileser who subjugated Israel; of his successor Shalmaneser who conquered the capital of the northern state, Samaria, and led the inhabitants away into exile in Assyria; and of Sennacherib who conquered many towns in Judah, among them Lachish, but whose siege of Jerusalem had to be lifted without success. There was an elaborate account of this siege and the miraculous way in which the city was saved:

> Therefore thus saith the Lord concerning the king of Assyria, He shall not come into this city, nor shoot an arrow there, nor come before it with shield, nor cast a bank against it. By the way that he came, by the same shall he return, and shall not come into this city, saith the Lord. For I will defend this city, to save it, for mine own sake, and for my servant David's sake. And it came to pass that night, that the angel of the Lord went out, and smote in the camp of the Assyrians an hundred fourscore and five thousand: and when they arose early in the morning, behold, they were all dead corpses. So Sennacherib king of Assyria departed, and went and returned, and dwelt at Nineveh. And it came to pass, as he was worshipping in the house of Nisroch his god, that Adrammelech and Sharezer his sons smote him with the sword: and they escaped into the land of Armenia. And Esarhaddon his son reigned in his stead.
>
> (2 Kings 20: 32–7)

This account had inspired many subsequent poets and formed a part of the cultural baggage of the Christian world as one of the most pregnant images of the power of the Jewish God. None has written more eloquently on the topic than Lord Byron in the poem 'The Destruction of Sennacherib':

> The Assyrian came down like the wolf on the fold,
> And his cohorts were gleaming in purple and gold;
> And the sheen of their spears was like stars on the sea,
> When the blue wave rolls nightly on deep Galilee.
>
> Like the leaves of the forest when summer is green,
> That host with their banners at sunset were seen.
> Like the leaves of the forest when Autumn hath blown,
> That host on the morrow lay wither'd and strewn.

Esarhaddon, the next king of Assyria, does not figure prominently in the Bible. In fact, it is only with the destruction of Nineveh that we really hear more of Assyria, first of all in the book of Nahum, the jubilant account of the final moments of the great city:

> The chariots shall rage in the streets, they shall jostle one against another in the broad ways: they shall seem like torches, they shall run like the light-nings. He shall recount his worthies: they shall stumble in their walk: they shall make haste to the wall thereof, and the defence shall be prepared. The

gates of the rivers shall be opened, and the palace shall be dissolved. And Huzzab shall be led away captive, she shall be brought up, and her maids shall lead her as with the voice of doves, tabering upon their breasts. But Nineveh is of old like a pool of water: yet they shall flee away. Stand, stand, shall they cry; but none shall look back. Take ye the spoil of silver, take the spoil of gold: for there is none end of the store and glory out of all the pleasant furniture. She is empty, and void, and waste: and the heart melteth, and the knees smite together, and much pain is in all loins, and the faces of them all gather blackness. . . . Woe to the bloody city! it is all full of lies and robbery; the prey departeth not; the noise of a whip, and the noise of the rattling of the wheels, and of the pransing horses, and of the jumping chariots. The horseman lifteth up both the bright sword and the glittering spear: and there is a multitude of slain, and a great number of carcases; and there is none end of their corpses; they stumble upon their corpses. . . . And it shall come to pass, that all they that look upon thee shall flee from thee, and say, Nineveh is laid waste: who will bemoan her? whence shall I seek comforters for thee? . . . Thy shepherds slumber, O king of Assyria: thy nobles shall dwell in the dust: thy people is scattered upon the mountains, and no man gathereth them. There is no healing of thy bruise; thy wound is grievous: all that hear the bruit of thee shall clap the hands over thee: for upon whom hath not thy wickedness passed continually?

(Nahum 2–3)

These passages, in their graphic description of the attack on the city, are closely related to many of the scenes on the Assyrian reliefs discovered by Layard in the palaces, although they depicted the enemies of Assyria in the role as vanquished victims. On the palace walls one saw the thundering ranks of chariots, showers of arrows raining down on the defenders, city walls falling and the prisoners, women and children taken away together with the enormous booty.

It is pure hatred that radiates from the lines in Nahum, not least in the final, mocking shout, and one can understand this hate as the release, the jubilant joy felt by those who finally saw the oppressors, the merciless warriors from Nineveh, suffer the same fate they had inflicted upon others. One can hardly wonder that Assyria and Babylon have come to symbolise violence and decay in the western tradition. Strangely, the Bible completely avoids telling us who were responsible for the conquest and sack of Nineveh, just as Nahum does not mention the name of the last ruler in the city; the curious 'Huzzab' which appears to be the name of the queen should really be understood as a title rather than a name.

This is great and shocking literature – but what was Layard to do with these accounts? Was it really possible that his two periods could correspond to this biblical story, so that the first palace in Nimrud had been built by king Nimrod himself? Or at least, since this appeared rather unlikely, did the building reach back into a past which was nearly as distant? If so, who then were the kings in the later dynasty – could they be the Assyrian kings who were referred to as the enemies and conquerors of the Jews?

All this had to be understood in combination with another set of stories about Assyria, those which appeared in certain Greek works. The two sources did not exactly coincide, and the Greeks had unfortunately been just as vague as the Bible, even though they too had taken a special interest in the final drama of Nineveh's fall.

The Greek literature on these subjects had a special background in political and cultural conditions which had coloured the sources in various ways. With the conquest of Mesopotamia, Persia, India, large parts of Central Asia and Egypt by Alexander the Great at the end of the fourth century BCE the basis was laid for the Hellenisation of the Near East, with Greek traditions penetrating everywhere at the expense of local political, religious and cultural patterns. The Greeks were of course mildly interested in the many cultures they now dominated, but this did not go terribly far, however. Whatever can be said about the intellectual achievements of the ancient Greeks, they appear to have been chiefly interested in themselves, which meant that relatively few works were written about these strange foreign countries (Momigliano 1975). Assyria and Babylonia are no exceptions, despite Alexander's own fascination with Babylon, the city he planned to make the capital of his world empire. He died here in 323 BCE, and a few decades later a Babylonian priest known as Berossus decided to write a work in Greek on the history and culture of his country, apparently in an attempt to educate the new masters a little in the achievements and traditions of the ancient culture they had subjugated. His effort met with a strictly limited success, and his work has not survived; all we have are fragments which stem from quotations and references to his text in various other works which made use of his history (Burstein 1978). Such references, combined with a few other works based on knowledge gained from the Persians, constituted the sum of knowledge available for later generations, and they were accordingly also the basis on which nineteenth-century Europe could attempt to create its understanding.

According to this Greek tradition there were two important figures in the very earliest history of Assyria: King Ninus and his queen, Semiramis. Ninus founded Nineveh around 2200 BCE according to the Greek authors and he conquered vast areas, from Libya to Bactria in central Asia. Semiramis was married to a certain Menon, the head of the royal council and governor of Assyria, but her beauty and wisdom so enchanted Ninus that he married her himself and made her his queen. She survived him and became an even greater conqueror and ruler than her dead husband. She defeated Ethiopia and conducted a successful campaign against India, and the Greeks appear to have been deeply fascinated with this extraordinary woman. According to Diodorus she was 'the most renowned of all women of whom we have any record' (Diodorus 1968: ii, 4). Her son Ninyas was known as a weak and effeminate ruler who did not conquer anything, and he was succeeded by a series of thirty kings of Assyria. The thirtieth was Sardanapal, about whom there is a whole group of stories.

He was described as the archetypal despotic king, inactive, self-indulgent, effeminate and of course morally utterly depraved. A Median chieftain named Arbaces decided at some point that he should be removed and started a revolt supported by and inspired from Babylon, and it all ended with a siege of Nineveh. Just before the fall of the city, in despair at the prospect of having everything fall into his enemy's hands, Sardanapal had an enormous pile of wood set up in his palace yard and covered it with all his gold, silver and precious clothes, placed his eunuchs and women from the harem inside the pile in a special room, set fire to the whole thing and threw himself into the flames. This cruel story held a special fascination for subsequent European writers and in the nineteenth century it became the subject of one of the masterpieces of romantic painting, Delacroix's *Death of Sardanapal*, which created a sensation when it was first shown at the Paris *Salon* in 1828 (see Plate IV).

Sardanapal's death was not the final end of Assyria, however, for he was followed on the throne by Arbaces, and some years later Nineveh was again conquered and sacked, this time by a combined force of Medes and Babylonians. From then on Assyria's power was broken and Babylon became the new political centre.

With some effort it was possible to create a combined picture which drew upon both of these traditions and which enabled historians to reconstruct a history of Assyria. This was precisely what generations of world histories had done. One had names, events, romance and even dates for most of this. The Assyrian kings mentioned in the Bible from the late period could be located in the gap between Arbaces and the final destruction of Nineveh and Assyria, so the tradition postulated a history of Assyria which fell into two distinct episodes or phases: the founders who created Assyria and constituted no more than one or two genera-tions, and the final period with Sardanapal, Arbaces and the 'biblical' kings Pul, Tiglath-pileser, Shalmaneser, Sennacherib and Esarhaddon.

The question was, where was Layard in terms of time? Was it thinkable, as some seemed to believe, that the Northwest palace at Nimrud could have been built by that Nimrod who according to the Old Testament lived no more than a couple of generations after the Flood, the man who was the first real political figure in man's history? In spite of the tempting similarity of the names neither Rawlinson nor Layard were keen to connect the discoveries too closely with the biblical tradi-tion. In their correspondence we find constant references to the Greek authors and their confusing lists of Assyrian kings, but none of them was inclined seriously to entertain the notion of the grandson of Noah as the builder of the palace. Layard was presumably deeply sceptical with regard to the literal truth of the biblical accounts, and Rawlinson appears to have felt much more at home among the Greeks than among the Jews. He was clearly extremely proud of his classical erudition, and then there was his brother in Oxford who was deeply orthodox and heading for a career in the Anglican church. The brother who had declared that the inves-tigation of the Assyrian palaces should be stopped because it came uncomfortably close to the holy text – an attitude Rawlinson had characterised as 'downright rot'. Eusebius and Diodorus appeared safer than Moses and Noah, for the Greek works did not claim to represent infallible truth and could therefore be used with a pleasant flexibility.

It is accordingly no surprise that Rawlinson's guess was that the man respon-sible for the earliest palace at Nimrud was Ninus, rather than Nimrod of the Bible. He quickly became aware that this identification was somewhat problematic, however, for this king had both a father and a grandfather who were provided with the same title which Rawlinson wanted to understand as 'King of Nineveh'. The conclusion was that whereas 'Ninus' was the first king to build a palace with sculptures and inscriptions, he was hardly the founder of the town as such. The Greek king lists, which differed from one author to the next, referred to no less than six kings with the name Ninus, and it could be one of the later ones. As late as January 1848, as Layard was busy writing his book, Rawlinson maintained that it could yet have been the oldest Ninus who built Nimrud, but somewhat confusingly he dated him to not much earlier than 1000 BCE, thus much later than the Greek authors who placed him a millennium or so earlier.

In hindsight one must wonder why Rawlinson did not contemplate the possibility that the late Assyrian kings mentioned in the historical books of the Bible were the ones who appeared in the texts from Khorsabad, Nimrud and Kuyunjik. In fact, he had at one point seriously entertained this idea, as can be seen from one of his first letters to Layard, while he was still at the embassy in Constantinople. In August 1845 Rawlinson presented his speculations with respect to the different variants of the Assyrian cuneiform script: there were two types, he felt, the first represented by various non-Persian rock inscriptions and the texts from the area round Lake Van, whereas the second type was represented by Botta's texts from Khorsabad.

> Mons. Botta will not admit of this distinction and he certainly has bestowed more labor on the investigation than I have – but I nevertheless adhere to my opinion and attribute the 1st class of Assyrian writing to the dynasty which ended with Sardanapalus and the 2nd class to that what comprised Pul, TiglathPilesar, Sennacherib, Esarhaddon and the other kings mentioned in Scripture.[91]

It is of course impossible to determine with certainty what induced him to leave this splendid idea, but it is hard to free oneself from the feeling that he simply wished to avoid finding these kings with all the religious agitation they would drag into the debate. Much rather Sardanapal and Ninus whose names were not loaded with religious significance.

Of course, there were traps into which one could all too easily fall, and it was especially perplexing that the Greek tradition completely ignored precisely those kings who were so well known from the Bible. Instead we are told that the Median Arbaces conquered Nineveh and Assyria, and it was widely assumed that this had happened *before* the biblical kings; in other words, Tiglathpilesar, Sennacherib and so forth were later and Rawlinson speculated that they might have been Median vassals, too unimportant to find mention in the Greek tradition. Rawlinson accordingly did not expect to find them in the material at all but stuck to Sardanapal, the king who died in the great fire with his harem, as the last ruler in the material found by Botta and Layard. For this reason both Rawlinson and Layard were blocked by the notion that there had been two Assyrian dynasties, separated by an unknown number of years, probably centuries, and that Sardanapal's death marked the ending of the tradition. The biblical dynasty was, according to Rawlinson, not at all represented in the finds from Assyria.

But if Rawlinson's date for the founding of Nimrud was correct, this meant that the Assyrians were much later than the Egyptians, a notion which could also lead to controversy. It appeared to be in direct contradiction to the biblical account, which located mankind's earliest history in Mesopotamia, and it was probably not with any great pleasure that Layard faced the idea of leaving the most distant past to the Egyptians. He was no doubt romantically tied to the notion of the dawn of history, viewing his excavations as a decisive part in man's search for origins, for the beginning, the most ancient. The older his discoveries were, the more significant.

This was presumably one of the main reasons why he insisted on the great antiquity of Nimrud, a conviction which somewhat impeded his otherwise excellent good sense. In view of his feeling for stylistic criteria one cannot but wonder why he could not draw the correct conclusion from the connections between Assyrian art and the very early sculptures from Lydia and other places in Asia Minor and Greece. When he presented his results to the French Académie in Paris on his way back from Assyria he had in fact suggested that the earliest Assyrian reliefs came from 'the last six or seven centuries of the Assyrian empire, and thus should belong to the eleventh or twelfth century before Christ, 100 or 200 years before the Trojan War'. Such a dating would, it is said, add to their importance in terms of the history of Art, and they would be 'the very earliest models for Greek Art' (Anon. 1847). It seems that he dropped this idea, although it must be admitted that it is difficult to get a precise notion of the datings which were considered most likely at these early stages of the investigation.

In fact, a debate about precisely these matters had run in the pages of the journal *Athenæum* even before Layard's return to England. In the issue from June 1847 there was a very extensive report on the first of Layard's sculptures which had just arrived at the British Museum, eleven reliefs and two fragments of colossal bulls. All were described with great care, and the writer Joseph Bonomi speculated on their age:

> We may conjecture from the magnificence and vastness of both the structure described by Mr. Layard and that discovered at Khorsabad by M. Botta – as well as from the elaborate detail of the sculptures – that they are of a very remote antiquity; possibly of the earliest period of the first Assyrian empire.

He dismissed the idea that they could belong to the time of the kings mentioned in the Bible, the time of Sennacherib, whose army was defeated before the walls of Jerusalem, 'for the terrible calamities which followed that event, and the total dismemberment of the Assyrian empire which took place so few years after, could not have allowed sufficient time to accomplish such magnificent works as these monuments attest'. Without directly mentioning names and dates, Bonomi therefore placed the Assyrian palaces in the time of 'that primitive civilization of the human race of which we have such abundant proof in the books of the Old Testament'. Although they cannot be valued for their beauty as works of art, they do testify to a 'high state of civilization'.[92]

There was a quick reaction from one of the leading art theorists in England, Richard Westmacott Junior. His father was a professor of sculpture at the Royal

Academy and in that capacity automatically adviser to the British Museum in all matters concerning the purchase and display of sculptures. He was also responsible for the large frieze above the main entrance to the British Museum, which figures on probably millions of snapshots. When the father died in 1856 the son took over his posts, but at this time in 1847 he was still a coming man. Like Bonomi he found the Assyrian reliefs technically advanced but without artistic value – Rawlinson's and Layard's debate in the letters exchanged between Baghdad and Mosul simply marked the beginning of this debate. However, Westmacott had a theoretical schooling which allowed him to draw more sophisticated conclusions with respect to chronology.

One of the dominant notions of the time in art history was the idea of progress in art, a kind of art-historical theory of evolution which went from the most primitive to the most advanced, encapsulated in the phrase the 'Chain of Art'. There was an attempt in various museums in Europe to actualise such ideas through the physical arrangement of the sculptures and other works of art, so that the museum could become 'a school of arts and ... an authentic archive of its history'; done properly, such a display would, it was assumed, have a 'civilising influence on the people' (Jenkins 1992: 57). The older Westmacott had to some extent accepted this scheme as the basis for the organisation of the British Museum, even though he subordinated it to aesthetic or picturesque principles.

In his debate with Bonomi Westmacott Junior based himself on an evolutionary understanding, which of course meant that locating this technically advanced Assyrian sculpture among the very oldest works of art in mankind's history was problematic, not to say intellectually unacceptable. He pointed out that the reliefs were distinguished from what he called primitive art through their attempt to provide an anatomically correct rendering of humans and animals; primitive art is not at all interested in imitating reality and exhibiting beauty. He did not assume that there was a direct line connecting all art in the world in one single chain, but rather that within each cultural tradition one would always have the same sequence of principles shown by the works of art. The well-documented Greek development from primitive to archaic and fully evolved classical art must be used as a model for how art will advance in any society, and in line with this idea he must conclude that the Assyrian reliefs were the end result of a long local development.

He goes even further, however, pointing out that Assyria must have been in contact with other civilisations in the Mediterranean area, and that this allows for a meaningful comparison between the reliefs and other, already known artistic traditions. These should not be seen as further developments of Assyrian art, but they must have been aware of its existence:

> If Art was of the advanced state of the marbles at the extremely remote date that has been claimed for them, how can it be accounted for that the sculpture of Asia Minor was at the comparatively late period of 600 BCE so rude and primitive, – and when there had been probably some hundred of years' communication between these countries? I cannot help fancying that the improvements – or what may with greater accuracy be called indications of advancement – traceable in these marbles correspond in no slight degree

with the character of sculpture of about the date above mentioned among some of the nations referred to; – that is, some of the countries of Asia Minor.[93]

Westmacott is struck by resemblances in the rendering of, for example, knees with 'some of the earlier Greek and Sicilian forms'. He compares the lions and bulls with the earliest coins of Macedonia and Posidonia, pointing also to Xanthos and a relief in Rome. He concludes that his argument from an art-historical point of view leads him to date the sculpture to 650–620 BCE.

This was the first competent evaluation of Assyrian art, and it is remarkable how it was totally rejected. When Layard was confronted with these ideas at a meeting of the Royal Asiatic Society on 15 April 1848, he rejected the notion of 'stages of Art in one nation', at least when combined with the idea of development and advancement; instead he maintained that in Assyria one could see that the oldest reliefs were the most perfect and beautiful. In his book he stuck to this point of view, claiming that Assyrian (as well as for instance Egyptian) arts 'do not appear to have advanced, after the construction of the earliest edifices with which they are acquainted, but rather to have declined' (Layard 1849: II, 157–8). In fact, he develops a kind of art-historical counter-theory, suggesting that art generally can be seen to degenerate or decay during the course of a civilisation's life. During the first childhood of a nation the main emphasis necessarily had to be on a rendering of nature itself, since there was no great historical events to be inspired by; later on there would be a tendency for art to harden and become fixed in precisely defined codes – and he points to Egypt as the typical case where religion is supposed to be responsible for the ossifying conservatism. Instead of imitating nature art now imitates art as it has been transmitted, and this process necessarily leads to a general decline.

No doubt there were other motives than the pure wish to reach an understanding of Assyrian art behind these remarks; Layard himself points to the significance of his observations for a modern context and thus he joins the criticism of the dominating Classicist ideology in his own London: 'It is to be feared, that this prescriptive love of imitation has exercised no less influence on modern art, than it did upon the arts of the ancients' (Layard 1849: II, 283). This is clearly directed against the Westmacotts who were both deeply anchored in the established artistic elite whose goal and aim was the purest Classicism.

Layard's very first evaluation of Assyrian art was offered in an article in the journal *The Malta Times* (in which he had acquired a financial interest) where he described the discoveries made by Botta. Having had an opportunity to see the drawings of the reliefs from Khorsabad he had been struck by their beauty; he was also willing to consider a far more recent date for them at this time:

> We have alluded to the variety of the subjects described by the sculptures, but the spirit and beauty of their execution form the widest field for astonishment and conjecture. To those who have been accustomed to look upon the Greeks as the true perfectors and the only masters of the imitative arts, they will furnish new matter for enquiry and reflection. I shall, I think, be hereafter able to shew that even if they cannot be referred to a period much

antecedent to the earlier stages of Greek art, they have nevertheless no connection with it, and are perfectly original both in design and execution. Whilst probably contemporaneous with many of the most ancient sculptures of Egypt, they are immeasurably superior to the stiff and ill proportioned figures of the monuments of the Pharaohs. They discover a knowledge of the anatomy of the human frame, a remarkable perception of character, and wonderful spirit in the outlines and general execution. In fact the great gulf which separates barbarian from civilised art has been passed.

(Layard 1845: 2)

Westmacott would probably have objected to the last sentence, but he might have found the ideas about the dating reasonably acceptable. In Layard's lecture to the French *Académie* on Christmas Eve 1847 we get a glimpse of his first evaluation of the reliefs he himself had discovered at Nimrud. He had explained already on this occasion that the oldest reliefs were the most perfect, and that accordingly the sculpture from Nimrud surpassed that from Khorsabad with respect to dignity, movement and diversity; they had 'more style and yet more realism, especially in animals and the hunt'. He was particularly impressed with the lions and horses and went so far as to claim that these latter, which represented the purest Arabic breed, could be compared with 'the most noble Greek models, not excepting the horses from the Parthenon'. The editor felt obliged to add a sceptical question mark at this point; even though he had of course never seen any of the reliefs Layard was discussing, it must have seemed to him almost sacrilegious to place them on the same level as the Elgin Marbles (Anon. 1847).

CHAPTER TWENTY

THE MYSTERIES OF CUNEIFORM

——— •◆• ———

While Layard was busy writing his book on Nimrud the decipherment of the Assyrian-Babylonian cuneiform system of writing was entering a decisive phase, and he must have been terribly frustrated by not being able to include in his book any readings of just a few of the many texts he had found. The solution seemed so close, and Rawlinson's letters promised much. After a new visit to the Bisutun rock in September 1847 he claimed that he could now prove that his previously established alphabet was nearly one-hundred per cent correct. Not only that, he was now in a position to add a large number of new values, 'and I have moreover a vocabulary of between two and three hundred words in the determinate rendering'.[94]

This clearly had to mean that Rawlinson was on the brink of the final breakthrough which would allow him to produce translations of the texts and definitive readings of the royal names. If Rawlinson could give him translations of just a few of the important texts, his own account would take on a completely different and conclusive character since he would be able to tell his readers who had actually built and lived in these palaces. In fact, it would become possible to begin to write a history of Assyria. It was therefore a colossal disappointment to be told by Rawlinson that he did not expect to be able to provide such translations in time for the publication of Layard's book.

The immediate excuse was that he lacked texts, he who had access to more texts than anyone else in the world; he complained that he had so few texts from Nimrud, and wrote that 'before I could work out the matter I must see *all* your copies, particularly the pavement slabs, & those I fear it will be impossible to obtain until you publish'.[95]

Furthermore, he was constantly hindered in his work on cuneiform by being bogged down in administrative matters in the Residency, yet he used every spare moment. In the following letter he expressed confidence that he would soon be in a position to read all the inscriptions, and he had – 'now not the slightest doubt that I will give the general meaning of all the Inscriptions both of Khorsabad and Nimrud, in the course of another year'. Further study has made him a little worried, however, for it seems that there were more substantial differences between the Babylonian and the Assyrian texts than he at first assumed – 'but I can now confidently say "land in sight",' he claims.[96]

The problem for Layard was that Rawlinson confined himself to such non-specific generalities and seemed quite unwilling to even hint at what he was reading in the texts. Their correspondence had now been going on for two years in this fashion, and it is understandable that Layard's patience was getting strained. Rawlinson had claimed before that he was 'pretty certain' of his readings of the texts, and now when he appeared to be on the brink of the final breakthrough there was no end to his caution. It must have been tempting for Layard to conclude that Rawlinson was withholding his real results in order to be in a position to publish them himself in triumph and gain the maximum of honour and prestige. Indeed, it is understandable if the major in Baghdad found it somewhat unsatisfactory to supply Layard with the fruits of his toil in order that they might be published in the book on Nimrud.

It is also possible that Rawlinson was not so close to the breakthrough as he liked to claim; in fact, he may even to some extent have used a deliberate strategy of creating a smoke screen which could confuse and deter his rivals. It is clear from the correspondence that he felt threatened not only by Layard, who was actually working hard on the texts, but especially by a certain Dr Hincks who is mentioned again and again in his letters.

This man, who Rawlinson clearly regarded as his most dangerous rival, even though he also claimed that he was 'losing himself in a quagmire', had written a series of learned articles on Egyptian hieroglyphs as well as cuneiform studies. He was an elderly country parson in Killyleagh in County Down, a man who had no special training in 'Oriental studies' apart from his knowledge of Hebrew. He had first taken an interest in Egyptian and his work on cuneiform was apparently motivated by a desire to see if the same principles which were valid for hieroglyphic writing could apply to cuneiform (Davidson 1933; Cathcart and Donlon 1983; Cathcart 1994; Daniels 1994).

These two men were to complete the initial phase of the decipherment, but not in a spirit of collaboration and friendship; rather, their joint achievement was marked by rivalry and competition. The complex and often strained relationship which developed between them had its roots in their divergent perceptions of what happened during the final phase of the decipherment of the Old Persian script, the one found in the first column at Bisutun. It will be remembered that with Rawlinson's report from 1838 the decipherment was greatly advanced, but some fundamental problems were still unexplained, the most serious one of which concerned the very basis for a correct decipherment, the nature of the script.

It was assumed by all, including Rawlinson, that the Old Persian script was simply an alphabet, but this led to sometimes very strange readings. Many words appeared to give consonant clusters to such a degree that they seemed to be unpronounceable, and the interpretation of the script furthermore led to a situation where there were two or three signs available for several consonants. The distinctions which appeared to be introduced by these many different signs were hard to reconcile with any 'normal' phonetic linguistic structure – how many different 'm'-sounds could a language have, to take an example? When Rawlinson in early 1846 sent off his monumental manuscript which contained his rendering of the Bisutun inscription these problems were still unresolved.

It was in this situation that Hincks first showed his exceptional gifts as a decipherer in his work on cuneiform. In June 1846 he gave a lecture in Dublin in which he solved the puzzle of the many consonants in the Old Persian script.

In effect, his discovery was that the script was not simply and purely alphabetic in nature, but that it was a mixture of alphabetic and syllabic principles: there was a sign which had the value /m/ or /ma/, but there were others which were to be read /mi/ and /mu/. The consonant itself was the same in all these signs, which meant that there was no need for the supposition that the Old Persian language had been based on an incredibly complex phonological system.

These ideas were presented in short form in a letter published in the London magazine *The Literary Gazette* in July 1846,[97] and Hincks announced his discovery in a letter to Edwin Norris, the secretary of the Royal Asiatic Society in London, where he sent a more extensive report in August. At about the same time Rawlinson sent off from Baghdad a revised version of his own transliterations in which he based himself on precisely the same principles which had been announced by Hincks. He claimed to have reached this understanding independently, and this has been accepted by all who have published accounts of the decipherment. It is certainly possible, in my view even likely, but it should be pointed out that others at the time were convinced that Rawlinson had taken over his idea from Hincks. Certainly, one of his friends in London, Mr Renouard, who was also a correspondent of Rawlinson's, was in no doubt; he wrote to Hincks: 'it is evident that Major R. caught the idea of simplifying his alphabet ... from you. Your hint in L.G. 25 July would have escaped most readers, but ... he availed himself of a clue which scarcely anyone else could have followed ... ' (Davidson 1933: 138–9; Borger 1975–8b: 18).

It is of course entirely acceptable to build on the ideas formulated by others, but Rawlinson was accused of dishonesty in claiming that he had in fact had the idea independently of Hincks. This accusation, it should be said, was followed over the years by several others of the same nature.

It is not clear whether Hincks was personally convinced of Rawlinson's guilt, and he did not publicly accuse him at the time; instead, he stated in a review of the major's publication that his letter with the '*rectification* of his Alphabet' was sent 'between two and three months after the reading of the paper alluded to, but before any account of it would have reached him'. Hincks's review is indeed very complimentary, and concludes that whereas Rawlinson's contribution to *deciphering* the Old Persian texts was 'very small', 'that of *interpreting* them is for the most part his' (Hincks 1847).

Whether or not these suspicions were justified, the fact was that the Old Persian texts could now be read, and one might have thought that this would make it a relatively simple task to confront the Babylonian-Assyrian script. It should be possible first of all to find names of persons, lands or cities which could provide secure readings of signs in the Babylonian column, the method which had been used originally by Grotefend to make the initial attack on the Old Persian column. However, as already mentioned, Rawlinson was hindered here by the fact that precisely personal names often were given by way of complex and learned ideographic writings and were thus not written phonetically at all. When attacking the

Assyrian texts he was furthermore blocked by his curious insistence to look for the names of kings and dynasties in the classical writers, avoiding the names from the Bible.

One must remember, however, that all of the fundamental questions, which had to be cleared up before a proper decipherment could be reached, remained unanswered. It was not known which *language* these texts represented, and there was no certainty even with respect to the question of which linguistic family it might belong to. It was not improbable that it was of the Semitic type, and we can see from the letters that Rawlinson initially searched through general books on Semitic in order to find clues, even though he and most others working on the problem considered this to be just one of several equally probable possibilities. At one point Norris, the secretary of the Royal Asiatic Society, was 'deep in Babylonian and swears it is fine Biblical Hebrew', according to Rawlinson, but this solution was dismissed by the major in Baghdad,[98] just as he ridiculed Isidor Löwenstern's attempt to read the Khorsabad texts as Esarhaddon's annals written in good Semitic (Löwenstern 1845).[99] Hincks, in the letter already mentioned, had also claimed quite unequivocally that the Babylonian inscriptions and the third column at Bisutun were written in a Semitic language:

> This language is clearly of the class which has been called semitic. I have noticed the feminine termination, different ways of forming the plural, a variety of pronominal affixes, and three preformations of verbs. It, however, appears to differ from the semitic languages hitherto known much more than they do from one another, and to have relations with the Median, and through it with the Indo-Germanic languages.[100]

In June 1846, at about the same time Hincks wrote his letter to the *Literary Gazette*, Rawlinson had written to Layard that 'The language as I have often told you has to be reconstructed "ab origine". It is in my opinion utterly unrelated – correspondents do not exist in any available speech, Semitic, Arian or Scythic – so how we are ever to interpret it with any thing like certainty I am at a loss to divine'.[101]

The character of the script itself was also debated; even though it made use of more than a hundred signs – in fact, a good deal more when the new material from Khorsabad and Nimrud was taken into account – it was far from clear how this *system of writing* was to be understood. It had been suggested that it was purely ideographic in nature, and it seemed reasonably clear that it could not be a simple alphabet – even though the same Löwenstern had offered an interpretation based on the idea that the script, like other Semitic systems of writing, was purely consonantal (Löwenstern 1847). Hincks claimed that 'the characters are partly alphabetical and partly syllabical; and a few represent more than one syllable'. Yet, he also says that 'no vowel which ought to be sounded was omitted'.[102]

These ideas were apparently very close to the ones entertained by Rawlinson, who insisted that Babylonian cuneiform was at least partially alphabetic in nature. Consequently, where he had felt that the Persian phonetic system was complex, the Babylonian one was as he saw it on a completely different level of complexity.

At this time, from late 1846 to mid-1847, a sense of urgency is apparent in Rawlinson's letters, for this was when he was becoming aware of the work of the

Irish parson. The first reference to Hincks in Rawlinson's letters is from 14 October 1846, where he wrote:

> Cuneiforms are at present in great favor at home & a certain Dr Hinkes(sic), an Irishman, has got much further than I am pretend (sic) to have reached. ... Dr Hinkes is certainly on the right track & a long way before me.[103]

He had not seen any of the articles written by Hincks – whose name he is not even able to spell correctly – and his information is clearly derived from Edwin Norris.

As already mentioned, at this time Hincks was (probably erroneously) beginning to suspect that his own good ideas were somehow filtering through a number of personal contacts to Rawlinson in Baghdad, and he attempted unsuccessfully to stop this flow. His friend Renouard in February 1847 sent Rawlinson a letter which told him in detail what Hincks had achieved. Rawlinson immediately felt a great sense of relief, as he wrote to Layard:

> I was afraid you know of Dr Hinkes but having received a private tracing of his alphabet by this post in which he professes to give the value of 76 Babylonian characters I am much relieved for he has not above a dozen correct identifications and these were self evident to any one looking at the Persepolitan translations.[104]

He wrote in a similar vein to Renouard, who immediately (18 May 1847) communicated to Hincks Rawlinson's precise words:

> if he (i.e Hincks) had the more extended data which I am fortunately able to command, he would discover evidence of fluctuating phonetic powers ... that would, I think, fairly stagger him. ... The day however is still, I think, far distant in which we shall be able to read and understand independent Babylonian and Assyrian inscriptions, for we want the grand desideratum of language.
>
> (Davidson 1933: 141)

Rawlinson's sigh of relief at discovering that his rival was not so dangerous after all was somewhat premature, however. He was convinced that 'fully one half of the powers he has assigned, I can prove to be wrong from the orthography of the names at Behistun; and many of the others which he has taken from the Persepolitan names, he has so tied up by his introduction of a system and a precision unknown to the alphabet, that they are hardly recognizable'. Slightly later he wrote to Layard about Hincks (finally able to spell his name correctly), describing him as 'the best Egyptian scholar living, but he is I suspect going a little too fast in Cuneiforms, if I may judge by his Median & Babylonian alphabets'.[105] After this Rawlinson refers to Hincks in a tone of condescension, bordering on contempt, but that was hardly justified.

The list of seventy-six signs had been presented by Hincks to the Irish Academy in November and December 1846. Twenty-three of the values were entirely correct, and a number of others were 'nearly' correct, in the sense that Hincks had the right consonant in a syllable but was wrong about the vowel. He gave the value RA for a sign which should be read RI, NU for NI and so forth. Counting these almost correct readings one reaches the conclusion that he had hit upon (or nearly) the correct reading for no less than forty-two of his signs in the list. It also appears that he now regarded the script as syllabic and had dropped the idea of an alphabetic element. On that background we must ask how secure was the basis for Rawlinson's readings, given that he could be so far wrong in his evaluation of Hincks' results.

Part of the reason for his dismissal was probably that he was irritated. One should remember that Rawlinson was a perfectionist, who hated the idea of publishing anything before he was absolutely certain that he had it right; and this Dr Hincks did not suffer from the same kind of pusillanimity but freely offered his newest ideas – fully prepared to withdraw them shortly afterwards to replace them with something more convincing. Sitting with his notebooks which he filled with minute observations and elaborate theories, Rawlinson was deeply frustrated by Hincks' unhesitating frankness.

> As for old Hincks, I am tired of him – he gives a new alphabet every month and ultimately perhaps by way of guessing may arrive at something – as all his theories however are propounded in the same tone of dogmatic confidence, people will be puzzled at last to know which to believe.[106]

Rawlinson's notebooks, which he used during these years in Baghdad in his attempt to penetrate the mysteries of the cuneiform writing, are now in the British Library (see Figure 20.1). They show first of all his tireless toil through several years during which he was searching for the key. No one can claim that he did not work hard or with the utmost determination when he confronted this intractable script which continued to confuse and evade him. Night after night he sat in the Residency in Baghdad, making notes, drawing up lists of signs, copying inscriptions and trying out different readings. Unfortunately we cannot follow the process in a chronological order, for he made use of a series of notebooks at the same time, which means that each one contains results from several different years.

In October 1847 Rawlinson finally felt able to express real confidence that he would soon be in a position to read all the inscriptions – 'I can now confidently say "land in sight" – and despite all Hinck's(sic) pretended discoveries I can affirm that he is losing himself in a quagmire'[107] – and this was because he had at last got hold of a reliable version of the Babylonian column at Bisutun. As mentioned above, he had returned to the cliff in September 1847 and in a letter to Layard he explained his success:

> Having first satisfied myself that a considerable portion of the tablet was legible, I got hoisted up on the opposite precipice and found a little nook in the scarplet to work with my big telescope. The letters are only distinguishable for a couple of hours during the day that is from ten to twelve and even then a novice would I suspect make a sad hack of the writing. However the results have exceeded my most sanguine expectations – for I have actually recovered almost one half of the Inscription. I have taken two independent

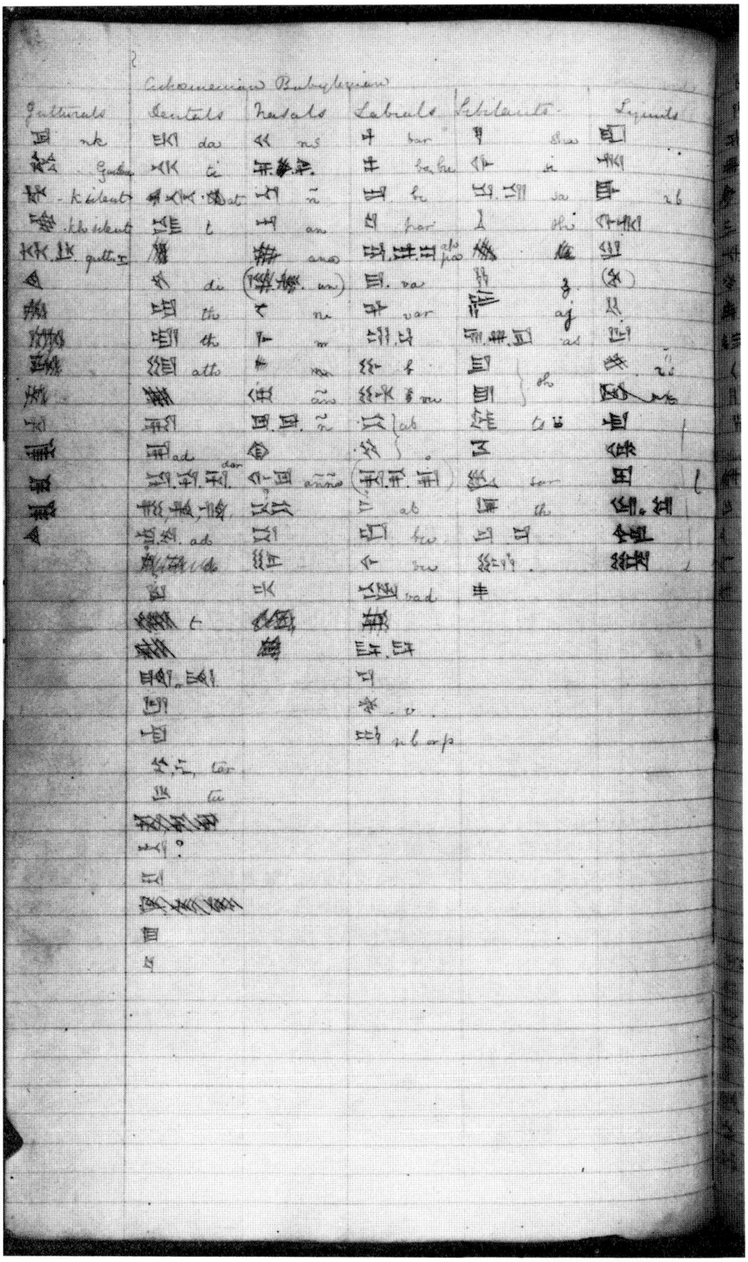

Figure 20.1 A page from one of Rawlinson's notebooks (BL 47620) with his attempt to create a list of sign-values. Reproduced by courtesy of the Trustees of the British Library.

copies to guard against the chance of error and for the sake of reference have also bribed two Kurds (the only two individuals in the country who could or would venture on the scarp) to take a paper impression. [108]

Returning to his desk armed with this new text he concluded that the results were extremely gratifying. The new version in Babylonian made it possible to make many new comparisons with the Old Persian version, and he quickly reached the conviction that his previously established alphabet was nearly one-hundred per cent correct. Not only that, he was now in a position to add a large number of new values, 'and I have moreover a vocabulary of between two and three hundred words in the determinate rendering'.

The Babylonian column of the Bisutun inscription was therefore of immense help to Rawlinson in his further work, and without it he probably would not have been able to reach an understanding of, for instance, the language of the texts. In one of the notebooks he provides an extensive table of the sounds of the language, a list that follows after the copy and some analysis of the Babylonian version of the Bisutun inscription; it is presumably therefore to be dated to the first part of 1848. Characteristically he is – like Hincks – much more confident with the consonants than the vowels associated with them. On the other hand, he still seems to regard the system as primarily alphabetic in character; one notes, for instance, that he provides a list of no less than six different signs which are all given the reading /l/; the correct readings for the six signs in question were **LA, UL, LU, LAM, IL**, and **LI** – which indicates that he was right in thinking that they all had the element /l/ in them. At the same time he does give syllabic values for other signs, so he appears to have been somewhat uncertain on this point, and one understands readily how this imperfect understanding fills him with despair and makes him complain that the system is so loose that anything seems possible!

It is not entirely clear whether he had at this time cracked the problem of language, although it seems probable that he was becoming more convinced that it was of a Semitic type. However, in January 1848, several months after he had begun working on the Bisutun key, he wrote:

> Mr Norris also tells me in a letter I have lately received from him that Burnouf has declared he can read and *understand* the Khorsabad Inscriptions, and that he is now preparing a paper on the subject. I really however cannot believe this, for where the deuce did he get his language from. A few common Semitic affinities are obvious – but I can find nothing in any of the languages of that family, which can be used as a key. . . . In fact it seems to me that if the Assyrian language were as well known as the Syrian or Hebrew, there would still be great doubt in interpreting the Inscriptions – and I thus look with great distrust on these announcements of a sudden and complete solution.[109]

His real worry was Hincks, however, who might reach decisive results if he was placed in possession of a really extensive textual material, he feared; the most extraordinary aspect of Hincks' previous successes was perhaps the fact that he had worked on the basis of an extremely limited number of texts. To avoid more danger from that side Rawlinson implored Layard not to supply 'Dr Hincks with materials before I can also have access to them – otherwise I fear he might give me the gobye'.[110]

Directly contrary to Rawlinson's wish Layard took the initiative to contact Hincks so that the Irish country parson gained access to at least some of the texts brought back from Nimrud. When we consider the total lack of concrete information which was characteristic of the letters he received from Baghdad it is not difficult to understand that he decided to try to get more facts from another source. He accordingly started a correspondence with Hincks.

At that same time Botta was working hard on cuneiform in Paris, although he attacked the matter from a slightly different angle. He began with the observation that several different signs could occur in apparently free variation in the writing of the same word; in one text one might find both

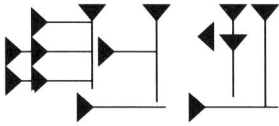

and

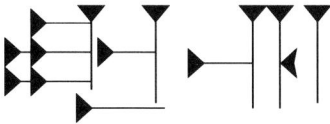

Clearly, the only difference is the last sign. At the same time he could show that both these writings could be replaced by a single sign:

which again could be replaced by a much more complex sign:

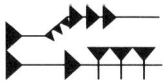

All these writings had to represent the same word.

Botta drew up a list of the variants he found in his own material, but he refrained from offering actual readings of any signs. Instead he concentrated on the question of the reason for this strange practice, which was clearly an important feature of the writing system since he could point to no less than ninety-eight examples in his texts.

It seemed obvious, in an example like the one just provided, that some of the writings, using just a single sign to represent a whole word, should be understood as ideographic in nature. They therefore rendered the meaning of the sign without giving a clue to its phonetic reading. Botta knew that the writings presented above all referred to a word which meant 'king', for that could be deduced from the Persian writings. The two first writings which used two signs presumably gave a spelled-out version of the word, and the variation at the end of the word might be caused by the word appearing in different types of sentences where in one case it was a nominative form, in the other a genitive. Other similar instances could be explained as different verbal forms, and if the language hiding behind the script was Semitic in type, one might begin to explain variations in the first sign in the writing of verbs by way of the paradigms of forms known from Arabic or Hebrew: 'he wrote' would in Hebrew be *jiktob*, whereas 'we wrote' would be *niktob*.

Botta accepted all such explanatory models as probably relevant, one did not exclude the other, but he felt certain nevertheless that in the majority of cases he was faced with real identity; the signs in other words stood for the same word in the same form. He did not suggest that they were truly homophonous, rendering *precisely* the same sound, but that the system was based on a distinction between *nearly* identical sounds. He also considered the possibility that the writing was really a mixture of an alphabetic and a syllabic system; a sign could therefore simply represent /b/, while others stood for /ba/, /bi/, /bu/ and so on.

Botta's list was potentially very useful because it could help to identify the value of signs which appeared as variants of signs whose value had already been established. If it could be said with a high degree of probability that a certain sign should be read **BA**, and if this sign was found to occur as a variant of other signs, it was logical to conclude that these other signs should also be read **BA** or something very similar. Layard had already made use of this method at Nimrud and had discussed it with Botta in Paris, where they had exchanged variants. Rawlinson had distanced himself from this method in his article on the Bisutun inscription, but privately he was in fact working along the same or similar lines, as can be seen for instance from his six signs which he all gave the reading /l/. The observations which had now been collected and systematised by Botta probably led Rawlinson into further fits of confusion and desperation, as he had expressed it earlier:

> The more indeed I penetrate into the phonetic structure of this ramified Babylonian alphabet, the more am I staggered at its extraordinary laxity, copiousness & uncertainty. System there was evidently none – any word of two syllables may be written some degree different ways and I really doubt if our organs of speech will admit of ever representing many of the compound and fluctuating articulations.[111]

These variant writings continued to confuse as can be seen from the fact that as late as 1850 Rawlinson surprisingly claimed that they in fact represented different sounds, suggesting that they should be seen as an indication of a wish to provide 'so minute and elaborate' a phonetic rendering of names, especially foreign ones, that the 'artist was perpetually liable to confound the characters' (Rawlinson 1850a: 30). In 1846 when he wrote the letter just quoted he certainly did value Botta's work very highly, for he complains bitterly that it has not yet appeared in print:

'I wish to goodness Botta would publish his table of variants. It would save me an infinity of labor – for otherwise I should have to go over exactly the same ground as himself and I do not know anything more tedious than the mechanical proofs of interlineation'. However, this type of snivelling is of course quite contrary to the major's whole attitude to work, so he immediately corrects himself and says: 'to obtain results in any path labor must be undergone, and the more severe the more one enjoys the results – so we had better make up our minds to put our shoulders squarely to the wheel'.

The problem with Botta's list was that it remained impossible to say in which instances the variants represented the same or nearly the same sound, and where one was faced with other types of variation, based for instance on grammatical or even semantic differences. His list would be of great value once the wall of misunderstanding and ignorance had been pierced, but it did not provide an adequate tool for that task itself.

So what about the country parson in Ireland? Layard wrote his first letter to Hincks in January 1848, a few weeks after his return. It appears that he was working hard on what he called 'an analysis of the standard inscription of the earliest palace of Nimroud', but he complained of a lack of time which had prevented him from making more than scattered observations while he copied the texts and compared the different versions. However, he ended with a promise that he was at Hincks' disposal if he should wish to have further information (Davidson 1933: 145).

This was an offer too good to pass over, of course, and the letter must have been a marvellous surprise for Hincks; he answered the very same day he received it with a long epistle. His attitude is clear from the very beginning:

> I was this morning favoured with your letter of the 20th. I wish, as you have received my papers, to make a few remarks in explanation of them. The account of the Babylonian language given in the first paper of the second Oct(?) is in many respects incorrect; that in the following paper, though materially improved, is still very inferior to what I should *now* give. I have corrected many values; & I think that I now know beyond the risk of error 100 distinct characters – not to speak of trifling variations ... You will see if you read the Van paper, that I give the *meanings* of several Assyrian & Babylonian words & refer to passages in the Great Inscription of the E(ast) I(ndia) C(ompany) & those of Botta, as if the meaning was *fully ascertained*. I consider it to be so. The interpretation of many words & even of entire sentences I think I have placed beyond question.

Here is a man who is totally unafraid of being right! Not only is he willing to present his ideas and happy to revise them when presented with good enough arguments, but he is capable of defending them when he feels on safe ground. In this one letter there was more concrete information, or at least more interpretations, than Layard could expect to receive in ten letters from Rawlinson.

One of the most interesting points was that he has found the reading of one of the elements which form part of several of the difficult personal names, no less than the name of the main Assyrian god, Assur. He could therefore say – with absolute conviction! – that the name of the king who built the Northwest palace at Nimrud began with the element 'Assur'; Rawlinson's suggestion that it should be read Ninus could accordingly be entirely discarded.

He also dealt with the question of dating and gave Layard one more nudge in the right direction – one that he unfortunately chose to reject. Hincks thought that he had found the name of the capital of the Jewish northern state, Samaria, in texts from Nimrud. His reading was wrong, but one cannot complain about his conclusion: 'This limits the age of the inscription between about 900 & 700 BCE'.[112]

Hincks was not really in a position to help Layard with the essential matters yet, he could not read the texts any more than Rawlinson, and it is unclear whether Layard appreciated the very real advances that Hincks had in fact made.

In his book he chose the safe solution: he accepted practically all of Rawlinson's theories and referred to the learned major repeatedly whenever he felt the need to draw in the leading authorities in the study of the Assyrian language, writing and history. Accordingly, the great builder at Nimrud was Ninus. Hincks was banished to the footnotes.

CHAPTER TWENTY-ONE

BACK TO
CONSTANTINOPLE

——— •◆• ———

Layard did not spend much time in London during 1848. Most of the year he lived with his mother in Cheltenham on the River Severn. There may have been a brief pause in his visits to cousin Charlotte, but we have no reason to believe that the mutual attraction had become too much of an obstacle, so that either he himself found it most convenient to stay away, or that he had perhaps discreetly been asked to limit his visits. In fact, in August and September he accompanied Charlotte and her husband on a tour of Scotland, where they visited manors to take part in the delights of the hunting season. Lady Charlotte was engrossed in Carlyle's book on the Middle Ages which she read with deep fascination. At the end of October the large farm show took place at Canford, and Layard again visited. He lectured in the Town Hall of neighbouring Poole, where he kept his audience in a spell with his account of the excavations at Nimrud. He seems now to have spent most of his time together with the Guests (Bessborough 1950: 223).

For a man like Layard, who had no formal classical schooling, there was a lot to catch up with before he could write a truly learned book, and the final result shows how he must have been studying with great perseverance and energy. No one can rightfully complain of a lack of references to classical authors or an insufficient level of erudition. Naturally, the discussions which draw upon this kind of material have a somewhat quaint and old-fashioned tone today, but as long as the Assyrian inscriptions themselves continued to be stubbornly silent he was forced to labour with the confusing references to Ninus and Sardanapal. In the middle of this he suddenly received a summons to Oxford where he was given an honorary degree. This was both unexpected and extremely welcome and Layard, who had never had the chance to study at a university, was beside himself with pride. He wrote a letter to Samuel Birch, the assistant in the department of antiquities at the British Museum, telling him that he had been called 'rather unexpectedly & in a very flattering manner to receive the distinguished honor of a honorary degree of DCL'. He felt that this meant that he had received all the honours which could possibly be his due, and it was now simply a matter of getting his results before the public so that it could 'take an interest in it & understand its importance'.[113]

The book which became the result of these months of toil contains an account of his excavations and an analysis of Assyrian history and culture, based on his finds and on the references in classical writings and the Bible. The first part was thus his personal story where he could draw upon his memory, diary and note-books. It must have been a pleasure for him to write this part which he finished in a few months; when he wrote to Birch in July he was already done with one of the following, more analytic chapters, which was 'now in the process of reduc-tion into a legible handwriting' – sigh! if only some more of his letters had been given the same treatment.

Despite frequent attacks of malaria he had accordingly been working with furious energy, and he succeeded in finishing a manuscript which was published in two volumes and comprised some 900 pages. At the same time he worked on the volume with drawings of the reliefs and he supervised the publication of the inscriptions. The practical work on this last book, taken on by the British Museum, was in the hands of W.S.W. Vaux, a man who was employed at the Museum in the depart-ment of medieval medals and manuscripts. He was probably expected to be a careful and competent editor, but he had never before taken any interest in cuneiform, so Layard was somewhat worried about the result.[114] Considering that all these tasks demanded his attention it is understandable that he had little time left over for a social life, but then one does not get the impression that he was terribly much in demand.

In September Layard finally decided to withdraw from the Border Commission. He wrote to Lord Palmerston and to Canning asking for permission to resign, and this was granted; he then had to face the fact, however, that the promised salary of £250 a year also fell away. He had to return to the embassy at Constantinople to function once again as an unpaid attaché – which meant that he was still depen-dent on Canning's private funds. All the worry about the future which had been expressed in his letter to Rawlinson half a year before turned out to be justified. He had to realise that despite all his efforts he still was a nobody.

And this was not the only disappointment he had to face at this time. Shortly afterwards arrived the shipment with some fifty boxes which had been waiting first at Basra and later at Bombay. These were the first important finds from his exca-vations and he could not wait to get the boxes open so that all could see what treasures he had brought to the country. However, when the lids were taken off Layard could see that everything had been taken out, and that the objects had been repacked in a quite unsatisfactory way: they were not properly wrapped and the smaller objects were lying helter-skelter in the boxes in a completely different order than the one he had arranged. His careful notes about the contents of each box, and thus the information about the provenance of the individual objects, had in other words become valueless. Even worse, several of the objects had been damaged and others were entirely missing.

It had been clear for some time that something had happened in Bombay. In the *Athenæum* of 6 February 1847, one could find a note about an exhibition there of 'a collection of Sculptured Figures and Cuneiform Inscriptions from the mound of Nimrod, south of the village of Nunia, opposite Mosul, on the Tigris'. The boxes had been landed at Bombay in January and deposited in the harbour, apparently with no real supervision, until they had been loaded on the brig 'Jumna' on 12 April 1848, in order to be shipped to England. They had been opened and an exhibition had been arranged; a certain Mr Buist had even held public lectures in which he explained the meaning of the Black Obelisk and showed both original pieces and casts made on the spot. About thirty boxes with smaller finds were in a scandalous state and many objects had been damaged. The glass vases, which had so fascinated Layard, were simply gone.

The journey onboard 'Jumna' had been quite dramatic as well. Eleven days after the departure from Bombay the brig had hit upon a violent storm, had lost its mast and been in acute danger of sinking; somehow it had been kept afloat and had reached Trincomalee in Ceylon, where it had been repaired (Gadd 1936: 48–9). This was one of the reasons for the long delay, but the real disaster was of course the damage done to the objects in Bombay, and Layard was beside himself.

Newspapers and magazines gave extensive coverage of the finds and were suitably enraged over the scandal at Bombay, but one particular article in the *Athenæum* of 18 November – published after Layard had left England again – was extremely unpleasant for him. Bonomi, who had earlier written extensively about the reliefs, ended a long new article with a strongly worded attack on Layard, in which he expressed his outrage at the fact that Layard had sawed most of the reliefs in half. First, he had made them lighter by having the backsides sawn off, but he had also had most of the blocks cut into two pieces horizontally. In the Northwest palace most reliefs were placed in two panels over each other, separated by a band of writing, and Layard had let the local stone mason remove these inscriptions. The intention was of course to lighten the load, making the blocks easier to transport, and Layard had quickly realised that the text in these bands was an identical repetition of the so-called 'standard inscription' which was found everywhere on the walls. He concluded that it was unnecessary to waste money and effort on the transportation of these extra kilos of stone all the way to London. This was indeed an unfortunate decision which cannot meet with approval from a modern archaeologist; it means that the relationship between the upper and lower panels in the decorative scheme of the palace rooms is sometimes difficult or impossible to establish now, but, even so, it is not easy to be too scandalised when we consider Layard's working conditions and the attitudes of his time. Bonomi had no idea that the texts which had been removed were duplicates of known inscriptions, and he was thoroughly outraged and described Layard's action as 'a vandalism not to be left undenounced in the nineteenth century'. Layard was naturally deeply hurt, but he now sat in Constantinople and could do no more than write a personal letter to Bonomi to defend himself.

Already before this happened he had been forced to realise that England did not offer any sudden, happy and unexpected possibilities, no orange fell into his turban, so there was nothing to do other than go back to Constantinople. He arrived in the Turkish capital at the end of December 1848, in time to say goodbye to the members of the Border Commission who were leaving on their mission. One wonders whether he regretted his decision.

While he sat down to take up his duties in the embassy together with Canning, to whom he had a somewhat strained relationship, the storm of praise finally broke in London. His book *Nineveh and Its Remains* appeared just after New Year and was an instant sensation. In magazines like the *Athenæum* and the *Literary Gazette* it was reviewed in enormous articles which ran over several issues, and it was described as 'one of the most interesting works of our day – a wonderful contribution to the history of a nation and glorious capital which had been lost and forgotten before the records of what we have hitherto been used to consider the most ancient histories of the world began.' Layard himself was praised for the 'bold and enterprising spirit which he has displayed, as well as the indomitable perseverance, intelligence, and tact with which he has pursued his object'.[115] This was the tone in all reviews, and uncle Benjamin and aunt Sara were practically in ecstasy. 'I cannot even think of you, most glancingly, without more emotion than is at all good for me! Shame upon my years! What a fortune your brains will be to you!' wrote Sara. Everyone was astonished and full of admiration for the book, which was 'not only considered perfect in style, astonishing in knowledge, but a *marvel* in its interest and completeness' (Waterfield 1963: 191).

In a letter to Murray, Lord Ellesmere, the president of the Royal Asiatic Society and one of the leading aristocrats and patron of the arts, characterised Layard's book as 'the greatest achievement of our time'. In his view 'no man living has done so much or told it so well'. Edward Hawkins, the newly appointed secretary of the British Museum and a close friend of Layard, took Prince Albert on a tour through the Assyrian antiquities together with the entire cabinet, and he explained to the exalted gentlemen that 'these things are without price; no thousands could buy them and they have cost the country nothing'. Now, finally, the government decided that a suitable ship should be sent to Basra to fetch the large bulls and lions which had been lying there for years.

Uncle Benjamin was in no doubt about the impact the book was going to have on Layard's future, and he was particularly pleased that his nephew had been able to present the story of the excavations in such a way that it became clear how poorly he had been treated by the British Museum. 'No one speaks of any other book than *Nineveh* & of its modesty. They abuse the Government & the Museum & praise your lenient treatment of them. Your course, my dear Henry, is now clear. *Nothing can stop you.*'

Layard had dedicated the book to his uncle and had not even mentioned Canning's name in his introduction. He appeared a little later in the body of the first chapter, where the reader is asked to join the author in a feeling of gratitude

> towards one who, whilst he has maintained so successfully the honour and interests of England by his high character and eminent abilities, has acquired for his country so many great monuments of ancient civilisation and art. It is to Sir Stratford Canning we are mainly indebted for the collection of Assyrian antiquities with which the British Museum will be enriched.
>
> (Layard 1849, vol. 1: 17)

One senses through the stilted phrases how many times Layard turned these sentences over in his head. Canning receives what is due to him, no more, and the uncle was perfectly capable of reading between the lines, for he wrote:

I have always felt, & do not hesitate to say, that your position at Nimrud was not put forward properly by Sir S.C. & no one at the Museum thought more about you than as a clerk or assistant, but thanks to your own plain, modest statement all now know better; but I cannot help expressing my opinion that Sir S.C. showed no particular kindness about it. It comes late but not the worse for that as it shows your moderation & all wonder how you could have gained such influence over a race of wild Arabs. Were you here now I fear your head would be turned, & it is well, therefore, you escape the intoxication.

(Waterfield 1963: 192)

Aunt Sara had a weakness for the grand ambassador with the white lion's mane, and she did not agree in this evaluation of Canning. She informed Layard that his employer had in fact ordered four copies of Layard's book. In Constantinople the ambassador pretended not to have read it, though, and he did not wish to read or discuss the reviews, so the atmosphere between the two men, who spent several hours daily in each other's company, must have been strained. Sara Austen felt that Canning was simply testing Layard's reactions by his apparent lack of interest, but he found that hard to believe. In his letters to her he gave what he felt was clear evidence of the ambassador's intense jealousy; thus, Canning maintained that it was he who had first realised the potential of the Assyrian mounds after having read Rich's book – 'which I lent him in order to back my repeated suggestions as to excavations in Assyria!! What can be done under such circumstances?'[116]

Influential people in London now finally set the machinery in motion which could secure Layard a permanent position, and Lord Ellesmere wrote to a certain Charles Arbuthnot, who was a close friend of the great hero the Duke of Wellington; he in turn forwarded the letter to Lord Palmerston, a text in which Layard was recommended in some memorable sentences:

He is one of those men of whom England seems to have a monopoly, who go anywhere, surmount anything and achieve everything without assistance, patronage or fuss of any kind.

(Waterfield 1963: 194)

When several members of the staff at the embassy died in a new cholera epidemic in the Spring of 1849, it finally became reality: Layard became a salaried attaché.

The publication of the book naturally led to a strong resurgence of the interest in Assyrian antiquities and the reliefs which were now installed in the British Museum. The galleries with the Assyrian finds were constantly thronged with curious visitors, and when merchant Ross visited London and appeared in the Museum, a large group of people gathered around him and asked him about Assyria and Nimrud. Hormuzd Rassam, who lived and studied in Oxford, was also invited to parties in fine houses where he became the central figure who was supposed to entertain the company with stories about Layard and his excavations. In May Layard was awarded the gold medal of the Royal Geographic Society, its greatest honour, and his uncle received it on his behalf, making a small speech in which he characterised his wandering nephew:

When he left England, he had no letters of introduction, and no patronage or assistance of any sort; but, though young, his character was formed. Firm and energetic, with courage which nothing could daunt, he combined an indomitable and enterprising spirit with the most amiable disposition.

(Waterfield 1963: 196)

From Baghdad came a small peep: 'Every one writes to me "Of course you have Layard's book" and accordingly no one sends it'. He had read the long reviews and seen excerpts from the book, 'and judging from the Extracts, cannot think the compliments paid to you at all exaggerated. The style is certainly most pleasing and the matter full of novelty'.[117] It must have felt very odd for Layard to sit in Constantinople at this time, when he was finally receiving the attention and honours for which he thirsted, and therefore without the means to use the situation to his advantage. Had he been in London, his head might have been turned, as the uncle feared, but he would have been in the middle of all the success and would have lectured to learned societies and been invited to parties everywhere. Precisely now was the time when he might have secured for himself the connections which would have led to a meaningful career.

One of the consequences of the great interest was that the British Museum inevitably would have to make certain that the excavations could continue, and there was of course no one other than Layard who could be asked to work at Nimrud. But on which conditions?

The question was money. In an internal memorandum from the Museum Hawkins had made a list of the expenses for Botta's expedition, drawn up on the basis of information provided by Botta through Layard. And here we read of enormous sums: Botta had personally been given £5,000, Flandin £1,000; the latter's drawings had been bought by the state for a further £3,000; the excavation had cost £5,000, and the cost of publication amounted to no less than £13,000. When transport cost was added to this Hawkins reached a total of no less than £30,000, a veritable fortune. And, in fact, this was not the end of the matter, for Botta had received a kind of personal pension of £400 per annum, plus a promise that he could be sent as consul to whichever place he might choose. Both he and Flandin further received royalties on the publication, valued at some £10,000 for each man, so the total cost was at least £50,000! Of less importance financially, although probably very much appreciated, was the Grand Cross of the Legion of Honour given to Botta.[118]

At a dinner party at Montague Place Hawkins told the Austens that the government had decided to set aside a sum of £20,000 for new campaigns in Assyria and Babylonia, so it finally looked as if it would be possible to realise the grand scheme for excavations which Layard had put forward a year earlier.

It therefore came as a shock when it became clear that the Trustees had asked the Exchequer for a sum of £3,000, and when this was granted, they decided that it would be sufficient for a two-year campaign! This was meant to cover the expenses for travel, excavation and transportation; and Layard was supposed to excavate not only Kuyunjik and Nimrud, but to undertake a campaign in Babylonia and excavate some of the many mounds which were known to exist here.

Layard was shocked and scandalised, and in his letters to the family he did not mince words. To Henry Ellis, the head librarian at the British Museum – and consequently the administrative head of the entire institution – he wrote to say that the sum was completely inadequate; in fact, from a personal consideration he found it directly inadvisable to take on the task on these conditions; he would, however, attempt to do his best, and he added: 'My private resources are far from considerable, but such as they are they shall be devoted to the undertaking'.[119]

The staff of the expedition was supposed to comprise a doctor, Humphry Sandwith, who was already in Constantinople, and who was supposed to care for Layard whose health was not very good; an artist who should make drawings of the finds, first of all the sculptures and inscriptions, and then of course Hormuzd Rassam. He was not happy to have to leave Oxford, however, for he enjoyed life here to the full, but he came when Layard called. 'I would rather be a chimney sweep in England than become a Pasha in Turkey', he wrote.

It appears that the artist was chosen by the Austens. He was a young man of twenty-eight called F.C. Cooper, and he left London in Hormuzd's company after a teary farewell scene with his pregnant young wife.

Instructions were sent to Layard from the Museum in the middle of July, and this time they were couched in a different language. We now hear that 'Mr. Layard is intimately acquainted with the whole subject, and particularly with the Assyrian antiquities already deposited in or acquired for the Museum'. With respect to Mr Cooper's position, it is said that 'in order to assist in making Plans, Drawings and Copies of Inscriptions the Trustees will attach an experienced artist to the Expedition'. In contrast, the letter makes it plain that the gentlemen at the Museum found it difficult to understand precisely why Layard would need the services of Hormuzd:

> The Trustees are given to understand that in Mr Layard's opinion the services of Mr Hormuzd Rassam are almost essential to the full efficiency of the expedition. The Trustees do not object to Mr H. Rassam's employment nor to his receiving such remuneration as Mr Layard may think fit on account of his travelling expenses to Mosul and Salary.[120]

CHAPTER TWENTY-TWO

MOSUL REVISITED

—— •◆• ——

A few days before his departure from Constantinople Layard sat down to write a letter to his old friend Ross, explaining that he intended to take a new route to Mosul: by boat to Trabzon on the Black Sea coast and from there by the caravan trail to Lake Van, where there were many ruins and inscriptions. The last trek from Van to Mosul passed over some very high mountain passes and went through areas inhabited by both Kurds, Nestorians and Yezidis.

> The funds given by the Museum are, as you know, exceedingly small. I scarcely know what I shall do to carry on the excavations. I have much less than I had last time – fortunately I have made a little money by my book and that will help me to keep above water. A medical man, a Dr. Sandwith, accompanies me. He is a very clever and amiable fellow & will be a great addition to our party. Mr. Cooper is rather green but will soon be broken in. Rassam is just as ever – buying all manner of trumpery to astonish the ‹natives.[121]

Canning, who was still officially Layard's employer even though he had leave from his position at the embassy, wrote an official note the following day in which he set out his instructions. Also here one sees the difference from the first instructions written four years earlier. The letter is considerably more urbane than the first one, and the ambassador expresses his complete satisfaction that Layard is the best-qualified person to evaluate the archaeological problems he may have to face. Canning does find it pertinent to remind him that he now goes to Mosul as a person who is officially attached to the embassy. 'It is the more incumbent on you to abstain carefully, as heretofore, from any language or proceeding likely to wound the national feelings or religious convictions of the people with whom you may have to deal'.[122] Clearly, the ambassador still did not really trust Layard's discretion, and the affair with the Cadi on the Tigris continued to influence his view of the young man.

One undecided matter irritated Layard a great deal, namely the lack of a new firman from the Turkish authorities, which would permit him to excavate and to send home what he found. For various political reasons Canning was not interested in approaching the Sultan at this particular time, and he felt that the old

firman could still be used. He did promise Layard, though, to see to it that excavation permits for both Assyria and Babylonia would be acquired as soon as it
was politically opportune; despite the lack of such a permit he emphasised the
importance of expanding the activities to the south.

It was a large group which left Constantinople on 28 August 1849. Layard now
travelled as an important man, and gone were the days when he rode with Mitford
from village to village, free as a bird. On this trip he was accompanied by several
guests, and he also had both servants and guards; one of these was the faithful
soldier, the *cawass* Ahmed Agha, who was described by Dr Sandwith as a man
with shining black eyes, jet-black beard, and with the regular features of the ancient
Assyrian kings. Another travelling companion was Yusuf, the leading Yezidi priest
or 'cawal', who had spent some time in Constantinople together with a group of
his colleagues.

This particular sect, into whose rites and secrets Layard had been partly
initiated during his first visit, and for whom he felt a strong personal sympathy, had been exposed to a great deal of persecution after his departure. This
was due first of all to a new order stating that all Yezidis had to serve in the
Turkish army. In Islamic countries the tradition had been that only Muslims
could fight for the state and the faith, but one of the many new reforms introduced during these years extended the duty to perform military service also to
the Yezidis. Their lives were governed by elaborate rituals and rules which determined the smallest details of their daily existence, so for them this new order
was a catastrophe. Rather than living uninhibited lives of debauchery and abandon,
as many thought these so-called 'Devil worshippers' did, they were restrained
by rules which interfered with all aspects of their existence: the colour blue was
anathema to them, and in the Turkish army they had to wear blue; and much
of the food served to soldiers was forbidden to Yezidis. Moreover, the brutal
officers in the army had no inclination to make special concessions towards this
group, which was regarded as made up of political and religious enemies. Naturally,
there was opposition among the Yezidis and this was repressed with the utmost
severity; in fact, the sect as such became the target for a general campaign of
persecution, and the Yezidi leaders had no way of establishing contact with the
political leaders to negotiate a settlement. Therefore, when it was rumoured among
them that Layard was back in Constantinople, it was decided to send cawal
Yusuf together with four other priests to the capital in order to appeal to him.
This was a most dangerous mission, but the men did find Layard who passed them
on to Canning, and after long negotiations the whole affair had ended with a
compromise which went some way towards recognising the special religious taboos
of the Yezidis.

Because of these successful negotiations the journey from Lake Van to Mosul
became a veritable triumphal procession. In the first Yezidi village they reached
Layard's large party rode to the central square, and cawal Yusuf, who had covered
his face with a scarf, ordered in a commanding tone of voice the villagers to find
food and beds for the men. The local people thought Layard's group were Turkish
soldiers, the worst possible visit a village could get, and Yusuf kept up the charade
with the terrified people for some time before finally making himself known.

Everyone was then overjoyed; such practical jokes were extremely valued by all, and Hormuzd in particular was a master in this sport.

There was no end to the joy, once Yusuf had been recognised, for he had been given up for dead, killed by the Sultan in Constantinople. Now he was placed in a house together with all the leading men from the village and he had to give a minutely detailed account of what everyone had said and done, and how all had ended with a great result – thanks to Layard and Canning. It is easy to imagine what this meant to these people, to find themselves suddenly under the protection of an order from the Sultan, to have their religion recognised and to be promised peace and liberty. One can immediately understand the warm feelings of gratitude which poured over Layard. It was to him the Yezidis had turned and he had proven worthy of their confidence. It was of course Canning who had worked out the actual compromise, but he was 1,000 km away. Layard was here, and he had returned to his friends.

The following morning the village was filled with visitors coming from all the neighbouring Yezidi settlements, and a caravan consisting of hundreds of singing and shouting people followed Layard's group to the next larger village, where a sumptuous meal awaited them.

> The men had assembled at some distance from the village, the women and children, dressed in their holiday attire, and carrying boughs of trees, congregated on the housetops. As I approached sheep were brought into the road and slain before my horse's feet, and as we entered the yard of Akko's house the women and men joined in the loud and piercing 'tahlel'.

Once again cawal Yusuf had to tell the story of his mission to Constantinople. After this lunch the company continued and was met once again by a large crowd of people which consisted of both Yezidis and Christians; two Jacobite bishops joined the procession which proceeded to a large Christian village, where greetings were exchanged. From here the steadily growing group continued to a small town, Redwan; on the road they met three further *cawals* accompanied by many Muslims, so it was a triumphal procession which entered Redwan.

Layard's purpose in providing such an elaborate description of his reception among the Yezidis was to describe the genuine and spontaneous gratitude shown by this 'much maligned and oppressed race'. He wishes to argue against 'those, unfortunately too many, who believe that Easterns can only be managed by violence and swayed by fear'. There was no need to interfere in their authority or compromise their natural dignity in order to deal with them; instead, one should build on their sincerity and seek to lay 'the foundation of real attachment and mutual esteem' (Layard 1853: 45).

They expected a somewhat different reception in the Kurdish village Funduk, whose inhabitants were renowned for their ruthless brutality shown during the campaign directed against the Nestorians a few years earlier, the war which had been led by the notorious Beder Khan Bey. Layard had no intention of stopping here, even though they arrived in the evening, so the party rode slowly through the narrow streets in the gathering darkness, while people were preparing for sleep on the rooftops around them. The young artist Cooper was shaking with fear because Hormuzd had amused himself by telling him horrendous details of the countless robberies and raids of the people of Funduk. As a group of men suddenly came running up to them Cooper panicked and drew his double-barrelled pistols. It turned out, however, that the men came from the chief of the village who insisted that it would be intolerable for his reputation if such eminent travellers should pass by without eating and sleeping there. Layard and his company had to turn around, and spent the night in the chief's house.

They were now close to Mosul, and when they arrived at the small Christian village Tel Kef, three hours' ride from their final destination, they were met by several of Layard's old headmen and workers who came to greet him. Toma, with the nickname 'Shishman', or 'the fat', Mansour, Behnan and Hannah. In the village waited the Vice-Consul Christian Rassam, Hormuzd's brother, who had prepared a feast in the house belonging to the Chaldean bishop.

The next morning they met more well-known faces, first of all Layard's old horse Merjan, who waited to serve his master again:

> the noble animal looking as beautiful, as fresh, and as sleek as when I last saw him, although two long years had passed; former servants, Awad and the sheikhs of the Jebours, even the very greyhounds who had been brought up under my roof. Then as we ascend an eminence midway, walls, towers, minarets, and domes rise boldly from the margin of the broad river, cheating us into the belief, too soon to be dispelled, that Mosul is still a not unworthy representative of the great Nineveh. As we draw near, the long line of lofty mounds, the only remains of mighty bulwarks and spacious gates, detach themselves from the low undulating hills: now the vast mound of Kouyunjik overtops the surrounding heaps; then above it peers the white cone of the tomb of the prophet Jonah, many other well-remembered spots follow in rapid succession; but we cannot linger. Hastening over the creaking bridge of boats, we force our way through the crowded bazars, and alight at the house I had left two years ago. Old servants take their places as a matter of course, and, uninvited, pursue their regular occupations as if they had never been interrupted. Indeed it seemed as if we had but returned from a summer's ride; two years had passed away like a dream.
>
> (Layard 1853: 59)

Not all was as it had been, however. He immediately sat down to write a long report to Canning in which he described the journey and commented upon the political condition of the region. The entire Pashalik of Mosul and the steppes west of it leading into Syria were in a 'disgraceful state of disorganisation'. The Bedouin had plundered all the villages and he doubted whether there was a single inhabited settlement left on the right, western banks of the Tigris. Marauding bands of tribesmen now stood less than five km from Mosul.[123]

Both Muslims, Christians and Yezidis had expressed that they would rather see the return of the Kurdish chief Beder Khan Bey than suffer under this total anarchy left by the Turkish authorities. The new Pasha at Mosul was a cultured and intelligent man, a former ambassador to Berlin who had known Layard in

Figure 22.1 The mound Kuyunjik, probably drawn by Layard himself.
(From Barnett 1976: 3)

Constantinople. Unfortunately he suffered from great indolence and lack of energy, and he tended to become irritated when things did not go exactly as he wished them to; he would then suddenly erupt in fury and take drastic decisions which he would later regret. But the decisive element in the situation was that he was the sixth or seventh Pasha at Mosul since Layard's departure; this rapid rotation meant that no Pasha ever had the time or the inclination to truly learn about the problems of his province – much less address them.

Layard's old friend Abd-ur-rahman, the sheikh of the Abu Salman tribe, complained bitterly over the situation; one of the many reforms had deprived his. tribe of their essential traditional grazing lands, and he wailed that he and the tribe now lived in abject poverty.

After a few courtesy visits and a round of letter-writing, Layard and Hormuzd took Cooper on a tour of the excavated rooms at Kuyunjik the following morning. Ross, who had been placed in charge of the continued excavations here, had left for England so the task had now fallen to Hormuzd's brother. All he had done was to keep the operation going in order to make clear the continued British interest in the place. Fat Toma, the man in charge of the mound, took them through

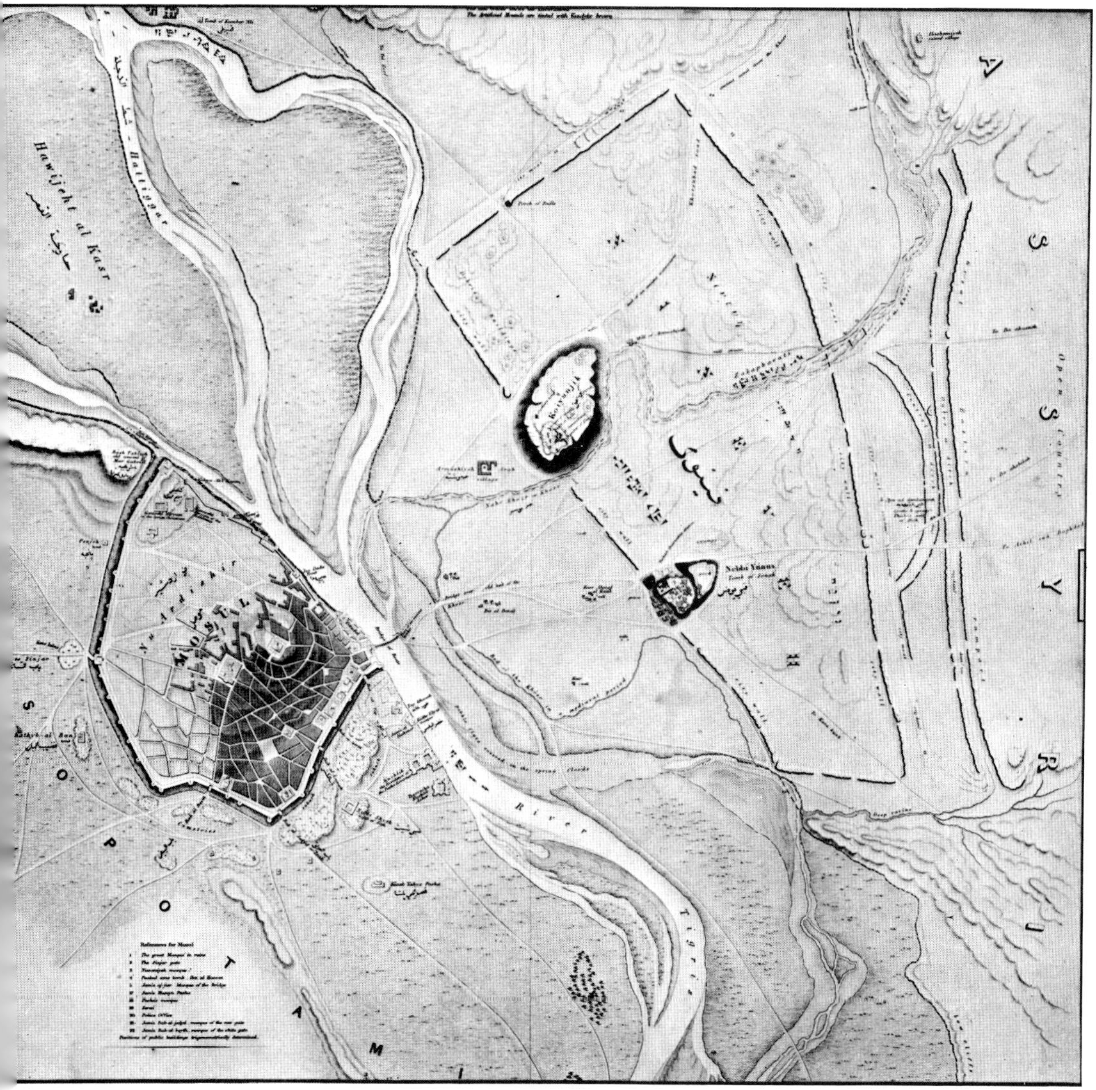

Figure 22.2 Captain Felix Jones' map of Nineveh. The walls can be seen, with a series of outer walls towards the east; the two mounds Kuyunjik and Nebbi Yunus are prominent in the empty landscape. Today the entire middle area of Nineveh is filled with new buildings, with Mosul expanding across the river. (From Barnett 1976: 1)

the rooms which Layard had never seen. In accordance with the instructions from the British Museum, his own trenches had been filled in, but there were many rooms with a great number of reliefs.

Everything was heavily damaged by the fire, but Layard was struck first of all by the contrast to the palace at Nimrud. Here at Kuyunjik everything was different. Certainly, the building was as large as, perhaps larger than the Nimrud palaces, but the reliefs showed clear stylistic differences. They were rather closer to Botta's finds from Khorsabad, even though nuances were evident. Most reliefs showed scenes of war, and the religious and cultic scenes which were so prominent at Nimrud appeared to be missing. He saw none of the large demonic figures with the head of an eagle or with large wings, and the sacred tree, a recurring motif at Nimrud, was nowhere to be seen. The individual relief blocks were not divided into two registers, but the scenes spread over the entire surface of the block. Many of the individual figures were accordingly quite small, since they were scattered over large compositions which must be described as landscapes. In the palace at Nimrud all figures were of the same size and stood on a firmly drawn line at the bottom of the relief. But in Kuyunjik the artists had attempted to work with a kind of perspective and each landscape had been carefully described with details such as hills and mountains, rivers, roads, vineyards, marshes and so forth. Layard also felt that each room in the palace was meant to tell one coherent story, in most instances the account of a military campaign: one would see the Assyrian army leaving, the battles in the foreign lands which always culminated in a victory and the deportation of prisoners and vanquished; they might be paraded in front of the king himself on his throne. It seemed clear that inscriptions at the top of the reliefs had indicated which country or city the campaign was directed against, but since the rooms were nearly all badly damaged, such inscriptions were in most cases destroyed (Reade 1979a, 1979b, 1980; Winter 1981, 1983; Russell 1991).

In fact, the palace had suffered very greatly from the fire that had marked the end of its existence. The enormous logs carrying the roofs, and which – as we now know – were made of mighty cedars taken from the forests on Mount Lebanon, had of course been destroyed; in those places where the palace had had more than one storey, the top floors had crashed down and badly damaged the ground floor rooms. Most reliefs were only preserved to about one meter's height, and even those remains were very brittle and threatened to decay completely. The large figures that had guarded the most important doorways were also in most instances preserved only as big feet, sometimes with a little of the body of the bull to be seen. It was clearly going to be very difficult to remove and transport these reliefs.

Ross had excavated in the normal fashion in open trenches, but after his departure Christian Rassam had moved the activities to a new spot in the hope that better preserved sculptures might turn up there. It turned out that the palace here was covered with such a massive layer of later accumulations that it was very difficult to reach the reliefs in the normal way from above, so Fat Toma had devised a new method of excavation by way of tunnels, like shafts in a mine (see Figure 22.3).

Figure 22.3 The strange and unfortunate tunnelling which was used at both Kuyunjik and
Khorsabad at least provided a picturesque scenery. (From Layard 1853: 104)

The hardness of the soil, mixed with pottery, bricks, and remains of buildings raised at various times over the buried ruins of the Assyrian palace, rendered this process easy and safe with ordinary care and precaution. The subterraneaous passages were narrow, and were propped up when necessary either by leaving columns of earth, as in mines, or by wooden beams. These long galleries, dimly lighted, lined with the remains of ancient art, broken urns projecting from the crumbling sides, and the wild Arab and hardy Nestorian wandering through their intricacies, or working in their dark recesses, were singularly picturesque.

(Layard 1853: 69)

Layard, and in fact many later archaeologists working at Kuyunjik, made use of this method, which is of course extremely unfortunate, if only because it leaves the rooms themselves untouched. There are places on the mound where it is easier to reach the Assyrian levels and where the method was not used, but as a slightly later visitor explained, most of the large palace was approached through tunnels:

The tunnels and galleries pierced by Mr. Layard through the bowels of the enormous mound are still perfect as when he ceased his excavations in 1852, the hardness of the sun-baked bricks through which they were cut preventing the sides from falling in. They cross and recross each other, diving at one time deep into the recesses of the mass, at another ascending, when least expected, to the surface. A number of slabs, the inscriptions and bas-reliefs which were not of sufficient interest to induce their removal, still line many of the passages in their original position, traces of fire being observable distinctly on most. One corner of the great mound, some 2500 yards in circumference, was perforated like a honeycomb with the numerous shafts which had been driven through it.

(Ussher 1865: 393–4)

Contemporary drawings and watercolours show these tunnels where the light from the regularly spaced shafts running up to the surface throw a dramatic and eerie illumination over the long rows of reliefs.

Work was now resumed and reorganised and new workmen were hired: Fat Toma was placed in charge of Kuyunjik where several teams began extending the trenches and tunnels. Layard also placed some gangs on other parts of the mound, and a group was ordered to tackle one of the gates in the wall which surrounded the entire city. Arabs from the Jebour tribe made up the largest group of workers, but the actual digging was done by the Christian Nestorians, whose strength and good sense Layard had more confidence in.

An engineer from the Border Commission, a certain Lieutenant Glascott, had made an exact map of Kuyunjik which he gave to Layard (see Figure 25.2). The palace he was uncovering was located at the southern tip of the mound, whereas the ruins of a modern village were found in the north. The palace is on high ground, but in the middle of the mound there is another considerable rise which indicated the existence of some important building. From the northern tip close by the village is the only road which leads up onto the mound, whose sides are otherwise nearly vertical; there are several ravines, however, where rainwater had dug deep into the flanks of the tell. These places seemed to be promising locations for an excavator who could tunnel directly into the ruins at those spots where remains of buildings stuck out of the sides of the ravines. There was obviously more than enough for him to do here.

CHAPTER TWENTY-THREE

AN ENCOUNTER
ON NIMRUD

—— ·•· ——

In Mosul Layard was visited by cawal Yusuf who invited the entire company,
including the Vice-Consul, to the holy site of the Yezidis to take part in the
great annual feast. Layard had already been there once, but this time he was the
guest of honour and was expected to explain in detail what the new agreement
with the Sultan meant. This became a memorable event where he was allowed to
take part in all the most secret and closed ritual events. He wrote down the texts
of the hymns and prayers which formed part of the rites, and in his book one
even finds in an appendix the notes to the accompanying music.

Back at Mosul in mid-October Layard received a letter from Edward Hawkins,
the leader of the Antiquities Department at the British Museum. He had been ill
after having taken part in an archaeological conference at Salisbury, where most of
the participants came down with cholera; this was clearly bad enough in itself, but
he had even more depressing news to impart after having been to a new meeting
with his superiors, the Trustees of the Museum. He declared that he was unable
to even think about Layard's situation without 'infinite vexation':

> I continue to discover more of the motives for the smallness of the grant,
> besides the general pressure upon the finances of the country; they were afraid
> that a large grant would encourage a less careful watch over expenses
> disbursed, and a too great readiness to excavate imprudently. I acknowledged
> the correctness of the general principle but insisted strongly upon the injus-
> tice of it in your case, a proved and tried man. It was all unavailing, but I
> certainly drew from the conversation my own conclusion that more money
> *could* be got when it was really wanted, and with this we must be content
> *for the present*.[124]

That was how far the trust of the Museum went! Layard felt he had to pinch and
scrape because the fine gentlemen in London were worried that he might squander
their money. Hawkins also explained that all the finds from the first expedition
now were in the Museum, except for the great lion and bull which continued to
wait at Basra. Everything was causing great interest, but, as he added in a post-
script to the letter: 'It is your own book which has done every thing for you, the
greatest assistance I have been to you was instigating you to write it'. He also

wanted more finds as soon as possible, and preferably some gold! Hawkins felt that there must be a great chance of finding treasures which had been buried in the days before the final fall of Nineveh.

All the workmen were now in place, having arrived from the various camps and villages, and Layard had about one hundred men at work on Kuyunjik in twelve to fourteen teams. Having started the whole thing he went to Nimrud together with Hormuzd on 18 October in order to revisit his beloved ruins. He met old friends and spent a long evening in the village talking to the men about all that had happened since he had last been here, the harvest, taxes and the new system of military service which also here created violent opposition.

The following morning at sunrise he and Hormuzd ascended the mound in order to plan renewed activities.

> The mound had undergone no change. There it rose from the plain, the same sun-burnt yellow heap that it had stood for twenty centuries. The earth and rubbish, which had been heaped over the excavated chambers and sculptured slabs, had settled, and had left uncovered in sinking the upper part of several bas-reliefs. A few colossal heads of winged figures rose calmly above the level of the soil, and with two pairs of winged bulls, which had not been buried on account of their mutilated condition, was all that remained above ground of the north-west palace, that great storehouse of Assyrian history and art. Since my departure the surface of the mound had again been furrowed by the plough, and ample crops had this year rewarded the labors of the husbandman.
>
> (Layard 1853: 98)

The aim of continued excavation here was to uncover many more rooms in the Northwest palace, also those which did not have reliefs, to discover more about the enigmatic central palace, and finally to investigate the large 'pyramid' at the northern tip of the mound.

The second morning he saw a group of horsemen on the mound when he arrived, and on reaching them was shown in silence a figure swept in a rug who was lying asleep at the bottom of one of the trenches. It was Rawlinson.

Layard had of course been expecting him for some time, even though in his book he describes the meeting dramatically as a complete surprise. At any rate, it was a most important occasion, for this was the first time Rawlinson visited the excavations. During the entire first expedition the two men had met only in Baghdad, and even though Rawlinson had several times laid plans to go north to Nimrud, he had never found the time to do so. Now he was finally here, passing through on his way back to England.

They had a great deal to discuss, of course. Layard could show his guest around both Nimrud and Kuyunjik, for the first time showing the major what he had found and giving him an impression of the buildings he had uncovered, but it did not in fact turn out to be a truly successful meeting. Rawlinson was unwell and extremely tired after his ride from Baghdad. In the end all they managed was only a very brief tour around Nimrud, after which they had to retire to the village because Rawlinson came down with an attack of fever. When his condition deteriorated during the night they decided in the morning to ride to Mosul and get Rawlinson to bed; he stayed there for two days without venturing outside the house at all. Finally, on the third day he was well enough for a hasty tour of Kuyunjik and the rest of Nineveh, and he then left for Constantinople.

It appears that this was not a happy meeting. Layard is naturally extremely discreet when writing about it in his book, but it is hardly a coincidence that he added a footnote to his brief passage about Rawlinson's stay in which he referred to another visit; a certain Captain Newbold also passed through Assyria at about the same time and we hear about the happy hours they passed together, and how this gentleman 'in spite of hopeless disease, and sufferings of no common kind, maintained an almost unrivalled sweetness of disposition, and never relaxed from the pursuit of knowledge and the love of science'. Presumably, this is Layard's way of saying that Rawlinson behaved in the exact opposite manner – unfriendly, bad-tempered and more interested in his own comfort than the ruins Layard so wanted to show and explain to him. We are not really in a position to speculate about the reasons for the lack of warmth and interest, but Rawlinson was no doubt ill and had reason to worry about his health. But the fact is that Rawlinson was not very interested in ruins; he had indicated in his letters to Layard that he intended to travel as fast as possible, even making it clear that there was no need for Layard to come to Nimrud to meet him there. All he wanted was to make a brief survey of the place and look at the inscriptions which might be visible.

In his diary Layard wrote about their first day at Nimrud that they rode round the ruins looking for inscriptions, and they had 'much interesting talk on Assyrian matters'. The next day: 'Ride into Mosul with Rawlinson, who was suffering much from fever and weakness, & he remained during the day in bed'. This was true also of the next day, and then finally: 'Rode with Rawlinson to the Mound, & go over the ruins with him. He then leaves for Constantinople'. That is all. Then follows a long story about Abd-ur-rahman who has been thrown into jail for refusing to pay his tithe.[125]

Rawlinson was clearly interested only in the texts and could quickly get enough of ruins. In fact, Layard knew as much from his letters, but it must have been extremely disappointing to meet the major's lack of interest or understanding of the material world in which the texts belonged and which they reflected. The situation reminds of the reception of the very first reliefs at Baghdad, when Layard in a similar way was exposed to Rawlinson's indifference.

The major's own account of these days in the diary which he kept during his travel from Baghdad to Europe does not add much which can throw light upon the meeting; he writes about the visit to Nimrud: 'Looked over the ruins and excavations partly then & partly in the afternoon, but did not enjoy it much, as I was suffering all day & Layard had no medicine to relieve me'. He did learn a little, though, the genealogy of a king, but the ruins as such do not appear to have made any impression on him. In Mosul Layard sat at his bedside during the first day and they discussed Assyrian history; Rawlinson noted that a new king was mentioned in a text, and he found the reliefs describing the transport of the great bull 'very curious'. His visit to Kuyunjik was unsuccessful, however, for Mrs

Rassam insisted that he should ride on her horse, and as he was taking it out of the gate it kicked her guard in the groin and killed the man. Rawlinson was of course quite blameless, but the face of the poor wretch rolling on the ground continued to haunt him. So, for one reason and another he was unable to show much interest in Layard's glorious ruins.[126]

This was the more disappointing, since the letters which Layard had received from Baghdad during the preceding months had been promising, filled with revolutionary news about Assyrian history and interpretations which turned previously held opinions upside down. As early as March Rawlinson had hinted that his studies had led him to drastic revisions of his theories. He now doubted whether king Ninus had ever existed, and said: 'I throw all Greek traditions regarding Assyria to the winds. The only names that at all suit are those of the Median dynasty of Ctesias – but it does not follow that the age he assigned the family was the true one'.[127] Another conclusion was that the gap between the builder of the Northwest palace at Nimrud and the king at Khorsabad must be reduced to about one hundred years.

If the Greek traditions have to be discarded, then what about the Bible? Rawlinson had been sent a copy of an inscription from a hitherto unattested king, a text found in a different location and brought to Nimrud, and he felt that here he was finally dealing with one of the kings from the Old Testament; it was, he said, the youngest Assyrian text he had ever seen and he suspects that the king's name was Tiglath-pileser. It would have been interesting to know what his basis for this for once entirely correct reading was, but he does not – of course – inform Layard of that. The surprising aspect is that he is now willing to consider finding one of the biblical kings:

> it is the most modern Assyrian Inscription I have seen, the only one indeed I think we have of the lower dynasty – it is indeed a most valuable link between the Babylonian and the old Assyrian and being chiefly historical & geographical with very little of the pantheistical trash that takes up so large a part of the standard tablets of Nimrud Khorsabad & Koyunjik, will prove of real service in working out the chronological series – unfortunately there is no genealogy – but if you ever light on the place from where it was brought to Nimrud, there will assuredly be other memorials of the same family. I have a suspicion that the king named is the Tiglath Pilesar of Scripture and this as I said before is the latest monument we have.[128]

The fact that he wishes to date the text to a very late period is presumably due to his interpretation of its nature and content, and such a remark might lead us to believe that he was in fact able to read the text, but this is clearly not the case; he could see that it contained fewer names of gods and more of cities and countries, simply because these were marked by determinatives.

Two weeks later he feels utterly lost again with respect to chronology, even though he remains convinced that the Greek traditions must be discarded. 'I can give now very nearly as <u>literal</u> & as <u>certain</u> a translation of the obelisk Inscription, as I did of the Persian record at Behistun but I still say I <u>know</u> nothing of the age of the record and am very loth to set about guessing'.[129]

Finally, in the next letter he lets himself go with a long account of his ideas – having first complained of 'rheumatism and a lazy liver', but that is part of his normal letter style. He views his results as primarily of geographical and historical interest, and he starts dramatically with the claim that he has found many references to Jewish cities, even Jerusalem, 'though the name is so transmogrified that I have had difficulty in recognizing it'. In fact, his reading was mistaken; he read the name written *Gar-ga-mish* (the city Carchemish on the Euphrates) as *Sha-lu-ma*.

However, he dates the texts to the period of the Judges: 'I think that I have found repeated mentions of the Jews (the 12 tribes as they are called "worshipping the one and the Supreme God") and I believe accordingly that I can fix the epoch of your earliest Nimrud ruins at about 1400 BCE'. The Assyrian palaces are accordingly still removed by several centuries from the historical kings mentioned in the Old Testament, and even the name Tiglath-pileser, which he had read a few weeks earlier, is given up. This single fact, that he continues to steer clear of the Bible, shows that he still cannot read the royal names, for if he had been able to do that, he would have found Sargon and Sennacherib and the other 'biblical' kings in the texts.

So what could he read, and what was the factual basis for his sudden optimism? He was clearly able to read quite a lot of the running text in the inscriptions, and he could recognise many place-names; he now knew that Nimrud is not Nineveh but Calah, and he had even been able to read accounts of the foundation of the city. So where was Nineveh? Somewhat surprisingly Rawlinson maintained that it had yet to be discovered:

> It was not Koyunjik, the name of which I am unable to read, though I see it was a famous place in the time even of the Obelisk king and that the king whose name appears on the bricks, Bulls &c only reedified it – nor was it Khorsabad, which was named specially after its founder.

He now realised that 'there must be 20 times as much to be discovered as we have yet got hold of', and that the founder of the Northwest palace at Nimrud was not at all the first Assyrian monarch, 'probably half way down the line', he said. The so-called 'lower dynasty', that is, the kings mentioned in the Bible, were still utterly unattested, and he was finally convinced that the Greek dynastic lists were entirely fictitious.

One senses in this letter that Rawlinson felt himself to be progressing rapidly, the gate is opening for him, and he provides more information in this one letter than in scores of normal ones to Layard. Obviously, he was delighted and so enthusiastic that he somewhat forgot his caution, but at the end he does suddenly realise that he has perhaps written more than he intended, and he asks Layard to keep all this to himself. It is in order to inform Canning, if he should be interested – obviously because he is not a potential rival; he also promises to tell Layard what he may need to know when they meet later, but 'pray do not communicate the contents of my letter in your correspondence either with Birch or Norris'.[130]

It is frustrating to read letters like this, which appear to contain a great deal of information in the form of lists of names which Rawlinson claimed to have read, but which is entirely silent with respect to actual, precise readings of textual passages. His speculations continue in the following letters, but hard facts are still extremely rare. He notes that royal names 'are expressed almost always either partially or wholly in bona fide *ideographs* – that is by signs, which have no doubt phonetic power, but which are not used phonetically in these cases, but rather as symbols or ideographs of the Gods'.[131] Yet, when he finally produces a king-list the following year, he reads the names phonetically.

All of the kings belong to the same dynasty, he says, and this ruled from about 1400 to 800 BCE, ending with Sardanapalus; in fact, Rawlinson is again poring over his Greek texts looking for clues, especially Polyhistor who is now the great authority. Having concluded his work on the Nimrud texts, he started making an analysis of the Khorsabad ones, but found it much harder; he praised the text on the Black Obelisk for its 'severe simplicity' which would in fact allow anyone to grasp its general meaning without being able to read any of it:

> I shall not be at all surprised to see Hincks come out with something good. As far as analysis goes he may have made the same progress as I have. The only advantage I must necessarily have is in my alphabetical key and in a few hints towards translation afforded by the Bisitun Babylonian. However I hope to explain all this to you when we meet at Mosul.[132]

In this phase of his work the interpretations of individual features keep changing, and his theories develop continually. Shortly before his departure from Baghdad he has returned to the matter of the name of the king who built the Northwest palace at Nimrud, and he now reads it Sardanapal! On the other hand, Nineveh is now Kuyunjik, and he is certain that this city was much older than Nimrud: it was

> the usual place of residence of kings who built palaces at Nimrud & you are certain therefore of finding records there of the early kings if you only dig in the right place. At present you are merely excavating a Palace of the son of the Khorsabad King, built perhaps 1000 years after the original foundation of the city.[133]

Unfortunately, we do not have copies of the letters Layard sent in reply to these accounts from Baghdad, but it seems that he must have expressed some doubts about various points. Layard had a unique knowledge of the sites and the buildings, and he felt less than enthusiastic about some of Rawlinson's theories. The major was not amused and wrote:

> You do not appear to appreciate the progress now made in reading, or at any rate in understanding the Inscriptions – there is no occasion now to have recourse to secondary data, the Inscriptions tell their own story and connect all the names ... in one continuous line of 10 kings.[134]

These 'secondary data', now no longer of any interest or importance, are not further defined, but Rawlinson clearly refers to the archaeological finds, buildings, reliefs and so on. For him only the texts were important, for they constituted history, and history alone can justify their pursuit in Assyria and is of any relevance to modern man. In this way the two men obviously had to disagree and probably clash with each other, for Rawlinson's views reduced Layard's efforts and ambitions to unimportance. We already know from the previous correspondence that he regarded Assyrian art as utterly valueless, *as art*; the reliefs may be of interest as illustrations to a historical analysis, but the texts obviously are of infinitely greater importance in such a perspective.

Rawlinson represents the dominant attitude in his country and his time, even though he held unusually strong and, one must say, somewhat naive views. For an Englishman, or any educated European, world history was a well-defined process, with a beginning, a middle and a provisional culmination – the best of all worlds, which was realised in the present. 'Culture' is Europe, all other traditions must be measured against it and will invariably fail. With the Parthenon sculptures as the artistic culmination and the perfect example it goes without saying that all other artistic traditions pale into insignificance. Victorian England knew the end result, and the proper task was therefore to uncover all the interesting – but in themselves unimportant – equations which together led to this result.

This traditional view of history clashed with a more nuanced, less Eurocentric one in the meeting between the two men. In contrast to Rawlinson Layard was genuinely fascinated and impressed by the Assyrians and their art, not simply as a stage on the route, but as an independent human and artistic phenomenon. This may be connected with their different personalities, backgrounds and so forth, and probably also with the practical relationship each man had to the remains of the past. Rawlinson had his entire understanding of the ancient Assyrians from his studies at the desk, whereas Layard had been digging and uncovering their palaces and their reliefs.

To others the most important practical consequence of Rawlinson's theories concerned chronology. Canning wrote an ironic letter after he had spoken to Rawlinson in Constantinople and been informed of his new views:

> I know not how to console you for the loss of those fifteen centuries of which Major Rawlinson is determined to curtail you. Your disinterred monarchs are getting quite modern in our enlightened apprehension, and we are in danger of losing half our respect for their antiquity. Pisani [a man at the embassy] begins to think that he remembers the youngest of them. ... I can recommend nothing better than that you should find an antediluvial dynasty as fast as possible either under the old mound or somewhere else.[135]

Very funny. One of Layard's friends at the embassy, Longworth, wrote about the same matter and expressed his confidence that Layard would pay no attention to Rawlinson's theories, 'as you will feel pretty certain that in the course of another revolving moon he will probably make out these remains to be fifteen centuries older than you presumed them to be'.[136]

Of course, Rawlinson was on the right track, even though he did not go far enough since the Northwest palace must be dated to roughly 900 BCE, but it was in fact a little odd that everybody turned this against Layard, for the major had been just as certain of a much older date for the palaces. Moreover, it is uncertain where those 1,500 years really came from, for Layard had hardly suggested a date that remote for the palaces at Nimrud. The fact is, that Assyria was now seen as Layard's personal domain, so the age of the buildings reflected upon his prestige. Obviously, he would want them to be as old as possible, the more ancient the more interesting. Rawlinson's new dates could therefore serve to take Layard down a peg, duck the newly famous young man a little. Jealousy was a key concept in the relationships which connected these men. Rawlinson acknowledged as much in a letter he wrote to Layard from Constantinople, describing his view of Canning:

> Your previous letters and explanations had prepared me for Sir Stratford's sly remarks – but I am I confess astonished to find feelings of jealousy in such a man as the Ambassador.[137]

Such emotions had flared up also in London while all this went on. In his rectory at Killyleagh in County Down Hincks had been reading Layard's book, and he had been upset by being ignored. The old Irishman felt that Layard had treated him unfairly by giving priority to Rawlinson for a number of discoveries he had made himself. He sent a letter to the *Literary Gazette* in which he expressed his disappointment at seeing his own discoveries awarded to another person; it is quite a reasonable and calm note, except perhaps for one passage which grated on the ear of any Englishman, not least of Rawlinson:

> It was not likely that an author who sought popularity at the present time in England, should, without necessity, have introduced the name of a native of unhappy Ireland; – one who had not, like Major Rawlinson, the good fortune to be so long transplanted from it, that his connexion with it by birth might be forgotten.

This was paranoia and surely unfair to Layard who would hardly have been led by such political concerns and awarded the honour for what an Irishman had done to an Englishman. Considering the relationship between the two countries at the time it is understandable that Hincks might have such a suspicion – even a paranoid can be persecuted – but after this passage it did not help much that he acquits 'the author of having been intentionally guilty of this injustice'.[138]

Hincks mentioned two points, which may seem trivial: who had first read the name of the king Nebuchadnezzar, and who had first realised that the inscription on a clay barrel was partially identical to the text on a stone tablet which was in East India House in London. Each of these observations had some significance for the further understanding of the script, especially the last point, because it provided a direct link between the cursive script used on clay and the monumental one found on stone. Rawlinson had in fact privately acknowledged that it had been of very great importance for him:

> How Dr. Hinkes succeeded in sinking his first shaft, I hardly understand – but sunk it he certainly has, and unless I look about me, he will anticipate all I have to say on the subject. I am indebted to him indeed for a most notable discovery, one in fact which has proved of more use to me even than

my Behistun key. In his letter of July 18th to the Editor of the *Literary Gazette*, I found it stated that the fragment in Porter, Plate 78. Vol 2, at which before I had hardly looked, contained a transcript in the cursive character of passages of the great Inscription at the India House. Once put upon the scent, of course I immediately detected the parallel passages.

(Davidson 1933: 138)

It may seem almost comical to focus so much attention on such points, but let us remember that even today we know of academic conflicts over the right to scientific insights, and where these now concern fields such as medicine or particle physics, in 1850 the decipherment of cuneiform was clearly a matter which was expected to be of sufficient public interest to make it worthwhile debating such points in a leading magazine.

Rawlinson wrote to Layard that the proper reading of the name Nebuchadnezzar had probably been independently established by both men, which is possible; but his claim to have been the first to have noticed the identity of the two texts is contradicted by his own letters. He may of course have forgotten how he knew this, but there is certainly room for doubt about his sincerity.[139]

Otherwise Rawlinson's letter from Constantinople was friendly in tone and it is impossible to read any indication of disagreements between the two men into this text. They kept up the façade and chose as good Englishmen 'to disagree without being disagreeable'.

CHAPTER TWENTY-FOUR

RAWLINSON IN PARADISE

—— •◆• ——

The major had lived in the East for more than twenty-two years, so his return to London was one of the crucial events in his life. He was already a well-known figure in learned circles in London, the admired translator of the old Persian inscription at Bisutun, and the writer of a number of articles in the journals of the Royal Geographic Society and the Royal Asiatic Society. He slipped with ease and pleasure into the social life of London, the intelligent, learned and incredibly erudite soldier who had seen and experienced so much in the Empire. A portrait from this year shows us the forty-year-old major, a sensitive man with a surprisingly youthful, almost childish face, who sits leaned over his notebooks and copies of Persian cuneiform inscriptions (see Figure 24.1).

He became a member of the Athenæum Club, one of the respectable clubs which stood for learning and solidity, and here he could have daily encounters with many of the leading scientists, scholars and intellectuals of the day. Darwin came here regularly, and he loved it; when he dined here it made him feel 'like a gentleman, or rather like a Lord', he confessed (Desmond and Moore 1992: 253). It was a grand meeting place for London's elite, located in a palatial building at Waterloo Place, looking out over the Mall to St James's Park. The house had been built in 1830 and its façade was marked by an enormous Doric pillared entrance; inside one found oneself in a hall designed to look like the Temple of the Winds in Athens, where marble pillars with golden capitals support a carved ceiling. On the left a door leads to the large dining room in Pompeian style with five tall windows towards the garden; a monumental staircase under a chandelier 18 m above the floor leads to a landing where a statue of Athena surveys the hall. Up here one finds in the whole width of the building a sitting room with twelve pillars, red damask walls and three large marble fireplaces. Rawlinson's first letter to Layard from London was sent from here.

He explains that he has visited the British Museum without meeting anyone interested in cuneiform matters. He was not very impressed with the Museum, which he presumably saw for the first time in his life. He had been shown round by Norris from the Asiatic Society, but apart from the library it all seemed somewhat a joke compared with the museum in Berlin, which he had visited on the way. He was particularly irritated to find the Assyrian monuments so miserably displayed, and to see that the best reliefs had still not arrived.

Figure 24.1 Rawlinson in London in 1850, by Thomas Phillips. The famous and learned colonel sits with his notebooks and copies and is clearly quite satisfied with his results. (From Rawlinson 1898: 164)

The most important thing is, however, that he is going to have 'a night at the Asiatic Soc. on the 17. of January, when all the Savans in turn are to attend & I am to explain the obelisk and give a general sketch of my notions on Assyrian history'.[140] This was going to be the real test. A lot was at stake for him, for this was his opportunity to make a truly positive impression on all the men in London who meant anything.

Lord Ellesmere, president of the society, led the meeting, which was a resounding success for Rawlinson. He presented in detail his readings and interpretations and dazzled his listeners with his erudition. Birch from the British Museum wrote to Layard the following day, explaining that 'all London was moved' by the Major's lecture. 'I was highly delighted & astonished – and am even now writing to see the machinery. It is a most triumphant discovery – and will make the French & Germans stare'.[141]

Rawlinson explained to his audience that the large Assyrian ruin mounds could now be given their proper names: Nimrud was Calah, whereas Nineveh should be sought in the depths of Nebbi Yunus; Kuyunjik was a suburb of Mespila, a some-what bizarre notion which reaches back to the account of Xenophon. Khorsabad was an independent city named presumably after a king by the name of Sargon – a happy guess. These identifications represented a radical break with the previous theories, first of all those propounded by Layard who maintained that Nimrud was the original Nineveh.

Rawlinson next approached the question of chronology, the complex issue which contained so much potential controversy. He now dated Layard's palace at Nimrud to the 13th or 12th centuries BCE, and he still maintained that the kings who appear as the enemies of the Jews in the Bible were not attested in any material. Therefore, the Sargon who gave his name to Khorsabad obviously had to be a namesake of the one who is found in the Old Testament. But now for the first time we are finally told how he read the names of the Assyrian kings, for it was clear he had to present a dynastic list – even though he cautiously stressed the uncertainties involved in the reading of names. His list was the following: Hevenk I, Alti-bar, Assar-adan-pal (who was identical with Sardanapal of the Greek traditions), Temen-bar, Husihem and finally Hevenk II. The king who built the Northwest palace at Nimrud was therefore Assar-adan-pal or Sardanapal. All of the kings belonged to the dynasty which started with the (probably mythical) figures Ninus and Semiramis; they did not, however, belong at the beginning of this line, but rather at the end. The builder of Nimrud was not identical with the last king who had the name Sardanapal, the depraved ruler who perished in the flames; it had to be an earlier ruler of the same name.

Not one of these names was correctly read or interpreted. The only one which comes close was Assar-adan-pal, whose name should really be read Ashur-nasir-pal. The first element, the divine name Ashur, had been correctly interpreted by Hincks long before this. It is interesting to consider how Rawlinson reached such readings as Hevenk or Husihem for names which should have been read Adad-nirari and Shamshi-Adad; the latter was written with five signs which we may render with their common phonetic values as:

AN - UTU - SHI - AN - IM

The first of these signs is a determinative indicating divinity, so that the second sign is marked as the ideogram for a god; in this case it is the divine sun whose name was Shamash. The third sign is a phonetic marker which indicates that the preceding word ends with the syllable /shi/, which tells us that the word *Shamash* was to be read *Shamshi*. We then have the determinative for god again and finally the ideogram for the weather-god Adad. The name therefore is to be read *Shamshi-Adad*, which means 'The god Adad is my sun'.

^{d}Shamshi^{shi-d}Adad

Rawlinson knew that the first sign was the divine determinative, but he read the god's name 'Husi'. The ideogram for the sun-god can be read in various ways, for instance as UTU, UD or U, and he then combined this with the nearly correct reading 'SI' of the third sign. Again, in the case of the name of the weather god Adad he was both right and wrong: the sign does have the reading IM or EM when used phonetically, so his 'Hem' was not far off the mark. His real problem was of course that he was unable to combine his various more or less correct observations to form a correct whole, for he was blocked by the complexity of the ideograms.

The important thing was, however, that the learned and influential Londoners felt convinced that this man knew what he was talking about. The head librarian of the British Museum, Sir Henry Ellis, expressed his great joy and satisfaction with the lecture, but he still found grounds for some reservations, pointing out that much was so speculative that 'we are still not in a luminous condition'.[142]

Rawlinson was immediately asked to give a further lecture in the middle of February, and this time the chair was to be taken by none other than HRH Prince Albert. The report on this meeting in *The Athenæum* is enormous and extremely detailed, for this was clearly a matter which was felt to be of the highest interest to the reading public.[143] The presence of the Royal Consort on the podium obviously lent a special significance to the event.

The walls of the room were hung with a series of paper casts of original inscriptions, most of which came from the investigations of the speaker of the evening. The main attraction was naturally the cast of the Babylonian column of the Bisutun inscription made for him by a couple of Kurdish boys. Rawlinson claimed that this was as important for the decipherment of cuneiform as the Rosetta stone had been for the hieroglyphs. The gathering had an opportunity to study these paper mouldings, which convincingly demonstrated the scope of the major's intellectual achievement in making sense of such materials.

According to the report Rawlinson began with an account of the very foundation for his decipherment, explaining how some one-hundred signs could be read on the basis of parallels in the Persian inscriptions, while nearly fifty further signs could be interpreted on the basis of 'a diligent collation of inscriptions'. In his view the writing system was of Egyptian origin and consisted of a mixture of ideograms, syllabic signs and what he called 'literal characters', by which he meant letters in the alphabetic sense. He could not accept that it was entirely syllabic in its phonetic part, even though

Figure 24.2 Scene from the British Museum in 1850, from *Illustrated London News* (26 October 1850: 332). The British archaeologist Campbell Thompson remarked that 'these enormous Assyrian bulls had something very much in common with the ponderous, conservative philosophy of the Mid-Victorian period, with its unshakable faith in this best of all possible worlds, with its definite social castes duly prescribed by the Catechism, all doubtless to be maintained *in saecula saeculorum*' (Thompson and Hutchinson 1929).

there was, no doubt, an extensive syllabarium; and the literal characters, more-over, required a vowel sound either to precede or follow the consonant; but such vowel sound was rarely uniform, – and he preferred, therefore, distin-guishing the literal signs as sonant and complemental, and leaving the vowels to be supplied according to the requirements of the language.

This was one of the fundamental flaws in his system, and one that held him back from a true breakthrough.

He proceeded to give an elaborate account of the language which resulted from his readings. The Bisutun inscriptions, he could explain, pointing to the cast on the wall, had allowed him to make a list of more than 200 Babylonian words, 'of which the sound was known approximately and the meaning certainly'. He stressed that the decipherment was far from finished, but he claimed nevertheless to be able to 'interpret the historical inscriptions pretty closely, and to ascertain the general purport of any record of whatever age, or on whatever subject'.

He now knew that the language was Semitic in nature, and he could describe Babylonian grammar 'in considerable detail', as the reporter wrote. The verbal forms were then analysed 'with even greater minuteness' – and one now senses that the reporter feels he could live with a slightly less detailed account; what did the righteous Prince on the podium think? Did he perhaps feel that he now knew more about Babylonian grammar than he needed to know? Rawlinson went on, classifying conjugations and distinguishing persons by affixes and number by suffixes. Despite the details, however, he admitted that the verb was characterised by 'the singular want of precision . . . in failing to discriminate between past and present time'. He concluded that these languages were the most primitive Semitic tongues known.

He then embarked on a historical analysis, which meant that he had to consider Hincks' theories. The old Irishman had claimed that the biblical kings Sennacherib and Esarhaddon had built the palace at Kuyunjik and the Southwest palace at Nimrud, and Rawlinson went through the arguments *pro et contra*. Two points seemed to him decisive and led him to reject Hincks' theory: one was his (erroneous) reading of the names of the later Assyrian kings as *Arko-tsena* for Sargon (as we now know), *Bel-adonim-sha* for Sennacherib, and *Assar-aden-assar* for Esarhaddon; and the other argument was that

> there were many cuneiform records of Assyrian kings posterior to the builders of Khorsabad and Koyunjik; and these kings were evidently not less celebrated warriors than their predecessors. If then the line he was now considering were really Shalmaneser, Sennacherib, and Esar-haddon, who, he asked, were the later monarchs?

In fact, there was only one important king who came later, Esarhaddon's son and successor Ashurbanipal. Rawlinson admitted that this reasoning did not amount to a direct proof that Hincks was wrong, but he felt personally convinced that the Assyrian kings must be dated to the period 1250–1100 BCE and that the biblical kings remained unattested in the Assyrian texts.

One gets the impression that the meeting must have lasted for hours, for after this he is said to have presented a detailed account of all the inscriptions from Khorsabad, after which he 'continued to describe all the campaigns of the Assyrian monarchs in succession'. He then went into the question of the so-called 'Scythic' element in the writing system, which he said was due to the nomads as opposed to the sedentary people, irrespective of 'nationality'. He proceeded to discuss the texts from Van, after which he passed to Babylonia, where he spoke at length about Nebuchadnezzar. The name Babel was never used until this king, previously having been called Shinear. He ended with the texts from Susa which were quite distinct, and he concluded his lecture with a plea for many more texts and research.[144]

Was anyone awake at the end of all this? Or should we assume that the gentlemen in their stiff collars and whiskers hung on his lips and swallowed every word with passionate interest? In any event, Rawlinson had now proven himself, behaving in a competent and intelligent manner, sufficiently convincing to persuade his

Figure 24.3 Letter from Samuel Birch, who liked to use the official stationery of the British Museum, dated 2 March 1850. Reproduced by courtesy of the Trustees of the British Library.

audience to accept him and have trust in his theories. Layard's publisher Murray was apparently not present at the meeting, but he explains how Lord Ellesmere said that Rawlinson read the inscriptions 'like an old newspaper'. He was in great request in London Society – 'in fact a *lion* of the Season. He has dined with me only once – I got Bunsen, Grote, Murchison, Dean Milman & a few more to meet him'.[145] Fine company, indeed, with leading historians and intellectuals who were happy to be introduced to the learned major.

And Layard sat in Mosul reading these accounts, thinking back on his own year in London and England. Clearly, this was the moment when the rewards could be reaped, and it was his own book which had laid the foundation for the enormous interest in which Rawlinson could now bask. Layard had to read the newspapers and magazines in order to discover what the major had found out, for he had of course never received this information in the many letters they had exchanged. Not surprisingly, his response was somewhat sour, and he could not bring himself to accept most of Rawlinson's conclusions, in particular his theories with respect to the proper names given to the various Assyrian ruins.

Botta and Layard had of course hunted for the one city whose name everybody knew: Nineveh, and they had interpreted their finds accordingly. Their books both claimed to describe the discovery of this great, ancient metropolis: *Monument de Ninive découvert et décrit par M. P.E. Botta* and *Nineveh and its Remains*. In fact, Layard had convinced himself that ancient Nineveh had comprised the four major mounds: Khorsabad, Kuyunjik, Nebbi Yunus and Nimrud, and the fact that the first and last were separated by some 40–50 km did not bother him; the Old Testament, after all, said that it took three days to traverse the Assyrian capital. A couple of years later Joseph Bonomi in a book on the Assyrian discoveries discussed this problem in detail, comparing Babylon, Nineveh and London, a city which had grown phenomenally in the course of a few decades; Babylon covered an area of 225 square miles, he assumed, with an enormous exaggeration; Nineveh some 216 and London just 114 square miles. Bonomi suggested that the total number of inhabitants in Nineveh had been about 600,000, which was only a quarter of London's population, and he explained the enormous size with the existence of large gardens, even fields within the walls of the ancient city (Bonomi 1852: 45).

As early as 1846 the engineer Ainsworth who lived in Mosul had ridiculed the many ideas with respect to the location of Nineveh, pointing out that this city had first been located at Mosul, then Botta had moved it to Khorsabad, and now the British wanted to move it to Nimrud. As he said: 'there will be a native Nineveh, a French Nineveh, and an English Nineveh'.[146]

For Layard it was hard to get used to the idea that his beloved Nimrud was not Nineveh, but he was particularly irritated at Rawlinson's suggestion that Nebbi Yunus alone represented the ruins of the ancient capital. After all, this mound is not very large, and it '*unquestionably* forms part of the group of which Kouyunjik is the principal ruin; it is but a second building – palace or temple – of a town or the quarter of the town'. In fact, Rawlinson's notion concerning Nebbi Yunus is hard to understand, for he had after all taken a ride around the ruins, and, as Layard points out to Birch: 'Anyone examining the ruins will see at once that it *must* be of the same period as Kouyunjik'. Clearly, the major did not notice very much on his visit to Nineveh. On the other hand, Layard continued to maintain that Nimrud 'was the real capital by whatever name it may have been known and that Khorsabad and Kouyunjik are either more recent cities or quarters or royal residences added on to the old city'.[147] So, Rawlinson made Nineveh too small, Layard made it too large.

The interest created in London by the finds from Assyria was intense and in fact surprised Rawlinson. 'People talk of you more than ever I suspected, at any rate wherever I go I hardly hear of any thing else than Nineveh & Babylon', he wrote to Layard. At the same time he begged for more material, for he was clearly reaching the limits of what he had brought with him, and in order to be able to present new sensational discoveries he needed more texts from Layard. Yet, all was not Assyria for him anymore, for he found himself deeply immersed in society and even began to look with an appraising eye on available young ladies, a theme which otherwise appears to have been kept very much under control. Clearly he enjoyed the charm of female company in London, but the thought of having to return to Baghdad made him recoil:

> I don't think there is much chance of my marrying. I know Baghdad too well and besides I have seen very few girls indeed who came up to my ideal standard. Hitherto I have been going out a good deal, every night in fact to 2 or 3 places, but I am now going to shut myself up and work steadily.[148]

Birch also noted that Rawlinson was so popular that he had little time for his studies. How he enjoyed it! Apparently he did not do anything, except go from one party to the next, two or three every night, watching the elegant young ladies, making conversation with grand and admiring gentlemen in the cigar smoke, talking about his experiences in the exotic East. He rented a flat in fashionable St James's Street, on the corner of Piccadilly and just across from Albemarle Street; less than 50 m away he had the house where Layard's publisher John Murray resided – and where the firm still has its offices. He wrote to Layard, explaining that everybody was excited by his activities in Assyria, and that the reports about the discovery of the Assyrian royal throne were the constant topic of conversation. 'If you could now find Sardanapalus's toilet table or his "pot de chambre", people would be in ecstacies'. All very well, but he was the one who could write in a casual note that he had dinner at Buckingham Palace a few days before, speaking a whole hour with the queen about Nineveh and Babylon, and it was he who was to chaperone the royal family during their impending visit to the British Museum where he was supposed to guide them through Layard's reliefs.

> All classes indeed from the Queen and Duchess of Cambridge downward threaten to lay my services under contribution after Easter to act as 'showman' to the Nineveh Gallery in the Museum. Except, however in the case of the really pretty ones, like Lady Jocelyn, I shall certainly brush off this duty.[149]

In the next letter he finds London's distractions 'quite dreadful – what with visitors during the day, parties at night & the calls that other Societies make on me, I have really very little time indeed to devote to mere Cuneiform Study'. He is working on a lecture dealing with what he calls 'the Comparative Geography of Babylonia & Chaldæa' for the Royal Geographical Society, and after that he is 'doomed' to give a lecture at something called the United Service Institution, so he is quite unable to find time to finish his monograph. He has found the time, however, to escort Lady Jocelyn and Lady Eddisbury through the collections at the British Museum – 'I certainly would not do this for every one – but Lady Jocelyn is so pretty one can refuse her nothing'.[150]

Part of the summer he spent in Scotland where he visited a number of manor houses and took part in the hunts of the season, and when he returned to the leather sofas and red damask of the Athenæum Club he sat down to answer letters from Layard. It now appeared that open conflict was about to break out between the two men, and Rawlinson felt constrained to assert that he had supported and praised Layard at all times and in every connection. At one point he had accused 'others' of an excessive degree of 'over confidence' in their interpretations, but this referred to Hincks.

> I have, I believe, uniformly backed you and took occasion in my address at the United Service Institution to make your 'eloge' in due form, though really you have no need of anything of the sort – and moreover in my simplicity I fancied you rather preferred being criticised to being puffed.

But, Rawlinson! surely it is the entire situation which is beginning to unnerve Layard to such an extent that he can no longer keep his jealousy under control! Rawlinson did not understand but went on naively with more details from his wonderful life:

> I am enjoying myself most amazingly, being quite overwhelmed with attentions from all parties, that is from Princes & Dukes downwards – and really when one knows the value of these things and there is thus no danger of having one's head turned, the whole thing is very enjoyable.

He has been promoted to the rank of Lieutenant-Colonel and has hopes of a K.C.B., the only honour he has any wish to get, he says. He is now planning to spend a month in the country with his family in order to get a little work done; 'after which I shall take another month's run amongst the English country houses, shooting, talking, flirting'.[151]

Rawlinson was in Paradise and he knew how to enjoy it to the full. 'I find Society so appealing after having been for 23 years in the East, that I cannot persuade myself to stick to my closet & work', he wrote with disarming frankness.[152] Layard also heard from Murray about the impression Rawlinson was making in London as 'a man of superior intellect immense tact & great sagacity'; Murray finds him 'most agreeable in society. He is a capital Diplomat – & though I am sure up to all kinds of fun – he is too cautious to commit or compromise himself'. Moreover, his theories are generally considered sound and people 'confide in them'.[153]

Some of the more knowledgeable people had their reservations, however. Birch at the British Museum felt that 'Rawlinson gives forth very extraordinary news but he is much puzzled and vacillates in his philological ideas'.[154] Rawlinson himself did not apparently see any great problems, and his references to the only serious rival, Edward Hincks, are generally dismissive. He sees the situation as one where Hincks continues to accept Rawlinson's basic ideas – and in fact often appropriates them as his own. There is no reason to expect any great conflict between them, for the only point where they disagree now is the name of the man who built the palace at Kuyunjik; Hincks continues to claim – correctly – that it was Sennacherib, whereas the colonel maintains his position that the biblical Assyrian kings are absent from the texts.

It is of course impossible to say precisely what it was that blocked Rawlinson on this point, but it is difficult to avoid the suspicion that he was suffering from a degree of fear of too close a contact with religious issues. In fact, the now existing agreement with respect to the broad dating of the Assyrian finds was enough to create difficulties and make some people nervous. As Birch wrote to Layard, the relatively recent dates given for the palaces at Nimrud and Kuyunjik surprised many:

> Assyria compared to Egypt is a beardless boy in the History of mankind. Perhaps older remains will turn up – but is the old Biblical antiquity of Assyria and Babylon a fable? This will be no slight matter here. I expect a controversial war. I have all along foreseen it and shall hold myself still till it ensues. I am constantly consulted by both parties upon Egypt – and you are opening daily the trenches of a great religious war.[155]

Birch was in the British Museum exposed to the constant and inexhaustible interest of the general public in such questions and their religious significance. He clearly felt between the devil and the deep sea when he had to answer the urgent questions with some degree of soberness, presenting the latest scholarly theories, under pressure from both the atheists and from orthodox church groups. From his point of view it was a war. Rawlinson moved in other circles, and he had a quite different experience from his talks with cultured and wellbred people; he was met with a far more open religious attitude than he had expected:

> I have even discussed the probable spuriousness of a great portion of Daniel, with several members of the Bench of Bishops without scandalizing them & I am strongly urged by many people to put forward the arguments against the authenticity of the book in print.[156]

I hardly need to say that of course he did not do anything so rash as this. On the contrary, he now started a collaboration with his religious brother George, signing a joint contract with Murray for a new edition of Herodotus in English; the translation was to be done by George, whereas Henry was to be responsible for the geographical and historical commentary.[157]

Birch felt unable to decide whether Rawlinson or Hincks was right in the question of the identity of the palace builder at Kuyunjik, but he clearly regarded the Irishman as a minor player in the game, not in any way the equal of the colonel. Rawlinson himself characterised Hincks' latest published paper on the Khorsabad inscriptions as 'almost as wild & unintelligible' as his previous contributions; what was correct can be reduced to 'a few fortunate hits'. Layard's latest discoveries were in his opinion making it clear that his theory was correct, 'and supports me against Hincks and the French party who *will* try and force every thing into synchronism and accordance with Scripture'.[158]

It is in fact rather surprising that Rawlinson can maintain such a negative attitude towards Hincks at this time, especially in view of the fact that already in May 1849, nearly a whole year before the major's famous lectures, Hincks had given a lucid presentation of the principles of cuneiform in a lecture to the Royal Society of Literature in London. True, the lecture as such was not published at the time, and it had been announced under a rather misleading title, but the *Literary Gazette* had carried a very extensive report of the main points, and these amounted to a succinct analysis of the character of the Assyrian script. Moreover, Hincks had anticipated Rawlinson's conclusions concerning the nature of the language as Semitic, 'approximating to the Hebrew and Aramæan'.[159]

The rivalry between the two men began to draw in others, however, and the conflict broke into the open with an anonymous article in *The Athenæum* in mid-1850. The writer emphasised the huge importance of the decipherment of cuneiform, which together with the reading of the hieroglyphs was 'among the chief literary triumphs of the present age', a fact which made it even more important that the honour was given to the right person. Dr Hincks, it is claimed, occupies a foremost place among the scholars who have contributed to this breakthrough: 'Indeed, in sound scientific method, boldness of conjecture without rashness, and felicity in seizing upon such points as admit of being chronologically determined, he is unrivalled'. Rawlinson's work on the Bisutun Inscription is praised, and the fact that both men have reached nearly identical conclusions at the same time is seen as indicative of the correctness of their theories. But the decisive point is that Hincks established the understanding of 'the Ideographic element' in the writing system, a discovery which has since been 'adopted in a great measure by Major Rawlinson, who now reads, for example, Aser-aden-pal (Sardanapalus), where he previously read Ninus, thus approximating to Dr. Hincks, by whom the same name has been always read Assurhadin'. So, even though Rawlinson has undoubtedly contributed in important ways to the decipherment, it is to Hincks that the real honour should be given, and the article concludes as follows:

> Discoveries which are worth claiming ought at least to be fairly recorded.
> In the bye-ways of learning, injustice is easily and often done by mere suppression of the truth.[160]

Rawlinson saw it differently. When the two men appeared together at the annual meeting of the British Association for the Advancement of Science at Edinburgh in the summer of 1850, a society which comprised practically all branches of learning and where Hincks was one of the vice-presidents in the section on historical geography, Rawlinson 'found that the Dr had pretty well adopted all my readings and was inclined to appropriate them. There is hardly any difference now in our systems of interpretation, though my alphabet is the more extensive'.[161]

In fact, Rawlinson's position in London's society was now so well established that the strange country parson from Northern Ireland was no more than a minor nuisance. He certainly could not prevent the colonel from enjoying life to the full. Rawlinson was so pleased with his new situation that he found it distasteful to consider a return to Baghdad; actually, he admits that he dislikes the idea so much 'that I dare say when the time comes, I shall throw up'. He cannot consider more than a further two years' service on the Tigris, and only because it would give him opportunity to study cuneiform.[162]

He spent Christmas at Woburn Castle as the guest of Lord John Russell, the Prime Minister, who was promised a guided tour of the British Museum to admire the Assyrian reliefs:

he is determined to get introduced to the Nineveh marbles before the opening of Parliament & it is just as well to have him on our side if we meditate asking Govt. for any money. I thank my stars that I am entirely independent of the Trustees and can snap my fingers at them – for such a pigheaded overbearing set I never saw.[163]

Rawlinson had been in contact with them a few times and was angry because they refused to buy the collection of antiquities he had brought with him from Baghdad for £300; they tried to beat him down to two hundred, which offer he indignantly rejected. But he had also had a meeting with them where he was asked to express his views on the possibility of continuing excavations in Assyria. The Museum was considering asking for more money from the government and wanted the advice of the learned colonel. He declared that in his view there was now enough examples of Assyrian art in the Museum, but that there was a great need for more inscriptions, especially historical ones. It was therefore necessary to continue excavations in many different places, both in the north and the south. In future it would hardly be necessary to send back to England all the heavy blocks with inscriptions, and he suggested that paper mouldings would be sufficient. Apparently, it was not even necessary to make casts of the sculptures found.

Such views were expressed by others, for instance in a leading article in *The Athenæum* at the end of 1850, in which the writer declared that he was

satiated with these repeated recurrences of the same formulæ of expression, – and little disposed to recommend that an inch more of the valuable space in our Great National Building shall be given up to them. It is sufficient for the national honour that this country was among the first to possess any of these primitive specimens of sculpture, with the valuable lessons which they teach.[164]

CHAPTER TWENTY-FIVE

PALACES AND
TREASURES

—— •◆• ——

At this time Layard was busy excavating more reliefs for the Museum, making surprising and unique discoveries in these months. The palace at Kuyunjik was a lively place where room after room was being uncovered – or at least the walls which the tunnels were following were cleared, and a kind of plan began to reveal itself. Large halls, some of them perhaps interior courtyards, surrounded by suites of smaller rooms constituted a series of pivotal points in the plan of the palace, and these complexes were connected by way of narrow corridors. All walls were covered with reliefs, but many were very badly damaged; of those which were well enough preserved to allow a true impression of the large landscape scenes, one group in particular impressed Layard. There was a series of reliefs which showed the large bull colossi being transported all the way from the quarry to Nineveh where they were installed in the palace (see figure 25.1). In great detail he could study the technological feats of the ancient Assyrians and conclude that their handling of the extremely heavy bulls was almost precisely identical with his own.

The reliefs covered the walls of an entire room and showed how a bull was drawn on an enormous sled by a whole army of men who pulled on large ropes; we find ourselves close to the quarry and the men are clearly prisoners of war – Assyrian headmen and officers stand ready with their long sticks to let them fall on the backs of those who are not pulling hard enough. Others are engaged in the quarry itself, some carrying away the boulders left over from the work, and the entire scene takes place at the banks of a river (surely the Tigris) where unconcerned peasants are busy hauling water from the river up into irrigation ditches. On top of the bull one sees a small group of men who lead the enterprise with shouts and gestures, and not far away, on a small hill, stands the king himself in his chariot under a parasol, reviewing the entire procedings. Behind him are wooded hills with bushes and vines.

In another scene one sees the finished bull being installed in its final resting place. It has been raised and is supported by a wooden scaffolding, and it is being pulled in place on a sled which is drawn forward on rollers. Next to the bull one sees rows of men carrying tools and pulling carts loaded with large ropes, and there are several headmen with sticks to encourage the workers.

Figure 25.1 One of Sennacherib's bulls on its way to the palace. This scene is part of a vast composition, and in its details there are many resemblances to the mode of transportation devised by Botta and Layard. (From Layard 1849–53, II, plate 13)

It was a quite extraordinary feeling for Layard to stand here, face to face with these images which proudly tell the story of the construction of precisely the palace his men were busy uncovering. These ancient Assyrians seemed almost as fascinated by technology as Layard's own time was, and they had clearly been very practical and energetic people who took an intense interest in all aspects of their world. This was obvious also from the scenes which showed wars and conquests, for the artists had attempted to render with precision the landscapes and towns visited by the Assyrian army, giving detailed pictures of strange buildings and other people's way of dress.

He soon discovered a room which contained a description of a campaign in a mountainous country, and the journey through the wild scenery was described on the stone; birds' nests with young indicated the time of year, the windows in the local houses were shown to have had central bars in the shape of Ionic columns, and the Assyrian soldiers were carrying away booty from the conquered city such as large beds which had to be carried by two men and high-backed chairs. It was

PLAN
of
EXCAVATED CHAMBERS
of
KOUYUNJIK.
No I.

GRAND ENTRANCE

GRAND ENTRANCE

N.B. The shaded parts are the remains of building actually excavated those in outline restorations.

(The roman letters refer to the Plan
in vol. 2 of Nineveh & its remains)

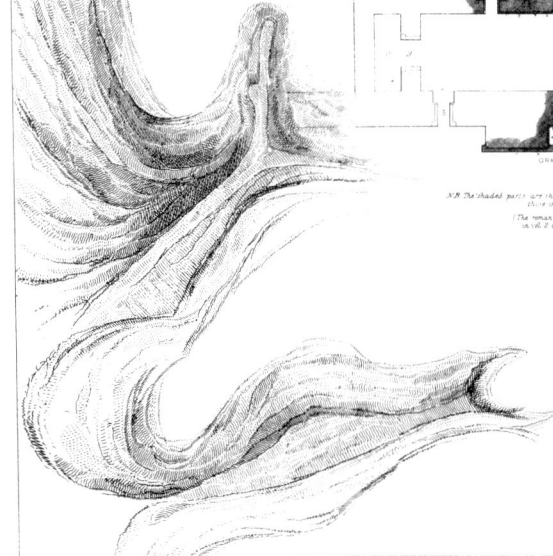

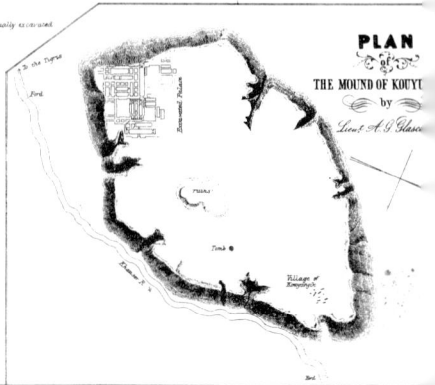

PLAN
of
THE MOUND OF KOUYU
by
Lieut. A.G. Glascock

John Murray Albemarle St. 1853

a complete world which began to reappear in these scenes, and it was quite different from what Layard knew from Nimrud.

His excavations went on without any clear plan in different parts of the building, whose shape and size it was impossible to guess. They were in the middle of the palace, but Layard wanted to find a façade, and he moved some workmen to the eastern end of the area, to a place where a large bull had been discovered in 1848 during his first expedition. They started at a spot where he assumed an important gate had been located, and it turned out that he stood by an entire façade where colossal bulls flanked several doorways; this had to be one of the main entrances to the palace, he thought (see Figure 25.2).

Botta and Flandin had found a real façade at Khorsabad, and their plans and drawings showed what Layard's must have looked like when the figures still stood in their full glory, for it was obvious that the two palaces were quite similar. There were remains of ten enormous bulls on this façade together with six very large human figures; he called these latter the 'Assyrian Hercules' – a name which is as good as any other, since we still do not truly understand the significance of these figures. It is one of the traditional heroes in Mesopotamian iconography, armed with what looks like a boomerang and holding a lion carelessly over one arm. This hero, whoever he may have been, and the large bulls were protective spirits that guarded the main doorways in the palaces (see Figure 16.1).

The entire façade could not be uncovered, for part of it had disappeared in a ravine which cuts into the mound at this spot, but Layard estimated the total length as more than 60 m; the reconstruction which was made by the architect Fergusson after Layard's ideas gives a reasonably good impression of the grandeur of the façade itself (see Figure 31.1). Admittedly, it is likely that these gates did not constitute the outer façade of the palace, but that they marked the entrance to the throne-room from a central courtyard (Russell 1991). This means that the palace continued and the building he uncovered presumably constitutes only about half of the total; much of the rest has disappeared into the ravine.

How frustrating it must have been to wander through these rooms, studying all these images – and yet not know who had built this palace! As already mentioned, Layard had suggested in his book that it could have been Sennacherib – a pure guess – and Hincks had presented a reading of the name of the builder which also concluded that it was Sennacherib. But there was very little certainty, and Rawlinson stubbornly refused to accept the idea. However, the bulls from this façade were to provide the final answer to the riddle, for they carried a long inscription between their legs, a text which finally settled the question. Layard made careful copies of

---

Figure 25.2 The vast palace of Sennacherib at Nineveh was partly excavated by Layard and Hormuzd Rassam. The plan only shows the walls, for most of the rooms were never cleared. The impressive eastern entrance at the bottom of the plan actually leads directly into the throne-room, which functioned as the link between the private sections and those areas to which visitors could gain access. The large ravine just outside the façade has destroyed what must have been a large courtyard with the outer sections of the palace (Russell 1991). Layard's plan therefore probably shows only about half of the entire complex. (From Layard 1853: 65)

this inscription, but he could not know that he was finally faced with the solution, so he had to make do with further speculations.

Also at Nimrud there were great new discoveries, and Layard travelled back and forth in order to supervise and organise. The first task was to complete the job inherited from the first expedition: the removal and transportation of the great human-headed lions from the Northwest palace. These were the sculptures which had first shown the potential of the mound, whose heads had created such commotion in Nimrud and Mosul as resurrected spirits from a distant past. They were still here, guarding the ruins of the palace, but the British Museum had expressed a distinct wish to have them brought to London. It would be in order, it was said, to saw them in half, but Layard would not contemplate such an act. These lions had a very special place in his heart, and he was deeply impressed with their beauty and perfection. In no way could he think of doing harm to them.

He had to construct a veritable highway through the palace in order to make way for their transportation down to the river, and the removal of walls which this entailed led to various interesting finds, such as a subterranean drain running underneath the unfinished Southwest palace and which was built as an arched tunnel.

At the end of January the road was ready for the lions. Layard visited them the evening before they were to be moved, watching the soft moonlight glide over

> the stearn features of the human heads, and driving before it the dark shadows which still clothed the lion forms. One by one the limbs of the gigantic sphinxes emerged from the gloom, until the monsters were unveiled before us. I shall never forget that night, or the emotions which those venerable figures caused within me.
>
> (Layard 1853: 201–2)

This was a moment for reflection, in the moonlight which threw its eerie brilliance over all of his activities here. He knew that in some deeply significant sense it was wrong to remove these monsters from their old place and drag them to London where they would stand in a different world as dead messengers exposed to the careless glance of bored visitors. As some of these ancient animals from Nimrud stand now in the noise of the British Museum, squeezed by a children's bookshop, it is hard not to regret their fate.

It took three days to transport a lion to the river, and it turned out to be such hard work that Hormuzd had to use all of his imagination and inventiveness to spur on the workers. The enormous cart which carried them kept sinking into the soft earth – the result of recent showers – and the Arabs were tempted to give up. At one point it was decided that it was the dull artist Cooper whose presence was causing all the difficulty; all the workers refused to pull any further until he had been removed from the mound, and a little later it was agreed that it would bring luck if one of Layard's guests, Charlotte Rolland, would ride the lion. She readily consented, but it did not help for long. Hormuzd then appointed a small, scrawny boy to lead the entire operation, for he was obviously the proper sheikh for such a bunch of weaklings. That brought the cart a bit further; when it stopped again he appointed a ninety-year-old man, and after that the most unpopular man among the workers was forced to lie down in front of the wheels, and he was not allowed to get up until they were right on top of him. At last, Layard had to throw off his jacket and pull on a rope himself, and after enormous trouble the exhausted men finally succeeded in getting the lions down to the riverbank.

The level of the water was extremely low at this time, however, so there was no hope that they could send them down to Baghdad on a raft as yet; Layard had to leave them here, waiting for more water in the river, and when that finally came, it turned out to be excessive – but we must not anticipate what was to happen.

New rooms in the palace were opened up during this entire process, and in one of them a large collection of metal objects appeared. Layard had to spend weeks getting these fragile things out of the ground. They were found in a rather strange room which must have been close to the outer wall of the palace towards the river and the quay; there was a well in the room, and as it was uncovered it became clear that a true treasure had been stored here. Bowls, dishes, bells and other metal objects appeared; in very large bronze bowls lay some eighty bells, cups and dishes as well as various ornaments used to decorate horses' harnesses, furniture and chariots. Lion feet from chairs and tables could be recognised from the images on the reliefs, and so could the details of elaborate harnesses – the bells belonged to them. Perhaps the most fascinating aspect was the decoration of several of the bowls and dishes, both in raised work and engraving. Some of the objects seemed almost purely Egyptian in style, others were at least heavily inspired by Egyptian art, whereas others again were Assyrian. There were two deep bowls which had medallions in very high relief and which reminded Layard of early Greek art.

Some one hundred and fifty dishes, bowls and cups came to light here, in what was often referred to as the 'kitchen'; most of the objects were in very poor condition, and this was true also of the bronze weapons found here: swords, daggers, shields, parts of chain-mail and tools such as hammers and saws. All together these objects constituted the largest treasure of metal objects ever found in Assyria, but in fact there were many other objects in the room. Several complete elephant tusks were found together with carved ivory, one object apparently an ivory sceptre. Two complete and several broken glass flasks were of quite special interest, because they carried an inscription which identified the owner of the treasure as the king from Khorsabad.

The reading of his name was not secured at this time, but it was obvious that he was the builder of Botta's palace at Khorsabad, so this gave a date for the treasure, long after the Northwest palace at Nimrud had been built. The old palace had apparently been restored by the later king, who might have used it as one of his houses while he was waiting for the new palace at Khorsabad to be completed. Layard may have known that in France scholars were now convinced that the name of this king was Sargon; in the catalogue for the new 'Nineveh Hall' at the Louvre, which appeared in 1849, the famous Oriental scholar Adrien de Longpérier wrote with cool conviction that the inscriptions referred to 'Sargon, the great king, the mighty king, king of Assyria' – and he dated him to 710–668 BCE (Longpérier 1849).

This identification and dating had a special significance for the finds Layard was making. Many of the objects had, as mentioned, a clear Egyptian inspiration and could reasonably be expected to have their origin in the Levant; it was either Sargon himself or his predecessor Shalmaneser who had captured and sacked the capital of the Jewish northern kingdom Samaria, and it was tempting to speculate whether some of the ivory objects could have come from the treasury of the palace or from the temple of that city.

Together with the glass vases he discovered a lens of rock crystal, and he thought that it had been used as a magnifier by the goldsmiths who had decorated the fine dishes and bowls. The one find that more than any other captured the imagination was the so-called royal throne. It stood in a corner of the room and could easily be made out to have been a throne, even though it was so poorly preserved that it fell to pieces at the slightest touch. It had been made of wood which was now entirely gone, but it had been decorated with bronze plates, engraved and filigree, and these were partly preserved. Layard could immediately make out that the motifs were the same he had already seen on the reliefs, especially on the embroidered ornaments on the king's dress which had been so lovingly rendered by the sculptors.

Layard appears to have found the remains of various pieces of furniture here and his reconstruction has been disputed, although there is no doubt that one of the main pieces was in fact a throne, possibly the one which had belonged to the builder of the palace, Ashurnasirpal II (Curtis 1988: 85). It must have been a masterpiece when complete, and even in its dilapidated state it was obviously a quite unique find. One cannot but sigh at the thought that it was discovered at this early time when the archaeological technique was quite incapable of handling the task of saving and restoring such an object. Layard could not extricate the entire throne, obviously, and all he could rescue were 'numerous fragments', but this discovery has also suffered a rather sad fate after his time. In 1853 he noted with bitterness that some of the fragments which he had packed with the utmost difficulty and sent to London, now appeared to be falling to pieces. Even now, one hundred and fifty years after its discovery, there is still no scientific publication of the material, neither of the throne nor of the many metal bowls and other objects (Barnett 1967; Barnett 1974; Curtis and Reade 1995: 121–7 especially 133–47). To some extent this is undoubtedly due to Layard's imperfect excavation technique, but he did what he could and cannot be blamed for later neglect.

One of the most prominent features of the mound Nimrud was the large 'pyramid' north of the Northwest palace, and it was obviously necessary to find out what was hidden here. Both Layard and Rawlinson had for some time speculated whether it could be a grave of one of the most important Assyrian kings, covered with a monumental building. The colonel had recently suggested that this was where one could find the remains of Sardanapal, and Layard had suggested that it could be the grave which had been built by Semiramis for her husband King Ninus. Old engravings which build on the Greek traditions often show this grave as a kind of pyramid just outside the walls of Nineveh.

Layard put a team to work on this mound, and they dug a tunnel straight through it without finding anything; the mound appeared simply to be a solid mass of mudbrick. A new tunnel was made at the very bottom of the mound, and here the men ran into a powerful wall of stone; as this was followed into the darkness of the mound it turned out to be a square wall which seemed to have marked the front of what could have been a large tower. Layard concluded that it was a stepped tower rather than a pyramid – several successively smaller storeys had been placed on top of each other. The top of the Black Obelisk had this shape. Layard still felt that it was a grave, and this idea appeared to be confirmed when while digging a further tunnel higher up his workers ran into a long vaulted room which ran through the building. This chamber or gallery, which was some 30 m in length, 4 m high and 2 m wide, remains a mystery. It was empty, and Layard noted that someone long ago had dug into it from the outside, presumably grave robbers. However, the building is unlikely to have been or even contained a grave, for it was the first excavated example of a so-called *ziggurat*, a type of high temple which is known to have existed in many cities in ancient Mesopotamia. The most famous example is the Tower of Babel, described by the Greek historian Herodotus, who called it the temple of Bel, 'the Babylonian Zeus':

> The temple . . . has a solid central tower, one furlong square, with a second erected on top of it and then a third, and so on up to eight. All eight towers can be climbed by a spiral running round the outside, and about half way up there are seats for those who make the ascent to rest on. On the summit of the topmost tower stands a great temple with a fine large couch in it, richly covered, and a golden table beside it. The shrine contains no image, and no one spends the night there except (if we may believe the Chaldeans who are the priests of Bel) one Assyrian woman, all alone, whoever it may be that the god has chosen.
>
> (Herodotus 1954: 86)

Such high temples make up a central part of the religious compounds in many cities, and it is a building tradition which has its roots in the very first city-states built by the Sumerians on the southern alluvial plain in the fourth millennium BCE. In this landscape, endless, monotonous and flat, such temple towers have stood out, rising above the wall of the cities and visible like small mountains over large distances. But no other *ziggurat* has contained a chamber or gallery like the one found by Layard, and there is simply no good explanation for its existence.

CHAPTER TWENTY-SIX

GUESTS

———— •◆• ————

Despite such complex and demanding tasks Layard also found the time to relax and to make explorations in Assyria. When the leading men of the Yezidi sect came to Mosul to take care of some business with the Pasha they were of course invited to Layard's house where a large feast was arranged for them in the courtyard to give them an opportunity to sample the wonders of the Turkish cuisine (see Figure 26.1). Dr Sandwith has given a lively description of the events of this night. Like all of the others, he was acutely aware of the nervousness and suspicion of the Yezidis, for under normal circumstances a member of this sect would be as good as dead if found within the walls of Mosul after dark when the gates closed. The twenty guards who escorted the priests were extremely hesitant to put away their weapons, but after a time the mood became jolly and relaxed as the dinner progressed:

> We were all seated in a large circle round the courtyard, and a crowd of servants brought in a succession of dishes overflowing with grease, which were attacked with the energy and perseverance of men who habitually lived in the saddle, and who had ridden forty miles to dinner. The feast was almost interminable, from the number of dishes, for it was a point of honour to make our guests over-eat themselves if possible. At last a huge pilau made its appearance, which is a sign of the end of the dinner, as a sweet pudding is with us.
>
> Pipes and coffee were now brought, and each guest loosed the folds of his shawl and settled down to enjoy comfortably the hour that passes between dinner and bed. Just at this time a strange muffled noise is heard at the door, as if a number of people are trying to force a passage, and yet refrain from speaking aloud, then at once bursts upon the ear a wild, unearthly yell, and a troop of half-naked Arabs, with torches in one hand and naked sabres in the other, rush in upon the Yezidees. These latter, unarmed, astonished, with faces expressing indignation and horror at being thus betrayed to death, start to their feet, mechanically search for their arms, and with their backs to the walls seem prepared to meet their fate with indignant resignation. The Arabs approach, wave their gleaming swords above their heads, and turn off suddenly, and amidst shrieks of laughter commence their war-dance.

Figure 26.1 The interior courtyard of a wealthy house in Mosul, drawn by Flandin. It was probably in such a scene that Layard's party for the visiting Yezidis took place. (From Flandin 1853–76: Plate 33)

Some little time elapsed ere the Yezidees quite recovered their equanimity, so sudden and terrible had been the start. It was a practical joke of somewhat dangerous character. Fortunately each guest was unarmed, or some one must have fallen.

Always good for a joke, that Hormuzd! For it was of course he who had arranged this little party entertainment. When all had calmed down again the night was spent with music and dancing, and the good doctor had a wonderful time:

> The whole courtyard was filled with Arabs – there were about 180 of them – many of whom held torches in their hands, whilst numbers of them joined in a wild but graceful sword-dance. Their naked limbs, the simple drapery of their costume, and their often handsome faces and figures, showed well in the torchlight. It was a beautiful sight, worthy of the pencil of Rembrandt.
>
> (Ward 1884: 68–70)

At the party were also the Rollands, Captain Stewart Erskin Rolland and his beautiful wife Charlotte (that name again), who had joined Layard's party as they passed through Mosul. This was for a time a most satisfactory arrangement, for Charlotte especially was deeply interested in archaeology and not afraid to do some hard work. Captain Rolland was fascinated with Layard and quite blinded by his personal charm and energy. His main contribution was not in the trenches, however, but he wrote a series of admiring and almost enraptured letters to friends in England, and some of these were subsequently sent to various newspapers which printed them. In one of them he wrote:

> Layard is the most delightful companion I have ever met. . . . I never in my life was so well or so happy as I am at present. My wife, too, thoroughly enjoys the wild life. . . . You can have no idea of the difficulties Layard has to contend with, or the energy, talent, perseverance and shrewdness with which he surmounts them; or the exquisite tact and good humour with which he manages the different people he has to deal with. . . . I do not believe any other man living could do it so well or at one tithe of the expense; an influence can only be acquired amongst Arabs by feasting them and making them small presents, as there is nothing they hold in such an estimation as generosity. Such, however, is the respect they hold him in, that one of his friends might travel Mesopotamia unhurt and untouched, though in the midst of tribes at war with each other.
>
> (Waterfield 1963: 204–5)

One of his letters was printed in *The Times* and created a minor sensation, both because of the admiring description of Layard and by its violent attack on the meanness of the British authorities who refused to provide him with adequate funding. Layard did not care for this kind of public interest, but Rolland was not alone in writing at this time, for several visitors from England passed through Mosul and Nimrud; after their brief visits they sat down to write an account which often contained rather inadequate and strange descriptions of the finds Layard was making. This situation in fact became rather unpleasant and led to a controversy with his employers at the British Museum, who were not happy to read in the newspapers about the fantastic discoveries being made, but which Layard had not found it worthwhile to inform them about. In March Hawkins wrote him a letter in which he told him that it would be wise to 'advise your friends at Mosul to be a little less communicative. ... Let them say as much as they please about your want of money, but you must make them dumb about your success'. He explains that reports of a wonderful throne of gold and ivory have appeared and led to all kinds of questions to the Museum.[165]

But Layard was not pleased with his employers either, and he did not like the idea of writing long reports directly to the Trustees, preferring the more informal style he could adopt in letters to Hawkins, who could then present the relevant information to the lofty gentlemen. Layard was quite aware that this was creating difficulties, for he wrote to Canning that he was 'in disgrace' with the Trustees for not 'condescending' to send home sufficiently full reports. Some of the reports which appeared in the newspapers he suspected had been planted by employees at the Museum, but he does not mention any names. He fears 'that mischief has already been done'.[166]

The articles began to create problems even in his relations with the Turkish authorities. Layard still had no official permit for the activities of his second campaign, and Canning was unable to secure one until December 1850; when it finally materialised, it was limited to only six months and there were further restrictions. The change in the Turkish attitude which was plainly to be read from this vizierial document was explained by Canning in a letter to Lord Palmerston at the Foreign Office:

> The <u>causes</u> of the change are rather to be conjectured than ascertained. Among them, no doubt, is an incipient desire at the Porte to collect materials for establishing a museum of its own. To this may be added the rival solicitations of other antiquarians, particularly of the French, and a general feeling of jealousy excited by Mr. Layard's success, and the frequent exaggerations respecting it which have figured in the public journals since his return to the field of discovery.[167]

Some of the articles contained very sharply worded attacks on the British Museum and the government for the stinginess with which Layard, it was felt, was being treated. In his own letters to the Museum he never let an opportunity pass to remind them that he had very little money, but it was of course the public debate which was an embarrassment to the Trustees, having to read in the papers about their own pettiness and lack of good will. The reports of sensational discoveries led to a new appeal to the Exchequer in March, when a further £500 was given, but in Layard's view such a small sum was practically useless, and then it was followed by a very clear statement which said that this was in no way to be seen as a commitment to continue to support the excavations.

During his first expedition Layard had been entirely on his own and had only Hormuzd to assist him, but the social situation now had changed dramatically. He experienced the effects of his growing fame in England, and all travellers in the

Near East naturally saw his excavations as an obvious stopping point; who would not want to see the intrepid young man who had overcome so many obstacles, and who could resist the thought of actually witnessing ancient palaces being taken back from the earth? There was a coming and going, which of course had its positive sides, but which sometimes could become rather tiring. The basic team was not very satisfactory either, and Dr Sandwith soon turned out to be very little help, for he had only one interest: hunting. His nephew has described his uncle's own experience as he had told it to the family:

> He was young, romantic, carried away by the novelty of the scenes through which he was passing, a keen sportsman, ignorant of Oriental antiquities, and as yet little given to political reflection. This journey was a central event in his life. The year among the Armenian mountains and in the deserts stamped itself so vividly upon his memory, that in after-years his friends and family used laughingly to charge him with beginning half his stories with the words '*When I was in Mesopotamia*'.
>
> (Ward 1884: 43–4)

The artist Cooper, who according to Sandwith was 'rather out of his element in the Desert', made his plans and drawings, but he suffered terribly from homesickness and longed for his wife in London. Captain Rolland was also interested chiefly in horses and shooting.

The real annoyance came from the Vice-Consulate in Mosul, however, where the parents of Mrs Rassam, the missionaries Badger, were staying. Like Botta before him, Layard developed an intense loathing for these people, whose bigotry and condemnation of himself and his party created constant difficulties. It is hardly possible now to unravel the various intrigues which came to characterise this excavation, but it seems clear that most of them were centred around Charlotte Rolland. Layard mentions several times how she was treated in an insolent and unfriendly manner by the women of the Rassam household. She was a beautiful, lively and charming young woman, who was probably not terribly ladylike in her fascinated immersion in the work of the excavation, and one may reasonably suspect that the severe and unforgiving Mrs Badger looked with disgust at her behaviour. It also seems clear that Charlotte had a very free and open relationship with Layard, based on a mutual affection which the people around them could not help noticing. So there probably was a great deal to talk about and be scandalised at, and the Badgers were not the kind of people who would hesitate to proclaim their views in public.

Layard did get away from Mosul several times, however, and found time to make an extended trip round Assyria, visiting other mounds. His instructions spoke of excavations in the entire region, including Babylonia in the south. He attempted to conduct an investigation of the main ruins in the north, and he had ordered his trusted foreman Awad to open trenches in a number of other mounds. One or two of them turned out to contain remains from the Assyrian period, which was shown for instance by bricks with inscriptions, but the investigations were largely unsuccessful seen from Layard's point of view. He did not discover further palaces, and that was of course what he was looking for.

He took a special interest in Khorsabad, and it was really not very proper for him to tackle this place, which was Botta's discovery and clearly a French area of interest. In his instructions Layard had been reminded that he must maintain good relations with the representatives of other European nations, and it should hardly have been necessary to stress that this meant he had to stay away from mounds which were already 'taken'. Yet, he sent a rather large team to Khorsabad to clean up and investigate various untouched parts of the ruin, and this became a quite substantial operation which involved the uncovering of new reliefs.

Botta's trenches were falling down and practically nothing remained of the reliefs he had left behind. Exposed to sun and rain the brittle stone did not last long but crumbled to dust. A few weather-beaten heads of the colossal bulls were still visible above ground, but the buildings which Layard uncovered were so destroyed that his fairly large operation in the end yielded a rather poor result. He dug a little in other mounds in the neighbourhood, but with little or no success. The only thing he could understand was Assyrian monumental architecture; prehistoric villages with modest mudbrick houses and large quantities of painted pottery did not constitute meaningful finds for him – or for anybody else at this time.

His work was hindered on several occasions by the unsettled state of affairs in the north. Bedouin from the desert operated uncomfortably close to Mosul and Nimrud, and more distant districts were often very dangerous. While Layard was staying at Nimrud in the village it was attacked one early morning, as the fog covered the steppe and hid the robbers during their approach. He woke up to the sound of gun salvoes, screams and shouts, and he rushed out to see what was going on. The situation was chaotic and dangerous, with a group of robbers who were trying to drive away the cattle of the village, while the local people attacked them with all available weapons, spears, pitchforks, sticks and guns. The vital thing for Layard was to prevent anyone from being killed, for that would automatically lead to a long feud with constant raids. He got on a horse and rode up to the leader of the raiders who had been recognised as a certain Saleh, brother of the sheikh of the Tai tribe.

> He saluted me as I drew near, and we rode along side by side, whilst his followers were driving before them the cattle of the villagers. Directing Hormuzd to keep back the Shemutti, I asked the chief to restore the plundered property. Fortunately, hitherto only one man of the attacking party had been seriously wounded. The expedition was chiefly directed against the Jebours, who some days before had carried off a large number of the camels of the Tai. I promised to do my best to recover them.

After some discussion Saleh agreed to hand back what had been taken – out of respect for Layard – and then followed a truly bizarre scene: the villagers had to point to their property in the hands of the robbers, who were not particularly happy to release the things again, and Layard's workers from the Jebour tribe now decided to create some serious havoc and had taken up position on the mound itself, ready for an attack. Others rushed up to the returning robbers, waving swords, spears and pitchforks and shouting shrill war-cries. The situation soon became very tense and the hysteria was helped by the women who rushed around among the mounted raiders and demanded their blankets and jackets and shawls. But the crisis was averted by a hare which found itself in the middle of this commotion and suddenly decided to make a run for its life, disappearing into the steppe.

> My greyhounds, who had followed me from the house, immediately pursued her. This was too much for the Arabs; their love of the chase overcame even their propensity for appropriating other people's property; cattle, cloaks, swords, and *keffiehs* were abandoned to their respective claimants, and the whole band of marauders joined wildly in the pursuit. Before we had reached the game we were far from Nimroud. I seized the opportunity to conclude the truce.
>
> (Layard 1853: 168–9)

Layard had to promise to visit the camp of the Tai a few days later in order to seal this new alliance, and he went off with Hormuzd towards the east to the large plain which surrounds the town Erbil. This was where the Tai had its pastures. The extremely rich agricultural land was full of ancient remains and Layard took the opportunity to investigate a couple of mounds, but without any luck. He returned a few months later, when he had been prevented from approaching the southern Assyrian site called Kalah Shergat which was located further down the Tigris, because the region was being raided constantly by the Shammar Bedouin. But even in the Tai district there was now war; a few days before Layard's arrival a group of Shammar had attacked some Kurdish nomads in the region, and since these had an alliance with the Tai which allowed them to graze their animals here, they were under Tai protection. The tribe therefore had to raid the Shammar in order to revenge the attack on the Kurds, but a raid led by the same Saleh had ended with a defeat and the loss of nearly fifty horses. Layard arrived at a dejected camp.

In the tent of the sheikh sat the leading men of the tribe discussing the defeat. An emissary from the Shammar had arrived together with Layard, and his task was to gather information about the captured horses. This guest was welcomed in the tent without hostility, for he was on a traditional errand whose purpose was known and accepted by all. The Iranians are known to say: 'After women, horses..'. and there were stories of warriors wounded in battle whose last words to their adversary was an account of the name and descent of the mare they were riding. After every major battle men would therefore be sent to the losers to be told about the horses, going from tent to tent where they would be well received and even invited to drink tea.

Layard continued his archaeological activities as well, visiting the important rock reliefs close to the village of Bavian which had been discovered by the French consul Rouet a couple of years before. These are sculptures from the time of Sennacherib which have been carved directly into the rock face, and which show images such as religious symbols, winged bulls and the king in cultic scenes. There are also three long inscriptions, and one of these is located in an inaccessible spot; Layard had himself lowered from above, and hanging over a deep chasm he made a copy of the text.

While he was digging and investigating and entertaining guests, the interest in his activities grew in England, where also Rawlinson's lectures and theories helped to keep the attention of the public riveted on Assyria. The number of visitors to the British Museum continued to grow, and Layard's book sold extremely well and appeared in several printings. As early as October Murray could inform him that 800 of a new printing of 2,000 had been sold, and a couple of months later it had sold out. The publisher was convinced that there was still a great interest in the book and he suggested that Layard should prepare a cheap edition, somewhat abridged and with fewer illustrations. This became the one-volume edition, published in the series 'Murray's Reading for the Rail' which was sold in kiosks all over the country in very large numbers. It was a series of 'cheap books in large readable type: suited for all classes of readers – for various tastes – and for old and young of both sexes'. The price of Layard's book of 360 pages was five shillings (Layard 1852). As long as he sat in Mosul Layard really did not have the time to revise his text, so he suggested that the second half should simply be cut away, the analytical section which had a more academic character, and that references to the Bible should be added to the running text.

He began to make real money on the book and Murray could promise him at least a further £800 for the fourth printing of the two-volume edition.[168] At the end of February the account now shows £1,276, and a new edition of 1,250 copies in print.[169] Obviously, this commercial success had to be pursued, and Layard was quite aware of where public interest lay, so he suggested to Murray that the abbreviated edition should contain descriptions of 'each Basrelief as it was discovered and pointing out what Biblical or ancient heathen custom art or fact it or any of the details illustrate'.[170] This version, which in fact included even more illustrations than the first one, became a colossal success, and a great many ladies and gentlemen must have made the long train journeys fly away by joining Layard at Nimrud and on the plains of Assyria. Murray also told Layard how he had personally experienced the immense interest which continued to be generated by the books:

> Your discoveries & all your proceedings continue to be regarded with the greatest interest in all parts of the Kingdom. I myself last Autumn was one of a numerous congregation assembled in a *wee Kirk* in a small Scotch village called Fairly ... who listened with the greatest interest to a lecture delivered by the Minister upon you & your discoveries – & the same thing has gone on in countless obscure places.[171]

CHAPTER TWENTY-SEVEN

PASTORAL

—— •◆• ——

As spring arrived Layard began to make plans for an excursion. The only major river which joins the Euphrates after it has rushed down from the mighty Taurus Mountains in southern Turkey and glides majestically through the wide Syrian steppes is the Habur. This river drains a very large area and a host of smaller streams, which have their origins in the southern slopes of the Taurus, form the sources for the Habur. The area that is touched by all this water is one of quite extraordinary fertility, and through many periods from prehistory it has been very heavily populated. At this moment the Habur region is the centre for the most intensive archaeological exploration in the entire Near East and dozens of mounds from just about every period since the earliest Neolithic are being excavated. In Layard's time, however, the area was not just unknown in an archaeological sense, it was nearly empty of human habitation.

In the autumn of 1846 Layard had visited the areas west of Mosul, without having an opportunity to investigate the Habur district itself. That time he had carried with him instructions from Rawlinson to establish precisely which rivers ran here, and he was particularly interested in finding out if the large *wadi* (a river which has water only during the rainy season) Tharthar, which runs parallel to the Tigris from north to south, was part of the Habur complex. The southernmost section of the Habur had been investigated by the British Euphrates expedition, but most of the region was virtually blank. It is extraordinary that such relatively simple geographical problems in this quite well-travelled country still lacked authoritative solutions at this time.[172]

Layard knew that a very large number of ruins were supposed to exist in the region and he had long wished to go there on an extended visit. From his Arab friends he kept hearing that the place was a veritable paradise: large forests, lots of water, wide meadows with great herds of animals. The Jebour tribe who lived around Nimrud, and whose members formed the majority of Layard's workers, had another branch which spent a great deal of time in the Habur. The chief of this group was an old acquaintance, so Layard regularly received invitations, but he did not react to these until he was also informed that two bull colossi had suddenly appeared in one of the mounds there. This clearly had to be investigated.

It was not easy to arrange an expedition to Habur, however, for Captain Rolland's claim that any friend of Layard's would be welcome among all Arabs was not only highly optimistic and exaggerated, it would have been extremely dangerous to put to the test. He knew that the Shammar tribe controlled the regions to be traversed, so it was important to secure their protection. He turned to sheikh Suttum, who was the head of one of the subsections of the Shammar, and asked for his help.

Suttum arrived at Mosul on 19 March with his camels who were to carry the large party and its baggage. There were twenty-five in all plus a large number of horses, and the group leaving Mosul counted more than a hundred people. Layard brought about fifty of his most experienced workmen, among them both Jebour Arabs, Nestorians and Yezidis; Cawal Yusuf joined them, and a number of Jebour decided that this was a good opportunity to visit their kinsmen in the Habur. Dr Sandwith, Cooper and Hormuzd were of course in the group, together with the Rollands.

Suttum, the guarantor for the safety of the caravan in the desert, was described by Layard as the perfect Bedouin, exceptionally intelligent and known for his diplomatic skill as well as for his courage in battle. He was an impressive man, despite his moderate height and a limp caused by a gunshot wound (see Figure 27.1).

> His features were regular and well-proportioned, and of that delicate character so frequently found amongst the nomads of the desert. A restless and sparkling eye of the deepest black spoke the inner man, and seemed to scan and penetrate everything within its ken. His dark hair was platted into many long tails; his beard, like that of the Arabs in general, was scanty. He wore the usual Arab shirt, and over it a cloak of blue cloth, trimmed with red silk and lined with fur, a present from some Pasha as he pretended, but more probably a part of some great man's wardrobe that had been appropriated without its owner's consent. A coloured kerchief, or keffieh, was thrown loosely over his head, and confined above the temples by a rope of twisted camel's hair. At his side hung a scimitar, an antique horse-pistol was hung by a rope tied as a girdle round his waist, and a long spear, tufted with black ostrich feathers, and ornamented with scarlet streamers, rested on his shoulder. He was the very picture of a true Bedouin Sheikh, and his liveliness, his wit, and his singular powers of conversation, which made him the most agreeable of companions, did not belie his race.
>
> (Layard 1853: 239–40)

The season is the most paradisical in this country, which most of the year lies brown and scorched, but which during its brief spring explodes in colours, fragrance and beauty. The caravan travelled through a countryside which was green and fresh, with an apparently endless carpet of grass stretching to the horizon, and whose lush green colours were only broken by splotches of large fields of bright red tulips and the shadows from the countless mounds among which they moved. It was almost impossible to keep the caravan together, for even the Bedouin could not think of the dangers of attack, so all scattered over the green carpet, singing and smiling. Suttum had to ride back and forth all the time, trying to make people

Figure 27.1   Sheikh Suttum drawn by Cooper. (From Layard 1853: 239)

understand that it was dangerous to become isolated from the group, but it was a very difficult task.

One of those furious and sudden storms, which frequently sweep over the plains of Mesopotamia during the spring season, burst over us in the night. Whilst incessant lightnings broke the gloom, a raging wind almost drowned the deep roll of the thunder. The united strength of the Arabs could scarcely hold the flapping canvas of the tents. Rain descended in torrents, sparing us no place of shelter. Towards dawn the hurricane had passed away leaving a still and cloudless sky. When the round clear sun rose from the broad expanse of the desert, a delightful calm and freshness pervaded the air, producing mingled sensations of pleasure and repose.

(Layard 1853: 242–3)

In the area south of the low Sinjar chain the landscape is dotted with ancient mounds and Layard rode among them in the company of Suttum who knew this land from his childhood and had names for every single mound. They found only potsherds, of course, and no traces of reliefs or large palaces. One of the mounds mentioned by Layard as particularly impressive has a special place in my own memory of this country. He calls it Tell Ermah, 'Mound of Spears', and explains how he and Suttum rode to it alone because it was somewhat away from the path of the caravan, but so large that it could be seen from a long distance. It was clearly worth a visit. I visited the British excavations here, directed by David Oates, in 1964, when the mound was known as Tell Rimah, and I remember a day of burning sunshine, one of those afternoons when the heat grabs you and holds you in its grip, making it difficult to breathe. I was sitting in the shade under an open tent together with Barbara Parker (later Lady Barbara Mallowan), an archaeological veteran from Assyria who had excavated at Nimrud for years; one of the other archaeologists brought us three small lumps of dirt which he claimed were cuneiform tablets, and sure enough, as they were carefully cleaned line after line appeared under the brush. This was my own first experience of a completely 'fresh' tablet which no one had read for more than three thousand years.

The British expedition to Rimah went on for several years and a number of interesting buildings were discovered, among these a large temple complex on a tall platform. This was what Layard and Suttum had seen on the horizon over the steppe. They ascended the mound and enjoyed the sight of the green land around them which spread like an endless sea. While Layard walked around and examined the mound, Suttum stayed on the summit and he spotted something which was moving towards them far away in the steppe. When Layard came up to see he was unable to determine what it was through his telescope, but Suttum's falcon eyes told him that it was a messenger from his father's camp who was coming to meet them.

The party turned northwards towards the low Jebel Sinjar with the fortified settlement at Tel Afar, the next goal for the caravan, but they did not get that far this day. They struck camp in the middle of another field of ruin mounds and received a visit of a group of Turcomans from Tel Afar, whose leader was an old friend of Layard's. They had a conflict running with the Pasha at Mosul and sought Layard's help. In the evening he climbed the largest mound and saw the sun slowly descend over the darkening steppe.

On all sides, as far as the eye could reach, rose the grass-covered heaps marking the site of ancient habitations. The great tide of civilisation had long since ebbed, leaving these scattered wrecks on the solitary shore. Are those waters to flow again, bearing back the seeds of knowledge and of wealth that they have wafted to the West? We wanderers were seeking what they had left behind, as children gather up the colored shells on the deserted sands. At my feet there was a busy scene, making more lonely the unbroken solitude which reigned in the vast plain around, where the only thing having life or motion were the shadows of the lofty mounds as they lengthened before the declining sun.

(Layard 1853: 245)

He could see not less than two hundred mounds from where he sat, a sign of the richness of the land and of its long history. But they continued on their way and soon arrived at the large Yezidi village called Mirkan; Layard had visited it earlier in the company of a Turkish Pasha who had destroyed the settlement, and the belligerent inhabitants were once again in direct confrontation with the authorities. The situation was further complicated by the fact that the village was at war with several other towns located to the north of the Sinjar chain, and there were regular raids with dead and wounded. Layard and Cawal Yusuf argued with these people and tried to make them understand that after the new agreement in Constantinople there was a real chance of peace and prosperity, if only they were willing to stop fighting. The presence of the leading Yezidi priest had its effect, and the talks ended with an agreement that peace should be established with the other settlements. This meant that the two peacemakers had to engage in a diplomatic mission to the neighbouring tribes and villages.

Apart from the constant strife and the all too common raids, the conflicts which erupted with depressing regularity among villages, tribes, religious groups, nomads and sedentary Arabs, Layard's main interest was concentrated on camels and horses. In this period, before railways and cars, most European travellers shared the Arab's intense passion for noble horses; hours of discussion and endless anecdotes about the descent, beauty, strength and stamina of individual horses took up most of the time during his visits to the tents and huts *en route*. Suttum's elder brother, Sahiman, rode a horse whose reputation for beauty, strength and speed was such that the entire tribe's self-definition hinged on it, and it was easily the most admired horse in the Syrian desert. Suttum himself rode a so-called 'deloul', a fast dromedary which normally carried two riders and which was nearly as highly prized as a fine horse.

When the caravan arrived at the camp of Suttum's father they were received with a gigantic feast, and as the companion of Charlotte Rolland Layard was allowed to visit the women's tent. With enthusiasm he describes the beauty of the young girls, their skin, the large almond eyes which are so expressive and shine with an incredible radiance and fire; their black, thick hair falls in masses of curls down their backs, and their carriage is proud and graceful. But, sadly, their beauty lasts only until the end of their early youth, and with few exceptions they quickly change into 'the most hideous of old hags, the lightning-like brightness of the eye alone surviving the general wreck'.

Suttum's wife Rathaiyah was one of these not quite young women, even though she had retained much of her previous beauty.

There was more than the usual Bedouin fire in her large black eyes, and her hair fell in many ringlets on her shoulders. Her temper was haughty and imperious, and she evidently held more sway over Suttum than he liked to acknowledge, or was quite consistent with his character as a warrior.

(Layard 1853: 264)

She was in fact his second wife, but her power was such that shortly before this time she had forced him to return his first wife, who was younger than herself, to her family. Obviously she had got rid of what she must have considered a dangerous rival, but since the younger wife now lived in a camp in the Habur area, there was an evident risk that Suttum would be reunited with her there. Accordingly, the dominating lady had insisted on following the caravan all the way to its destination. Layard had no problem with this, of course, and may have found the situation amusing, but difficulties soon arose. Rathaiyah refused to sleep in the tent Layard had offered Suttum, an ordinary white tent which closed in the normal English way at the ends; she went so far as to leave Suttum's bed in the night and sleep under the open sky on the grass – and one may imagine what kind of gossip this would have caused if others noticed! Her view was that it was improper for a true Bedouin to sleep in a closed tent, something fine ladies from the city could do, so Layard had to exchange Suttum's tent with a traditional black tent which had been given to the kitchen personnel. Here, in a tent open to all sides, she claimed that she could again breathe and feel like a Bedouin.

One day they ran into a group of Shammar Arabs from another branch of the tribe. They were on their way north, having just robbed a Turkish government caravan, and many of them were grotesquely dressed in various military uniforms which they had taken from the dead soldiers. Their action would obviously result in strong military reprisals from the Turks, and the other branches of the Shammar had tried in vain to get their kinsfolk to hand back what they had stolen. In fact, this meant they were in direct confrontation with the paramount chief of the Shammar, and Suttum's protection was very precarious in such a situation. It was a tense and unpleasant meeting, where the possibility that Layard's company were going to be the next victims was a constant threat, and it was extremely unpleasant to have these wild men strut around the camp, fingering everything with lusty eyes, especially the clothes of the English visitors; they wanted to know all about their price and quality. In the end nothing happened, however. On the other hand, the riches of Habur were now truly becoming evident. The horses of the caravan moved through endless fields of flowers and they could soon see the river in the distance.

The Khabour flows through the richest pastures and meadows. Its banks were now covered with flowers of every hue, and its windings through the green plain were like the coils of a mighty serpent. I never beheld a more lovely scene. An uncontrollable emotion of joy seized all our party when they saw the end of their journey before them. The horsemen urged their horses to full speed; the Jebours dancing in a circle, raised their colored kerchiefs on their spears, and shouted their war cry, Hormuzd leading the chorus; the Tiyari sang their mountain songs and fired their muskets in the air.

(Layard 1853: 269)

249

Figure 27.2 The Arban mound on the Habur. Part of the mound has been eroded by the river, and this had revealed the Assyrian bulls. (From Layard 1853: 273)

Shortly afterwards they reached their final destination where they were received by sheikh Mohammed Emin. He pointed to the large mound which was on the other side of the river and pointed out the two bulls which were the direct cause of Layard's visit. The mound was directly on the river, which had undermined part of it and thus uncovered the bulls (see Figure 27.2). They stood a little above the water and waited, but since the mound was on the right, northern bank of the river which could not be crossed at this time, Layard's caravan struck camp opposite the ruins. As his tent had been raised, visitors began arriving with gifts, of which the most important was a falcon named Fawaz. It came originally from the region around Takrit on the Tigris, and it had first been given to Firhan, the paramount chief of the Shammar, by Sadoun-el-Mustafa, chief of the Obeid tribe; it had then been presented to Moghamis, Suttum's uncle as a sign of friendship, and he now offered it to Layard. It was placed on its stand in the middle of the tent and it remained with Layard during his entire stay in the country.

The following day they crossed the river and established their camp next to the mound. Layard had planned carefully and was able to settle as a true sheikh; a tent which could contain nearly two hundred people was set up close to the river in order to function as *museef*, the formal reception area where he could entertain guests; his own tent was placed at the very back of the camp where no one else was allowed to come, giving him an opportunity to retire whenever he wanted to be alone. He also normally had his meals here, often in the company of Suttum and Mohammed Emin – and of course the other Europeans. Dr Sandwith had a special tent where he could receive patients, and there was no shortage of those. The black Bedouin tent of Suttum was placed at the very outskirt of the encampment, so that Rathaiyah could avoid contact with the other members of the party.

The first day Mohammed Emin arranged a large party for Layard's company, and his own *museef*-tent soon became a favourite goal for visitors from all around, people who wanted to have a look at this unusual guest. A sheep was always slaughtered when such visitors arrived, and if the party could not eat it all, the rest was given to the workers, since it was regarded as unacceptable to keep food for the next day. Layard had ample opportunity to study local custom and made elaborate notes about cooking, diseases, childbirth, the beloved dromedaries, warfare in the desert and so forth.

Suttum's family problems blossomed when they arrived at Arban. His young wife Adla with her small child had fled to her father Moghamis, and Layard was asked to try to organise some kind of agreement with Suttum and especially his new wife. In the end it was Hormuzd who took the matter in hand.

> The Sheikh was afraid to meet Adla, until, after much negotiation, Hormuzd acting as ambassador, the proud Rathaiyah consented to receive her in the tent. Then the injured lady refused to accept these terms, and the matter was only finished by Hormuzd taking her by the arm and dragging her by force over the grass to her rival. There all the outward forms of perfect reconciliation were satisfactorily gone through, although Suttum evidently saw that there was a different reception in store for himself when there were no European eye-witnesses. Such are the trials of married life in the Desert!
>
> (Lanyard 1853: 301)

In fact, Layard had not too dissimilar problems rather closer at hand, as can be seen from his diaries and letters. His relationship to the beautiful Charlotte Rolland developed into a mutual attraction which began to have an influence on her husband. In the middle of April Layard took her on a trip to Moghamis' camp which was located a couple of hours' ride from Arban; they rode together with Suttum, and Layard had Charlotte behind him on his newly acquired *deloul*.

> The face of the Desert was as burnished gold. Its last change was to flowers of the brightest yellow hue, and the whole plain was dressed with them. Suttum rioted in the luxuriant herbage and scented air. I never saw him so exhilarated. 'What Kef (delight)', he continually exclaimed, as his mare waded through the flowers, 'has God given us equal to this? It is the only thing worth living for. Ya Bej! what do the dwellers in cities know of true happiness, they have never seen grass or flowers? May God have pity on them!'
>
> (Layard 1853: 301)

In his diary Layard wrote that he 'never saw anything as beautiful as the desert today', and he noted that 'Charlotte's good nature and kind manner had made a great impression on the Arabs' (Waterfield 1963: 210).

His main concern was, of course, archaeology and during the three weeks which they spent at Arban he investigated the mound with vigour. The two bulls had only been partially uncovered by the landslide, and as they appeared it became clear that they were both smaller and more primitive in style than the ones from Nimrud and Kuyunjik. To begin with he saw them as older than the other finds he had made, coarser and rather clumsy in their rendering of anatomical detail. They carried a brief inscription, and he could see that it was the regular formula which was supposed to mean 'Palace of ...'. The name was different, however, and he noticed that there was no royal title after it, nor the name of the country ruled from the palace. He was therefore not certain that he was dealing with the name of a king.

There were apparently no walls associated with the two bulls, and the excavations were extremely difficult since the Assyrian levels were almost at the bottom of the mound which towered over the bulls to a height of many metres. Clearly, this place had been continually inhabited for a very long time after the Assyrian period, and there was a succession of levels on top of the ruins he was interested in. At the very top there was in fact the remains of a medieval minaret from a long disappeared mosque. There was no other way than depending on the technique which had already been practiced at Kuyunjik: tunnelling. They began to dig their way through the mound.

After five days they ran into a new couple of bulls, identical to the others and carrying the same inscription, but Layard's workers still could not find any walls. Also, it seemed that there were no reliefs in the building which the bulls somehow had to be associated with. Instead, his workers found a lion which in size and style corresponded exactly with the bulls. They also discovered a stela which was badly damaged; it had a rounded top and a carving of a male figure, but there was no inscription. Together with some minor finds this was the result of Layard's Assyrian excavations at Arban; finds from other periods were made, though, and the most interesting was a small collection of Egyptian scarabs, most of them dated to the reign of Thutmosis III, i.e., the fifteenth century BCE. Egypt had then had a brief period of imperial expansion into the Syrian area.

Layard concluded that Habur yielded far fewer antiquities than expected, and it is fair to say that his expedition as an archaeological venture was a failure. His method of excavation was not at all suited for a mound like Arban, where there were no monumental buildings with stone walls as in Assyria proper. Three weeks is naturally a very brief period for a real excavation, even if one uses one hundred workmen. Modern archaeologists know from bitter experience how one can dig for several seasons at a site before one *perhaps* makes the discoveries that were anticipated. Later excavations at Arban (now known as Tall Ajaja) has shown it to contain the ruins of an Assyrian provincial capital called Shadikanni, and the name on the bulls is to be read Mushezib-Ninurta. He was the local governor here around 800 BCE at a time when the central power in Assyria was partially paralysed, and he was therefore able to grab so much local power that he could set up monuments in his own name (Mahmoud and Kühne 1993–4).

When the excavations were given up Layard's company took a tour of the region to look at other mounds, and also to visit the volcano called Kawkab, 'The Star', which is a dominant feature of this part of the desert. The mood in the party was somewhat depressed, and Layard's irritation with Captain Rolland, Cooper and Dr Sandwith continued to grow. Apart from making his drawings Cooper was of no use whatever, and Sandwith was obsessed with his shooting rifle; hunting was all he cared about. This was not the kind of company Layard wanted around him after the disappointments of Arban. To make things even worse, Hormuzd suddenly came down with a violent attack of fever which forced them all to stop for several days.

Shortly after his return to Mosul Layard wrote a letter to his friend Ross which contains not the slightest hint that he was having difficulties with the Rollands; in fact, he thinks that they

> appear to have enjoyed themselves exceedingly. She is very delicate, but a very nice person and anxious to do everything. She was very much admired by the Arabs – and used to ride with me on a Dheloul, a swift camel, which I purchased. Mrs Rassam has behaved very unkindly to her – all the fault of those cursed Badgers who are a regular pest.[173]

But he also wrote on the same day to his aunt, and here we become aware that there are serious problems. It seems that the captain has married beneath himself, and that 'her position in society was inferior to his. Instead of endeavouring to raise her he appears to do everything in his power to keep her down'. Layard has no respect any more for the man who is described as 'one of the most selfish, illbred, unfeeling and conceited men I ever met'. The captain, moreover, appeared to be suffering from such violent moods that Dr Sandwith was beginning to regard him as suffering from a kind of madness, and shortly before Layard sat down to write to Sara Austen Mr Rolland had thrown another fit which had alarmed the doctor because of the effect it had on the young woman. As Layard wrote: 'You may conceive the position of a young woman isolated from every one, without a friend to turn to, exposed to continual neglect'; not only that, but she is, as he writes, 'thrown entirely amongst strangers, & those strangers young men'.[174] The latest scene took place in Layard's house, and he felt he had to refrain from explaining precisely what took place, but as a result he gave Charlotte a room of her own in his house. One wonders whether that was a very prudent arrangement, assuming that part of the problem was the captain's strong feeling of jealousy towards Layard.

Nearly a month passed in this manner, a most tense and unpleasant time, which culminated in a new confrontation which this time directly involved Layard. The entire party had been at Nimrud for a time and on 10 June was on its way back to Mosul; during the ride Rolland spoke only once to Layard, throwing an insult at him. He decided to let it pass unnoticed, and as they reached Kuyunjik where their tents were pitched, Charlotte as usual went to the large common tent, but her husband dragged her away with him and coming hastily up to Layard insulted him in the most deliberate manner. He chose not to respond, but only turned his back upon him. But the affair was not finished with that.

> A few moments afterwards I heard violent screams proceeding from his tent, which was left completely open on two sides. One of my servants running in at the same time cried out that Mr. Rolland had thrown his wife to the ground and was attempting to murder her. I had only one course to pursue and calling some people we separated them and secured him. He was in a most violent state – uttering abuse which I need not repeat and calling for his arms – because I had dared to interfere between him and his wife.[175]

He was later released, of course, but he then attacked Layard and had to be held by the servants. After some hours he finally calmed down and apologised to Layard for having struck him, but it was clear that this could not go on. Rolland was asked to write a formal letter of apology in which he took the blame for all that had happened and declared that Layard had behaved with total correctness; and Layard demanded that both should leave at once for England.

We are naturally not told in the letters what exactly Captain Rolland shouted to Layard, but it seems safe to assume that the 'insults' were accusations of adultery involving Layard and Charlotte. Whether the captain's suspicions were groundless or not is hardly possible to decide now, but it is not unlikely that the couple had behaved in such a way that Rolland found it easy to interpret the situation in this manner. Layard was clearly deeply involved in the fate of this young woman, and his concern alone would have been enough to rouse the anger of the apoplectic captain. A little later Layard wrote to Ross that he was going to feel the loss of her, but that was for purely practical reasons: 'she is the only person who has given me the slightest assistance – copying inscriptions, notes MS. etc., and taking bearings – in fact always making herself most useful'. He attached a letter to her and expected her to send him a discreet reply through Ross.[176] Somewhat later he returned to the matter:

> I am very anxious to hear how Mrs. Rolland got on after her departure and her letter greatly relieved my mind in many respects. I hope she will reach England safely and receive that protection, which she so much requires, from her parents. The Badgers & Rassam have acted most infamously – I may except old Rassam, who is a donkey & hardly those precious friends of his. I am disgusted with the whole circus & shall probably never put my foot in the house again. After all I have done for the Rassams I confess I am astonished at the manner in which Mrs. R has acted, alltho after the unprincipled acts which we both know her jealous & vindictive temper led her to commit, I might have expected anything.[177]

CHAPTER TWENTY-EIGHT

DISASTERS AND
NEW DISCOVERIES

——— •◆• ———

Matilda Rassam, the object of Layard's anger, was waiting in Mosul with a story that was not likely to put him in a better mood. It concerned the packing and transportation of the two lions from the Nimrud palace, which had been left on the river bank waiting for the waters to rise; her husband was supposed to take care of the practical details. The story of what happened is contained in a letter she wrote in the middle of April, and her lively account deserves to be quoted:

> Your two rafts have started at last & a precious job we have had. Mrs. Badger Rassam & myself started for Nimrood on the 8th the river was then high, but when we reached the village of Nimrood to our great surprise we found that the Lions were half under water & the villagers making every prepara- tion to leave for the Mound. Although we could see what rapid strides the water was making towards the village we still laughed at their fear. After taking a walk to the mound, we found on our return that all the people had deserted the place, & Awad came in while we were at dinner & told us that we barely had time to reach the excavations before the road would be impass- able. At the same moment Hannah came in for a shroud to bury the body of a young girl, about 10 years of age, which they had found floating down into the pond where you used to catch such delicious fish. A second Corpse was also floating but could not be recovered. It is supposed they had been about two days in the water. After hearing all this, we thought it high time to decamp & after giving orders to have all your things removed to the mound, we set off & were soon lodged in a black tent. The men bearing your effects, at least those that were portable, reported that the water was knee deep in your rooms. Hannah and Behnan still remained in your house & determined not to leave it; I of course sent for them immediately & after locking all the doors (which was of little use as some parts had already fallen) they left your mansion. By this time the whole plain was covered with water to the foot of the mound & they waded through it up to their waists. It was about midnight when they reached us, the poor fellows shivering & shaking with cold.

The rain now began to fall in torrents, & there were we servants, workmen &c &c huddled together in a miserable black tent which admitted a greater part of the rain. As soon as it was light we went to the edge of the Tel to take a view of the village, but there was little or nothing of it to be seen, the whole plain had the appearance of a rolling sea dashing against the foot of the mound.

We were now quite at a stand still nothing could be done the rain was coming down awfully & did not cease the whole day, the river also continued rising. I never remember spending a more miserable day, & we did nothing but wish for the morning, but as fortune would have it, the morrow was worse than the preceding day. Rassam now resolved to remain till next morning & rain or no rain to start for Moossul. During that night we were literally swimming & the servants were engaged baling the water out of the tent.

... Seeing no chance of the river falling & our situation was so miserable we returned to Moossul leaving orders to have the Lions embarked as soon as the river fell. Sultan Agha had just returned with the intelligence that the raft started yesterday, at 12 o'clock, but I am sorry to tell you that one of the Lions broke into two pieces just as they were putting it on board. It has not in the least injured the piece, for if it had been cut through with a knife it could not have been done better.[178]

Matilda did not tell him (perhaps she did not know) that someone had seized a chance to hack the snout off one of the lions, presumably a superstitious peasant who wanted to be absolutely sure the beast was dead. The piece was found again, however, and the damage proved to be fairly negligible. But Layard was beside himself and immediately sat down to write long excited letters to London to explain what had happened. Undoubtedly, he felt a twinge of conscience which he hid in his anger, for there was no denying the fact that had he stayed in place instead of going on an excursion to the Habur, this would hardly have happened. He did not reason like that, however.

After the labor and anxiety which the removal of these fine specimens have cost me I cannot but feel deeply vexed at these occurrences which cannot but be, to a certain extent, the results of carelessness, and my regret is not diminished when I reflect that these accidents are mainly to be attributed to a parsimony truly unworthy of an undertaking which has excited so much interest in England, and the results of which had proved, before the second expedition so important in an archæological point of view. Had proper means been placed at my command, the Lions would have been embarked under my own superintendence. As it is I have been struggling thro' the winter and spring to make ends meet, and have been obliged to defer from day to day and from week to week that which ought to have been done at once. I have made use, as far as I prudently could of my own resources, as the last accounts sent to you will show, and I would cheerfully do so to a greater extent were I able.[179]

He points out that Rawlinson had paid no less than £350 for two lions from Khorsabad, which he bought from the French consul at Mosul, and how on earth was he supposed to be able to find that kind of money in his tiny budget to pay for the transportation of many more objects to Basra?

Things were going from bad to worse, however. A week later he received a letter from Captain Felix Jones who commanded the British river steamer on the Tigris, and he announced how he had been surprised and annoyed to discover that only one of the two rafts sent down from Mosul had arrived at Basra. The other one had been dragged into an enormous swamp which had been created as the result of a breach of the Tigris banks; it now lay about 1 km from the river itself.

> Passing it at night on our way down we were nearly meeting the same fate for, ignorant of the irruption, we were steaming along as usual and were nearly drawn into the influx – though steaming certainly at 11 miles an hour allowing for the current. It was not surprising to me therefore when I heard one of the rafts had been swept in against the efforts of the Kellekchis (the raft-men) – and the other was only kept from a similar accident by the boat and the whole of the people using every exertion to prevent it. It was while so engaged that the smaller one with only two men at the oars came within the vortex and, unmanageable as these machines are, was quickly hurried into the gut by the impetuous stream that carried it a mile into Mesopotamia before it could be brought to the bank – where I found it on my way up – deserted by its people who were compelled to beat a retreat with starvation staring them in the face and no chance of doing any thing had they remained.[180]

Captain Jones took his steamer through the breach into the newly formed swamp and managed to reach the stranded raft. The smaller cases with reliefs he could get transferred to the steamer, but he was very uncertain whether it was going to be possible to save the other lion.

Again Layard took up the pen and wrote to London, and again he felt constrained to complain at his lack of funds, for even though this was an accident which could have happened at any time, he felt that it was largely his empty purse which was the cause of all the mishaps which now appeared to hit the expedition.[181] In fact, Jones succeeded in saving the lion on his next trip to the place, so what looked like a major disaster turned out relatively well.

On the other hand, both Dr Sandwith and Cooper now came down with the fever which always took its toll among the Europeans when the weather began to get really hot. Both were so badly affected that it quickly became necessary to remove them from Mosul to the mountains, and this could not have happened at a worse time, for very important discoveries were now being made both at Kuyunjik and at Nimrud.

Matilda Rassam had explained in her letter about the terrible rain that very beautiful things had appeared at Nimrud while Layard was in the Habur; the workers were busy clearing the area around the so-called 'pyramid' and had run into what appeared to be the entrance to a temple. There was a large stela which excited her:

Several beautiful things have come out of the pyramid unlike any previous sculptures. There is one slab containing a king cut as it were in an arched frame with their Deity the Crescent & a kind of bell just over the king's head. His Majesty has a double necklace on, & one of the ornaments is as perfect a Malta cross as any I have seen. In front of the figure is a round stone standing on lion's claws, & in the center of the stone there is a round hole, which I fancy was used for burning incense in. The King & the Lions are covered with inscription. But there is a most beautiful statue about 3½ feet high covered with inscription & made of the finest Italian marble, the feet are broken off but there they are, in one hand it has a sickle the other resting on the breast.[182]

They had discovered one or possibly two temples which had been built as part of the sacred complex in which the *ziggurat* was a prominent feature. None of these temples were fully excavated by Layard and most of the work here was done by way of tunnels, so it is limited what he could say about them. The most remarkable thing about them were the entrances (see Figure 28.1). The largest building had two gateways, separated by some 10 m, and one of them was guarded by two colossal lions with human heads and wings; at the other stood tall relief blocks with images which had no parallels in the palaces: on both sides the doorway was flanked by a human figure who held up one hand in greeting and had a plant with three flowers in the other. In the entrance itself one was met by two large monsters who were being chased out of the temple by a divine figure (see Figure 28.2); the monsters were very strange, dragon-headed, with lions' paws, and wings and lower body like an eagle. They were rendered with a dramatic and very powerful intensity which impressed Layard, and he interpreted the scene as the god's fight against evil, represented by the demonic creature who appeared to be related to later ideas and representations of devils and wickedness. To the right of this entrance stood the relief Matilda had described with an altar in front of it.

The temple itself was largely empty and very damaged by fire, but he did discover a large floor-slab which was covered with a very long inscription on both sides, as well as a few smaller objects which had escaped the looters. Some of the old cedar beams from the Amanaus mountains in the Lebanon were so well preserved that his workers used them on their campfires. He could smell the incense-like fragrance from the cedar wood in his tent.

The smaller temple was really only one room with a monumental gateway flanked by two naturalistic lions, somewhat smaller than the others and without wings. Here too they found large blocks of stone as floor-slabs covered with inscriptions. It was here the statue mentioned by Matilda was discovered, without a doubt the most perfect example of Assyrian sculpture in the round ever found and one of the treasures of the British Museum. The temples were dedicated to the goddess Sharrat-niphi and to the warrior-god Ninurta, the figure who chased out the demons.

At Kuyunjik the workmen had been just as industrious and lucky. In continuation of the very long gallery, some 75 m, where Layard had found the reliefs showing the transportation of the bull colossi, they ran into a kind of corridor which began to descend. They were here nearly at the edge of the mound itself

Figure 28.1 The entrance to the Ninurta temple at Nimrud. The tunnel disappears into the darkness of the mound. In front of the stela, which shows the king and divine symbols, stands a typical Assyrian altar. (From Layard 1853: 351)

Figure 28.2 This dramatic scene, which shows the god Ninurta chasing a demon out of his house, met the visitors who entered the temple itself. (From Layard 1849–53, II: Plate 5)

and the rooms they had been working in were already very deep, so it goes without saying that it was exceedingly difficult to pursue a descending passage. Layard expected it to lead down to the ancient riverbank. On one wall there were reliefs showing servants carrying luxurious food, clearly meant for a sumptuous feast: fruits of various kinds, dates, pomegranates on a string, apples and grapes; sticks with dried grasshoppers (obviously a delicacy), hares and birds; then followed a couple of men who carried tables laden with cakes and fruit, and the procession concluded with a long row of servants who brought vases with flowers. All this was presumably meant for a wonderful picnic which would take place in the palace garden at the foot of the mound.

The opposite wall shows prancing horses being brought out by finely dressed servants. Unfortunately, Layard's workers could not follow these scenes to their conclusion, for they were now working at a depth of 15 m and there was a growing danger that the tunnels close to the edge would collapse on top of them. They had therefore been forced to abandon this place, where the reliefs were so well preserved, and they had tackled the other end of the long gallery.

Here they opened a fresh tunnel which ran alongside a series of short walls on the right hand side of rooms and corridors, and they pursued it through four doorways. The last one of these was very unusual, for it was guarded by some strange figures which looked like a mixture of a man and a fish (see Figure 28.3).

Figure 28.3 One of the fish-men flanking the entrance to a tablet room in Sennacherib's palace. The men are probably hoisting cuneiform tablets to the surface in the basket. (From Layard 1853: 342)

Such figures were already known from a cylinder seal Layard owned, and he saw them as representations of the god Dagon, who was known from the Old Testament. But there was another account which could fit their weird appearance, a story told by Berossus in his Greek work on the history of Babylonia and Assyria; he described how at the very beginning of time a fish-man called Oannes rose from the sea to teach the people in southern Mesopotamia's oldest cities the joys and arts of civilisation. Such traditions had to be closely linked, Layard felt, and what could be more meaningful than Oannes standing guard over the entrance to three rooms which turned out to be filled with thousands of cuneiform tablets, what appeared to be a complete library (Burstein 1978).

In a compact mass some 30 cm thick they found documents of all kinds, part of the gigantic palace archives from the time of the late Assyrian kings. In no time they had filled ten large boxes with tablets and the first room was not half empty yet. Most of the tablets were unfortunately broken in pieces, but there were many large fragments. Layard speculated that this was the archive of the empire.

Until this time most of the inscriptions found had been monumental in nature, cut in stone, either alone or in connection with reliefs. Other types of texts had been discovered, primarily in southern Mesopotamia, both 'barrels' and 'prisms' of clay covered with writing, as well as lots of bricks which carried either stamped or handwritten inscriptions. Finally, there were the so-called 'tablets' of clay, which are not of gravestone dimensions such as innumerable illustrations depicting Moses carrying the Tablets of the Law have led people to think, but normally quite small objects which vary in size from a matchbox to a cigar-box.

Clay was the most important raw material in southern Mesopotamia where the first cities grew up and where writing was invented. It was a simple matter to make a small pillow-shaped lump of fine clay, and when that was reasonably dry it formed an ideal base for scratching or impressing drawings and signs with a simple stylus. Once it had been allowed to dry in the sun it became hard enough to handle without any risk that the signs would be damaged, and if the tablet carrying the message lost its interest after some time, one could simply make it wet again and reuse it. If, on the other hand, it carried a message which was deemed of extraordinary importance, and which should be kept for posterity, it could be fired to terracotta and was in effect indestructible. It could be broken, of course, but the pieces – if found – could be stuck together again. By far the majority of the approximately 500,000 tablets which have been found in the Mesopotamian earth since the days of Botta and Layard were not burnt in antiquity, and most are damaged in some way after their millennia of sleep in the ground; after careful excavation, cleaning and firing in our museums they are, if not as good as new, then at least perfectly legible. If one is faced with tablets which were fired in antiquity, either deliberately or because the building which housed them was burnt down, they can be virtually pristine.

It is this writing practice which has secured us such an enormously detailed documentation from the old civilisations in Mesopotamia, for tablets sometimes virtually leap from the ground when excavators have had the luck to find the archive rooms of a palace or a temple or, say, the private house of a merchant who had an extensive correspondence and many contracts in his archive. After the collapse of the ancient Mesopotamian cultures other media became normal for writing, papyrus, paper and leather, and this unfortunately means that we suddenly have no or very little source material, for it was obviously only under very lucky circumstances, or in very special climatic conditions, that such materials could survive.

Layard stood here on the threshold between the two fish-men looking into the first great archive room ever discovered. An upper floor of the palace had clearly fallen on top of the original room, and the plan reveals that the walls in this section of the building were very heavy, obviously because they carried a superstructure; this had crushed all of the tablets. His workers dug out fragment after fragment which were placed in boxes and taken to Mosul where they began to accumulate. It is difficult to say with precision how many tablets were found in these rooms, for other very large discoveries of tablets were made in other parts of the mound later and in the British Museum archives most of the texts were simply labelled 'K'. – for 'Kuyunjik'. Neither Layard nor his immediate successors had any awareness of the importance of keeping track of every object found in order to allow later scholars to determine precisely in what context they were found. But in all more than 20,000 tablets and fragments came out, and the task of putting together these pieces has occupied generations of scholars in the Museum, a gigantic puzzle with tens of thousands of individual pieces (Reade 1986a; Parpola 1986).

At Nimrud Layard had not found a single tablet and it has been claimed that this must simply be because he did not realise what they were; he found many tablets here, it has been said, but threw them away as some strange kind of potsherds. This is the accusation found in the only book we have about the history of Assyriology, written in 1925 by a man called Wallis Budge, a later keeper at the British Museum. For that reason alone one has to be sceptical, for although Budge's book for generations was the authoritative account of the history of exploration and decipherment, it is in fact shot through with the author's personal sympathies and antipathies – and the author did not like Layard. In fact, Budge is probably the most completely unpleasant person in the history of the field, and his book can now easily be seen to constitute a strange mixture of truth and downright mendacity.

> The fact is that many tablets were found both at Kuyûnjik and Nimrûd by Layard. ... The natives thought they were bits of pottery decorated in an unusual manner; and Dr Birch told me that Layard thought the same until 1849, when he brought home a few specimens of the 'strange pottery' and showed them to him. When Birch told them what they were, and showed him the plates in Rich's 'Second Memoir', Layard sent out to Kuyûnjik and ordered Mr Christian Rassam to collect all the pieces of the 'strange pottery' he could find, and to put them in baskets until his return to Môsul. Similar orders were sent to Nimrûd, but it was too late; for the tablets and fragments had been thrown on the piles of earth that had been excavated, and had since been carried away by the natives to make top-dressing for their fields.
>
> (Budge 1925: 83)[183]

There is nothing in the available contemporary evidence which supports this claim, and even if it had not been Budge who had made it, one would have found it difficult to trust this accusation, which is clearly designed to ridicule Layard. One would have thought that he, with his intense interest in the writing system, would have been able to see that the signs on tablets were identical with the ones on stone as they appeared on the walls of the palace. In his correspondence with Rawlinson there are repeated discussions of inscriptions on cylinders and bricks, so both men were clearly aware that the writing system was used on clay. No doubt tablets could have been found and thrown away without being recognised for what they were, for the excavations were not exactly conducted with the meticulous care which a modern archaeologist would demand, and there were long periods when they proceeded without any supervision by either Layard or Hormuzd; however, Budge's story is not to be believed.

In fact, it is not very likely that the Northwest palace at Nimrud, where he worked during the entire first expedition, would have contained archives, for this building had certainly not been in use when the town was captured and destroyed. At the time when the conquerors rushed through the streets on the citadel putting all the temples and palaces to the torch, the Northwest palace was already a ruin, for which reason it escaped being burnt down; it is not terribly probable that archives would be kept here – although individual tablets thrown away by an Assyrian scribe might have ended up in the ruins. There is no very good reason to believe that Layard's workers found any tablets here – nor that Botta found any at Khorsabad without realising it.

It may be that the discovery of the archive rooms at Kuyunjik sharpened his awareness that such objects in fact could be expected to appear, and that he instructed his people from then on to be on the look-out for them, but as it stands Budge's story is surely 'a pack of lies', as pointed out by Saggs, who added the warning that 'no statement of Budge about Layard should be received without careful examination' (Saggs 1970: 45, n. 1). In any event, Layard immediately realised that this discovery would throw a strong light on the Assyrians and the details of their world. He was faced with what had to be the archives of the realm.

In the middle of all this excitement Layard found time to write a long report to his employer, Canning, based on his observations during the trip to the Habur. He felt that the Turks had excellent opportunities for controlling the tribes of the desert, simply by way of a steady advance of military power and a system of carefully placed strongpoints. An all-out attack would simply drive the Bedouin into the desert, but they could be made to coexist with the settled population. The revolts and raids which the tribes had been involved in during the present stupid system, which was characterised by 'the extreme treachery and misconduct of the local authorities', should certainly not be punished, and he envisaged that his plan could lead to a nearly idyllic situation in the region:

> The produce of their immense flocks of sheep and camels would become a fruitful source of trade with the towns & villages & be gradually the means of leading them to peaceful occupations, whilst their horses might furnish the finest light cavalry in the world. In fact from being dangerous enemies they might become useful subjects of the Turkish Government.[184]

He was dealing with urgent problems which he knew only too well from personal experience, for Turkish control of Mesopotamia was in deep decline during these years. Even Nimrud had been attacked and the entire area along the banks of the Tigris towards Babylonia in the south was subjected to constant raids. The great marshes south of Baghdad were in open revolt against the local Pasha.

CHAPTER TWENTY-NINE

SUMMER IN THE PALACE

—— •◆• ——

It was now getting extremely hot in Mosul and Dr Sandwith and Cooper were quite incapacitated by the heat and came down with fever. They were entertained by a large number of guests who came through the town and visited Layard and his party, two married couples on their way to Baghdad, a military man named Walpole who later wrote an account of his visit, a priest called Malan who had artistic abilities and made a number of drawings of Layard and the excavations, and a further priest, Mr Bowen, who was on a tour of inspection to the churches of the East. None of them created any problems, it seems, and Layard enjoyed playing host, but the doctor and Cooper became weaker and it became necessary to send them up into the cooler mountains. Layard and Hormuzd were also beginning to suffer from malaria again, but luckily not at the same time, so when one was down, the other could work. It could not last.

On 11 July Layard shipped the first large collection of sculptures from Kuyunjik to Basra and then left Mosul for the mountains, 'in the middle of the hot stage of fever, and half delirious'.

Having fetched Cooper, who stayed in a convent relatively close to Mosul, they arrived the following day at the place where Sandwith and Walpole had pitched camp.

> We had no difficulty in finding our European fellow-travellers. The first Kurd we met pointed towards a well-wooded garden; above its trees peered their white tents. As we rode into it, however, no one came out to welcome us. I entered the first tent, and there, stretched on their carpets, in a state of half-consciousness, the prey to countless flies, lay the Doctor and Mr. Walpole. It was with difficulty I could rouse them to learn the history of their fever. The whole party were in the same state; the servants prostrate like their masters.
>
> (Layard 1853: 367–8)

It took some days before they were able to continue further up into the mountains. They now had to pass through desolate and trackless regions inhabited by Kurds and Nestorians, but they also met other groups, such as a caravan of Jewish nomads who drove their cattle through these high mountain passes. The goal for

Layard's party was Lake Van, where they arrived in near-total exhaustion. This area is filled with ruins and there are several cuneiform inscriptions on the rocks, but the most important thing was the wonderful climate which makes the summers here very pleasant. Layard immediately set out on expeditions, visiting several Armenian churches and talking to their priests, but the rest of the party continued to be plagued by fever and took refuge in a convent which was even higher up. It did not really help, however, and it became clear that both Dr Sandwith and Cooper were in risk of losing their lives or at least suffering permanent damage to their health if they stayed in these wild regions. Layard decided to send them to Constantinople together with Walpole. This left only Hormuzd –

> once more I was alone with my faithful friend, and we trod together the winding pathway which led down the mountain side. We had both suffered from fever, but we still had the strength to meet its attacks, and to bear cheerfully, now unhindered, the difficulties and anxieties of our wandering life.
>
> (Layard 1853: 411–12)

'Now unhindered ...' Cooper carried a letter addressed to Canning in which Layard wrote that 'neither of these gentlemen were at all qualified for an expedition of this kind & I have received little or no assistance from them'. Several years later Layard received an apologetic letter from Dr Sandwith in which he wrote that he had been suffering from a feeling of guilt for years because of his laziness in Assyria; but the fact of the matter was – he preferred to shoot (Lane-Poole 1888: 91). In general, Layard felt that he had good cause to complain of 'the shabby & careless manner in which the whole thing has been done in England', and he was absolutely clear in his mind that nothing could induce him to stay in Mesopotamia for another year. When Layard came back to Mosul he wrote a letter to Ellis at the British Museum to explain the situation and ask for a new artist to be sent out to complete the work started by Cooper; however, it must be a strong and healthy man, for the experience with Cooper should not be repeated.[185]

Also his trip to Van resulted in a long report to Canning, this time concerned with the situation of the Christians in the mountains. It was a sad and depressing account of constant encroachment on their rights by both Kurds and Turks. 'The Kurds took our lives, but the Turks take our livelihood', was the complaint from all the places he went. Even the Yezidis were again submitted to persecution and Layard was deeply depressed and disillusioned with regard to the good faith of the Turkish government or its ability to create reasonable conditions. During these months a controversy raged in England after the publication of an extremely anti-Turkish book, and Layard had planned to write a defence of the Turkish government, but 'after what I have seen during the last month I have not the heart to take up my pen in defending a government who permits the injustice & oppression I have described within its dominions'.[186]

The difficulties for the Christian communities were not created by the Kurds and the Turks only. Catholic and Protestant missionaries were very active there and their influence was nearly as destructive as the Turkish persecution, for the traditional village priests, who had a very limited education and often were illiterate, became easy prey for the campaign of intimidation which the missionaries inflicted on them. Layard met with the Nestorian patriarch Mar Shamoun who told him about the terrible doubts and the unbearable fear created in the hearts of these simple people by the descriptions of the consequences they were going to suffer on their souls because of the heretical religion they practised.

It was an annoyed Layard who returned to Mosul to find that the Trustees had expressed their displeasure at finding that the expenses from the excursion to the Habur appeared in his accounts to them; clearly, they did not feel that it had been a serious archaeological venture, and Layard disgustedly asked that the relevant expenses be removed from the account he had sent, so that he personally paid for it all. He also saw that Canning still had not obtained the necessary papers for his trip to Babylonia, where he was planning to go in early October.

But while Layard and his party had escaped from the Mosul heat, his workers had struggled on, and since most of the men from Nimrud had been transferred to Kuyunjik progress was rapid. A number of rooms had been uncovered and a new kind of relief had appeared.

Many of the rooms in which they were now working lay almost on the edge of the mound, and it seemed that the outer walls of the mighty palace had at one point crashed down to the ground below, for what they found had to be interior walls. The men had first discovered a large hall, or rather an interior courtyard, nearly 50 by 40 m, and even though it was in part badly damaged a number of interesting reliefs were in fact preserved. They showed scenes from a war which took place in a landscape dominated by a great river, and Layard interpreted them as renderings of a campaign directed against southernmost Babylonia where the enormous marshes stretch to the mouth of the Persian Gulf. Of special interest was a picture of the Assyrian king in his might on a chariot, not least because Layard could see clear parallels to the classical historians' descriptions of the splendour of the Persian monarchs. Quintus Curtius has given us a striking account of the Persian army, and Layard felt that he was watching a very similar scene. In the case of the Persians we hear that the procession began with altars on which the holy fire burned, followed by priests and 365 young men who represented the days of the year; then came a chariot dedicated to the highest god, drawn by white horses, and after that first a great stallion, 'the Horse of the Sun', followed by ten carts decorated with reliefs in gold and silver (see Figure 29.1).

> These were followed by the cavalry of twelve nations of different cultures, variously armed. Next in line were the soldiers whom the Persians called the 'Immortals', some 10,000 in number. No other group were as splendidly bedecked in barbarian opulence: golden necklaces, clothes interwoven with gold, long-sleeved tunics actually studded with jewels. After a short interval came the 15,000 men they call 'the king's kinsmen'. This troop was dressed almost like women, its extravagance rather than its fine arms catching the eye. The column next to these comprised the so-called 'Doryphoroe', the men who usually looked after the king's wardrobe, and these preceded the royal chariot on which rode the king himself, towering above all others. Both sides of the chariot were embossed with gold and silver representations of the gods; the yoke was studded with flashing gems and from it arose two

Figure 29.1 King Sennacherib returning from one of his victorious campaigns. (From Layard 1849, II: 137)

golden images (each a cubit high) of Ninus and Belus respectively. Between these was a consecrated eagle made of gold and represented with wings outstretched.

The sumptuous attire of the king was especially remarkable. His tunic was purple, interwoven with white at the centre, and his gold-embroidered cloak bore a gilded motif of hawks attacking each other with their beaks. From his gilded belt, which he wore in the style of a woman, he had slung his scimitar, its scabbard made of precious stone. His royal diadem, called a 'cidaris' by the Persians, was encircled by a blue ribbon flecked with white.

(Rufus 1984: 30–1, Book III, 3)

This description, in which one notes with particular interest the reference to the images of Ninus and Belus, must – despite the obvious exaggerations – remind one of the Assyrian reliefs and their representation of the kings in triumph. The numbers of men involved are certainly smaller, although we do not know precisely how many men took part in the battles fought by the Assyrian army. Belus was no Persian god, but in antiquity was known as the main god of Babylon, to whom, for instance, the *ziggurat* was dedicated. One is accordingly struck by a sense of continuity, where the ancient Mesopotamian traditions were still alive among the Medes and Persians who had made an end to first Assyria and later Babylonia as independent states. It is not easy to translate the grey reliefs into living pictures, but the splendour described by Quintus Curtius gives us a glimpse of the impression which the great Assyrian kings must have made on their contemporaries. And it is not difficult to imagine the feelings of awe and joy which went through Layard when he first confronted these images, many of which have unfortunately perished. It is much more difficult for us now to evaluate the expressive power of these reliefs, for the ones we can see in places like the British Museum are out of context and one cannot move through rooms for which they were created and in that way experience the impact they once must have had on their time, when they were complete and fresh.

The large courtyard had a well-preserved façade on its western side with three monumental doorways, the middle one with bulls more than 6 m high. The doors led to a smaller room without reliefs, which again had three doorways, the middle one with bulls, leading to yet another room, where unfortunately the reliefs were poorly preserved; finally, a new set of three doors opened on three smaller rooms, the middle one again with bulls. The architectural effect of this row of monumental bulls must have been truly stunning; a person standing in the courtyard would see a series of bulls which disappeared into the semi-darkness of the rooms, and the perspective and the sense of distance was enhanced by the progressively smaller size of the bulls, from more than 6 m to less than 4 m for the last one.

The room which was reached by way of this impressive sequence is the only one which has been even partially preserved today, as the so-called 'Lachish Room' in the British Museum. The story told on its walls was about Sennacherib's campaign directed against the Jewish state of Judah, and it concentrates on the most important event during that war – seen from the Assyrian point of view: the conquest and looting of the city of Lachish (see Figure 29.2). The account in the Bible does admit that this town was conquered by the Assyrians, but the main thrust of that story is of course the abortive siege of Jerusalem which ended with the withdrawal of the Assyrian army.

When Layard saw these reliefs, he did not know what was depicted, for he could not read the captions which are placed in various places on the reliefs and which give the names of both the town and the Assyrian king. Moreover, the reliefs were in very poor condition and he could see no reason to try to take them down and send them to London. When it became clear, after the texts could be read, what the decoration of this room was about, it was decided by the British Museum that the reliefs must be saved at all costs, and it fell to Hormuzd Rassam to take them down with immense care, so that they could be shipped to London where they are now and constitute the most impressive example of the art of Sennacherib's palace.

It is not that these reliefs are in any way unusual or of higher quality than the others, which were left at Kuyunjik. It was simply the fact that they described an event which was so well known from the Bible which was the reason for the extraordinary interest shown.

The fact that we have most of the decoration of this one room gives us a unique opportunity to try to understand how a visitor to the great palace would have experienced the decorations. We have to imagine a world where pictures are something very special, so unusual that most people rarely see any at all. A reasonable parallel is perhaps constituted by the frescos in many Romanesque village churches

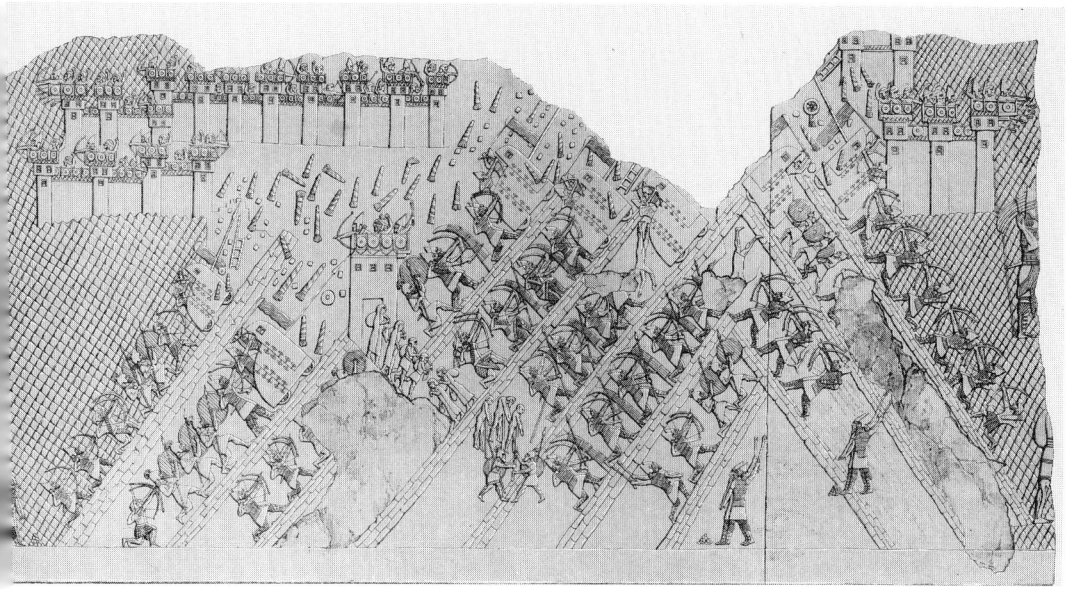

Figure 29.2 Detail from the reliefs in the Lachish Room. One sees the central scene where the city is attacked by the Assyrian army. Armoured siege-engines, lancers, bowmen and sling-throwers are involved; captured enemies are hung on poles as a warning to the defenders on the walls, who answer with a rain of bows, stones and burning torches which are meant to set the siege-engines on fire. (From Layard 1849–53, II: Plate 21)

and the impression they made on the worshippers. But Sennacherib's architects went much further, so that the person who entered a room like the Lachish hall, which is *c.* 7 by 15 m, was exposed to a virtual visual storm, something which can perhaps be compared to the 'surround' movies where one seems to become part of the events.

Entering the Lachish room one was faced on the back wall with the depiction of the most violent part of the battle itself; the town Lachish, a large city on a mound, with high walls and towers, is under heavy attack by Assyrian forces. Thousands of defenders stand on the walls and send a rain of arrows down on the advancing enemies. This was the climax of the whole scenery, but it all began on the wall to the left of the entrance, where one sees the Assyrian army preparing for battle, long rows of soldiers, bowmen and lancers and men with large shields; they advance on the city itself from the left; in the front large screens were held up to protect against the arrows of the defenders, side by side with very big siege-engines which could ram the gates and undermine the walls; then come the lancers hiding behind shields, followed by row after row of bowmen and sling-throwers. The culmination is the attack itself which advances on high ramps of earth thrown up against the walls in the middle of the scene. One senses the ferocity of the attack and sees the vain attempts of the defenders to keep the Assyrian soldiers at bay by hurling burning torches down upon their screens and siege-engines.

On the right the battle is already over and the Assyrian soldiers drive prisoners out of the city and carry loot away on carts and camels. This turns into an ordered procession where the leading men of the city are led before King Sennacherib who is sitting on his throne in front of his tent with his victorious generals, ready to let representatives from Lachish do homage to him. Over his head is a short inscription which says: 'Sennacherib, the mighty king, king of Assyria, sat on the throne while the booty from Lachish passed in front of him'. With him is a detachment of cavalry, and his own glorious chariot stands ready behind him. The scene takes place in a hilly landscape with palms, fruit-trees and vineyards, and behind this procession – which dominates the right-hand wall of the room – is the peaceful contrast to all that has passed before: we see the Assyrian camp where men are busy with different tasks; it is a carefully planned camp, oval in shape, surrounded by a wall and with a road leading through it; in the upper left corner stands the sacred chariot with divine emblems and two priests in high hats are carrying out some rite in front of it; in other tents one observes men who make a bed, set a table, cook food, and enjoy a cup of beer in a quiet moment.

Lachish itself has been excavated since then and the great Assyrian attack-ramp has been found thrown up against the wall. There is every reason to regard the reliefs as a reasonably accurate account of the town's capture (Ussishkin 1982).

In another room close by, Layard found a series of damaged reliefs showing scenes from another mighty battle, but it was immediately clear that these were different from anything else he had discovered. They were made of a different kind of stone which was harder and had many fossil encrustations, and there were obvious differences in the rendering of details of weapons and dress. These reliefs were from the reign of Ashurbanipal, Sennacherib's grandson who had used the old palace and redecorated some of the rooms.

They show the further development of the Assyrian relief style and their technical perfection is on such a level that one must deplore the fact that only six blocks were reasonably well preserved. Again the battle progresses from left to right, and the first scene shows two armies clashing in a furious, open battle with hand-to-hand combat everywhere. It was a decisive battle fought between Assyria and Elam, a state in southwestern Iran, and it took place on precisely the same battlefield where war after war has been fought through the millennia involving armies from the Iranian highlands and from the Mesopotamian plains; the last battle in this series was fought here some fifteen years ago in the war between Iraq and Iran. The British archaeologist and specialist in Assyrian art, Julian Reade from the British Museum, has described the scenes:

> On the far left is the charge of the Assyrian army, chariots, cavalry, and helmeted infantry. A critical factor in the victory was probably the Assyrian skill at close-quarter fighting; the Elamites seem to have relied overmuch on bows and arrows. The enemy, most of whom can be recognized by their headbands knotted at the back, are already giving ground. Some of them are running down a steep slope, presumably the mound of Til-Tuba on which they have been stationed. Further to the right the composition is divided into three horizontal bands. The retreat turns into a rout, and the enemy are finally

Figure 29.3 An idyllic scene from the palace garden at Nineveh. King Ashurbanipal and his wife sit under the vines enjoying a cup of wine accompanied by a variety of delicacies; four servants fan the air, while others stand ready with new delicious titbits and a small orchestra entertain the royal couple. In the midst of the sound of birds and harps hangs the cut-off head of the Elamite king brought from the battle-scene at Til Tuba.
(From Place 1867, III: Plate 57.2)

driven into the river behind them. For three days, according to Ashurbanipal, the river was choked with corpses. Against this general background of confused fighting, the fate of the Elamite king is recorded in a series of episodes. Some are explained in captions carved on the stone, others in the tablets which refer to this cycle of sculptures.

(Reade 1983: 61)

The Elamite king is shown together with his son in scenes which are scattered over the large relief; first he is seen in a chariot which crashes and turns over so that both men fall to the ground; he is hit in the back by an arrow but the crown prince drags him along to a small thicket where they hide and attempt to resist the Assyrian advance. The caption over their heads says: 'Teumman in his despair said to his son Tamritu: Shoot with the bow!' but their fight is in vain and both are killed by an Assyrian soldier who cuts off their heads. The diadem of the Elamite kings falls to the ground but is picked up by another soldier, and when the heads are brought to the scribes who are counting the spoils of the battle ('body count' it was called during the Vietnam War), it is discovered who they were; the head is brought under military escort to Nineveh, where it is presented to the king who did not personally take part in the campaign. The final scene shows Ashurbanipal and his queen in the garden house under the vines at Nineveh, where they enjoy a cup of wine and the music from a small orchestra (see Figure 29.3). The head of the vanquished Elamite foe hangs in one of the trees in the garden.

Layard walked through the corridors and rooms, choosing which pieces were to be packed and sent to London, and all of his time for the next month was spent on this task. He did have an opportunity to make a brief excavation at Nebbi Yunus where he found inscriptions and made paper casts of them. In the beginning of October he sent off one hundred cases with reliefs and other finds, and he had a further fifty to one hundred ready for shipment within the following week. In fact, he was preparing to leave not just Nineveh, but Assyria for good. He wrote to Palmerston asking permission to go to England in the spring in order to give him an opportunity to work on his finds. Excavations at Nimrud stopped and he prepared to go south to Babylonia in order to try his luck during the cold season where the climate was acceptable on the flood-plain.

CHAPTER THIRTY

BABYLONIA

—— ∙◆∙ ——

The political situation in the country was rapidly deteriorating. Caravans were attacked and plundered a few hours' ride from Mosul, and one of Layard's own rafts was attacked on its way down-river. 'The men I had hired to accompany it defended themselves well, and after killing 25 of the assailants & wounding a considerable number compelled the remainder to retreat', he wrote to Canning; this was war – a battle with twenty-five dead![187]

When Layard finally decided to leave Mosul he had to make an arrangement with a sheikh from one of the branches of the Shammar tribe, who accompanied him on the raft down to Baghdad; the son of the sheikh rode the whole way along the river in order to explain to possible attackers who fancied a nice little robbery, that they had better keep away from this one.

They passed through Takrit, birthplace of the great medieval warrior Saladin who created such difficulties for the Christian knights during the Crusades – and of Saddam Hussein of a somewhat shadier reputation – further down they reached the nearly deserted town Samarra and saw the strange minaret which has an outer spiral path to the top. This was once the capital of the land and during the Middle Ages it was one of the most splendid cities in the Near East, but Layard saw a small town with decrepit hovels which crouched behind a town wall of mudbrick. After Samarra the river became wider and calmer; in November, the time of this particular journey, there is so little water in the river that one glides along imperceptibly as one approaches Baghdad. Slowly the raft swam through endless datepalm groves which mark the proximity of the large city. An enormous mosque with two golden cupolas, the Kathimain complex, was at that time located just outside the walls of the town, and having passed it they glided slowly into Baghdad (see Figure 30.1).

> We pass the palace of the governor, an edifice of mean materials and proportions. At its windows the Pasha himself and the various officers of his household may be seen reclining on their divans, amidst wreaths of smoke. A crazy bridge of boats crosses the stream, and appears to bar all further progress. At length the chains are loosened, two or three of the rude vessels are withdrawn, and the rafts glide gently through. A few minutes more, and we are anchored beneath the spreading folds of the British flag, opposite a

handsome building, not crumbling into ruins like its neighbours, but kept in repair with European neatness. A small iron steamer floats motionless before it. We have arrived at the dwelling of the English Consul-general and political agent of the East India Company at Baghdad.

(Layard 1853: 473)

In Rawlinson's absence his post as Resident had been taken over for the time being by a certain Captain Kemball, who was kind and helpful. It was more than ten years since Layard's first visit to the city and nothing had improved since; on the contrary. He estimated that Baghdad had no more than 50,000 inhabitants, and epidemics raged constantly in a community devoid of the most elementary sanitary installations. The landscape around the city was so plagued by Bedouin that it was very dangerous to venture outside the walls; the official contact with Basra was maintained by way of the British river-steamer, for traffic overland was subjected to constant attacks.

> The physical state of the Pashalic is no less deplorable than the political. Dams, watercourses & any other public work have been allowed to go to ruin. The result has been that during several months of the year Baghdad stands, like an island, in the midst of a vast pestilent marsh. From the effects of the malaria, according to the Government returns which are undoubtedly far beneath the mark, 11,000 persons died last year in the city alone! This year altho' the mortality has been less the number of deaths has still been very considerable. One dam alone now protects Baghdad – if that were to give way suddenly as seems not only possible but even probable as no attempt whatever is made to keep it in proper repair, the city would be swept by a torrent about nine feet deep.[188]

Layard had brought thirty of his most experienced Jebour Arabs from Nimrud, and he now set them to work on a few mounds located just outside the walls of Baghdad, but he did not feel it safe to leave the city before he had a formal permission from Constantinople to excavate in the south. He was worried that the local authorities would refuse him permission in the absence of a firman, so he waited for nearly six weeks until the beginning of December. He was not happy to move away from the safety of the walls with this large party without clear guarantees.

In the meantime he had received a letter from England which informed him that a new artist had been appointed, a certain Mr Bell who had been recommended by Sir Richard Westmacott himself. He had been given what was deemed to be ample instructions, and had for instance been trained in the use of the Talbotype camera, which would permit him to make photographs in Assyria. Layard wrote back, asking that the artist be sent directly to Baghdad, where he assumed he would need his services.

The governor of Baghdad, Abde Pasha, had finally decided to tackle the Bedouin to put a stop to their marauding. He had hatched the plan to divert the water from the Euphrates which otherwise went into one of the enormous marshes where the most difficult tribe was hiding, in order to force them out into the open country

Figure 30.1   Flandin's drawing of the palace of the Turkish Pasha in Baghdad.
(From Flandin 1853–76: Plate 41)

where they could be confronted. This plan involved a huge dam which was to be built at Hindiyeh south of Baghdad, and Layard finally decided to ride to the Pasha's camp to introduce himself. It turned out to be a very pleasant interview which convinced Layard that he might after all try to work in the south without a formal permit from the vizier in Constantinople. He therefore proceeded to Hillah, a small town south of the large field of ruins which covers the remains of ancient Babylon, and here too he was received with enthusiasm. The local people were in fact so happy at the prospect of work and wages that he decided to hire twice as many as he had originally planned.

Here he was, planning to excavate Babylon itself, a city whose fame surpassed even that of Nineveh and called forth images of fabulous wealth and power. Even today books are regularly published with the simple title 'Babylon', and they hardly ever deal with the ancient city, for the name itself evokes the theme of confusion and decadence in a metropolis. The name Babylon has become synonymous with sumptuous luxury, debauchery and dissolution – and all that is due to the Bible. That text has given us the images which also the men of the nineteenth century had in their minds when they thought of Babylon: the first great city where mankind had demonstrated its willingness to challenge the divine power by building the tower which was to reach all the way to heaven. This was where they had been punished with the Babylonian confusion and the creation of the many languages. Later on the city became the home of such kings as Nebuchadnezzar and Belshazzar, in whose palace gorgeous orgies was daily habit, and on whose walls the Jewish god had written the warning which alone could be deciphered by Daniel: 'God hath numbered thy kingdom, and finished it. Thou art weighed in the balances, and art found wanting. Thy kingdom is divided, and given to the Medes and Persians'. It was in this city that the Jews sat, 'by the rivers of Babylon', in their unwilling exile after Nebuchadnezzar had captured Jerusalem and deported its leading inhabitants. The fall of Babylon was prophesied by the fanatical prophets of the Old Testament; Isaiah and Jeremiah rage in anger and lust for revenge against the city which was the cause of the disaster of the Jews. And yet, reality was probably somewhat more complex. 'Babylon hath been a golden cup in the Lord's hand, that made all the earth drunken: the nations have drunken of her wine; therefore the nations are mad', sings Jeremiah, thereby revealing the fascinating attraction of the metropolis. When the Jewish elite was sent from the provincial outpost of Jerusalem to Babylon, it was somewhat the same as sending the intellectuals of Poznań into exile in Paris – it is a wonder that any of them wanted to go back after sixty years, and of course relatively few did; but those who chose to return were full of the rage of injured pride, a feeling they poured into their dreams and prophesies.

For those who took these accounts as literal truth a visit to the ruins of Babylon was both a shocking and elevating experience. One was obviously faced with the remains of what was once a gigantic city, but all was gone. As at Nineveh, long lines of mounds indicate where the enormous walls once ran, and several mounds along the river reveal where the most important buildings and cityquarters were. All is on a colossal scale – and all is desolation. No one lives here, and in the nineteenth century the place was home to lions and other wild animals. We have several descriptions of how it impressed the believers of the time who came here, strongly emotional outbursts which always end with the same triumphant realisation that this place, more than any other in the world, is manifest proof of the truth of the Holy Bible. A typical example of the fervour of this experience was expressed by the missionary Stern who came here shortly after Layard. He was shocked to see the 'utter annihilation and gloomy solitude' of the ruins. He exclaimed to himself: 'this is Scripture emblazoned in legible characters, and prophesy vindicated by the most evident verification'. Later on he took a stroll across the area, bewildered to see that no ruins are visible anywhere:

> I was indeed trembling when I took my Bible and read aloud the fearful threatenings of the Prophets over the guilty city; it was in vain to ask where are the glittering gates through whose portals flowed the mighty stream of luxurious nobles and proud merchants? Where the stately palaces, through whose re-echoing halls music poured her sublimest strains, and dissipation and gaiety perpetually dwelt? Where the hanging gardens, which even Grecian writers, who had been nursed in the lap of art and science, considered one of the wonders of the world; the impregnable walls; the hundred brazen

gates; and thousands of other beauties and splendours of an admiring world? The besom of destruction has entirely swept away the gorgeous and luxurious city. Here the sceptic must not question, and the infidel dare not scorn and ridicule the Divine source of prophetic revelation.

(Stern 1854: 59–60)

Layard had also been deeply impressed and moved when he first visited the ruins of Babylon in 1840, but his was not a religious experience – at least not of the same kind:

I shall never forget the effect produced upon me by the long lines and vast masses of mounds, which mark the site of ancient Babylon, as they appeared in the distance one morning as the day broke behind them. The desolation, the solitude, those shapeless heaps, all that remain of a great and renowned city, are well calculated to impress and excite the imagination. As when I first beheld the mounds of Nineveh, a longing came over me to learn what was hidden within them, and a kind of presentiment that I should one day seek to clear up the mystery. I have still the most lively recollection of that morning dawn when I first saw them, and of my entrance amongst them as the sun rose in unclouded splendour above the sea-like horizon.

(Layard 1903: 349–50)

Now he stood here again together with one hundred Arab workmen, ready to uncover what was hidden here and perhaps solve the mystery – however that might be defined. His men began digging at the mound called Mujelibe in mid-December, and he was from the very start uncertain whether the effort was going to prove fruitful, for it seemed obvious to him that all the mounds in the area had top layers which were very heavy and which had to be Hellenistic in date. And indeed, his workers immediately began to discover Greek artifacts, so he ordered a team to dig further down near the bottom of the mound in the hope of finding earlier periods which represented the 'real' Babylon.

After a month's work he closed the excavations with a highly disappointing outcome, and he wrote to Canning that 'the result of the excavations in the ruins near this place are not such as to encourage a considerable outlay, particularly in the present state of my finances'. He explains that the ruins consist of 'vast masses of brick-work, without sculptured ornaments or inscribed records as at Nineveh', so there is very little worth finding – and nothing worth removing to the British Museum. In other words, even if he had adequate financial means at his disposal, Babylon would not be a suitable target for his activities. He had discovered a very large building in the principal mound, but had given it up again, and his aim was to conduct 'mere experiments', unless directly ordered by the Trustees to tackle the site in a major excavation.

Instead he intended to go further south and examine a number of large mounds which were known to exist here, ruins with such names as Niffer, Sinkara and Warka. Since the area in question could not be reached after the rise of the waters in the Euphrates, that is in March, when the melted snow from the Taurus mountains arrives in these regions north of the Persian Gulf, he was in a hurry to move

Figure 30.2 William Kennet Loftus, the choleric and difficult man who excavated at several places in Babylonia, at the ruins of the Persian capital Susa, and at Kuyunjik. (From Barnett 1976: 2)

along. But he also worried about his eventual return to England and clearly did not wish to risk having to spend another summer in Mesopotamia; he pointed out that he had suffered very much from fever during the last six months, and that in fact Hormuzd had been even worse affected, so it was just about time to say goodbye to Babylonia and Assyria.[189]

That the mounds in the extreme south were known at this time was primarily due to the activities of a certain William Kennet Loftus, who had visited several of them and even conducted minor excavations (see Figure 30.2). Loftus had taken over the post left vacant in the Frontier Commission by Layard's resignation, having been appointed as geologist and natural historian in January 1849 (Harbottle 1958). His duties turned out to be very light, and he started to take an interest in the country and its ruins. In December 1849, about a year before Layard started his excavations at Babylon, Loftus went on a daring trip on horseback together with a colleague from Baghdad to the town Mohammerah, a journey which would take them across the entire central area in the south, ending at the lowest course of the Tigris. This region had practically never been visited by Europeans:

> In order that some idea may be formed of the difficulties and dangers attending a journey into Lower Babylonia or Chaldæa Proper, I may here mention, that, during spring and summer, when the Hindíeh branch of the Euphrates is closed, the greater part of the country, from above lat. 32°, is a continuous marsh towards the south, quite impassable except in canoes called terrádas. In these the natives are enabled to keep up communication among themselves on the spots of elevated land which raise their heads above the surrounding swamps. The heat, however, prevents the approach of travellers. In autumn these inundations rapidly subside, but the resultant malaria is so great as to deter any European from invading this *terra* (if it can be so called) *incognita*. The only season of the year, therefore, which frees Chaldæa from water and fever is the winter, when the air becomes rarified. . . .
>
> Under such unpromising circumstances, it is not at all surprising that this region has been so little visited, and that so many monuments of its past history still remain to be explored. In no other part of Babylonia is there such astonishing proof of ancient civilization and denseness of population. Some lofty pile is generally visible to mark the site of a once-important city; while numerous little spots, covered with broken pottery, point to the former existence of villages and of a rural population. Traces of old canal-beds prove the care with which the whole country was watered when the marshes were confined within proper limits, and the land of the Chaldees flourished.
>
> (Loftus 1857: 73–4)

This journey was the first which gave a real impression of the country where the very earliest civilisation in Mesopotamia developed in the Sumerian city-states, and Loftus' account to his boss, Colonel Williams, convinced the latter that it would be worthwhile to attempt to excavate some of the mounds. Loftus had been able to bring with him a sample of inscribed bricks which he had picked up on the surface, and copies of these had of course been sent to Rawlinson.

His excavations began at the site called Warka, a colossal ruin field which covers the remains of the Sumerian city Uruk, known from the Bible as Erech, one of the places supposed to have been ruled by King Nimrod. Loftus worked here for three weeks and discovered mainly a large number of graves. In fact, he had opened a cemetery from the Parthian period, which meant the centuries around the beginning of the Common Era; he excavated hundreds of the coffins typical of this period, made of glazed clay and shaped somewhat like a gigantic carpet slipper. Loftus had no idea of the period he was in, and Rawlinson saw his finds as evidence of a gigantic cemetery for the inhabitants of all Babylonia and Assyria.

The activities were then moved to the mound Sinkara, which is not far from Warka and covers the ruins of the ancient city Larsa; he dug here briefly and unsystematically, discovering a number of interesting texts from various periods.

All this was of course extremely attractive, not least for Rawlinson, who valued texts over everything else, but Loftus' activities can hardly be seen as anything other than a hasty raid, which, however, brought hitherto unknown types of material to light and showed the potential of the southern mounds.

Loftus came to play a not insignificant role in the further exploration of Mesopotamia in the years that followed. He was in several respects as unlike Layard as possible, apparently a deeply traditional man without much imagination, and a man who found it extremely difficult to discover anything positive to say about the inhabitants of the country where he worked. He wrote a book about his travels and excavations which contains several stories about situations in which he overcame the stupidity, meanness and wickedness of the local people by way of a suitable display of his own British superiority and mental strength. As he points out: 'it is well known among travellers that firmness and a show of superiority are a sure method of gaining the respect of an Oriental'. Many of Layard's conflicts with the Arabs were of course handled in precisely this way, but the difference is that he never appears to lose the basic respect for his opponents, whereas Loftus had no such feelings to begin with. Typical is his account of a tribe which lived in the border areas between Persia and Mesopotamia:

> it was the most extraordinary assemblage of animals bearing the human form that I ever set eyes upon. They had high shoulders, long legs, pucker-faces, and (if the Lamarckian theory of transmutation of species be true) perhaps also long tails, although I will not vouch for this fact, not having had an opportunity of making a minute zoological examination. They could not, however, have been so far advanced in the scale of progression as those men with tails, whom it is said the French naturalist, M. Castelman, heard of in Abyssinia, because the latter possessed benches with holes in them, through which they passed their tails; the Segwendís were not so civilized as even to construct a bench!

> (Loftus 1857: 359)

His descriptions are unusual, even for his time, and even considering that he most probably met with chicanery, stupidity and ill will. His biographer has generously described his account as 'a dispassionate but not unkindly view of the present primitive inhabitants and their corrupt rulers which seems well suited to contemporary English views' (Harbottle 1958: 200). Loftus' demonisation of Islam and his contempt for the people he insists on calling 'natives' is undoubtedly related to his extremely violent temper. He seems to have exploded at the slightest provocation, and became involved in difficulties as can be seen from a letter Hormuzd Rassam wrote to Layard a few years later about events which took place at Mosul. Loftus was leaving the city and Rassam and a certain Mr Berrington followed him across the rickety and narrow bridge of boats which took them to the other side of the river Tigris. Two Italian doctors passed the other way and one of them became incensed because the servants would not make way for him, so he struck one of them '& used a shameful language to us all. Mr. Loftus got in a dreadful rage, & as soon as all got over the bridge he jumped off his horse & ran after the Dr.'. Rassam followed but was stopped by the Pasha who was sitting on his balcony overlooking the river and who had seen it all. 'His Excellency asked me what was the matter and as I was telling him that a European Doctor had insulted us, 2 men came to me running & said "your friend is killed". Berrington & myself ran as fast as we could but Lateef Agha outran us & reached the spot just in time to keep the enraged Dr. from stabbing Mr. Loftus'. In fact, he had horsewhipped the doctor but was then overwhelmed by the other people in the Italian party, and Rassam came just in time to get him out of trouble.[190]

What did the 'natives' make of this? A complaint was handed to the Pasha, of course, the French consul Victor Place became involved, and the whole affair was deeply embarrassing. Nevertheless, despite his temper Loftus was considered to be 'active, intelligent, and thoroughly in earnest', as Rawlinson wrote to the Trustees (Gadd 1936: 36).

Reports about his excavations in the south in 1850 had been published in several places in England, and Rawlinson had expressed his great pleasure at the many new and exciting texts. Layard now sat here in Babylonia and had to conclude that the great discoveries he had been hoping to make seemed unlikely to be realised. In January he stopped work at Babylon and moved further south, to a village called Souk al Afaij, in whose neighbourhood there was a gigantic ruin called Niffer, the ancient city of Nippur. After a few days' activities here he had to realise that also Niffer was a disappointment and his results were exceedingly modest; he wrote to Canning: 'it still appears to me very doubtful whether the mounds of Babylonia contain remains of sufficient importance to warrant a considerable expenditure of money'. There were no finds which could be sent to the British Museum in triumph, and he could not advise them to spend considerable sums on a more extensive investigation.

Niffer was in fact the largest and apparently most promising ruin in Babylonia after Babylon itself; the mound is quite a lot bigger than Kuyunjik and most definitely not suited for a short reconnaissance of the type Layard had made. It was also extremely difficult to reach at this time because of the unrest which plagued the south; it was located at the edge of very large swamps so that Layard and his workers had to go there every morning in small canoes of reed covered with asphalt. Practically all roads were closed, and the disorder was expected to become even worse after the Pasha in Baghdad had been deposed in the middle of his campaign against the Bedouin. Layard was now ready to give up Babylonia for good, and he wrote with some bitterness that 'Major Rawlinson's exaggerated accounts of Mr. Loftus' discoveries have given rise to expectations which cannot I think be realised.'[191]

The entire expedition to Babylonia was, seen from an archaeological point of view, a signal failure – in the same way as the expedition to the Habur. These fruitless exertions illustrate the limitations of Layard's capability as an excavator and of his understanding of the character of the ruins he encountered. He clearly did not have the means to carry out a truly meaningful investigation of either Babylon or Niffer, but his approach was also governed by the simple view of the time that archaeology was a kind of treasure hunt: the goal was monuments and art destined for the museums of Europe. The mounds of Babylonia were much less productive than those of Assyria, for, as he quickly realised, there was no tradition for stone sculpture and reliefs in the south. Layard was the pioneer, the man who blazed the trail and showed the opportunities which existed, but he lacked the interest and the patience needed for the careful scientific project which was now on the agenda, including the development of a precise and coherent archaeological methodology and the reconstruction of the history of the country. One cannot help suspecting that his dedication to the entire project was just about at an end. In the following years it was openly rumoured that he declared in Baghdad that

> unless there was a Parliamentary grant of 25,000 pounds, there would be nothing to hope for from the site of Babylon; and that, if ever such a sum was given, he would ask to be spared the honour of being appointed to spend the money.
>
> (Fresnel 1855: 548)

It was becoming a great strain to expose himself to regular attacks of malaria and fever, and his physique was not what it had been. His depressive state of mind appears from a letter he wrote to his uncle in London, in which he said that just as he had begun with nothing, he would end up with nothing. He wanted no further honours, though, and was content with the knowledge that he had been 'useful'. He felt confident that he was able to fend for himself as long as he was not brought down by disease, and he was becoming more and more convinced that he could trust nothing or nobody. It is not clear precisely what caused this outburst, but he had obviously been severely disappointed, and he felt only disgust for the flattery which resulted from the kind of success he had achieved. No more was he going to let himself be taken in by it (Lane-Poole 1888: 94–5).

The simple, happy days from the first expedition did not return. Everything was more complicated, and Layard's personal relations to men like Rawlinson and Canning were clearly developing in a highly problematic direction. The great ambassador had not been happy to see Layard appear as solely responsible for the Assyrian discoveries in the eyes of the public, and right now it was Rawlinson who seemed to reap the rewards of Layard's work. Archaeology was no longer a truly satisfactory pursuit, and Layard probably sighed and agreed when he read a long letter from his friend Longworth at the embassy in Constantinople:

> What you write me on the subject of the excavations though to a certain extent satisfactory gives me uneasiness on your account both with respect to the outlay you have made on your own responsibility & the annoyance you have met with from the crude & contradictory speculations of the archaeologists who have taken up the subject of these antiquities – I must take the liberty as a friend of speaking my mind on these matters. I cannot help entertaining some uncomfortable forebodings – for I fear you are likely to be involved in endless polemics discussions & God knows what – & though I believe your clear judgement & sound sense would establish your superiority in this as in many other pursuits, it is a question whether the time it would necessarily occupy might not be otherwise employed with much greater benefit to yourself. As far as I am able to understand these subjects are much

too abstruse to occupy public attention long. There was something so marvellous & interesting in your discoveries that they became something more than a nine days wonder which in England is a great deal; the subsequent disputes of the learned do not I am persuaded attract much notice & I rather think that Rawlinson's theories are known to or appreciated by some half dozen people at most. With respect to yourself, I had thought & still hope you had a good diplomatic career before you.[192]

In the end the swamps at Afaij nearly cost him his life. The recurrent attacks of malaria and fevers now led to pneumonia, and he clearly had to get away from this most unhealthy spot, but he was unable to move. The only remedy he had was a blistering fluid meant for an injured horse, and he thought this saved his life, but even though it provided some relief, he was still unable to get up from his rug for several days. The rains were violent and as the water began to rise, the local Arabs left for safer areas, but it was only after Hormuzd had arrived to help him that he was able to attempt the journey back to Baghdad. With them were the thirty Jebour Arabs from the area round Mosul who had come south with Layard to dig, but despite the fact that they were a large company, the trip was nevertheless a dangerous one. He could hardly stay in his saddle, and there were constant alarms because of passing groups of Bedouin who threatened to attack them; the few villages they reached *en route* were most unwilling to let strangers in, for everybody was a potential enemy. They did reach the gates of Baghdad and Layard was put to bed and came under proper medical treatment which kept him in the city for several weeks.

In the meantime the letter from the Vizier in Constantinople had finally arrived with new permits for excavations. The permission was limited to a period of six months reckoned from the day he began his work, a condition he interpreted to mean from the day he resumed excavations after his return to Mosul from Babylonia. The Pasha at Mosul was ordered to send all duplicate examples of reliefs which might be found to Constantinople, whereas Layard was entitled to take all unique pieces. At this time the entire south was in a state of chaos after the Pasha had been deposed, and Layard gave up all thought of further work here – 'with great regret' he writes, but it is hard to believe him.[193]

CHAPTER THIRTY-ONE

GOODBYE TO ASSYRIA

—— •◆• ——

While Layard's commitment to the excavations appeared to be evaporating, Rawlinson was in full swing in London trying to raise money for a continuation. He had a meeting with the Trustees, in which he stated his disapproval at their failure to get funds, but he went further than that. Together with a small group of likeminded people he helped create a special 'Nineveh Fund', and they succeeded in getting Prince Albert to provide the first £100 for it. Layard's publisher John Murray accepted the post as official secretary for the Fund, and Rawlinson expressed his conviction that a sum could be raised which 'will at any rate enable you to *tap* most of the ruins in Babylonia'.[194] Murray also wrote encouraging letters about this matter, expressing the hope that Layard's disease would not prevent him from carrying out his difficult task 'until all is done that remains to be done in unravelling this great mystery – reconstitution of a lost nation. Such a golden opportunity may never again occur'.[195]

The Nineveh Fund was officially launched in January 1851 with the publication of a small pamphlet. It was stressed that the Fund had been started by 'persons interested in Eastern Science, and acquainted with Mr. LAYARD's position', but that he himself had no previous knowledge of the plans and consequently had not given his consent. The Fund was also completely without connection to the British Museum.

The authors pointed out that the funds allocated to Layard by the British government had been exhausted, and that he had been forced 'to abandon several new excavations which he had commenced at Nimroud and at Nebbi Junas, and which promised to lead to historical discoveries of the utmost importance'. This was clearly an incorrect description of the state of affairs, and it is somewhat difficult to believe that for instance Rawlinson did not know better. The pamphlet continued with the information that Layard now had gone to Babylonia in order to investigate the many ruins there. With some daring it claimed that Layard was 'prepared to devote the next six months to this particular object, and proposes, if unassisted from other quarters, to defray from his own resources the expenses of his preliminary survey, and of such excavations as he may find it practicable to undertake among the cities of Chaldea'. Those who had received letters from him during recent months must have known that he was not in the least willing to do such a thing, and one wonders whether this was also a somewhat crude and naive attempt on Rawlinson's part to put pressure on Layard. It must have been with a mixture of pride and irritation that he could read:

> As this object, however, of obtaining specimens of the early Art of the Babylonians, of accumulating historical documents regarding them, and of investigating generally the antiquities of a region which Biblical associations so much endeared to us, is one of national rather than of individual interest, it is thought that there are many noblemen and gentlemen in this country who would regret to see the expenses of the work thus thrown upon Mr. LAYARD, and who would willingly come forward with pecuniary aid, in order to relieve him from personal liability.

The objectives defined here were clearly Rawlinson's, but the committee behind the Fund consisted of the Earl of Aboyne, Sir John Guest, Bart., M.P., H. Danby Seymour, Esq., M.P. and Colonel Rawlinson. Murray explains in his covering letter that £600 has already been raised and that they expect soon to reach the figure £1,000. The list of contributors printed in the pamphlet names contributions of £100 each from Prince Albert, the Earl of Ellesmere and Sir John Guest; Murray and Rawlinson have given each £50, and one notes that W.S.W. Vaux from the British Museum, the artist George Scharf who collaborated with Layard on his book and the historian George Grote are among the contributors. Benjamin Austen appears under the pseudonym 'A.B.' with a sum of £100.[196]

No doubt these gentlemen meant well, but Layard was unhappy with their efforts. Had they asked him first, he would undoubtedly have rejected the idea. It was bad enough to be the agent of the condescending and apparently indifferent Trustees of the British Museum, but to enter into a kind of economic dependence on a group of private people, who counted Rawlinson as one of the most important members, was unacceptable. The Fund, one would assume, had to lead to complications with the British Museum, and through that institution with the Exchequer. In fact, a sum of money had just been allocated by the government, so how should that be spent? It was unthinkable that funds from official and private sources could be mixed.

Rawlinson was interested only in tablets and inscriptions and seems oblivious to the complications or the wider perspectives in the matter, but he was later to experience the difficulties such private funds could lead to. At the moment he was waiting impatiently to hear the results of Layard's expedition to Babylonia, for the tablets which had been brought back by Loftus had turned out to be full of interesting information. He described the tablets as a kind of 'Govt. bank notes, being in fact the regular currency of the country and payable in gold or silver at the Royal Treasury'. He suspected that the tablets found at Kuyunjik were of the same type. He was thus able to define the tablets from Babylonia as economic in character, but his interpretation was anachronistic: the tablets were not bank notes but recorded private economic transactions such as loans and the purchase of land.[197]

Layard had to disappoint Rawlinson, for he had virtually no results to show for his efforts in the south. At Nimrud and Kuyunjik he now also began to wind down his activities, planning for his final farewell to Assyria. The new artist, Bell, arrived and started drawing the reliefs. Layard describes him in a letter to Ellis as 'anxious to do all in his power to fulfil the objects of his mission. He draws nicely & carefully & will, I have no doubt, make good copies of the basreliefs'.[198]

Reliefs and tablets continued to be discovered in large quantities so there was a great deal of work waiting to be done, but Layard had clearly decided that enough was enough. In mid-April he wrote a long letter to Canning in which he explained his situation; he made it clear that he was preparing for a return to England, but he also stated plainly that he never intended to come back to Assyria. 'I feel that it is full time that I should turn my attention seriously to my profession', he wrote, echoing the recommendation given by Longworth some months before. He expressed bitterness over the lack of support he felt from the British Museum, but at the same time he refused to work for the Fund in London: 'The plan appears to me objectionable in many respects & I have declined availing myself of funds so collected'. Canning had apparently hinted in a previous letter that the Trustees felt Layard gave up too easily when faced with difficulties, but he wrote with some bitterness that if Canning had known 'how very inadequately I have been supported throughout and how many difficulties I have had to contend with I do not think you would concur'. Bell he characterises as 'a mere boy, very willing and industrious, but not the person any enlightened Govt would dream of sending out on such an expedition'. Many great opportunities have been lost because of a lack of funds and support, he wrote, and he concluded with some sadness that he felt 'heartily ashamed when I compare my published drawings with those of the French'.[199]

In the situation there was nothing he could do other than leave Bell with the responsibility for the continued excavations. Layard's last instructions to the young man were straightforward and unsentimental, and he left practically all initiative to Bell. His only concrete suggestion was that a connection should be established between the two monumental entrances to the large palace at Kuyunjik, in East and West, so that the building could be seen as a complete whole. Of course, he had to make careful plans and draw all reliefs, and Bell was asked to pay special attention to the collection of 'all small objects of interest such as inscribed tablets impressions of seals &c.'.[200]

A raft loaded with the last reliefs chosen was sent off to Baghdad; it carried seven large reliefs and three cases which contained parts of a winged lion and bull. These were destined for Sir John Guest. Two cases which each contained 'a winged figure' were for Canning, and there were finally three smaller boxes for the British Museum.[201] When all this was done he sat down to conclude his last official duty, a detailed account of the excavation for the Trustees, extremely detailed and covering every little item in his household.

He said goodbye to Nimrud and returned to Mosul, where he took a last stroll through the halls and chambers of the gigantic palace. He could look back on years of work here which had led to the opening of

> no less than seventy-one halls, chambers, and passages, whose walls, almost without an exception, had been pannelled with slabs of sculptured alabaster recording the wars, the triumphs, and the great deeds of the Assyrian king.

Figure 31.1 In collaboration with Layard the architect and art historian James Fergusson made a number of reconstructions of the Assyrian palaces. Like this one, which shows the entrance to the throne room at Sennacherib's palace, they give an impression of the power and majesty of Assyrian architecture, but in the details much is completely misunderstood. (From Layard 1853: frontispiece)

> By a rough calculation, about 9880 feet, or nearly two miles, of bas-reliefs, with twenty-seven portals, formed by colossal winged bulls and lion-sphinxes, were uncovered in that part alone of the building explored during my researches.
>
> (Layard 1853: 589)

The task completed was truly gigantic and he could well feel proud (see Figure 31.1). For us, who look back on his accomplishments, admiration must certainly also be a dominant feeling, but it is difficult not to think with sadness at the fact that very little is known about the two miles of reliefs uncovered by him. Even though the collections in the British Museum are very large, they represent only a small fraction of what was discovered, and for many entire rooms in the palace we have only the vaguest descriptions of the reliefs on the walls, and certainly no drawings or photographs. The young artist Bell had in fact brought with him a so-called 'Talbotype' camera, a device which had only very recently been invented by an interesting man called Fox Talbot who will reappear in this story; Bell had been trained in its use before he was sent off from London, but he did not leave us any photographs.

On 28 April 1851, Layard left Mosul headed for the town Alexandretta on the Mediterranean coast. His career as an active archaeologist was ended. It had started five-and-a-half years earlier, on 9 November 1845, when he had first dug at Nimrud together with his friend Ross. It had begun almost like a picnic, but it was a tired and somewhat disillusioned Layard who rode out through the gates of Mosul. He had, as he wrote to his uncle, started with empty hands, but he certainly did not leave 'with nothing' – even though he was inclined to think so in his darker moments. His entire life was to be closely linked to Assyria and his future career was to be based to a large extent on the fame and recognition he had gained.

Even though he was never to set foot in Assyria again, he was of course in no way finished with the palaces of this land. He now had to write his second account, find ways of making his discoveries coalesce into a coherent picture which could satisfy the still interested public. But even before he had left the Middle East Assyria sent him a last greeting. The young artist Bell had gone to Bavian in order to make drawings and plans of the reliefs there, and he liked to take a swim in the river Gomel which runs past. Fat Toma had warned him several times that the river was dangerous, but the young hothead had refused to listen and been irritated at Toma's concern which he felt was a personal affront. Of course, things went wrong and he was swept away by the current. All the Arab workmen ran after him and some even jumped into the river in an attempt to save him, but when he was found five minutes later it was too late.

Layard wrote to Ellis at the British Museum from Alexandretta in order to inform him about the accident, and he pointed out with some bitterness that Bell 'was unfortunately very headstrong & on leaving him I was under the apprehension that some accident would sooner or later happen to him'.[202]

How many times had Layard escaped from foolhardy adventures? Can he have avoided the feeling that he himself had used up all the luck?

PART III

VICTOR PLACE
AND HORMUZD RASSAM

CHAPTER THIRTY-TWO

RAWLINSON
GETS IT RIGHT

——— .◆. ———

Layard was back in London in July 1851. He had made clear announcements to everybody that his archaeological career was over, and his dream was naturally to find a niche in either the diplomatic corps or in politics, but the basis for such dreams was fragile. When he arrived in England he took the train directly to Canford where he was received by cousin Charlotte; she wrote in her diary that she was extremely pleased by this unexpected visit, but 'poor fellow he is sadly altered and tells me he has suffered much and been very ill' (Bessborough 1950: 275). From now on he was a daily guest and Charlotte gave a series of parties in his honour. She also went with him to the British Museum to help unpack some of his discoveries, and he entertained both at Canford and before the workers in the ironworks at Dowlais; he told a spellbound audience about his adventures in Arabia and his discoveries, and according to Charlotte he held his audience 'in a state of breathless attention'.

Sir John Guest was seriously ill and needed much care, so when Layard spent Christmas at Canford the ten children were entertained by him so that Charlotte could tend to her sick husband. At New Year's Eve he was invited to dinner at Charles Dickens' house in order to 'see the New Year in with such extemporaneous frolics of an exploded sort (in genteel society) as may occur to us' (Dickens 1882: III, 132). In London he joined a hectic social life and met many influential persons, but the political system was so pervaded by privileges and family connections that it seemed unlikely that he should be invited into it on the basis of his social background.

And yet, suddenly the situation turned and everything seemed rosy. The Prime Minister, Lord John Russell, asked him for an interview two days after his dinner at Dickens', and in February he was offered a post as embassy secretary in Paris at a salary of £500 per year. But even before he had become used to this another possibility appeared. He wrote a letter to Canning about it:

> When I announced to you a few days ago my appointment to Paris, I little thought that I should so soon have to communicate a further promotion. Altho' you will be, doubtless, much surprised, I have every reason to hope that you will not be displeased. You have always taken a most warm interest in my welfare, & I must ever bear in mind that it is to you I owe my first

true rise in life. The Queen has been pleased to approve of my being named Under Secretary of State for Foreign Affairs. I have today entered upon the discharge of my duties at the Foreign Office.[203]

This was a most unusual move by the government and one which attracted a great deal of attention in the press, for Layard was being asked to join the truly influential elite of the country. His letter to Canning may also indicate that he anticipated some concern on the part of the ambassador, who might suddenly find himself in a situation where he would have to take orders from his former employee. At any rate, the triumph did not last long since the government fell eleven days later. Even though Layard might have continued in his post he decided in the end to step down together with the other Liberal ministers. On the other hand, he was now so well established that his new political friends secured him the nomination as the Liberal parliamentary candidate for the town Aylesbury, and after a brief campaign he won a seat in Parliament in July 1852.

Archaeology retained a firm grip on him and his life, however. The books about the first expedition were still selling well and he had a nice, steady income from them; in fact, this was his only source of money, for the post as MP gave no salary, which meant that it was vital for him to write a new book about the second expedition. He was also quickly called to a meeting at the British Museum together with Rawlinson in order to discuss the possibilities for further work in Mesopotamia.[204] The Nineveh Fund was, of course, dead after Layard had declined to serve as its agent, but Rawlinson was still very eager to get hold of more texts and therefore wanted to renew the excavations. He argued for a new governmental grant, and in October Ellis could announce that the Museum had been informed by the Exchequer that they were ready to give two portions each of £1,500 for new excavations in Assyria and Babylonia, plus a further £500 for digs at Susa in southwestern Persia, the old Persian capital. All these activities were to be directed by Rawlinson, who was preparing for his return to Baghdad in order to resume his duties as Resident, and it seems to have been the intention from the start that Loftus should take responsibility for the activities at Susa, where he had excavated previously.

One of the main reasons for this renewed willingness to grant money was the announcement made by Rawlinson that he had finally achieved the decisive breakthrough in his studies of cuneiform (see Figure 32.1). His discoveries had been announced in a letter in the *Athenæum* in August; since all the learned societies were closed at this time of the year – the gentlemen were busy hunting and enjoying the summer at their manor houses – he had been forced to present his new ideas in this preliminary way. It was, he wrote, 'a most interesting and important discovery which I have made within these few days in connexion with Assyrian Antiquities'. He was obviously for once very eager to appear in print, fearing that Hincks might publish before himself.

The most important single discovery was that he had succeeded in 'determinately identifying the Assyrian kings of the Lower dynasty, whose palaces have been recently excavated in the vicinity of Mosul'; moreover, this had led to a new and better understanding of the historical inscriptions as a whole, so that he could

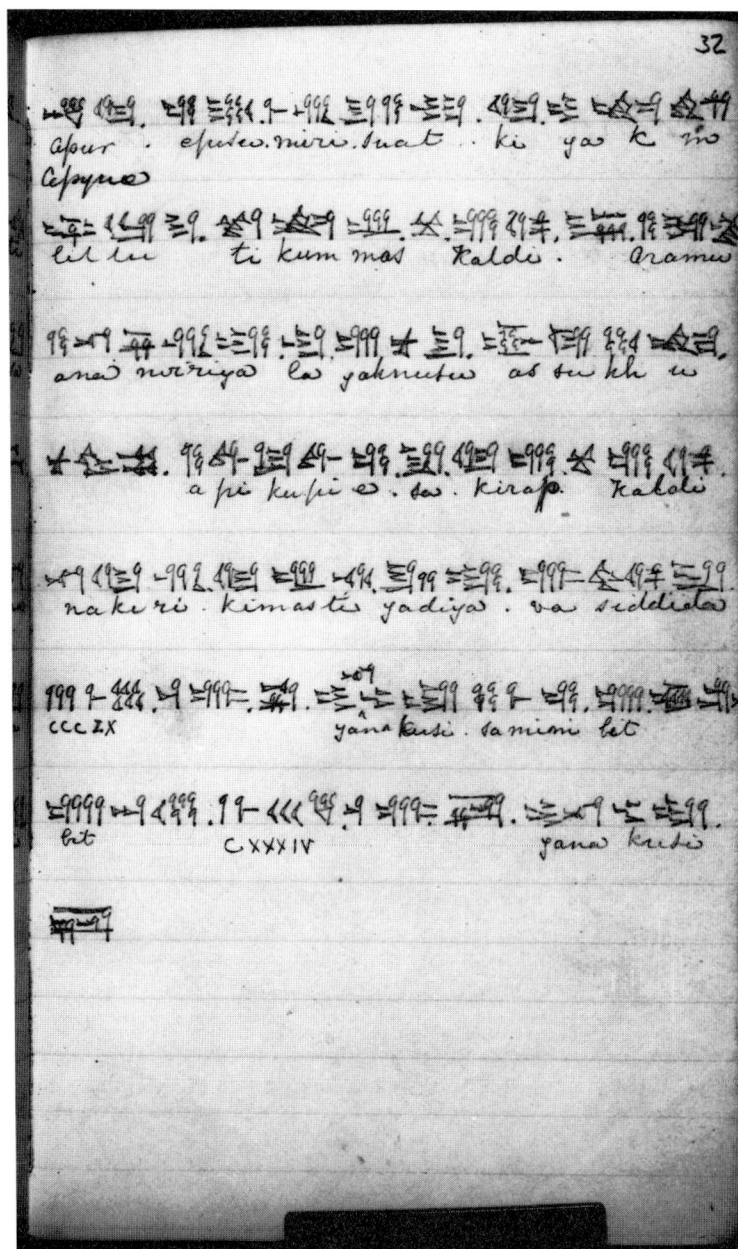

Figure 32.1 A page from one of Rawlinson's notebooks (BL 47624), probably from around 1851, with his attempt to read the Sennacherib inscription. Reproduced by courtesy of the Trustees of the British Library.

claim to have 'obtained from the annals of those kings contemporary notices of events which agree in the most remarkable way with the statements preserved in sacred and profane history'.[205]

These kings of 'the Lower dynasty' were precisely the persons who are mentioned in the Old Testament, the very men whose existence in the Assyrian texts he had until then so vehemently denied: kings like Sargon and Sennacherib. Hincks had of course long claimed that Sennacherib had built the palace at Kuyunjik, and French scholars like Longpérier had maintained that it was Sargon who had built Khorsabad, but Rawlinson had said no. Now he accepted these identifications, he read Sennacherib's name 'expressed entirely by monograms', as *Sennachi-riba*, which is remarkably close to the correct reading. He could also read the names Shalmaneser and Esarhaddon, and he could give a fairly detailed account of the stories told in some of the royal annals.

This was a major development – so one must ask what had happened? His key to this understanding came from the copies brought home by Layard of the inscription on the large bulls guarding the main entrance to the palace at Kuyunjik; it was here he had finally found convincing proof of a close relationship with the accounts from both the Old Testament and the Greek authors. It was the Assyrian report of the campaign directed against Judah and Jerusalem which was so close to what was already known from the Bible that there could be no doubt that the same events were being referred to in both texts.

The great public interest caused by Rawlinson's discovery had its roots precisely in this fact, that he was able in a convincing way to link the Assyrians with the detailed story in the Old Testament. For his contemporaries it was this connection which seemed of the greatest relevance, and it finally allowed him to bring some order into the overall historical framework. It could now be said with certainty which kings had inhabited the large Assyrian palaces, the texts could begin to be read and would soon provide detailed information about the history of the entire region; the Greek author's legends could be discarded – although the irrepressible Sardanapal continued to haunt the king-lists. Assyria was finally securely anchored in world history in those centuries where it belonged and has remained ever since.

Rawlinson's realisation was based on a real reading of large parts of the inscription on the Sennacherib bulls. The articles written at this time by Rawlinson, Hincks, Botta, Oppert and Longpérier in fact show that the cuneiform system of writing was by then largely deciphered – although this may not have been so apparent at the time. The principles on which the script was built were fairly well described, so it was known how the system functioned. Hincks was the one who had given the clearest and most perceptive analysis, in a lecture held in May 1849 to the Royal Society of Literature; this was reviewed in detail in an article in the *Literary Gazette* later that year, and from this one could get a precise impression of the special character of the script with a full understanding of many of its complexities.[206]

Hincks pointed out that the writing system was both phonetic and ideographic in character, and that in its phonetic part it was entirely syllabic in nature: signs could accordingly represent a syllable or an entire word, and each sign could be used in both ways. However, the syllabic system was more complex than one would perhaps expect, since he could show that each syllable 'might have two or more characters to represent it which were *perfectly homophonous*', that is, there would be at least seven different signs which were all to be read as *ba*. Apart from this difficulty the syllabic signs were fairly straightforward to understand, whereas the use of ideograms presented many complexities. It was not difficult to explain that a sign could stand for a word, for as pointed out earlier our own script makes use of such devices: the sign § of course stands for the word 'paragraph'. It was slightly more complex when several signs were linked to form new words; the word which had to mean 'palace' was formed by way of two signs, the first one of which alone stood for the word 'house', whereas the second one stood for 'great'.

Hincks knew that plural forms of nouns could be represented in two ways: the sign could be repeated ('house.house' would mean 'houses' just as 'p' stands for 'page' and 'pp' for 'pages'), or a special sign could be added which indicated that the word was in the plural. This could be understood as a determinative, one of those graphic indicators which are linked with words and show to which class of phenomena the words refer. There were many other determinatives: one sign would stand before names of cities, another before names of countries, a third before names of persons. The truly complex part of the system sprang from the fact that any given sign could be used in all these capacities, so that in one place it would function as a syllabic value, in another it would be an ideogram, and in a third it could appear as a determinative. And there was apparently no indication in the text itself which could tell the reader how the individual signs were being used.

Hincks had no convincing explanation for the origin of the sound values of the signs, i.e., why a given sign was used to render the syllable /ab/, whereas another stood for the syllable /ba/. Such values clearly had to reflect the phonetic structure of the language for which the script had been originally designed, and his suggestion was that this was of the Indo-European family.

In the Assyrian texts most words were, however, spelled out syllabically, which meant that the language could be analysed and understood. Hincks pointed out that it had to be related to such languages as Hebrew or Aramaic, that it was, in other words, of the Semitic family. This was by now generally agreed, and Rawlinson gave a fairly elaborate analysis of the grammar of the texts in his famous lectures in London the following year. Hincks surpassed him in his strikingly original interpretations of verbal forms, and he was able to describe central aspects of the language with surprising accuracy.

While Hincks was quite convinced that the phonetic use of the script was syllabic, Rawlinson found it extremely difficult to give up his notion of a much more mixed system in which certain signs should be understood as letters in the alphabetic sense; they might represent a syllable in some instances, such as /ba/, but in other places the sign should be understood to stand only for /b/. He took this principle from his study of Old Persian and also compared with Egyptian, which he thought was the origin of the cuneiform system.

Rawlinson's brief letter to the *Athenæum* did not really clarify the basis for his readings, and there was no reference to Hincks at all in the text. This was perhaps a little striking in view of the fact that he had accepted some of the basic ideas of the Irishman, but perhaps such a letter was not deemed the right place for comments of that nature.

We are accordingly never told precisely how Rawlinson achieved his breakthrough, but it seems that building on the many observations made by himself and by Hincks he was finally able to achieve 'critical mass', that so many individual conclusions on points of detail came together to make it possible for him to make the connection between the text on the bulls and the other accounts he knew.

In 1851 he published a long article in the *Journal of the Royal Asiatic Society*, which gave a more detailed explanation of his discoveries. It appears that his new realisation was based partly on the fact that he had gained access to a number of new texts, partly on some real new insights, but it was a hasty and incomplete piece of work which had to be published in a quite inadequate form, because he was about to leave England for Baghdad. Had he spent more time in his study and a little less in society and at hunting parties he might not have had to publish in this manner.

Instead of a comprehensive and detailed list of signs with values and meanings and a careful commentary he had to restrict himself to what he called an 'Indiscriminate list of Babylonian and Assyrian Characters', which contained 246 cuneiform signs taken from his little red notebooks. They are presented in a kind of phonological sequence, beginning with the vowels; the list gives first variant forms of the cuneiform sign, next 'Phonetic power', then 'Ideographic value', and finally 'Phonetic powers arising from Ideographic values'. Not all signs are given values at all, and there are several grave mistakes, but the system is basically in place.

His discussion of the alphabet begins with some remarks about the difficulties facing any decipherer working on the cuneiform material, and he states candidly that one must at the present time be very uncertain about the results one can reach: 'no amount of labour will suffice for the complete resolution of difficulties; no ingenuity, however boldly or happily exerted, can furnish readings of such exactitude as to lead at once to positive results'.

'On the very threshold of the inquiry' one is met with a series of difficulties which are inherent in 'the construction of the Assyrian Alphabet', and which tend to 'envelop all our subsequent labours in obscurity and doubt'. When compared with the Egyptian writing, which was at this time capable of being read with tolerable certainty, he notes that the systems are essentially the same, containing 'ideographs, determinatives, phonetics, and mixed signs', but he finds two special difficulties in Assyrian which do not exist in Egyptian:

> 1stly, There are no direct means of distinguishing between the various classes of Cuneiform signs; and 2dly, in the phonetic branch of the subject, which is of course the most extensive and important, there is no clue, as far as the alphabet is concerned, to the determination of one out of the many powers which may belong to a single character.

The second difficulty is the serious one. What he has accepted by this time is that the script is 'polyphonic' in nature, which means that each character can be read in several different ways when used as a syllabic sign. He has, however, a percep-tive explanation for this phenomenon, perhaps the most brilliant single observation in his presentation:

> The analogy of Egyptian writing would lead us to suspect that the Cuneatic signs were originally mere pictures, rude representatives of natural objects, which expressed in the first instance the actual object that was figured, but which came in process of time, and by a gradual transition from the repre-sentative to the symbolical system to express ideas. The formation of a phonetic alphabet, and the application of such an alphabet to the ordinary purposes of inscription, would then be a third step in advance, and might have taken place in the following manner: – each sign may have been employed phonetically to express the name, or names, of the object to which it was previously appropriated as an ideograph, and without any reference whatever to the sense.

The three steps or phases which he describes here represent first the development from a *drawing* to a *sign*, a process which results in a proper system of writing; next, the extension of the semantic field of each individual sign to ideas and concepts, so that a sign showing a foot may come to stand for words meaning 'to go' or 'to carry' or 'to stand'. Finally, the third step is the introduction of the rebus-principle, where the phonetic values of the signs are separated from their meaning as word-signs and can be used to represent syllables in the writing of any word: anyone can construct a writing for words like 'doughnut' or 'carmine', and if such a principle is systematised it will be possible to construct a complete syllabary. This analysis laid the grounds for a correct understanding of the special character of the cuneiform system of writing.

Polyphony comes in, then, because the signs as ideographs were used to repre-sent more than one word – as in the example I just mentioned, where the character based on the drawing of a foot could stand for related objects and concepts. In actual practice this sign could be read both as 'GUB' and as 'DU', and one value went back to a word meaning 'stand' whereas the other had its basis in a word meaning 'go'. In this way each sign could acquire several different phonetic read-ings and thus stand for a variety of syllables. Rawlinson's problem was that he had no idea which language the script had been created for (and he rightly rejected Hincks' suggestion of an Indo-European origin), and he was therefore unable to find explanations for the different readings. He certainly tried, however, and basing himself on the supposition that cuneiform had been created for a language of the Semitic family he looked around in the various known Semitic languages for clues to the phonetic values. He gave a single example, which is of course incorrect, although in principle he was right: he knew that the cuneiform sign which means 'land' had at least two readings, 'KUR' and 'MAT', and he pointed out that this could go back to the words *kura* in Arabic and *mat* in Chaldean. He had no way of knowing that the phonetic values of the signs (with few exceptions) are based on words in a language known as Sumerian, which is totally unrelated to Semitic in structure or vocabulary. The example chosen by him is even more complex, however, for the Sumerian word *kur* is the basis of the first phonetic value, but the second stems from the word *matum* which is Assyrian and Babylonian, and which of course also means 'land'. Such complexities could not possibly be understood at this time, however, and the important thing was that Rawlinson was right in principle.

He admits, however, that 'the practical inconvenience of such a variableness of power is excessive', an observation which quickly became the basis for some scepticism with respect to the correctness of the decipherment. However, even though the system of writing was clearly very complex, it turned out in practice that the texts could be understood once the fundamental principles had been established and more texts became available. In fact, one tends to lose one's breath when considering the speed with which the decipherment progressed from then on, how quickly the opaque wall of strange signs was broken down.

Rawlinson offered a detailed examination of only two signs which both referred to vowels; the first was

a sign which he gives the readings /ha/ and (correctly) /a/. This sound, and thus this sign, obviously appears in countless contexts, but he had noticed that it was the marker for first person singular in verbal forms. One particular sequence which was found many times in the royal inscriptions was:

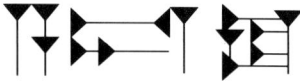

Rawlinson read these three signs as *ha-du-ku* (we would now read *a-du-ku*) and he analysed this as a verbal form meaning 'I smote' or 'I killed'.

The same sign could of course appear as an ideogram and it 'is commonly used to express the idea of "son"', interchanging with some other signs. Since the royal Assyrian inscriptions contain a wealth of genealogies, it goes without saying that these signs are not only very frequent, but also very important for an historical reconstruction.

Thus, scholars had the correct readings for a great many signs, the basic principles according to which the system functioned had been established, and now finally Rawlinson had also published both the Old Persian and the Babylonian versions of the Bisutun Inscriptions and provided a translation of them. This meant that a vocabulary could begin to be collected and that the grammatical problems could be tackled. A considerable number of nouns, pronouns and verbs could now be read, and the scholars were approaching the point where only the ideographically written personal names created truly serious obstacles, precisely those words which all had thought would provide the key to a decipherment.

Rawlinson's article was very important for the further development of the understanding of cuneiform, but true to his custom he presented his views as if they in all respects constituted new discoveries – despite the fact that other scholars had suggested similar ideas before him. Absolutely fundamental to his progress was the realisation that Hincks had been right all along in his claim that the cuneiform system was not alphabetic but syllabic in nature, but no one who read Rawlinson's article would be able to see that he had adopted the position of his rival here. In fact, he referred to his previous presentation as still valid, apparently claiming that he had no need to change his mind at all. In explanation of his position he points to the writing of the name for Cappadocia, *Katpatuka*, where the first syllable is written *ka-at*; he concludes that one of the two signs must represent 'a simple letter rather than a syllable'. He therefore still adheres to his previous statement 'that the Phonetic signs were in some cases syllabic, in others literal'. What he does not see (or will not admit) is that this in fact is a syllabic system, for even though the signs 'ka' and 'at' together give the syllable 'kat' they are still syllables and not letters in an alphabet. The vowels attached to such 'letters' were not, as he said, 'to be supplied according to the requirements of the language', they were as much elements of the sign-value as the consonants. His sign-list is therefore naturally based entirely on the syllabic principle.

Similarly, Hincks had long maintained that it was Sennacherib who had built the palace at Kuyunjik, a position which had been rejected by Rawlinson, but which he now adopted. One might have expected the colonel to make a graceful acknowledgement of this prior claim, but he did no such thing. It is true that Rawlinson was the first to present a truly convincing reading of this name, which Hincks had read *San-ki-ram* (Hincks 1850: 35–6), where Rawlinson read *Sennachi-riba*, which was much better; he could therefore reject Hincks' suggestion as a mere guess, but it is nevertheless striking that he completely ignored the fact that he was now adopting views which he had not long ago argued against in long articles.

Hincks did not immediately react negatively to this, however. After Rawlinson's initial letter to the *Athenæum*, in which he announced the readings on the bulls from Sennacherib's palace, and accepted the identification of the builder with this king, Hincks wrote a letter to the journal in which he congratulated him on his 'important discovery', refraining from pointing out that he was adopting his own position. He also corrected a few mistakes and introduced some others, but the tone was urbane.

When Rawlinson continued to ignore the old Irishman in the article in which he presented his sign-list it became too much, however. In vain Hincks searched for a single sentence admitting his own prior claim to these ideas, and he then sat down to write a long article which was to demolish his rival.

Reading these articles one hundred and fifty years later one is struck not only by the violent emotions, the rancour and jealousy which pervade the two men's relationship, but it is in fact difficult to understand that Rawlinson got away with it among his learned colleagues. The old parson at Killyleagh had a very sharp pen and the colonel was quite simply exposed. The truth is probably that Rawlinson's by now well-established position in England allowed him, as one of Hincks' friends wrote, to 'do things with impunity which the public would not suffer in a country Parson'. The writer expressed his conviction that truth would triumph, however, but he was at the same time worried that it would perhaps be 'unpalatable and must be administered with a little attention to the fancies of the patient' (Davidson 1933: 170).

In his printed answer Hincks did not mince his words, however; he first pointed out that Rawlinson had left his old system of decipherment based on an alphabetic interpretation and had now adopted his own syllabic principles, and he commented drily:

> For this substitution of truth for error, I of course cannot blame him; but I think I have a right to complain that he has omitted all mention of my priority in asserting that truth which he has so recently embraced.

The colonel had introduced a few corrections to Hincks' system, but he felt that they were either insignificant or wrong; even if they should be correct, however, they were not 'of such moment as to entitle him to claim more than the credit of improving another's work'. He then discussed these minor points before he delivered the truly decisive thrust:

> I think it proper to add in this place, that Colonel Rawlinson has not only adopted my system of classifying the characters, but my method of investigating their values by comparing different derivatives of the same root. ... If, then, it be alleged that Colonel Rawlinson was led to alter his views as to the *literal* nature of the cuneatic phonographs by his having adopted a better method of investigation than he had previously used, and not by the statements which I had made, I must reply, that this better method is itself to be found in my previous publications.
>
> (Hincks 1852: 306–7)

Few people read this learned article in the *Transactions of the Royal Irish Academy*, of course, and in the eyes of the British public Rawlinson was now the undisputed leader in the field, he had assumed the initiative in the further work on deciphering the script and reading the texts. One of the reasons for this was his brilliant ability to present his theories in a clear and convincing manner, and the contrast with Hincks is striking. The latter's articles could be nearly impenetrable even for his fellow scholars, for although the arguments were cogent and precise, he usually wrote in an extreme lapidary style, addressing himself to people who already knew what he was talking about. On the other hand, it would be quite fallacious to dismiss Rawlinson merely as an able populariser, for his learning and intelligence always meant that his articles were filled with relevant and knowledgeable information; the special quality lies in the combination of an understandable framework and a strongly technical content. All of his notes and the long quotations in strange languages, often using exotic scripts, were bound to convince the layman that there was substance behind his more simple problems and the claimed discoveries.

The decipherment of cuneiform was deeply embedded in personalities and in the cultural and social concerns of the time. This is particularly obvious in the case of Rawlinson's wish to steer clear of religious issues, an attitude which without a doubt blocked him in his work; on the other hand, his position as a socially acceptable English gentleman appears to have blocked not only Hincks' possibilities as a scholar, but also the proper recognition of his contribution.

Seen on that background it is clear that the decipherment of Mesopotamian cuneiform was the result of an unwilling and unrecognised collaboration between these two men. Both were extremely ambitious and touchy personalities, and it seems that Rawlinson in particular found it very difficult to entertain the idea that he might be bested by a man he did not even respect. As early as 1835 he wrote a letter to his sister from Kermanshah in which he declared his goals, and which shows that he knew very well what kind of a man he was:

> I aspire to do for the cuneiform alphabet what Champollion has done for the hieroglyphics ... my character is one of restless, insatiable ambition – in whatever sphere I am thrown my whole spirit is absorbed in an eager struggle for the first place.
>
> (Borger 1975–8a: 1)

Whereas the traditional view has been that Rawlinson was practically single-handedly responsible for the decipherment, a view strongly asserted by Budge who consistently referred to Rawlinson as 'the Father of Assyriology', a more balanced evaluation should take Hincks' great contribution into account. The latest statement on this question by Peter Daniels goes rather too far in my opinion: 'it is he (Hincks), and he nearly alone, who made it possible to read, once again, the memorials of the world's first civilization' (Daniels 1994: 54). It seems fair to sum up the contributions of the two men by saying that where Rawlinson was the hardworking, patient and extremely careful man, Hincks was the true genius whose intuition and flashes of insight constituted a very large part of the foundation for Rawlinson's painstaking work.

Anyway, these learned disputes, claims and counter-claims were of little interest to the public compared to the fact that the texts could now be read. People now discovered that the Assyrian texts really did contain information which was of vital importance for the correct understanding of passages in the Old Testament. With his new readings Rawlinson could give the main points in the history of Sennacherib as it appeared in the text on the bulls, and already the account of his first year contained mention of events which were known from other traditions. The first campaign of the Assyrian king was directed against a Babylonian revolt led by a certain Merodach-Baladan, who had also fought against Sennacherib's father – 'two important points of agreement being thus obtained both with Scripture and with the account of Polyhistor'. This Babylonian king appears also in the Old Testament where he is said to have sent envoys to Jerusalem in order to suggest an alliance directed against Assyria.

It was, however, the account of Sennacherib's third campaign which contained 'those striking points of coincidence which first attracted my attention, – and which being once recognized, have naturally led to the complete unfolding of all this period of history'. This was the story of Sennacherib's campaign against Judah and Jerusalem, and although Rawlinson could read a lot of the text, he also made some fundamental mistakes which led to a suggestion that there had been two different campaigns rather than one; on this basis a number of complex chronological problems arose which came to occupy much space in the learned journals for a time, and which appeared to point to discrepancies between the biblical and the Assyrian accounts.

All this just made the cuneiform debates even more exciting and interesting, however, and at this point, where Rawlinson was finally in a position to deliver the information which Layard had needed so badly three years earlier, when he was writing his first book, he decided irrevocably in favour of the old country parson in Ireland. We do not really know why, but it seems reasonably clear that Layard no longer had any warm feelings for the colonel, and he may have been genuinely outraged by Rawlinson's treatment of Hincks. Some years later he wrote about the matter, pointing out that the Irish scholar had been able to offer dramatic new discoveries on the basis of an extremely limited amount of material, whereas 'scholars in this country, whose learning was limited to the classics, were little inclined to accept these interpretations, and were rather inclined to reject them altogether as ingenious fictions' (Waterfield 1963: 233).

Layard wrote a long letter to Hincks and suggested a partnership over the publication of the texts from Nimrud and Kuyunjik, guaranteeing that Rawlinson would be kept out of it. It had been an unlucky accident which had placed the copies of the bull-inscriptions in the hands of the colonel, the ones which had subsequently enabled him to write his letter to the *Athenæum*, and this was not going to happen again (Davidson 1933: 168).

After Rawlinson's visit to Nimrud and Kuyunjik relations between him and Layard had been strained, and the two men who were so totally different in character kept up a polite façade but stopped the collaboration, which had in all events always been rather one-sided. This allowed them to go on communicating, and they had even joined forces in 1851 in an attempt to get Hincks moved to England, where a parsonage would better enable him to pursue his studies. We do not know if Rawlinson actually did anything positive about it, but at least he expressed his good intentions (Davidson 1933: 49–50). He had met Hincks a couple of times during his year in England and they had engaged in conversations which had apparently been quite friendly. Nevertheless, Hincks did not feel convinced that the colonel meant him well, and his frustrations grew in what he was beginning to see as his spiritual exile in Killyleagh.

> At my time of life (near 60) I would be most anxious to train up others to pursue what I have begun. I believe there is a great deal, *which would die with me*, known to myself alone – some of it in papers which in their present state would be unintelligible to others. A professorship, or something of the sort, instituted for me, would I think, be the best way of doing what I want. But were I in more independent circumstances & enabled to keep a curate, either by a civil list pension or by a good ... living *in England*, I would contrive to give such instruction as I think should be given: – provided only I could meet persons willing to receive it.[207]

The only pupil Hincks got was Layard. The attempts to find him a place in England continued all through 1852, but they were unsuccessful, so in the end Layard turned to the British Museum in order to have him appointed there and put in charge of the publication of the texts from his excavations. In October he went on a trip to Killyleagh to study with Hincks, and in a letter to his uncle he described the warm reception he had been given by the entire community. He was particularly interested in the many young ladies who paid a great deal of attention to the young, dashing visitor from London:

> The place swarms with young ladies – who at our dinners here have a proportion of three to one of the ruder sex. – speaking a rich brogue and having very free and somewhat universally affectionate manners – which render their society peculiarly agreeable. The Doctor is an original and spends his whole time in his study – we work hard and have already made good progress. He is wonderfully acute and logical – and has already made far greater progress than I anticipated in decyphering.[208]

In November Ellis wrote to Layard to inform him that the Trustees were considering his suggestion that Hincks should be given responsibility for the publication of the Assyrian inscriptions and copying the tablets which were in the Museum:

> I am directed by the Trustees to acquaint you, that they are prepared to consider the proposal for employing Dr. Hincks upon some arrangement to be definitely fixed, and request that you will be so good as to communicate with Dr. Hincks, and acquaint the Trustees with the result.[209]

This was progress, of course, but there were still many obstacles in the way. It turned out to be difficult to have Hincks released from his duties in Ireland, and money was even harder to get hold of. Hincks expressed his fear that it might be intrigues started by Rawlinson's friends in London which created these problems, but Layard did not think so. In fact, an arrangement was finally found which allowed Hincks to work for a period in the Museum, and he sat there filling two notebooks with transliterations and translations with elaborate commentaries, a work which was, however, never published.

CHAPTER THIRTY-THREE

NEW MEN,
NEW EXCAVATIONS

—— •◆• ——

Rawlinson's discoveries were not the only reason for the British government's renewed interest in excavations in Assyria; undoubtedly, it played a role also that the French had finally begun to take a serious interest in their unfinished work at Khorsabad. Even before Layard had left Mosul he had received a letter from a new acquaintance, R. Stuart Poole, who had seen Mr and Mrs Rolland after their return to England; he also had news from France:

> A particular friend of my uncle, & ourselves, M. Fulgence Fresnel, is now on his way to Mosul, as French Consul. You will doubtless become acquainted with him, & I therefore take the liberty of enclosing a note to him, not liking to write to such a remote part of the world without doing so. M. Fresnel is the brother of a celebrated natural philosopher, & is himself, as you well know, a distinguished orientalist. He is a man of very liberal mind, but I ought in confidence to mention to you that, although strictly honourable in intention, he is often indiscreet, through his enthusiasm, in speaking of matters of science, which should not transpire, &, I am sorry to say that he is very sceptical with respect to the truths of our religion.[210]

This appointment was bound to revitalise the French interest in Assyria, for Fresnel was a prominent member of the *Société asiatique* and one of France's leading Arabists; in the end he refused the post because of his appointment as the leader of a new French scientific expedition to Mesopotamia. The archaeological possibilities were therefore enhanced rather than diminished, and shortly afterwards the consulship at Mosul was given to another interesting man, Victor Place. Jules Mohl and the scientific establishment in Paris were now becoming fully awake to the possibilities, and the leaders of the Louvre Museum took contact with Place in order to interest him in the plans for a resumption of work at Khorsabad. He immediately agreed to this, and in his letter to the Interior Ministry in which he thanked them for the appointment at Mosul he wrote:

> I am aware that one of the most important interests attached to the consulship at Mosul is the discovery of the monument at Nineveh. The administrators of the Museum have encouraged me to concentrate my attention on this.
>
> (Pillet 1962: 11)

Figure 33.1 Gabriel Tranchand has given us the first photographic documentation of the Assyrian excavations. His pictures were not published but used as the precise models for engravings. This photograph shows Place himself in an informal situation in shirtsleeves in the garden of the consulate at Mosul. (From Fontan 1994c: 95)

The French Minister Léon Faucher had visited London where he had been very impressed by the new Assyrian discoveries which were being exhibited at the British Museum; in collaboration with the Louvre he took the initiative to have the French activities resumed and managed to get a grant of 70,000 francs through Parliament despite considerable opposition. The idea behind this large grant was to enable a team of scholars to carry out extensive investigations in the entire Mesopotamian area, including what was referred to as 'Media', the southern reaches of the Zagros in Persia. In this wider context the plans for a reopening of Botta's excavations at Khorsabad became only a detail, and a further 8,000 francs were sought, and granted, specifically for this purpose.

Fulgence Fresnel was put in charge of the expedition as such, and he had with him Jules Oppert, a German-French orientalist who had written about Old Persian (causing Rawlinson considerable irritation), and an artist named Félix Thomas. Clearly, the French were determined to reconquer the initiative from the British by way of a large-scale operation.

With Layard out of the picture it was unclear who should be sent out to represent the British Museum. Rawlinson was in charge of the activities, of course, but his work as Resident did not allow him to supervise the daily work, so someone else had to be found. Rawlinson suggested Loftus, but he was busy at Susa and the Museum felt that the main emphasis should still be on Assyria. Layard pointed to Hormuzd Rassam as the right man to continue his work, but he was in fact not very keen to go out alone. He wrote to Layard saying that even if the British Museum should wish him to go, he would never leave without him.[211]

Place only got away from Paris in September 1851 after the grant for Khorsabad had been cleared by the National Assembly in August. He had been given an opportunity to study Botta's report from Khorsabad and had prepared himself with some care for his task there. However, in Greece he suffered a serious accident which delayed him for several weeks, and he also had to make an extended stop in the town Samsun in eastern Turkey because of illness. Rawlinson was just then following the same route on his way to Baghdad, and he met Place at Samsun. The two men obviously got along very well and they made a kind of gentlemen's agreement with respect to their interests in Assyria. In Paris Rawlinson had heard that Place had been urged to reconquer Kuyunjik for France, despite the fact that Layard had worked here and that Christian Rassam had been instructed to keep a small workforce occupied on the mound after the death of Bell. When he actually met Place he was pleasantly surprised to find that they could easily agree on a settlement and he wrote to the Trustees that he was 'happy to find M. Place disposed to act in perfect harmony with us'. He emphasised that whoever was appointed to conduct the British excavation, it was essential to avoid misunderstandings with the French; Place had declared that he was going to ask for a permit to resume excavations at Kuyunjik, but he has promised 'that he will keep as far away from our trenches as possible' (Barnett 1976: 8).

The colonel agreed that Khorsabad was French territory, and he was also willing to divide Kuyunjik between the French and the British: the French could excavate the northern half, where no work had so far been done, whereas the British would keep the southern half where Sennacherib's palace was being uncovered. Rawlinson was worried that a proper British expedition would be difficult or impossible to establish, and he preferred that the French should dig at Kuyunjik rather than leave the mound untouched. He was eager for more tablets.

Place finally arrived at Mosul in January 1852, and three weeks later he started work at Khorsabad. He had brought with him a photographer rather than the customary artist, a certain Gabriel Tranchand who took a series of photos of the excavations; they are surely among the very earliest systematic excavation photos made anywhere in the world (see Figure 33.1). The precursor of photography, the Daguerreotype, had first been demonstrated in Paris in 1839, but Tranchand used a technique called 'calotype' which gives negatives on paper; this was the system developed by the British inventor William Fox Talbot and patented in 1841; in England it was usually called 'Talbotype'. It may be remembered that the unfortunate Mr Bell had brought such a camera with him from London a few years earlier. Place's systematic use of the camera is just one of several indications that he was a man of vision.

His instructions from the French Academy ordered him to

investigate the mounds which are close to the Tigris and by way of excavations which he will carry out there to procure the largest possible number of sculptures, vases, jewelry, cylinder seals and objects of all kinds which are used in daily life, and which the Assyrian Museum completely lacks.

(Pillet 1918: 2–3)

This formulation shows clearly the customary view of archaeology as a treasure hunt, where the emphasis is on the acquisition of museum objects for display alone. At the same time it indicates how little Botta had brought back to Paris. No doubt, Place agreed in principle with these aims, but he was also interested in making a much more systematic investigation. He was in some respects a pioneer, as his French biographer has stressed, a man of strong intelligence, but also a somewhat complicated and difficult man.

He had no background for this particular task, for he was a career diplomat. He was born in Corbeil in 1818 as the son of wealthy parents, but when he was sixteen his father went bankrupt and he had from then on to fend for himself. His consular career started relatively late in his life, and he had only held the post as consul, second class, at Santo Domingo, 1847–51, before he was appointed to Mosul. His work as consul appears to have been fairly demanding, and the excavations naturally had to come second, but at the same time he surely saw them as a wonderful opportunity to further his career and perhaps gain him fame, provided he could come up with discoveries to match those made by Botta and Layard.

There was accordingly the potential for a degree of conflict between him and Fulgence Fresnel's party who arrived at Mosul in March and stayed for a time in Assyria to study the ruins. The question was, who was in charge of the excavations at Khorsabad. The ministerial instructions appeared to say that Fresnel was in charge of all French activities in Mesopotamia, but Place could not accept this. He wanted to be his own master. Difficulties immediately arose between the two men.

Fulgence Fresnel is described by all as a most kind and considerate man, an opium-smoking man of the world, and it seems that he was only interested in reaching a reasonable compromise with the new consul. He tried to be accommodating and praised Place for his enthusiasm and intelligence, and he wrote kind letters about him to people in Paris. He was only too eager to transfer the responsibility for Khorsabad to Place once he realised what kind of a man he had to do with. Fresnel had no stomach for the constant trouble he would have had if he had insisted on his superiority.

On the other hand, Place had to face the fact that the activities at Khorsabad were only a minor part of the total engagement, and it was very little he could do with the 8,000 francs allotted to him. Moreover, problems arose after Fresnel had departed for Babylonia, for he had suggested to the minister in Paris that Nebbi Yunus should be tackled in a small dig which would cost only a few hundred francs, and the minister had responded positively. Such puny sums must not stand in the way of scientific progress, so, excavations ought to be started at once. When Fresnel received this letter from Paris he had to forward it to Place, who of course became deeply offended and wrote back to Paris to ask if he was supposed to receive his instructions through the hands of Fresnel. With that all communication between the two men stopped.

The French activities were to be haunted by misfortune. Already before Fresnel's arrival at Mosul they had heard with astonishment the news of the *coup-d'état* which turned the elected president Louis Napoléon into a self-styled 'Emperor', who thus abolished the republican constitution. This revolution created considerable turmoil in all the ministries in Paris during the next couple of years, with a rapid turnover of ministers, and in that atmosphere the expedition to Mesopotamia necessarily receded into the background. This meant that Place experienced constant difficulties, not just in getting his own personal salary, but even more in raising money for the dig at Khorsabad. Fresnel's expedition suffered serious financial difficulties as well in Babylonia.

Place quickly asked for permission to excavate at Kuyunjik and the painter Félix Thomas was very keen on the idea, but in the end Place decided to stick to Khorsabad. He probably thought that Layard had discovered the one palace that had existed at Kuyunjik and did not wish to spend his slender means on a fruitless search for more treasures on this mound which had proven so difficult to excavate. Instead he sent out agents to a number of other mounds in Assyria in order to occupy them for France, and in this endeavour he was in sharp competition with Rawlinson. He wrote about the colonel that he was a man of 'formidable energy, but I shall do what I can to exercise activities which can at least correspond to his, for I maintain that we must not let ourselves be outdistanced by England on a road which we ourselves have opened' (Pillet 1962: 24). Herewith the note was struck for the nationalistically based competition which was to characterise the French-English relations in Assyria during the following couple of years.

The British Museum could not really make up its mind about the man to send out as excavator, but they did dispatch an artist, a certain Charles Doswell Hodder, who like his predecessors Cooper and Bell was a young, inexperienced man without any knowledge of the Near East or any real idea of the job he was asked to undertake (Gadd 1936: 78–9). The always candid Mrs Rassam wrote to Layard: 'What in the name of all patience is the Artist to do when he comes here!! There is little or nothing to draw at Kiounjuk'. Her husband had employed a few workers on the mound but they had not found much; the most interesting discovery was a kind of cemetery with a few stone sarcophagi which contained jewelry and face masks of gold. She described these finds in several letters addressed to Layard, assuming them to be Assyrian, and she even sent some of the pieces to Layard in London. The news of this discovery spread in London and led to some sensational reports in which it was said that Rawlinson

> has opened out the entire place of sepulture of the kings and queens of Assyria. There they lie, it is said, in huge stone sarcophagi, with ponderous lids decorated with the royal ornaments and costume, just as they were deposited more than 3,000 years ago.[212]

In fact, the finds were from the Parthian period, some five to six centuries after the end of the Assyrian empire, and they were not nearly as spectacular as was said here; the report more than anything indicates the popular interest and the desire for new and fantastic discoveries (Curtis 1976).

Matilda also reported that Rawlinson had visited the excavations and with pleasure noted that many cuneiform tablets continued to be found; he gave instructions to Christian Rassam that they should be packed and sent down to him in Baghdad as soon as possible. Three large boxes filled with tablets could be sent off at once.[213]

Rawlinson was becoming worried that the British activities in Assyria might be in jeopardy and he wrote a series of pleading letters to the Trustees. He was of the opinion that a real Englishman should be appointed to lead the work – which of course meant that they should avoid Hormuzd Rassam. Rawlinson had little trust in 'Orientals' and regarded the Rassam family with special misgiving as dishonest and untrustworthy. It had to be 'a person of responsible character' – a description which presumably also excluded the artist Hodder who was not a success in his new job. The Rassams did not like Rawlinson much either and did not regard him as a good boss. Matilda packed all the fragile tablets from Kuyunjik and placed them carefully in the boxes, and she was hurt and annoyed that Rawlinson never with a single word acknowledged her unpaid contribution. Instead he hinted in his letters to her that he suspected her husband of spending Museum money on his own affairs, an accusation which she vehemently rejected. She also complained of his indecision:

> I dont think I ever met with such a feeble person as Col. Rawlinson is, one post, he says employ 6 Kirkhanas, the next reduce them to 3, then again employ 6 then 3 again. One post he writes that the Museum do not care about saving any more sculptures, they want Tablets & small objects, the next mail he says he does not feel justified in spending the Museum's money upon Tablets & Glass bottles. I quite expect to hear by this post that the mound must be given up & Mr. Hodder proceed to Baghdad. ... When I read the Colonel's letters they put me in mind of an Arabic tale called the discontented husband and runs thus 'A gentleman was always anxious to pick a quarrel with his wife, ...'. So is the Col. We do all in our power to please him but in vain.[214]

In fact, Rawlinson wrote to the Museum to find out if they were interested in any more sculptures, bulls and so forth from Kuyunjik; it seems that he was not, and he suggested that others should be allowed to take those reliefs which had already been uncovered and which stood available in the tunnels and trenches. He also returned to the still unresolved question of who should be sent out and wrote in plain words that he did not regard Hormuzd Rassam as the right person for the job; he pointed instead to Loftus who was extremely qualified, but the Museum was finally persuaded by Layard's argument that Hormuzd's prior knowledge and experience made him the ideal candidate. Because of the extremely slow mail between England and Baghdad Rawlinson was not informed of this until several months after the decision had been taken (Barnett 1976: 8).

Rassam left England in August and arrived at Mosul in October. Layard was worried for his sake and wrote to Ross:

> I am afraid he will not get on so well under the Colonel who is rather a hard task-master. Since I left little has been done. The Trustees mismanaged the matter as usual, and Rawlinson could not superintend the excavations from Baghdad.[215]

Shortly before reaching Mosul Rassam ran into Loftus who was himself on his way to Kuyunjik in order to start excavations there; Rawlinson had appointed him, apparently in the expectation that his recommendation to the Trustees would secure the job for him, but when Loftus saw Rassam's letters from the Trustees he had of course no other option than to accept the situation. The two men went to Mosul and took a look at Kuyunjik together before Loftus went on to Baghdad to report to Rawlinson that he was planning to go home. With a distinct lack of enthusiasm Rawlinson wrote to Layard:

> So Hormuzd is coming out after all. He is no doubt a good man to super-intend the 'diggins' – but I dislike the connexion. His brother is quite incorrigible as regards money – and I am resolved to have no accounts with him – though I hardly see now how I am to keep his hands out of the money bags.[216]

Rassam now took control of the activities, lowered the daily wages for the workers at Kuyunjik and sent a team to Nimrud to reopen the dig there. Since Place's workers were operating in the immediate vicinity of the mound, he was afraid they might find it opportune to take over the mound itself if there was no British work going on there. He did not think much of the French excavations, and neither did Rawlinson who wrote to Layard:

> The French Commission here is doing absolutely nothing – and is not likely to do anything either, stay as long as it may. Fresnel lives upon Opium and Oppert thinks of nothing but his pay. Place I believe up to the present time has found nothing worth speaking of. Khorsabad was exhausted, and it was quite foolish his continuing the work there.[217]

A couple of months later he noted that the French 'are wasting their money at Babylon absolutely for nothing. Place however has found a couple of Clay Cylinders at Khorsabad, which will be perhaps of interest, though from the description, they are, I suspect religious and not historical'.[218] These comments were not entirely justified, however, at least not with respect to Place. It is admittedly difficult to find out precisely what Fresnel and his team were up to at Babylon, since we have no real reports from there. Around the end of 1852 Fresnel wrote a long letter to Mohl which was subsequently published in the *Journal Asiatique*; in an accompanying note Mohl explained that he had in fact received several letters from Fresnel earlier, but he did not regard them as suitable for publication since they contained 'too many personal details and too many explanations about the difficulties he had met and the delays which he had been forced to accept'. Even the letter which was being published was revised to a considerable extent, and the introduction dealing with the financial problems of the expedition was simply dropped by Mohl.

The report itself reveals that Fresnel and Oppert have found it very difficult to work in Babylon, and that the majority of their finds are late, belonging to periods which must be placed after the Babylonian and Assyrian time. A large collection of glazed bricks, originally part of a colossal wall decoration, apparently constituted their most significant discovery. But it also appears that Fresnel's main interest was the study of the topography of the area and the question of the original extent of the ancient city; these are obviously matters of considerable scientific relevance, but such a preoccupation was not likely to result in glorious objects which could fill the halls of the Louvre. Mohl and the *Société asiatique* must have been worried (Fresnel 1853).

In a slightly later letter from June 1853 Fresnel again gives a detailed description of the problems of topography and asks urgently that a qualified surveyor should be sent to Babylon in order to produce an accurate map of the entire region. He and Oppert had already made extensive surveys and taken a special interest in the watercourses, claiming with some justification that the history of Babylon must be the history of the Euphrates. This interest in problems of cultural geography and ecology was remarkable and shows an awareness of questions whose importance has only much later been properly appreciated by archaeologists; not surprisingly, such priorities were not regarded as very meaningful by the bosses in Paris, although they would certainly agree that the still unresolved matter of the size of ancient Babylon was of considerable historical interest. One problem was to establish whether the ruins known as Birs Nimrud, located some 20 km from Babylon itself, and often regarded as the remains of the original Tower of Babel, had formed part of the metropolitan area of the city. Oppert had decided that the mounds there hid the ruins of a city called Borsippa. Fresnel refers to conversations with 'our happy rival, or rather our guide', Colonel Rawlinson, who is said to agree with their conclusions – although he is forced to admit that 'I do not know with certainty the results of M. Rawlinson's hydrographic researches'. The colonel was still wary of showing his cards, even to fellow scholars who so admired him.

Fresnel was clearly deeply frustrated at Babylon, as Layard had been before him, and the much longer and more extensive excavations and investigations which his party conducted here did not lead to the hoped-for results. He pointed out that it was immensely more difficult to excavate in Babylonia than in Assyria, and that it would be unfair to compare the results reached by scholars working in these two places:

> All those who have excavated at Nineveh have been lucky. MM. Botta, Layard and Place have exceeded expectations because they worked on a ground which is immensely rich, and which lay abandoned after the cataclysm of Sardanapal.
> (Fresnel 1855: 547)

At the time when this last letter was published, in December 1855, Fresnel's expedition had been dissolved and the work at Babylon stopped. There was no more money, so the team had to go home, but Fresnel refused to go back to France.

Figure 33.2 Place excavated a series of gates, both in the palace and in the city-wall, and some were almost incredibly well preserved, like this one which has been completely uncovered. Place and Tranchand stand on top of the bulls, and the tunnels disappear into the darkness. (From Fontan 1994c: 198)

He had dreams of establishing a permanent French school of archaeology at Baghdad, at the time an impossible dream, and he bombarded Mohl with letters full of plans and suggestions. Mohl wrote in a note to the letter that he had delayed publication for so long, 'in the hope that he would come to Paris himself to publish the results of the expedition whose leader he was'. The continued uncertainty with respect to Fresnel's plans had finally persuaded him to publish what he described as 'a fragment'.

A truly remarkable situation! Fresnel stayed on in Baghdad where he led a miserable existence, with his fortune lost, sick and penniless in the opium fogs. His servant remained with him, but no one else there seems to have lifted a finger to help him.

The artist Félix Thomas had left the expedition in Babylonia much earlier. At the end of 1852 a strange scene happened, described with obvious contempt by George Rawlinson in his book about his brother, the colonel. He claims that Thomas 'completely lost possession of his senses, and in this condition shot the Sheikh of Hillah, whom he imagined to have a design upon his life'. The reason was supposedly that he was excited by some discovery or other which he claimed to have made, and according to Rawlinson the result of this unfortunate episode was that a general feeling of alarm spread among 'the natives, who had always regarded it as a species of insanity, that Europeans should spend their time and money in digging up and carrying off old stones and bricks'. Since these natives were of course unable to distinguish between the French and the British, their resulting unwillingness to work for the 'mad foreigners' had unfortunate effects on all archaeological activities in the country (Rawlinson 1898: 179–80).

According to French sources it was an acute case of mental confusion caused by exhaustion, heat and dehydration which had caused Thomas to jump on a horse and rush away from the excavation; his close friend, who was a sheikh from Hillah, followed him to get him back, but Thomas fired at him and wounded him superficially. After a couple of weeks' convalescence in Baghdad Thomas was eager to come back, but Fresnel had lost faith in him and asked him to return to Paris (Pillet 1962: 44–5). Having waited in vain a few months for Fresnel to change his mind, Thomas went north to Place at Mosul, and here he became so entranced by Khorsabad and the new discoveries there that he decided to stay for a while to help make plans and drawings. This chain of accidents forms the background for the happy outcome which was a series of magnificent drawings and paintings from Place's excavations.

And great discoveries were being made at Khorsabad, where Place had extended Botta's palace considerably. He had pulled all his men to Khorsabad, abandoning the other excavations he had started, and employed some 100–130 workers. He was fighting to keep up his activities despite a spring season which had been uncommonly rainy and a summer which was unbelievably hot; the autumn then came with renewed violent rains. According to Hormuzd, who followed his work through rumours picked up in Mosul, Place was supposedly looking for 'a kitchen', a room like the one Layard had found at Nimrud full of metal objects, but he did not have much luck of that nature.[219] On the other hand, he attempted to clear the entire palace and he found some unbelievably well-preserved city gates, where not only the colossal bulls were standing as if they had been left the day before, but where the gate itself with its large, decorated arch was left intact, giving a powerful impression of the glorious architecture of the site (see Figure 33.2).

CHAPTER THIRTY-FOUR

JEALOUSY AND
ILL-FEELING

— •◆• —

In his final excavation report Place wrote about his relationship with English colleagues:

> The Museum in London was enriched with numerous sculptures found by Rawlinson and his collaborators, with whom I count myself happy to have had the most excellent relations. I mention with pleasure the unfortunately dead Mr. Loftus and a young artist of great ability, Mr. W. Boutcher. When a common love of research unites several Europeans in such distant countries, it is more useful to science, and more honourable to themselves, to unite their efforts in a generous competition in the service of good taste than to show discord, from which no one benefits. All excavators of Nineveh have had the happy attitude to recognise this principle.
>
> (Place 1867: I, 6–7)

Where is Hormuzd Rassam? Is it coincidence that Place mentions Rawlinson, Loftus and even the artist Boutcher, but excludes the man with whom he had most contact? Hardly. Hormuzd Rassam is present in the text as the counter-image, as the non-European who did not stick to the rules of generous competition and good taste. In his eyes the situation was quite different:

> It is a known fact that, whenever the British and French interests clash in foreign lands, there is sure to be jealousy and ill-feeling created; and, although I always avoided such unhappy results, my public duty forced me sometimes to brave it out.
>
> (Rassam 1897: 12)

Rassam was in no doubt that it was all a matter of national interests, that the claimed peaceful and noble competition among gentlemen was a smokescreen, and he was in fact faced with some unpleasant problems. The first one was the agreement Rawlinson had reached with Place at Samsun and which severely limited his own possibilities for work at Kuyunjik. From the start he tried to undermine the agreement about a partition of the mound by letting his workers open trenches which were as close to Place's area as possible; he quickly saw that interesting finds could be made here as well, quite some distance from the Sennacherib palace.

317

Without directly encroaching upon French territory there was little he could do, however, and the clashes came elsewhere.

Downriver from Nimrud, on the right bank of the Tigris, was a large ruin known as Kalah Shergat, where Rich had worked and where Layard had opened a few trenches. Since neither Khorsabad nor Kuyunjik were providing the stuff the excavators wanted, they both turned their attention to this spot, and Place had placed a few workers on the mound.

We now know that this was the site where the first Assyrian city was situated, ancient Assur, which had given its name to the country and which also boasted the temple for the national Assyrian god who was likewise called Assur. The ruins have been excavated carefully during a number of years at the beginning of the twentieth century by a German team led by Walter Andrae, and they made great and exciting discoveries here. However, there were none of the 'classic' Assyrian buildings, no large palaces with walls covered with reliefs and with huge bulls and lions guarding the gates. Most of the finds at Kalah Shergat were in fact from earlier periods, from the second and early first millennia BCE, that is, from a time before the Neo Assyrian empire (Andrae 1977). The older Assyrian kings had lived in much more modest palaces here, and when the great expansion began in the early ninth century BCE, Ashurnasirpal II chose to move his capital away from the old centre. Calah, the city at Nimrud, became his own city where he could build his vast palace and create new temples.

There was accordingly not much hope that either Place or Rassam would find the kind of buildings and objects they were looking for at Kalah Shergat, but they had no way of knowing that; the ruins themselves are so vast that both must have felt certain that something of great importance was hiding here, why not a gigantic palace?

When Place was forced to stop or at least severely limit his activities here, Hormuzd suggested to Rawlinson that he should occupy the site, and the colonel in Baghdad agreed. He suggested that a large team should be sent there as soon as possible. No doubt both were aware that such a decision was a little dubious, for Rassam wrote in his letters to Layard that he tried to prepare for the expedition in secret in order not to arouse Place's suspicion. He left on a raft while most of the workers followed on foot on the banks of the river. He was, however, overtaken by a rider who carried a letter from his brother in Mosul, informing him that Place had visited him to protest against the plans and that he had suggested that the expedition should stop and wait for a final decision from Rawlinson in Baghdad. Hormuzd refused and they continued downriver. At the mound they found a guard who carried another letter addressed to Hormuzd Rassam from Place, asking him to return to Mosul to discuss the matter. He had no intention of doing this but ordered his people to start digging. Some time later Place himself came down to Kalah Shergat and the two men agreed to divide the mound between them. The only major find to emerge from all of this was a well-preserved clay prism carrying a long inscription with the annals of the Assyrian king Tiglath-pilesar I.[220]

This is the version which emerges from Rassam's letter to Layard, but the French viewed the situation somewhat differently. Place argued that he had not in fact stopped the excavations in earnest, and he claimed the mound as French territory; it was purely a temporary situation that a single guard was left at the site, a man who was according to Place chased away by Rassam. He also says that Rawlinson was quite unaware of all this, and that it was his intervention which finally secured a reasonable settlement of the dispute (Pillet 1918: 10–11).

Rassam's subsequent account, which is contained in his book published many years later, is different from his letter in several respects. Here he says that while he was on his way to the mound he heard that a group of workers accompanied by some Shammar Bedouin were on their way to Kalah Shergat to reoccupy it for the French. Hormuzd's own men became so excited by this that they wanted to start an all-out attack at once, but he managed to cool them down. When they finally arrived at the mound, a group of his men went up to the ruins while the rest were being ferried across the river, and suddenly the air rang with war-cries and the sound of battle on top of the mound. Hormuzd's men were convinced that their comrades were being attacked:

> The Arabs who were with me at once took to their heels to help their comrades in the struggle. I tried all I could to quiet them, but to no purpose, as they said they were certain their fellow-laborers were being beaten and slaughtered, and their honor could not allow them to hear the sound of the war-cry and not run to their help. As I found that there was nothing for it but to allow the men to run on, I galloped as fast as my horse would take me, through the jungle, to prevent bloodshed.

No one was seriously injured, however, and a settlement was found (Rassam 1897: 16).

Whatever happened, it is obvious that it reflected, indeed unmasked, the intense nationalistic competition that characterised the relations between the local agents of England and France; Rawlinson and Place were barely able to maintain their status as polite, cultured gentlemen, but the real conflict came out into the open in the relationship to Rassam. They did not get along well after this and, in fact, things were quickly becoming even more complicated.

Shortly after these events Christian Rassam received a letter from sheikh Firhan, paramount chief of the important Shammar Tribe, who informed him that Place had tried to bribe him with large gifts in order to get him to chase the British workers from Kalah Shergat! 'You will be quite astonished if I tell you that all the time I was down at Shirgat Mons. de Place was trying to get Firhan the Chief of the Shammar Arabs to come and turn me away from that place', he wrote to Layard. He claims that he heard about this from a local Arab and says that it has since been confirmed by Firhan himself speaking to representatives of the Pasha and in the letter to Christian Rassam. Of course, Place denied the entire story.[221]

There is an official French correspondence about the matter, and Place wrote to his superiors in Paris complaining in strong terms about the behaviour of his British consular colleague, who had done everything in his power to make the accusation look reasonable. Hormuzd himself had behaved less than honourably, he felt:

while I was at Kalah Shergat Ormuz-Rassam already knew about the entire affair, since he had written about it to his brother. He saw me every day, but nevertheless he said nothing to me, even though he knew I was meant to visit Firhan on my way back.

(Pillet 1962: 33)

Rawlinson also became involved, and to begin with he found the evidence so convincing that he felt obliged to mention the affair in his own official correspondence with the embassy in Constantinople; even the little French colony in Mosul turned against Place, but he managed after a while to persuade everyone of his innocence. Rawlinson had to travel to Mosul, and after having seen the letters he became convinced that the accusation was false, fabricated by Firhan in order to extort money from both the French and the British, and supported by Christian Rassam, who undoubtedly had 'some dirty purpose of his own. Hormuzd is quite blameless, but I am thoroughly disgusted with the elder brother and must really break off all connexion with him'.[222]

In the middle of all this Rawlinson had great news about his work on the many tablets which came from Sennacherib's palace at Kuyunjik, texts which he was now for the first time able to study in Baghdad. 'They contain a perfect Cyclopedia of Assyrian science and are enough to occupy all the students of Europe for the next twenty years', he wrote to Layard, and to Rassam he described them as 'alphabets, syllables, vocabularies, grammers; treatices on arithmetic, astronomical formula, calenders and almanachs'.[223] Rawlinson was engaged in the very first reading of the gigantic scientific library which had been collected at the court of Nineveh and which is now known as the Library of Ashurbanipal, the last important Assyrian king who was Sennacherib's grandson. It was the result of a systematic collection of scholarly texts of all kinds and the creation of new ones by the many scribes and scholars who were attached to the court during the last half of the seventh century. Rawlinson's excitement was entirely justified and his expectation that these texts were to occupy generations of scholars has proven correct, for even today the study of Ashurbanipal's library is one of the main occupations of the Assyriologists of the world. When these tens of thousands of texts came to the British Museum in the following years, their presence there formed the basis for the creation of the new scholarly discipline which was called Assyriology.

In the course of the balmy spring season Hormuzd Rassam moved his men closer and closer to the demarcation line between the French and British zones, and reliefs and building remains were discovered in various places. In the centre of the mound he found a series of reliefs which were, he says, as fresh as if they had been made the day before; they showed a long line of soldiers, eunuchs and courtiers who were in some kind of procession, but he could not discover any building remains to go with them. They may in fact have been lining a passage or corridor linking the palace with another building in the immediate vicinity. Rawlinson felt that the reliefs should be dated to the period of the palace at Nimrud, which made them considerably older than the Kuyunjik palace.[224] In the vicinity he found a fragment of a very large white limestone obelisk, which had originally been similar to the black obelisk Layard had found at Nimrud, with reliefs and a long inscription, and in their search for the rest of this monument his workers unearthed in what he described as 'the pit' a large naked female statue, also in white limestone. It was rather badly damaged and unfortunately headless, but in the Assyrian context it was clearly a most unusual work of art; it carried an inscription dating it to the eleventh century – although this appears not to have been noticed at once.[225] In their search for more fragments of the obelisk Rassam's men were obviously running into much earlier levels.[226]

His workers were also busy at Nimrud, and here a very fragmentary obelisk was discovered in many pieces, but very few reliefs were coming out. His foreman there, a certain Bihnan, was, it appears, playing games with him; American missionaries and Place had been granted permission to take samples of reliefs from Nimrud by Rawlinson, but their efforts were not being rewarded by the kind of discoveries they were hoping for, first of all examples of the impressive scenes with the king confronting his courtiers. Rassam became suspicious when also Bihnan found nothing in those spots where he ordered him to dig, so he went to the mound himself.

> You may conceive how surprised & annoyed (though very much delighted) I was in finding different kind of sculptures in every trench I had opened, and when I asked Bihnan how he managed to miss those places he said that he quite forgot them. We have found 8 Kings, 5 Eunuchs, 3 Nisrochs and a great many Priests with garlands round their heads. The Americans are very much annoyed (and I dare say the French Consul will be doubly so when he hears of it) for they tried all they could to get a King but could not succeed.[227]

At Khorsabad all work had to stop in July because of the heat and for lack of money, but Place hoped for a new grant which would allow him to resume work in the autumn. He maintained friendly relations with Hormuzd, as we can see from his letters to Layard, but there was coolness between him and Christian Rassam. It turned out, however, that Place was ordered to stop his work at Khorsabad entirely in August, and the money granted to him was to be spent on the transportation of his finds. This was of course a huge disappointment, for he had plans for a complete uncovering of the palace which was clearly better preserved than any of the buildings discovered by Layard; he therefore felt that producing a complete plan of an Assyrian palace was his best chance of getting the upper hand in his competition with the British, who had many more single finds but no clear idea of what the palaces originally looked like. Place appears to have been in constant difficulties with respect to money, however, and in one of his letters to Layard Hormuzd tells us of a rather bizarre scheme he had for supplying himself with cash:

> I dare say you will be surprised if I were to tell you that before he left Mosul he became a dealer in iron and indeed I could scarcely believe it myself when I first heard of it. I believe I wrote to you some time ago about the mason's implements & iron chains which Mons. Place discovered at Khorsabad. It appears that they found at the same time a room full of iron some wrought

& some in pieces and which he brought to Mosul in cases under the name of antiques. Our Blacksmith came to me one day and informed me that a quantity of iron was offered to him for sale which was found at Khorsabad. He said he did not buy any of it as it was too hard for his work and he brought me at the same time a half of a pick axe to show me, and as I found it a curious relic I purchased it.[228]

The autumn was disappointing for Rassam. He found little at Kuyunjik and his excavations at Kalah Shergat did not produce the expected and hoped-for results either. One day in December when he was returning from there he met Loftus who was back in Mesopotamia where he was to excavate. His presence here was the result of a curious development in London which had led to the establishment of a new fund with the aim to support further excavations in Assyria; apparently a recreation of the old Nineveh Fund. As already mentioned, Layard had originally refused to have anything to do with this first fund, but he nevertheless appears to have been among the men behind the new one, joining among others his publisher John Murray. Once again Prince Albert was the main person among the contributors, who also counted some of the most influential men in England, but the real promoters of the 'Society for Exploring the Ruins of Assyria and Babylonia with especial reference to Biblical Illustration', which was behind the creation of the fund, have never been identified. It was called 'The Assyrian Exploration Fund', and the intention was to secure a continuation of the activities of Hormuzd Rassam whose funds were running out. However, Loftus and an artist called William Boutcher were sent off from England as early as October while Rassam was still busy at Kuyunjik, and it turned out that Rawlinson was strongly opposed to the whole arrangement. It would have been in order for Loftus to come after Hormuzd Rassam had completed his work, but 'that he should appear as a competitor is objectionable'. He therefore promised the Museum authorities to prevent Loftus from working in Assyria, and when asked to assist him by the fund suggested that he should concentrate on mounds in Babylonia instead (Harbottle 1958).

At this time Rassam was in fact running out of money and had to contemplate the end of his excavations. He had certainly accomplished a great deal, but he was still not happy with his results and was particularly bitter because of the agreement between Rawlinson and Place, which had effectively curtailed his work at Kuyunjik. The French consul maintained his right to the northern half of the mound, even though he showed no signs of doing anything about it. That was in itself cause for some satisfaction on the part of Hormuzd, for he would have had no option but to accept the situation if Place had sent some workers to dig a trench. But he was becoming more and more convinced that something of extraordinary importance had to hide in the French part of the mound, and he desperately wanted to make a truly sensational find. So far he had simply continued the work begun by Layard, and real success and fame – an intoxicating dream for the young Rassam – depended on discoveries which could rival those made by Layard in terms of importance and significance. His best chance lay on Kuyunjik, the colossal mound whose northern half had never even been touched.

But how was I to manage my project without the risk of being found out and stopped by him was the puzzle, as all the workmen knew that that part of Koyunjik was assigned to the French, and there were always spies ready to carry the news to my rival if they saw that I was excavating in his apportioned ground. So I resolved upon an experimental examination of the spot at night, and only waited for a good opportunity and a bright moonlight for my nocturnal adventure.

(Rassam 1897: 24)

What he writes here with an almost touching openness was in reality completely unheard of. His boss, Rawlinson, had entered into an agreement which he now cheerfully planned to violate, obviously fully aware that this was in direct conflict not just with the wishes of the colonel in Baghdad, but also with the repeated statements from the Trustees exhorting him to avoid conflict with the French. From the point of view of the French consul what he was planning was of course simple theft.

Characteristically, when he told Layard about the results of this manoeuvre he completely avoided talking about the background and just said: 'As I found the Northern part of the Kouyunjik mound not thoroughly examined I put a Karkhana to try a certain spot for a few days'.[229] As if there could not possibly be any problem involved in this!

The simple fact was that he knew he had to hurry if he was to accomplish anything at all before the money ran out, so on the night of 20 December 1853, he let his men begin their clandestine work. He had chosen the most reliable workers, but even they were not told about the true purpose of the operation, believing that he was planning another secret expedition downriver to Kalah Shergat.

Instead he sent them across the river after dark and let them dig with caution in three spots which he had marked on the surface beforehand. They were told to go deep, and the very first night they found evidence that they were in the vicinity of a major building: glazed bricks and fragments of reliefs. At dawn they stopped in order to return in the evening. He then gathered all the men at the most promising spot and they soon discovered the remains of a wall covered with reliefs, but it was so badly destroyed that nothing more than the feet of the figures were preserved. And worse, the wall faded out into nothing!

When Hormuzd received this report from his workers in the morning he was horrified, for he had already written letters to both Rawlinson and the British Museum announcing the discovery of a new palace; he knew that if he did not in fact produce one, he would be severely criticised for his adventure and become a laughing stock to boot. So when he returned to the mound that night it was with the sword of condemnation and ridicule hanging over his head; this was his last chance, for his undercover excavation was becoming known in Mosul and would soon result in a French intervention.

That night he personally supervised the excavations. He had his workers follow the damaged wall in the opposite direction and he soon discovered that it belonged to a passage which was gradually ascending. Layard had found such passages leading out of the large palace in the south of the mound, and Hormuzd hoped that this wall would eventually take him up into the palace itself.

> I therefore arranged my gangs to dig in a southeasterly direction, as I was certain that if there was anything remaining it would be found there. The men were made to work on without stopping, one gang assisting the other. My instinct did not deceive me; for one division of the workmen, after three or four hours' hard labor, were rewarded by the first grand discovery of a beautiful bas-relief in a perfect state of preservation, representing the king, who was afterwards identified as Assur-bani-pal, standing in a chariot, about to start on a hunting expedition, and his attendants handing him the necessary weapons for the chase. More than half of the upper part of the sculpture came into sight in an instant, as it happened that while the men were busily engaged in digging a deep trench inside what was found afterwards to be a long, narrow saloon, about fifteen feet wide, a large part of the bank which was attached to the sculpture fell, and exposed to view that enchanting spectacle. The delight of the workmen was naturally beyond description; for as soon as the word 'Sooar' (images) was uttered, it went through the whole party like electricity. They all rushed to see the new discovery, and after having gazed at the bas-relief with wonder, they collected together, and began to dance and sing my praises, in the tune of their war-song, with all their might. Indeed, for a moment I did not know which was the most pleasant feeling that possessed me, the joy of my faithful men or the finding of the new palace.
>
> (Rassam 1897: 25–6)

He had indeed found a new palace, and he could tell Layard a few days later that the reliefs he was now discovering were truly extraordinary:

> I venture to say that the art displayed in the treatment of both men & animals in these bas-reliefs surpass every thing yet discovered in the ruins of Assyria. ... I have no doubt that all these Sculptures which we have found will be wanted in England.[230]

He had found the first corner of the gigantic palace complex which had been built by the last major Assyrian king, Ashurbanipal, a man about whom nothing was known at this time simply because he was not mentioned in the Bible. He had been responsible, nevertheless, for the greatest expansion of the Assyrian empire, including the conquest of Egypt, and he was the king who had initiated the creation of the large scholarly library, parts of which had been found in the southern palace at Kuyunjik. The palace had been built originally by his grandfather, Sennacherib, but Ashurbanipal had restored it and made use of it for himself as well. He had then also built a new palace in the northern part of Kuyunjik, a building meant to surpass those built by his predecessors in beauty, elegance and technical perfection. The reliefs from this building are indeed in a class of their own, and one understands Hormuzd's excitement faced with such masterpieces.

The following day hundreds of people from Mosul streamed across the river to see what had emerged from the ground, and Rassam had his work cut out for him simply keeping them from crawling into the trench. There was in fact not much to see, but when his workers reached floor level in the passage it became clear that it was covered in tablets of the same type which had come from the other palace. The other part of the royal library was making its appearance.

Place had at this time reopened excavations at Khorsabad and he came from there to see what had been found and to lodge a formal protest. Rassam explains with a touching naivety that once he had explained to Place that Rawlinson really had no right to give away land which did not belong to him, the French consul appeared satisfied that his action was somehow justified. He congratulated him on his good fortune, although he also announced that he was going to appeal to 'higher authorities' (presumably this meant Rawlinson) against the breach of the agreement (Rassam 1897: 27).

Rassam wondered whether Place had not simply given up on the northern half of the mound in the conviction that Rawlinson had given it to him because he was convinced that nothing of importance was left there. In fact, Rawlinson had written shortly before that 'my own opinion is that the Mound is pretty well exhausted, and that there is no use in carrying on any more excavations there upon an extensive scale'. And about a month later he had said: 'I fear we shall be only throwing away our money experimentalizing any further at Kouyunjik – however in this respect you must use your own discretion'.[231]

Most probably Place had given up on Kuyunjik because of a lack of funds which forced him to concentrate work in one spot where he could be reasonably certain of results. He quickly bowed to the inevitable, in fact, and a month later Hormuzd could write to Layard that he had received two visits from his French rival who was extremely interested in all he saw and offered his assistance; the British artist Hodder was at this point so ill with an intestinal disease that he had to be sent home, and Rassam was here alone with finds which were of extreme importance. Place offered to let his own artist (by which he presumably meant the photographer Tranchand) assist Hormuzd, but this offer was not accepted, for Rassam was apparently worried that Rawlinson might resent such a close association with the French. He wanted to write to the colonel to ask for his permission first – something which had not been necessary when he opened the new trenches![232] He expected Loftus to take over the responsibility for the excavation shortly when his own money had run out completely, and there was of course an experienced artist, Mr Boutcher, in Loftus' party.

The halls that were being uncovered showed a variety of scenes, and some rooms were very poorly preserved where others seemed much better. There were a number of battle scenes, some of them showing campaigns directed against camel-riding Arabs from the desert, whose simple tent camps were put to the torch. Some of the most interesting reliefs showed a landscape close to Kuyunjik itself:

> There is a scene which is most interesting – there are *two* narrow rivers represented on these slabs & between these are lots of people (some walking & some riding) who are evidently making all haste to get out of the country & they are all running & looking backwards – unfortunately the slabs which come before these have been destroyed. On the other side of the *rivers* or

Figure 34.1 A section of the very large composition which described Ashurbanipal's lion-hunt. The precise and almost moving rendering of the wounded and raging lions place these reliefs among the absolute masterpieces of Mesopotamian art. (From Place 1867, III: Plate 50)

> above, there is a view of a large Palace showing very minutely the exterior architecture. The second story is built with pillars which have their bases on backs of lions & human headed Bulls with their heads turned like those found at Khorsabad. On the other slab there is represented a part of a Palace with a bridge having *3 pointed arches*; and what is more interesting & which I am sure will delight you more! they represent on a column a tablet with the King on it just like that one you found in the temple near the Pyramid at Nimroud & which you sent to England. It also resembles the rock tablets of Bavian. I wish very much that you were near that you might be able to come & see these interesting sculptures before they go to ruin.[233]

In fact, what he found here was a representation of Sennacherib's palace and of the gardens of Nineveh, scenes which give an idea of the massive power of these vast buildings. The palace must have risen high above the houses of Nineveh and must have been visible from far away as the concrete sign of the strength and might of its royal inhabitant.

Perhaps the most famous Assyrian reliefs are those depicting the lion hunt of Ashurbanipal (see Figure 34.1). The scenery is described in great detail and one can see that the hunt took place in a kind of arena, an area which was encircled with textile fabric stretched between wooden poles and along the sides of the enclosure stand soldiers holding large dogs in order to prevent the lions from getting away. A group of people are seen hastening up the slopes of a small wooded mound from where they can survey the enclosure. The lions are brought to the site in cages and released one at a time, and the king stands in his chariot shooting them with bow and arrow or cutting them down with his lance. In some scenes one sees him standing on foot in front of a lion which rears up on its hind legs to attack him, while he grabs its mane and coolly stabs it with his sword. The walls of these rooms were covered with wounded and dying lions, some crawl along with paralysed hind legs, having been hit by a precise shot with an arrow, others sit crouched on the ground, coughing up blood after having been hit several times. Men and animals are rendered with a realism and intensity which gives this whole gruesome scenery a gripping, even a deeply moving quality. This was the high point of Assyrian art (Barnett 1976).

Hormuzd was completely aware of the uniqueness of his finds and worked like a maniac in order to uncover as much as possible before he had to stop. One can say with the fine scholar Gadd that

> the discovery was most inopportune, though it seems ungrateful to use the word in such a connexion. For, in general, its excavation was conducted in a hurried and unobservant manner, without any such record as Layard had kept; little but sculptures and tablets were preserved, and there was no adequate planning.
>
> (Gadd 1936: 99–100)

As it turned out, little has been preserved from the palace of Ashurbanipal, even though the reliefs do fill a couple of rooms at the British Museum, but by far most of what was uncovered was lost or left and we have only inadequate descriptions of what was once there.

The conditions under which Rassam worked during these winter months were, in fact, appalling. The weather was ghastly, the cold was intense with the last snow-fall at Mosul on 9 March that year, and it rained incessantly. Hormuzd camped on the mound itself in order to be able to supervise the activities personally, and he recounts how one night when he was lying asleep in his tent he suddenly and without warning found himself sliding into a deep ravine, bed, tent and all. To his utter consternation he was in pitch darkness, with rain and hail howling around him, at the bottom of a hole which was rapidly filling up with water carrying mud and potsherds down over him. Some of his workers came to his rescue and pulled him out completely covered in mire, and he then realised that he had pitched his tent on top of one of Layard's old tunnels which had collapsed under him.

He continued until the end of March 1854 when Rawlinson ordered him to stop because the excavation had overspent the grant from the Museum. The dig was supposedly to be taken over by Loftus and Boutcher who worked for the private Assyrian Exploration Fund, but Rawlinson was still violently opposed to this arrangement and unhappy to leave the discovery of Ashurbanipal's palace to the two men. He therefore insisted that all antiquities discovered by them belonged to the Museum which had the right to the site granted by the Turkish government. He wrote to the Trustees that Loftus appeared to believe that he now was entitled to the sculptures, even those found by Hormuzd, but expressed his conviction that Loftus would 'find the old cock sparrow a troublesome customer' (Barnett 1976: 16).

The fund was apparently running out of donations and had entered into a some-what shady deal with the King of Prussia who was to pay a certain amount in return for a selection of sculpture from Assyria. Presumably Loftus knew that his activities were in reality dependent on such an arrangement which would secure the continued existence of the fund itself. Rawlinson in turn ordered Christian Rassam, a man he liked even less than Loftus, to resume limited excavations in the

Figures 34.2 and 34.3 F.C. Cooper, the artist on the second expedition, became a close friend of Hormuzd Rassam, and in the fall of 1851, while Rassam was in London, he painted these two portraits of his friend. Hormuzd was then 25 years old. One sees him in his two conflicting roles which he desperately tried to unite: as a British gentleman and as the subject of the Turkish Sultan. (From Barnett 1976: 3, 4)

palace in order to keep Loftus and Boutcher away. For a few months this farcical situation existed on Kuyunjik, with two competing English teams getting in each other's way, but in September 1854 Rawlinson was suddenly informed that the government had given a further £1,500 for Museum excavations in Assyria, and that the fund and the Trustees had reached an agreement according to which Loftus and Boutcher were transferred to the Museum's and thus Rawlinson's control.

Figure 34.3

Rassam's achievement on Kuyunjik is of course somewhat dubious seen from a strictly legal, or for that matter moral point of view, but he could rely on the practically unanswerable argument that he actually found what he was looking for. He was successful, and that is usually rewarded; it was in fact to be expected that his discovery would secure his personal fame, but events turned out somewhat differently. He became involved in other matters soon after his return to England and did not write the book which could perhaps have given him recognition; it took nearly forty years before such a report came out and then it was too late obviously. Also, he had to leave his discovery to others without having adequate drawings to place before the public, and instead his discoveries tended to be attributed to others, primarily to Rawlinson or Loftus; as appears from the quotation from Place's report, with which this chapter began, he was passed over in complete silence by his rival. Indeed, the French attitude has been consistently that the consul and the noble colonel got along fine in their gentlemanly competition, the troubles arose entirely because of the 'subordinate agents, especially the brothers Rassam, Chaldeans, and Rawlinson struggled to create peace' (Pillet 1962: 24–5).

Hormuzd Rassam is one of the most interesting personalities in this story, a man who saw himself as an 'Oriental', yet became more British than the most nationalistic colonel; a man who preferred being a chimney-sweep in England to a Pasha in Turkey; who became a member of the Anglican church and in his later life wrote extensively and vehemently in support of his adopted faith – his friend, the distinguished Assyriologist Pinches, said that 'like most Oriental Christians, he was a man of strong religious convictions, and having adopted evangelical views became a bitter foe of the high church movement' (Lee 1976), and he came to represent Britain and British interests in different places in the East, as the agent of the British Museum in several later excavation campaigns (see Figures 34.2 and 34.3). Once he had made up his mind that he was part of a fight over national prestige involving France and England, he dispensed with the niceties and probably did not at all understand or appreciate the fastidious politeness of Place and Rawlinson; he saw that in their actions they played the game to the full, occupying mounds under each other's noses. The problem was that Hormuzd was not a European and he did not play by the rules – whatever they may have been; in fact, one may wonder if they were capable of being obeyed by a man such as he was. Those people who could define themselves clearly and obviously as Europeans found him difficult to understand and could not really find a proper category for him. He was undoubtedly a clever and competent man and fully lived up to the requirements of the time for a good excavator, but he was no gentleman and there was no way he could become one. They knew it, he knew it, and he decided to define his own set of rules, declaring that Rawlinson had no authority to give part of Kuyunjik to Place, and constructing a rule which said that the first man to find a new palace automatically secured the right to it – irrespective of the way in which he made his discovery.

What he found was to a large degree if not stolen or appropriated by others, then at least attributed to them. The Ashurbanipal library was found by Layard and George Smith according to the next edition of the Encyclopedia Britannica, thus passing over Rassam completely; he pointed out himself that his discovery of the new palace appeared to have had 'such a bad effect on M. Place's memory that in the work he published in 1866–69 of his researches, entitled "Nineve et l'Assyrie", he quite ignored the fact of my discoveries, but made it appear that Mr Loftus, and even his artist, Mr Boutcher, were the successful discoverers' (Rassam 1897: 27, n.). When the finds were displayed in the British Museum his name was not mentioned, but Rawlinson was credited with the discovery of the Ashurbanipal palace; the same attitude was adopted by George Rawlinson in his book about his brother, for Hormuzd had of course been nothing more than the assistant whose name did not need to be mentioned.

His relationship to Rawlinson necessarily had to be strained and complex; one may compare it with the relations between Layard and Canning, adding that Rassam was not English and that Rawlinson had little respect for Orientals. In a correspondence from 1855 Layard complained to Rawlinson that he took the credit for both Rassam's and Loftus' discoveries, claiming that he was the one who had found Ashurbanipal's palace. The colonel answered that it had certainly been on his direct orders that Hormuzd had begun excavations on the northern half of Kuyunjik, 'which had hitherto been kept for the French. The passage which you quote from my letter refers to the Southern and Central parts of the mound, where I certainly thought there was no longer any use in experimentalizing'. This is therefore in response to the quote mentioned earlier, and it is very difficult to argue that Rawlinson is being truly candid in this letter. However, the fundamental point comes in the following sentences:

> I am quite ready to give Hormuzd every possible credit, and if you think it desirable I will write to the Athenæum on the subject and send it for your approval – but I must say that in regard to all the discoveries, whether made by Hormuzd, or Loftus, or John Taylor, I consider that I have an extensive right of *Seignorage* upon them – for my supervision was not as Oppert says mere monetary; but I selected the spots where they were to dig; in most cases I gave the officers involved detailed written instructions. I regulated the extent and nature of their establishments, and finally I determined what marbles &c were to be sent home. With regard to the present collection you must remember I picked out and marked every marble with my own hand. I also consider it of consequence that I worked gratuitously, while all the others were salaried. At the same time it is my honest wish that due credit should be given to all.[234]

A few months later Rawlinson became involved in a furious debate with Loftus over precisely the same kind of issue, ending with a letter of apology from the colonel which was printed in the *Athenæum* (Harbottle 1958: 212–13). Another letter was sent in which he explained that Hormuzd had in fact worked on Kuyunjik *against his express advice*. In the meantime Layard had explained to him, somewhat unkindly, that Hormuzd Rassam had been opposed to going out in order to serve under Rawlinson, and this made the colonel respond that he had regarded Hormuzd precisely as a subordinate agent and nothing else. He had been solely responsible for the excavations all the way through, so if he was to bear the responsibility for possible failure, he was entitled to be credited with the success. With some bitterness he added:

> You should also remember that I went out to the East again in 1851, at much risk to my health, as well as loss and discomfort, for the mere purpose of gratifying my antiquarian taste and advancing our Cuneiform knowledge, by directing and conducting the excavations which you had abandoned – and that had I not taken this duty on myself, neither could the Trustees have

applied for a Parliamentary grant nor have employed subordinate Agents. I believe that in strict fairness I have far more reason to complain myself, than I have ever given for complaint against me, but I am in real truth as little jealous as most people; moreover I hate controversy, and always wish to give credit where it is due.[235]

Rassam's strange, almost tragicomic view of himself as an English Oriental was shaped by such relationships and situations. Layard was clearly the most important person in his life, together with Pinches perhaps the only one who simply saw him as a friend, irrespective of nationality, creed or social background. Rassam's book about his excavations published in 1897 was therefore logically dedicated to the memory of Layard, 'the pioneer of Assyrian explorers, whose friendship of fifty years' standing was as true in my youth as it proved constant in my advancing years'. He also stressed that his only purpose in writing his book was

> to show how easy it is to get on with all the inhabitants of Biblical lands, especially the Arabs, provided they are not treated with unbecoming hauteur and conceit. I ever found Arabs, Koords, and Turcomans (all of whom are, of course, Mohammedans), most tractable people to deal with, and I always found them true, loyal, and most hospitable.
>
> (Rassam 1897: ix)

The racism and the prejudices with which he had to contend in his own personal attempt to cross one of the most formidable barriers of his world and be recognised as a 'real' Englishman, or even to be regarded as a competent, interesting person, is clearly in view in such a passage. The enormous pride he took in his discoveries merges with his self-understanding in a touching passage in which he quotes an article from the *Illustrated London News* in 1856, announcing the arrival of a new batch of reliefs from Ashurbanipal's palace; he notes that Rawlinson had been given the credit for the lion-hunt slabs, but this 'generous' article restored the balance:

> It must be not a little gratifying to that pioneer of Assyrian research [i.e., Layard] to find, through his example, an Oriental – generally indifferent to all works of art – so thoroughly interested in the undertaking and impregnated with the English energy to carry his individual labours to a successful conclusion.
>
> (Rassam 1897: 40)

Obviously, this 'foreigner in an Englishman's position', as the article called him, was equally gratified to be seen as the man whose eyes had been opened by his colour-blind friend, whom he loved and admired.

CHAPTER THIRTY-FIVE

WAR

—— .•. ——

While the conflicts raged in Assyria between Place and the Rassam brothers, battles erupted around them with wars being declared both on the personal and the international level. Let us begin with the smaller events which involved Layard, Hincks and Rawlinson, before turning to world politics and the Crimean War which was to have a decisive influence on activities in the Near East.

Layard's attempt to have Hincks appointed to a post at the British Museum was finally crowned with success in 1853. He tried to convince Rawlinson to accept this by pointing to the miserable working conditions under which the Irish scholar had been suffering in his isolation at Killyleagh, but the colonel was not in a mood to feel sorry for his rival or to be conciliatory. On the contrary, he declared himself to be deeply mortified at seeing Hincks taking the place which he regarded as his own by right:

> I looked on these tablets as a sort of game preserve – and Hincks I maintain to be a most unscrupulous poacher. The Irishman indeed has attacked me so wantonly and bitterly that I shall certainly retaliate and do all in my power to expose his dogmatism, excessive conceit and what I call his systematic dishonesty – we shall see who comes best off in the melée.[236]

Shortly afterwards, when Rawlinson had received reports telling him about the contents of Layard's new book on the second expedition, the tone became even harsher:

> I have not yet seen your book, but have of course numerous accounts of it in the letters of my correspondents – and am assured that the main drift of the antiquarian part is to exalt Hincks at my expense. You are of course at liberty to take any view you please of what the Irishman calls our 'controversy' – but the result of being thus run down is that it forces me to take up the cudgels – and this I shall do forthwith.[237]

It was not only the matter of Hincks' attachment to the Museum which fired his anger, of course, for part of the controversy was about the question of who was to be given the honour of being seen as the one who deciphered the cuneiform script in the eyes of the public, and consequently who could present the correct understanding of Assyrian history and its relationship to biblical interpretation. Both men must have been aware that the process of decipherment was to a large extent successfully completed, and it was now a matter of securing that the contemporary world as well as the future understood and appreciated Rawlinson's achievement and priority, as he saw it.

Considering Rawlinson's fundamental attitude and the self-image he had expressed already in the early letter to his sister, which has been quoted above, it had to be completely unacceptable to him to be bested by a man like Hincks, for whom he had persuaded himself to have little respect. No doubt it played a role that Hincks was a clergyman, a country parson, for the colonel appears not to have had a high regard for that profession, and it may have been important also that he was Irish, a kind of second-class member of the United Kingdom. Rawlinson had by now seen Hincks' biting and bitter comments to his own adoption of the syllabic principle for the cuneiform script, but he rejected vehemently that the Irishman should have the least justification in claiming any priority to any important discovery. The matter of syllables he left completely untouched – it would be difficult not to accept Hincks' argument on this point – and he concentrated instead on the question of who gave the first correct reading of the most important names. It was of course impossible to deny that Hincks was the first to suggest that the builder of the palace at Kuyunjik was Sennacherib, but he pointed out that this was not based on a real reading, but that it was nothing but a lucky guess; 'the Palestine campaign was the real *discovery*', he said, and that was of course his own. He declared himself now prepared for battle and intended to prove '50 cases of direct larceny against your protegé – and as I said in my last I will certainly do all I can to swamp him'. With bitterness he continues:

> You talk a great deal of Hinck's difficulties but is Baghdad 'a bed of roses'? My constitution is marred by this infernal climate and after 18 years laborious study on the Cuneiform Inscriptions I should like to have what single reward or encouragement I have personally received from the British Govt.[238]

War now having been openly declared he sat down to write letters to his many contacts in London and at the British Museum, and three weeks later he sent a long formal letter of protest to the Trustees. In this remarkable text, where anger and hurt boils under the formally correct surface, he tried to draw the rug from under Hincks and his planned work at the Museum. He maintained that an edition of the great Nimrud text on the basis of the fragments brought home by Layard necessarily had to be so defective that it was in fact meaningless to publish it. Since Layard had left Assyria much better preserved examples of the inscription had been discovered, containing many decisive variants, and these texts were in Rawlinson's hands in Baghdad. In that way a great deal of the justification for having Hincks work at the Museum at all was gone, in his view, and he went on:

> I will not dwell on the peculiar position which I occupy at present in regard to Dr. Hincks, but I appeal to the Trustees if after having devoted 18 years of my life to the decipherment of the Cuneiform Inscriptions, to the

sacrifice in various instances of my professional advancement, after having surmounted all preliminary difficulties, & aimed at that point when I might ultimately hope to obtain my reward by publishing the historical results of my discoveries, it must not be a source of keen disappointment to me to find myself at the last moment supplanted by a gentleman, who, however it may be sought to disguise the fact, is notoriously indebted in great measure to my published papers for his present undoubted proficiency.

The mortification indeed is the more severe as I certainly thought that my recent exertions in the service of the Trustees had given me a special claim on their consideration and as the delegation by the Trustees to Dr. Hincks of a duty which would seem naturally to dissolve upon myself, must give rise moreover to an impression that I have not been considered competent to undertake the task. I do not insist however at present on these details, I merely urge on the notice of the Trustees that in a matter which is of so much intrinsic importance & which so nearly regards the literary honor of our country as the publication & translation of the Nimroud annals, it cannot be proper to spend the public money on incomplete materials, when complete materials are available.[239]

While one can understand to some extent the disappointment felt by Rawlinson, it is difficult to sympathise with this letter which is hardly worthy of a great man. He had no formal right whatsoever to the texts found by Layard, and the fact that he had become used to regarding them as his private game preserve was really his own problem. Not only that, but one has to remember that he sat in Baghdad with thousands of tablets from the royal library at Kuyunjik, texts which he controlled and which would be enough to form the basis for many years of work and several scholarly careers. Feelings of liberality and generosity appear to have been beyond his human capacities in this matter.

And, of course, he got what he wanted, for the Irishman was no real rival in terms of connections and contacts. He was certainly hired by the Trustees in order to work on Layard's finds for a year and he did sit in the Museum during a couple of months, but this was not a happy experience for him after all. A year later he wrote dejectedly to Layard from Killyleagh, saying that his feeling was that people at the Museum had consistently tried to keep material away from him. He was allowed to look at certain texts only, and others that he asked for could not be found. The results of his one year's labour were contained in two large notebooks filled with transliterations, translations and commentaries which he had sent to the Museum, and he wrote to Layard that they contained

a mass of information, which is (I flatter myself – indeed I have no doubt) of *very great value*. I have no idea that the Trustees will *publish* it. I think it very possible that they will allow the use of it privately to some of their present employees, so as to enable him to carry on the work – *I being cast off*; and it may be that the person thus benefitted may not acknowledge the source from which he draws information. Rawlinson will be in London, I suppose, forthwith. He was expected before this. And I have no doubt that *he* will be allowed free access to all that the Museum possesses.[240]

335

He concluded his letter with the sigh: 'I am thus *disheartened* with respect to London', and he had good reason to be. A month later Ellis at the Museum wrote to Rawlinson about Hincks' notebooks, offering him full access to them and even suggesting that a copy of them could be sent to Baghdad (Cathcart 1994: 20). Half a year later Rawlinson had not returned to London yet, but one of his contacts in the Museum, Vaux, did the dirty work for him. The colonel had asked Vaux to find Hincks' manuscript for him, and he succeeded:

> Your letter arrived as you conjectured it wd. just as I was off for my vaca-
> tion and as I came back I was for a few days so busy that I had not time
> to think of Hincks. I have however now got his MSS from the Secretariat
> den and proceed to send you as much detail about it as I can cram into this
> letter. You wd. have been amused at the astonishment of Ellis and Co. when
> I asked to see H.s memoir. It was as good as a Comedy – if it had not been
> such a complete farce. At first he denied there being any memoir but the
> short printed notice, which appeared also in the Lit.ry Gazette, I think, in
> April 3. When I urged that the Trustees were not likely to have paid 100 £
> for that he began to reflect – and at length, when I pressed him further he
> admitted that there was such a Memoir. And that as he supposed it was
> useless – no one had looked at it. At length from behind a pile of dusty old
> books were dragged out two copy books containing H.s Memoir – and
> marked GH outside as having been sent in May 3d. I really believe that this
> proved Ellis's story is true & that no one had seen them till I ferreted them
> out, profiting by your letter. I asked to be allowed to read them at leisure
> which after some demur was granted & I have now had them for a fortnight
> in my drawer here. What wd. friend Hincks say if he knew all this? I shan't
> tell him – because I own I like the fellow – he is a queer cantankerous old
> chap of the Dominic Sampson school, but his bark is worse than his bite –
> and much of his crabbedness arises from his having lived such a mere student's
> life – and also from his coming from the Black North of Ireland. The first
> thing to be done is to give you a list of what he has translated or professed
> to have translated.[241]

Twelve closely packed pages follow which contain a detailed report on all of Hincks' results, give long extracts from his readings and translations, explain his system of transliteration and copy many of his notes and commentaries to the texts. Rawlinson got his revenge, and whether this is an example of what he himself called 'larceny' I leave to the reader to decide.

This sad story did not end here, however, for a couple of years later the note-books were still in Vaux's desk, and he happened to mention them in a conversation with a friend of his, the inventor of photography Fox Talbot, who often visited the Museum in order to discuss progress in cuneiform matters. Talbot then wrote to Hincks expressing his surprise on learning of the existence of a translation of the Nimrud inscription; he explained that in his conversation with Vaux he had said

> that I could not ask to look at your manuscript without your express sanc-
> tion and permission, to which he replied, 'Of course not', and thus, as you

were in Ireland, the MS. remained unseen by me. But as nothing can exceed the kindness and courtesy of Mr Vaux, I feel sure that if it depended on him to order the publication of your most valuable labours now in MS. in the hands of the Trustees, he would not hesitate to do so immediately, or to take any other step calculated to place your rights of priority in a just light. They are incontestable.

(Davidson 1933: 204)

What went through Vaux's head on this occasion? Did he suffer at all from a black conscience? The farce continued when Hincks wrote back saying that he disagreed with Vaux's attitude and wanted the manuscript to be available to everyone, and he then complained directly to the Trustees that the notebooks were being kept secret, while single individuals apparently had access to them. In some embarrassment the chief librarian Panizzi answered that only Mr Vaux had seen them, and that this was 'contrary to the wish both of yourself and the Trustees'; this was said to be regrettable and 'a complete mistake' (Davidson 1933: 216–17).

At the time when Vaux wrote his long letter to Rawlinson in Baghdad Europe was becoming entangled in a violent conflict that concerned the very survival of the Ottoman empire, the Crimean War. Layard was in fact at that moment on board a ship which was anchored in front of the Russian naval port of Sevastopol, Doctor Sandwith, his unfortunate companion from the second expedition was with Colonel Williams of the Boundary Commission in the city Kars in eastern Turkey where they were establishing themselves as heroes, and other persons who have appeared in this account played roles in this strange play.

One of the causes of the war was the 'Affair of the Holy Places' in Jerusalem, various sanctuaries which were at the centre of conflicts involving different Christian sects, and this brings us back to Botta. As French Consul-General in Jerusalem he was destined to play a central role in the political events which unfolded at this time, and which had a profound impact on the Near East.

He was, as already mentioned, appointed to the post as consul here at a time when the Dominican Valerga began to function as the so-called 'Latin Patriarch' in the holy city. As part of the Ottoman Empire Jerusalem had long enjoyed a special status with its majority of Christian inhabitants; these were split into several different groups, but the largest one was Greek Orthodox and the patriarch for this church had long had a leading position in the city as nominal head of the entire Christian community. The appointment of Valerga as leader of the Catholics there was clearly an element in a wider plan to change this situation, and it marked not only religious but also political interests, for the Greek Orthodox were seen as the allies of Russia, whereas the Catholics looked to France as their champion. When a silver star with a Latin inscription disappeared from the church in Bethlehem in 1847, this minor event became the starting point for open conflict; France demanded extensive Catholic control over a number of holy places, and it quickly turned into a controversy involving the right to control the keys to the Church of the Holy Sepulchre in Jerusalem and to restore the cupola for this building. In 1848 France was laying plans for its further strategy in this matter when the revolution came and changed priorities.

The matter did not disappear by itself, however, and in the course of 1850 various demands were expressed in an official letter to the Sultan. At the same time the Greek Orthodox patriarch applied for permission to repair and rebuild the roof of the church. There was no doubt that such a restoration would mean that the building would acquire a very clear Greek Orthodox look, and the French regarded the application as a most provocative intervention. Suddenly they demanded that the Turks should follow an old agreement from 1740, despite the fact that the French governments had never taken it seriously themselves; it now became the legal basis for their status in Jerusalem. Endless negotiations, claims and counterclaims followed, and the Russians began to make threatening noises, claiming to be the only protectors of the Christians in the Ottoman Empire. This claim was obviously seen as a threat more against the Turks than the French, and in 1851 a French-Turkish commission was established with the purpose of finding a settlement to the conflict. One of the members of this commission was Botta, who represented French interests in the Holy Land.

It worked during the whole of 1851, and Botta – who may have been inspired by his new-found religiosity which appeared in his letters to Disraeli – turned out to be a smooth and effective negotiator. He argued a French position which in effect would have given control over the most important holy places to the Catholics. Pressure from Russia became too strong, however, and the Turks – advised all the way through by Layard's old embassy friend Alison – attempted to find the basis for a workable compromise. A new commission was established, this time an Islamic one whose members were leading mullahs.

At the same time the coup d'état in France in December 1851 weakened the French position and made it essential for the new Emperor to compromise in order to gain the acceptance of the other major powers; thus, there was suddenly a possibility for a settlement which could be accepted by all parties. The Muslim mullahs presented a document which was filled with the most intricate and complex legal formulations which defined the rights of the various Christian sects in the country. The Greek Orthodox appeared to have come out best, but the Catholics could point to the fact that they were given the keys to the church at Bethlehem and that they were permitted to hold services in the Church at Jerusalem. The decision was passed to the French and Russian consuls at Jerusalem in February 1852, and Botta now arranged a strange performance. He got the Turkish emissary to read the letter from the Sultan to the Catholic community, hoping that this solemn ceremony might hide the fact that their demands had not been met; and he furthermore persuaded the Turks that a similar official ceremony was not to be held for the Greek Orthodox community. As a result all were dissatisfied (Seignobos 1921: 302).

Until the middle of 1852 Stratford Canning sat in Constantinople as British ambassador, and he appears to have seen it as his task to aid the reformist Turkish officials in their attempts to fend off both the French and the Russians. At his departure nothing had been definitely settled, however, and by then military interests began to appear in the matter. The Russians suggested to the British that the Ottoman Empire should now be liquidated and divided between the two powers, but England was not ready for such a policy.

At the end of 1852 the Turks offered a new proposal which went much further than the former one in an attempt to placate the French, and this time it was read only to the Greek Orthodox, but Botta did not complain. Anyway, the Russians rejected it. In February 1853 the Russian Count Menshikoff arrived at Constantinople with the final demands from the Russian Czar, and these in effect abolished all previous agreements.

It may seem distinctly odd that such local conflicts over some old rusty keys could exercise the minds of so many people, and one may imagine that the Turks occasionally looked upon this side of the conflict with some bafflement. In fact, this was only a minor part of the far greater and much more urgent problem of the survival of the Ottoman Empire as a multi-religious and multi-ethnic state. Violent conflicts involving the various religious and ethnic groups had erupted repeatedly and all knew that disharmony was lurking just below the surface. Since that time the world has seen several examples of the violence which can erupt when the central power in such socio-political units breaks down and no longer can control or hide the underlying potential conflicts. The Soviet Union or Yugoslavia are recent cases.

The Christian powers had earlier indicated their willingness to intervene in Turkey's internal affairs when their co-religionists were submitted to persecution which the Sultan was unwilling or unable to check. The Russians now went much further and demanded Turkish recognition of Russia's right to protect all Greek Orthodox Christians in the Ottoman Empire, a suggestion which would inevitably have had a deeply destabilising effect on the country by creating a kind of internal authority that could appeal to Russia at all times. Clearly, the Turkish government could not accept such a proposal, and the other European powers supported them in their rejection.

As the crisis now appeared to deepen the British government decided to persuade Canning, who had in the meantime become Lord Stratford de Redcliffe, to return to the post in Constantinople, and surprisingly he asked Layard to come with him as a special aide; even more surprisingly, Layard accepted.

Shortly before he had turned down an offer to take over the post as Consul-General in Egypt and a salary of £1,700 per year, a kind of compensation for his being kept out of the cabinet. When Rawlinson in Baghdad heard that Layard instead accepted to go to Constantinople for nothing to assist Canning, he found it difficult to hide his amazement and contempt:

> I cannot of course believe in a pure 'amor patriae', nor in any particular attachment on your part for the Elchee. The simple question seems to be what you are to get for volunteering again for the East. People of course cannot live on air, nor at your time of life can they afford to throw away a few years merely for éclat. I am not surprised at your declining Egypt, but to throw up 1700 £ a year and at the same time come to Consple on nothing, does I confess, pass my comprehension.[242]

He assumed that Layard was expecting to take over as the new ambassador at Constantinople once the present crisis had blown over, but it seems that Layard's decision to go was rather based on a feeling of obligation towards the man who had after all given him his first real chance.

The arrangement quickly turned out to be a total catastrophe for the two men who simply could not get along any more. Layard had no intention of acting as Canning's humble servant, being full of a feeling of personal achievement after his recent successes; his new book about the second expedition had just appeared and created a new wave of public interest, and he was now beginning to receive the honours he craved; shortly before leaving with Canning he had been made an honorary citizen of London. The ambassador, on the other hand, had suffered great disappointments and was beginning to have to face the fact that his political career was at an end. His hope of receiving the Foreign Ministry when the new government had recently been formed had been dashed, and he had with some bitterness been obliged to accept his new fine title as a for him small and unsatisfactory compensation.

The journey through Europe was according to Layard 'intolerable', and he declared in a letter to his aunt that he had no idea how he would have managed to survive it, had it not been for Canning's 'freaks' which at least gave rise to a few good laughs – behind the great man's back, of course. In Constantinople he then took a weary look at the absurd conflict which he felt was soon going to be over:

> The French and Russians have settled their quarrels – and I hope to hear nothing more of the Holy Places and the ridiculous squabbles about Greek and Latin saints and apocryphal tombs. One of the great subjects of discussion was whether the saints were to be painted with glories like plates round their heads after the Byzantine fashion, or with simple circles of gold which according to the fathers of the Catholic Church are the more authentic symbols of beatification. The great Powers actually threatened to go to war about such absurd matters! The Turks are now going to build the cupola themselves. The best thing they could do would be to turn all the Christians out of Jerusalem.[243]

He was already considering how to get out of this situation, for the embassy was a most uncomfortable place to be; the attachés referred to Canning's rule as a 'reign of terror'. He suffered for a month before going home again, but, of course, his analysis of the political developments turned out to be incorrect and the situation continued to deteriorate. Count Menshikoff delivered new, utterly unacceptable proposals or ultimatums, and these resulted in a more and more threatening military situation. Canning had the British Mediterranean fleet readied to be able to intervene, and in London Layard attempted to have Parliament debate the crisis and England's role. Since the government was rather unsure of its own priorities it did not wish to have a public discussion which might force its hand; the fiery pro-Turkish Layard was viewed with extreme scepticism, and he travelled the country giving speeches in which he explained that Russia, not Turkey, was the real enemy.

Then in July a Russian army crossed the border to Turkey and occupied a large area corresponding roughly to northern Romania down to the Danube, and this resulted in loud Turkish protests. Negotiations ensued which appeared to promise a result, so finally in August the government felt it safe to let Layard have his debate in Parliament. In his long and effective speech he pointed out that without the central government in Constantinople all of the Near East would fall apart and a chaotic political situation would arise, which would in effect force the western powers to intervene directly and militarily – unless they were willing to leave the entire area to the Russians. The expected settlement did not materialise, however, and in October 1853 the explosion came with a Turkish declaration of war with Russia (Goldfrank 1994).

These political events had a direct and profound impact on conditions in Mosul, of course. Seen in a local, Muslim perspective it was all a matter of war with the Christians, and no one here was willing or able to distinguish clearly between the various Christian sects. In the mountains around Mosul there was loud talk of *jihad*, Holy War, against the Christians, and the Chaldeans were extremely worried. There were rumours of freeing the old Kurdish warrior Beder Khan-Bey whose atrocities in his anti-Christian campaigns Layard had seen the effects of in the mountain valleys. When the Turkish military garrison was withdrawn from Mosul in early 1854 the tension became unbearable, and now Place decided on an ingenious scheme which could secure the lives and property of the Christian groups in the town. He had been ordered to stop his excavations, but he retained close connections with the Jebour tribe who had made up the larger part of his excavation team, and he now reemployed them to dig at Khorsabad; at the same time he made sure that they would come to Mosul once a week to receive their pay, and he arranged for them to parade through the streets of Mosul brandishing their guns and shouting their war-cry. He was convinced that in this way he avoided a situation where the Muslim religious leaders would encourage attacks on Christians and Europeans, for everyone knew that the wild Jebour, who were 'rather fond of plunder, always armed . . . ready for anything', were at his command if there should be a need for them (Pillet 1962: 41–3).

At first the Turks felt deserted by England and France, but it was in fact inevitable that these countries, however ill-prepared they were, should come to the aid of the Ottomans, and war was declared by both countries on 27 March 1854. Faced with this challenge the Russians withdrew from the occupied areas in the Balkans, and an army consisting of Turks, English and French troops settled down in the Bulgarian port of Varna. The matter was, in effect, cleared up, but now that large armies had been raised and sent to the Black Sea it seemed reasonable to end Russia's threat. In September 1854 the armies were therefore shipped to the Crimea where the aim was to capture and destroy the headquarters of the Russian Black Sea Fleet at Sevastopol.

In this situation it cannot cause wonder that authorities in both London and Paris forgot about the excavations in Assyria. No more money was forthcoming, and the war made such demands on the fleets that there was no hope that a ship could be sent to Basra to pick up Assyrian reliefs. So Place could only watch over his finds which had been brought to the banks of the Tigris across from Mosul as early as December 1853, waiting for a ship to be sent out. There were at least one hundred large cases. Rawlinson had been informed that the British Museum wanted no more than fifty cases with finds from Nimrud and Kuyunjik, for the somewhat altered national priorities meant that the Trustees felt unable to accommodate more sculptures. Rawlinson accordingly ordered Loftus to send no more than sixty cases, containing only the 'élite of your recent discoveries', whereas everything from Nimrud and the remains from Rassam's excavations were to be left behind. Place was to have a free hand in picking out slabs to be sent to Paris, an offer which was conditioned by a promise that the French ship which would come to Basra could also take on board the cases for the British Museum. Everything must then be drawn or photographed by Boutcher (Barnett 1976).

Layard had gone to the Crimea in order to witness the battles which led up to the final assault on Sevastopol. This had been a profoundly shocking experience, and he was filled with disgust at the suffering inflicted on the soldiers and the almost unimaginable waste of human lives. He was moreover horrified at what he perceived as the total incompetence of the English military, and returned to London filled with anger and loathing for a system which exposed the soldiers to cholera, hunger, cold and disease, sufferings which were placed in stark relief by the ineptitude of the officer corps. Ridiculous bureaucracy meant that supplies reached only as far as the storehouses at the naval port at Balaclava, often because the correct papers could not be signed which would release the food and medicine to the soldiers. Balaclava was pure hell:

> Ships arrived without notice in the congested harbour at Balaclava, and no one was quite sure what was in them. Sometimes they went all the way back across the Black Sea to Constantinople without being unloaded. . . . For days, for weeks on end, ships lay outside Balaclava waiting to come in and unload. And when they did so their crews, although well used to Eastern harbours, were appalled. Since the storm the ghastly pale-green waters were like a stagnant cesspool into which all imaginable refuse had been thrown. Dead men with white and swollen heads, dead camels, 'dead horses, dead mules, dead oxen, dead cats, dead dogs, the filth of an army with its hospitals', floated amidst the wreckage of spars, boxes, bales of hay, biscuits, smashed cases of medicines and surgical instruments, the decomposed offal and butchered carcasses of sheep thrown overboard by ship cooks.
>
> (Hibbert 1985: 206–7)

The military system was governed by aristocratic privilege. Younger sons in noble families could purchase a career as an officer, and nearly all commissioned officers in the British army in the Crimea had bought their commands; a real military education was according to the prevailing view all very well for such people as the Germans or French – 'and even for those officers who were unfortunately obliged to think of the Army as a career and to serve in India, but it did not do for gentlemen' (Hibbert 1985: 16).

After his return from the Crimea Layard made a speech in Parliament in which he launched a head-on attack against this system of privileges, which he felt should be abolished immediately. If this was not done, then the angry people of England would force the politicians to action (Waterfield 1963: 258–9). Palmerston, the Prime Minister, chose to see this speech as directed against the aristocracy as an institution in British life, and many saw it in the same way. Answering the charge that Layard set class against class, his friend Dickens said: 'The upper class had taken the initiative years ago, and it is *they* who have put *their* class in opposition to the country – not the country which puts itself in opposition to *them*' (Johnson 1986: 423).

It looked as if Layard was busy ruining his chances of having a normal political career, for his violence and his total lack of will to compromise created insuperable difficulties for him in Parliament. He was clearly a very troublesome man who insisted on being right, and he suffered from an unfortunate tendency to engage in strongly personal attacks on men he did not respect. But, as his biographer wrote, 'It is easy to be critical of Layard for not playing his cards well but amid all the confusion and slaughter his aggressiveness and refusal to compromise was a guide and comfort to many' (Waterfield 1963: 272). No one could really question his sincerity, even though his enemies did what they could, but he retained a deep sense of responsibility which was expressed in stirring words in his speech at Aberdeen when he was appointed Rector of Marischal College and University in April 1855:

> Had I been content to uncover the crumbling monuments of buried Nineveh, to gratify an idle whim – had they afforded me no instruction – had they given rise to no earnest reflection – had they proved of no further usefulness to this country than to satisfy a vulgar curiosity – I should, indeed, have been ashamed to allude to their discovery in such an assembly as this. I trust that even in the discharge of public duty, and in endeavouring to form my character as a public man, they will prove to me a continual warning, that the fate which befell Nineveh and Babylon may befall the mightiest of nations, when public virtue is no longer held in honour, when great principles no longer guide its counsels, and when the public weal is sacrificed and made subservient to private interests.
>
> (Layard 1855–8: 21–2)

CHAPTER THIRTY-SIX

SHIPWRECK

—— .◆. ——

Place's cases were lying at Mosul for sixteen months, from 5 December 1853 until 29 April 1855, while he waited for a message from Paris telling him that a ship was being sent out to Basra. It must have been very hard for him to watch them every day, thinking about all the things he could have done at Khorsabad if money had been allocated to him. On the other hand he knew that his finds were magnificent and would overshadow what Botta had already brought home to the Louvre; he had packed many more reliefs, two gigantic bulls and other very large sculptures. A number of tablets and clay prisms with inscriptions had also been found, but these had been sent home with Félix Thomas who had already left, so the cases contained primarily large objects.

He could look back on a massive achievement which had involved the opening of no less than seventy-eight rooms in the palace, he had uncovered one hundred and thirty-one doors, four large corridors and eight internal courtyards, and the area excavated by him covered more than 9,000 m² (see Figure 36.1). Compared with this, Botta's results were much less impressive, for he had uncovered no more than fourteen rooms, twenty-eight doors and four bulls. Nevertheless, the palace was far from fully excavated and it was with mixed feelings that Place prepared to send off his discoveries.

To make things even more complex, he had been told to move to another post. In November 1854 he received a letter from the ministry in Paris informing him that he was now Vice-Consul, second class, at a place called Galatz in Moldavia. He succeeded in convincing his employers that it would be intolerable for him to leave before the cases had been shipped to Paris.

Because of the demands on the French fleet during the Crimean War it had become necessary for the ministry to hire a privately owned ship, the threemaster 'Manuel' of 237 tons; according to the contract signed in December 1854 in Paris the ship was to arrive at Basra on 29 April of the following year. This meant that the journey was supposed to be completed in four months, which was extremely optimistic, since it usually took about half a year to get to Basra from Europe south of Africa. Place was informed about the contract in February 1855 and now had to prepare for the final trip downriver. He also had to pack all his personal belongings and the notes and plans from the excavation, all of which was placed in further cases.

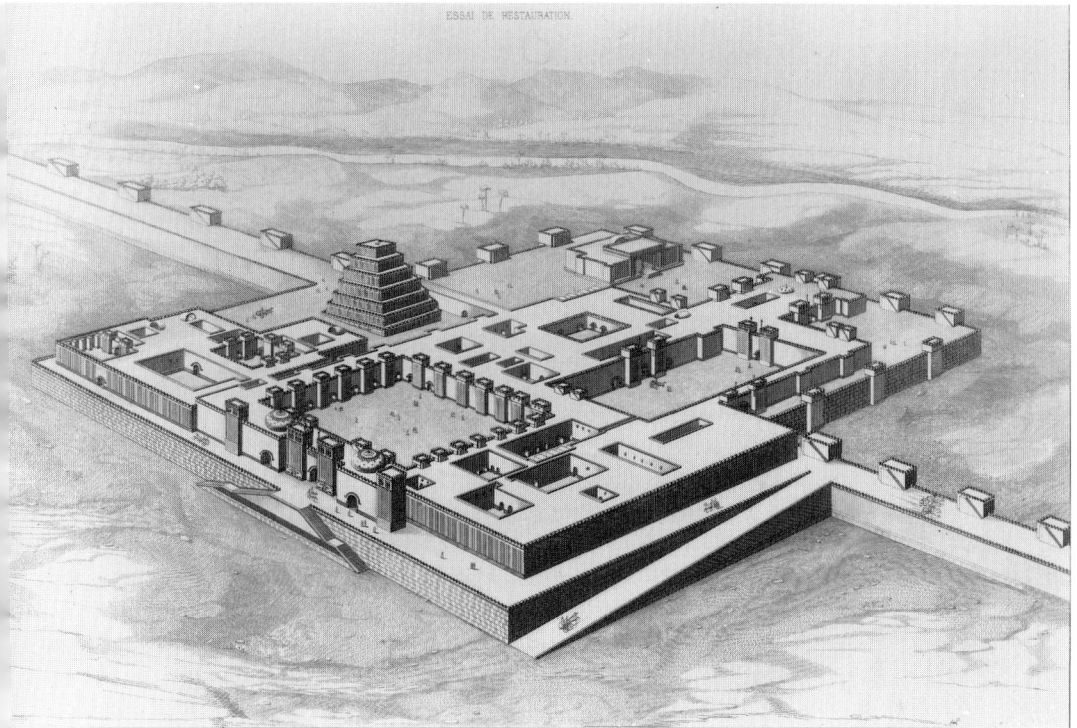

Figure 36.1 The palace at Khorsabad as reconstructed at the end of Place's work. Also in this picture there is a great deal which does not correspond to our views concerning Assyrian architecture, but the overall impression is convincing. It is noteworthy that the *ziggurat*, the temple tower, was a part of the palace complex itself, and later excavations here by an American team has shown the existence of a group of temples here. (From Place 1867, III: Plate 18)

He must have been relieved to be able to finally pack up and get the rafts constructed, but danger signs immediately appeared. Rawlinson wrote to him that a new large breach on the Tigris dykes had created a situation which was a thousand times worse than the one which had led to Layard's rafts being shipwrecked; furthermore, the unsettled political situation in the south had now resulted in a complete breakdown of order in the area around Basra, which was in effect being besieged by the Bedouin. Traffic between Baghdad and Basra had been cut, and only the strongly defended English steamer belonging to the Residency was able to navigate in some safety on the river (Pillet 1962: 71).

Place had no secure knowledge of when the ship would arrive, but he organised the departure from Mosul on 29 April, the very same day 'Manuel' was supposed to dock at Basra. The fleet of rafts arrived without mishap at Baghdad on 4 May, but here nobody had heard anything about the French ship. Place had received instructions that he should not go further south than Baghdad, and he was to stay here no longer than to the end of May, after which time he was to go directly to his new post.

He therefore had to face a situation where the most dangerous part of the journey had to be left to others, the stretch from Baghdad to Basra. It is unclear how he evaluated the problems, and he was later blamed for not having taken command of the last trip himself, but no one can know whether that would have made any difference. There were plenty of warnings, and even the Pasha in Baghdad tried to convince him to wait. The problem was: wait for what? The revolt in the south was not likely to be put down soon and the dyke was presumably never going to be repaired anyway. True, the 'Manuel' had not yet arrived at Basra, but its arrival was imminent, and it would probably leave again empty if the cases were not waiting for it on the quay. That would have been a real disaster.

The rafts were not in good shape either. Normally the cases would have been reloaded in Baghdad because the inflated skins which gave the rafts their buoyancy tended to deflate and become watersoaked (see Figure 36.2). A number of cases were in fact loaded onto a large boat, together with forty-one cases containing the results of Fresnel's excavations at Babylon, the cases from Kuyunjik which were destined for the Louvre and eighty cases for Berlin.

Place chose a certain M. Clément, a language teacher at Baghdad, to lead the transport, appointed him 'consular agent' and gave him detailed instructions, the necessary papers and gifts meant for the various Bedouin sheikhs whose areas were to be visited. The fleet sailed on 13 May, the large sailing ship of 50 tons and four rafts with a total load of 235 cases. Having watched the flotilla disappear downriver, Place mounted his horse and went north to Mosul again. He probably felt that he had done what was humanly possible to secure the transportation, but he must have been a deeply worried man nevertheless. While he rode north disaster struck on the river.

Everything went wrong from the very start. The sailing ship Place had hired had been exchanged for another one without his knowledge, one that was somewhat larger but much older and in very poor condition. It soon turned out to leak badly. M. Clément was onboard this ship, but he lost control of the crew; they landed again shortly after having left Baghdad in order to take on a large load of contraband, bales of silk which belonged to merchants in Baghdad and were meant for Basra. Since Place's transport was free from paying duties they presumably hoped to get their wares through customs too. M. Clément could not prevent this, even though he must have known that this spelled disaster, and since the captain of the boat in all likelihood was in cahoots with some of the Arab tribes along the river who were planning to steal the silk, this whole affair was to have drastic consequences.

After that the next five days were peaceful, but at the first confrontation with one of the Arab sheikhs M. Clément had to give up all of the presents meant for the trip. The customs authorities at Korna then demanded money despite a paper from the Pasha in Baghdad which declared the shipment free from duty, presumably because they found the bales of silk. M. Clément was now penniless and had nothing to give the sheikhs who came to demand gifts. The flotilla was subjected to constant looting and on 21 May the boat was boarded by a group of men armed with lances, swords and shields. The captain drove the boat into the riverbank, apparently on purpose, and this happened with such violence that the ship broke

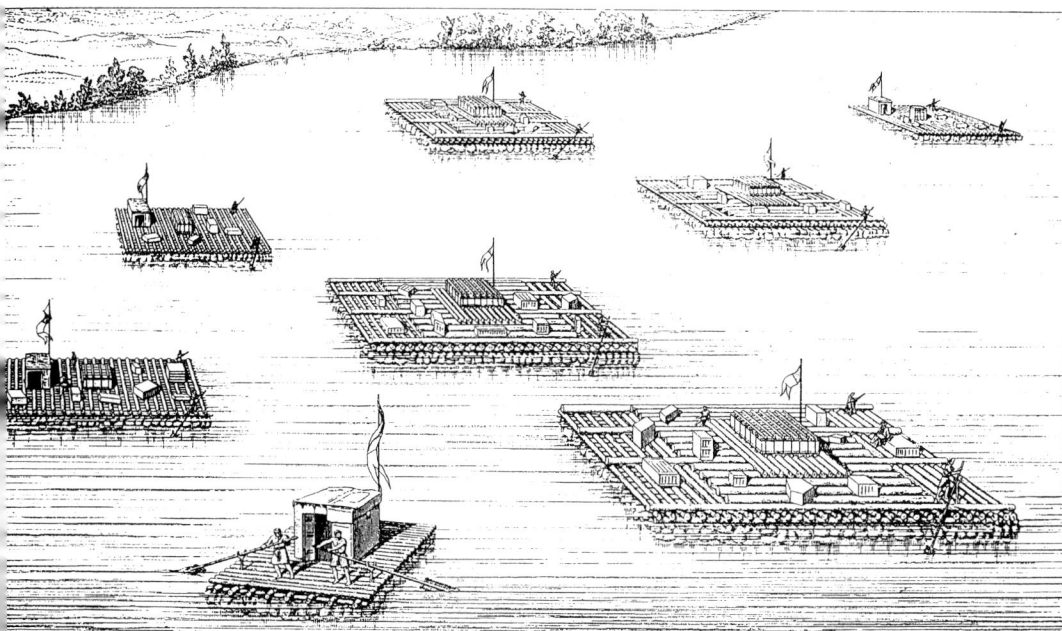

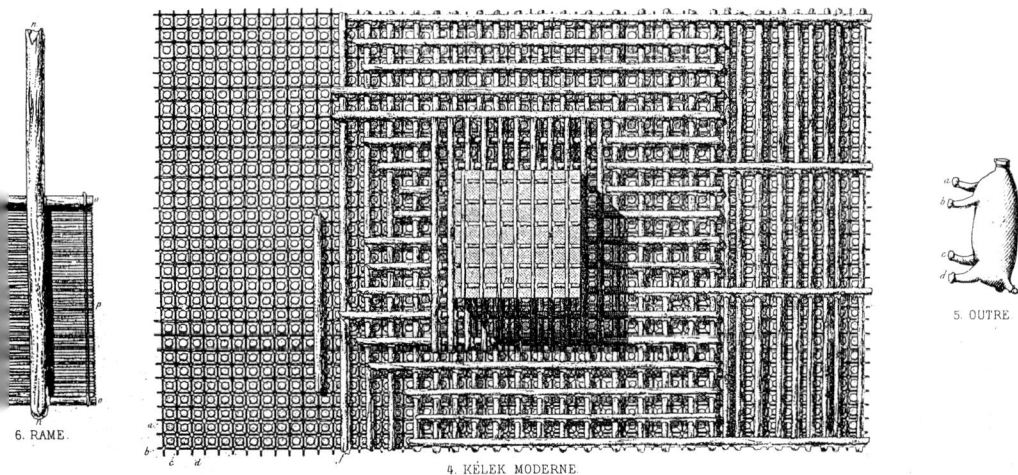

Figure 36.2 The proud armada of rafts on the Tigris on its way to destruction and shipwreck in the southern marshes. Below, a plan of a *kelek*, an oar, and one of the inflated sheep-skins which kept the whole thing above water. (From Place 1867, III: Plate 43)

347

in two and the aft part sank in three fathoms of water. The passengers had to abandon ship carrying only their personal belongings, and the pirates began to plunder the boat and break it to pieces to get the wood which was most valuable here in the treeless marshes. M. Clément was beaten and robbed; a Turkish naval ship watched the whole affair without intervening, but its captain afterwards gave some clothes and shoes to the naked M. Clément who was escorted to the British residence north of Basra.

The rafts were also plundered for all the wood that could be taken from them and they could hardly float after this treatment. One of them went aground close to Korna with its load consisting of a bull colossus which was lost and some smaller cases which were saved. Another sank in deep waters and was never found; the remaining two reached Basra before sinking and part of their cargo was saved, among other things the second large bull from Khorsabad. The rafts were then 1.5 m under the water and hardly visible on the surface. M. Clément arrived at the house of the French agent in Basra in a miserable condition, with bleeding feet; the men who were there to hear about his sufferings and misfortune sat down and wept.

Place arrived at Mosul on 23 May, a couple of days after the final catastrophe on the river. In a report dated 17 June he expressed worry over the fate of the transport, but it is difficult to understand that he should not by then have heard about it from the south. He was supposed to wait in Mosul for the arrival of his replacement, but having waited almost a month he suddenly decided to leave on 19 June. One can hardly escape the suspicion that he had by then been fully informed about the immensity of the disaster at Korna. These dates are those given by Pillet, based on the official reports to the ministry. According to Elisabeth Fontan, Place wrote a letter to his brother, Charles, already on 26 May – from Baghdad – in which he exclaimed 'Maudit soit le jour où je suis entré dans les fouilles de Ninive!'. What other evidence we have indicates that he was not in Baghdad at this time and that he could not have known about the disaster so early, but if Fontan is right his actions become even more desperate (Fontan 1994b: 14). At any rate, he could simply not stand any more but fled precipitately from the country which he never really liked, and which had now crushed his dreams and destroyed the fruits of several years' hard work. This disaster was unbearable and could not be handled in open confrontation with others; he had to be alone with his despair and jumped on a horse to get away from Mosul and Assyria. After ten days' ride he arrived at Diyarbakir in eastern Anatolia, and here he sat down to write a report about the disaster to Paris. He claimed that he had only just been informed, but that is hard to believe.

Even though one of the bulls was saved together with a few cases it is fair to say that he had lost everything. One of the most astonishing aspects of the affair is that Place had made no inventory of the shipment, so it is impossible to say precisely what disappeared in the waters of the Tigris, but it appears to have been nearly everything from Khorsabad, including all of his notes and plans which he had made during the years of excavation, as well as eighty-four cases containing his personal belongings. He lost all he owned, including his private library: two of his personal things were saved: a trumpet and a fish wrapped in a mat.

'Manuel' arrived at Basra on 8 June and attempts were made to salvage as much as possible, but without much success. Out of the 235 cases which we know with certainty were in the transportation twenty-eight were saved: one bull, one colossal figure of a man, sixteen cases with finds from the British excavations and two cases belonging to Place; we have no knowledge of what was in the remaining eight, but it is estimated that perhaps eleven reliefs from Place's excavations are now in the Louvre. Everything found at Babylon disappeared, together with nearly all the finds Place had brought to Mosul from Khorsabad.

When he arrived at Constantinople Place was informed in detail about the consequences of the disaster. He sat down to write a letter to his minister in which he explained first that all of his private belongings had been lost, but then added:

> But that is a purely personal accident and of minor interest compared with the consequences of a disaster where objects have disappeared which no one can replace. I hope that other explorers shall never have to experience such a painful disappointment.
>
> I am not going to tell Your Excellency about all that I have felt as I knew that the fruits of so much expense and hardship has been irretrievably lost. The hope of seeing our museum enriched by such beautiful discoveries has made me forget the fatigue and the annoyance I have suffered during four years. I thought indeed that when seeing the results Your Excellency would pardon me for the kind of passion which I have expended on these excavations and that you would not regret the good will and the generosity shown to me.
>
> One single moment has witnessed the capsizing of so many legitimate hopes, and nothing more remains for me to do than to ask you, Monsieur le Ministre, to please not reproach me for a disaster in which I am in any event the most unhappy person.
>
> (Pillet 1962: 83)

In Constantinople he had been informed that he was to go to the town of Yassi rather than to Galatz, and he arrived here in September in time to celebrate the fall of Sevastopol and the long-awaited end of the Crimean War. He was immediately granted leave to go to Paris to attend to his sick father, and he stayed there until June 1856. The cases from Basra arrived at the Louvre on 1 July, a few days after he had left again for Yassi. He was therefore not present when the cases were unpacked, and one again suspects that he fled in the face of the all too painful facts.

CHAPTER THIRTY-SEVEN

FATES

——— •◆• ———

Fulgence Fresnel was in Baghdad when he heard about the disaster which destroyed the results of his work at Babylon. It is unclear whether he really cared much about it any more, for he seems to have been living in a world of his own. His secretary stuck it out with him till the end, and he died in Baghdad a few months later, mentally broken, at the age of seventy-one. His close friend Jules Mohl gave a memorial speech at the *Société asiatique*, announcing that 'the society has lost one of its oldest and keenest members'. In a brief sketch of his life he pointed out how this man, one of the leading Arabists in France, and a wealthy man who conducted his studies as a hobby, had lost his considerable fortune because of an excessive generosity and some bad speculations at the *bourse*. He had then entered the consular corps and served in various places in the Arab-speaking world, for instance, at Jedda. He had chased after phantoms all his life, spending several years of his life on an attempt to establish a scientific expedition to Central Africa, where he was convinced the unicorn could be found. He sent agents into the jungles, but they returned only with loads of rhino horns. Mohl summed up his evaluation of Fresnel as follows:

> He was a uniquely gifted man who distinguished himself by the utmost cour-
> tesy, the most elegant conversation, a generosity which was destructive for
> his private fortune, an unusually lively wit, an amazing intelligence; he leaves
> behind him traces in science which will never be entirely obliterated, but he
> did not accomplish all that his talents promised, all the happiness his soul
> deserved, because he never learnt to discipline his spirit.
>
> (Mohl 1879: 81)

Fresnel never wrote a coherent account of his expedition, and it fell to the philol-ogist Jules Oppert to publish two volumes which appeared a few years later. They do not contain much information about the excavations, however; volume 2, which appeared first in 1859, contained Oppert's own systematic account of the deci-pherment of the cuneiform script, and it may be said to be the one presentation which finally brought some order into the further work on the texts, but it had little to do with Babylon. Volume 1 contained a kind of archaeological travel account from Babylonia and Assyria (Oppert 1859–63; Pillet 1922).

Figure 37.1 Victor Place remains an enigmatic figure. He stands here in 1852 together with Tranchand at one of the bulls of Khorsabad, a *flaneur* in Assyria, posing at a time when everything still seemed bright and rosy. Was he led to dishonesty by the disappointments he suffered in Assyria? Or was he in fact entirely innocent, a scapegoat for his country's disaster, and a man whose final destruction was just as unfair as his father's bankruptcy and the great shipwreck at Korna? (From Pillet 1962: Plate IX)

Place was in Moldavia, having lost not only all his finds, but also his notes from the excavation. The situation was not entirely hopeless for him, however, for he had sent long reports regularly to the ministry in Paris, and they contained detailed information about the excavation, so it ought to be possible to reconstruct a reasonable account of the work on the basis of this material. Tranchand's photographs as well as Thomas' plans and drawings were also available, having been brought directly to Paris (see Figure 37.1).

His work as consul was arduous, however, and he could not really do anything about writing a book until 1860. He then asked the prime minister for permission to have his old reports from Mosul sent to Yassi, but this request was turned down; his old father was allowed to copy as many of them as he could in the ministry in Paris, but since he was given only two weeks and the material comprised 387 folio pages he could obviously not do much. Place's final report in three volumes was therefore delayed and appeared at the Imperial Press only in 1867–70.

Politically he was in an interesting position at Yassi, for France was energetically pursuing a policy which aimed at creating a new, independent state in the area loosely known as Moldavia; both Turkey and Russia claimed this territory as their own, but there were special ties which bound France to these lands, first of all the fact that a Romance language was spoken here, related to French, of course; this formed the basis for a feeling of kinship which led to dreams of creating 'une petite France' here on the banks of the Danube. Despite resistance from all other major powers the French succeeded in establishing an independent state in 1859, the one we now know as Romania, and Place played a considerable role in the events which led up to this culmination.

In 1863 Place was moved to a post in Turkey, but he seems to have spent extended periods in Paris on leave, presumably engaged in the writing of his report on Khorsabad. In 1867 he was appointed to the post as Consul-General at Calcutta in India, a very important charge, but his real triumph came in 1870 with his appointment as Consul-General at New York. This was one of the most prestigious posts in the consular service, and the minister made it clear in his letter to Place that it was to be understood as an acknowledgement of his services. The salary was 60,000 francs per year. Place was fifty-two years old.

The job in New York had a special significance. France and Prussia were on a collision course and the political situation deteriorated rapidly; the French army, it was felt, needed guns. Place was ordered to buy a very large number of rifles from the Remington Rifle Company, one of the leading weapons manufacturers of the time, and one whose guns had been tested in actual battles during the Civil War which had ended a few years earlier. Place hardly got to New York before the war broke out with the hasty French declaration in July, and things quickly went badly for the French. In the battle at Sedan in September the emperor himself, Napoleon III, was captured by the Germans, and in January 1871 Paris capitulated after a long siege. The peace was signed in May, but already before this time Place's activities in New York had led to questions and accusations in the Parliament in Paris. He was said to have accepted a shipment of defective rifles in return for a bribe of 602,000 francs under the table, and he was recalled to France in March to answer his accusers.

In fact, the French armies were equipped with the *chassepot* rifle which was superior even to the German weapons, but there was a shortage of these rifles and accordingly guns were imported in large quantities from England and the USA. Eighteen different types poured into France during the war, and 'the French agents were not always skilful nor the foreign agents scrupulous'. During the battle of Le Mans in January 1871 a large proportion of the French soldiers were equipped with

> American muzzle-loaders left over from the Civil War. Their ammunition was soaked by rain and snow; it was of the wrong calibre; and the troops did not know how to load. Even had they been able to do so the defective mechanism of the rifles would have made them impossible to fire. No cleaning equipment was provided, but it is doubtful whether anything could have made any impression on the thick coating of rust which had accumulated since the Civil War had ended.
>
> (Howard 1961: 246–7 and 400)[244]

If these were what Place had been able to acquire in New York, one can understand the frustrated anger which led to the accusations against him.

He arrived at Paris a sick and broken man. Two of his children had died in New York of croup, and he and his wife brought their bodies home in coffins together with the two surviving children. At first he was acquitted by a court which did not find it to be proven that his motives had been criminal, but the government insisted on a retrial which resulted in a verdict of two years in prison. He seems to have spent no more than a few hours in prison, however, for President Thiers immediately issued a pardon. In January 1872 he stepped out of the prison gate and disappeared, and for many years it was unknown what had happened to him. It is now known that he went back to Romania, the country he had helped create and which had given him his wife, and he died in the town of Cascoeti in 1875.

Botta was by then already dead. In 1852 he had been appointed Consul-General at Baghdad, but he seems to have lost all interest in returning to Mesopotamia and did not accept the post; instead he stayed on in Jerusalem with the same title, and he sat here until 1855 when he was moved to Tripoli in Libya. At the age of sixty-seven he retired in 1869, and he died the year after in the village Achères just outside Paris. He appears never to have taken any further interest in archaeology or Mesopotamia.

The French interest in Mesopotamian excavations in fact disappeared after the disaster at Korna and the death of Fresnel. Jules Mohl, who had been the driving force behind these activities, was apparently so deeply affected by the loss of his old friend that he gave up any further attempt to advance the study of the ancient Mesopotamian cultures (Mohl 1879: xxxiii). Jules Oppert did go on with his Assyriological studies and had a distinguished career as a cuneiformist. The architect Félix Thomas had a reasonably successful career as a painter before him, but he became rather a strange character; it is told that in his old age he lived in a house at Pornic on the Atlantic coast, and that he could be seen here riding along the water accompanied by a pack of wolves (Fontan 1994a: 112–13).

It went considerably better for most of the Englishmen, except for Loftus who died in 1858 on his way back from India. He never wrote a book or substantial report about his excavations at Kuyunjik, so little is known for certain about the excavations there after Rassam had left in 1854 (Gadd 1936 with Appendix).

Hormuzd Rassam became an English official at Aden in the Yemen after his return to England, a post which Layard had secured for him. Before he left he asked Layard if he thought it would be a good idea for him to spend some time on writing a short report about his activities as an excavator.[245] Sadly, he does not appear to have done this.

He spent several years at Aden as assistant for the political Resident, and while he was there he was thrown into events which were as bizarre and picturesque as any that took place in the nineteenth century. There are several accounts available, a large work by Rassam himself, some governmental reports and unofficial books, and the story is far too complex to be retold in detail here. It all happened in Abyssinia where a local 'emperor' Theodore had taken the entire British colony, including the consul and some missionaries, prisoner at his mountain stronghold; he was angry because he had not received a polite answer to a letter he had sent in 1864 to Queen Victoria, in which he suggested a kind of alliance. Something had to be done, and the procedure chosen was to send an emissary carrying a personal letter from the queen to the emperor in the hope that this would secure the release of the prisoners. The choice of person for this task fell on Hormuzd Rassam, and where it would have been a most unusual assignment for any English official, it was almost unbelievably strange in the case of Hormuzd Rassam, who was suddenly elevated to the position as the personal agent of Queen Victoria. The semi-official report on the affair explains that he was chosen 'on account of his presumed knowledge of the native character and habits, which were considered peculiarly to fit him for any negotiations demanding great tact and delicacy' (Markham 1869: 90). In other words: a wily Oriental would be useful in negotiations with other 'natives'.

His mission lasted for four years. He was forced into a complex game with the unstable emperor Theodore, and from 1866 he was thrown in chains himself. He was seen by most people as having shown great skill and tact in an impossible situation, and he has been characterised as 'a supple and persistent man, not at all lacking in bravery' (Moorehead 1983: 216). The fact was, however, that the prisoners were not released, and as the affair dragged on it became increasingly clear that the government had to make up its mind about what to do. What was there to do? Declare war on Theodore? The knowledge available about this remote country in a corner of Africa was not extensive, but it was clear that it consisted of a series of extremely difficult and almost impassable mountain ranges which were bound to constitute a formidable obstacle to any invading force from England. The matter was debated in Parliament on 16 July 1867, and both Layard and Rawlinson took part. The colonel had a very clear view of the significance of the whole matter:

> I would say, then, that I look on 'prestige' in politics very much as I look on credit in finance. It is a power which enables us to achieve very great results with very small means at our immediate disposal. 'Prestige' may not be of paramount importance in Europe, but in the East, sir, our whole position depends upon it. It is a perfect fallacy to suppose that we hold India by the sword. The foundation of our tenure, the talisman – so to speak – which enables 100,000 Englishmen to hold 150,000,000 of natives in subjection, is the belief in our unassailable power, in our inexhaustible resources; and any circumstance, therefore, which impairs that belief, which leads the nations of the East to mistrust our superiority, and to regard us as more nearly on an equality with themselves, inflicts a grievous shock on our position.
>
> (Rawlinson 1898: 252)

The government was persuaded to declare war and send out an army after a few months of preparation; the final battle took place in 1868 at the mountain stronghold Magdala, where Theodore was killed and the prisoners liberated. Rassam returned in some triumph to England and received a sum of £5,000 for his efforts. In 1869 he married Anne Elizabeth Price, daughter of a captain of the 77th Highlanders, and during the 1870s they lived at 'Nineveh House, Spring Grove, Isleworth'.

He was later sent out to Assyria and Babylonia in 1877 as the agent of the British Museum, charged with the task of finding as many tablets as possible. Over four seasons he worked on mounds scattered over the entire region, and his activities of these years gave him a somewhat tarnished reputation as a primitive and careless excavator. He continued in the tradition of Layard and Place, and since he had a whole series of excavations going at the same time, it is obvious that he could not supervise them all in person. In fact, Hormuzd Rassam was not an archaeologist but rather a digger, and as such he was immensely successful. His task had been defined for him by the British Museum, of course, and he brought home some outstanding finds – such as the extraordinary Assyrian bronze gates from a site called Balawat and some 70,000 cuneiform tablets from the Babylonian city Sippar.[246]

Since he opened so many mounds at the same time it was inevitable that the workers saw their chance to steal, especially tablets from the trenches they worked in. Dealers in the bazaar in Baghdad soon realised that here was a new lucrative market to be explored, and the situation deteriorated after Rassam had returned to England. The British Museum was obviously bothered by this, not being particularly happy about having to buy tablets from their own excavations in the bazaar, and a young man in the department was sent out to investigate where the tablets came from. This man was Wallis Budge, who returned with a series of stories which seemed to imply that it was Hormuzd himself who with the assistance of other members of his family was organising this illicit trade. These stories were not made public, but the rumours circulated in London, much to Hormuzd Rassam's chagrin. Layard wrote to a friend about the matter, claiming that Budge spread his lies

> to supplant Rassam, one of the honestest and most straightforward fellows I ever knew, and one whose great services have never been acknowledged – because he is a 'nigger' and because Rawlinson, as is his habit, appropriated to himself the credit of Rassam's discoveries.
>
> (Waterfield 1963: 478)

Budge was Rawlinson's man and Layard disliked him intensely, but there is no sign that Rawlinson himself should have been involved in these intrigues or have stood behind the campaign directed against Rassam. Layard was convinced that his friend had to save his reputation by starting a suit against Budge, and he was to be the star witness because Budge had repeated his accusations to him in a private conversation in one of the exhibition halls of the Museum. In 1893 the case was tried and Budge lost, but the outcome was nevertheless ambiguous; Hormuzd had demanded £1,000 in satisfaction and received only fifty, and Budge was promoted at the British Museum where a private collection was arranged in order to help pay his legal fees. In this atmosphere of complete disunion and discord it became impossible for Rassam to find an English publisher for his large book on his archaeological career, so it had to appear at an American press in 1897. He lived to a ripe old age, raising a son and seven daughters, dying in 1910 as a forgotten and neglected man who never received the recognition that was his due (see Figure 37.2). Budge, on the other hand, published a long series of books, many of them on Egyptological subjects, and in the eyes of many scholars of questionable quality. In 1921 he wrote the so far only book on the history of Assyriology, and one can imagine the treatment given of men like Layard, Hincks and Rassam, whereas Rawlinson is hailed as 'the father of Assyriology'.

The colonel had returned from Baghdad for good in 1855 and one of his first actions had been to write a memorandum to the British Museum, in which he laid out a detailed plan for the publication of at least some of the cuneiform tablets which had by now accumulated in the Museum. He suggested that a selection of texts should be published in two volumes, apparently copies only of the cuneiform, and with no translations or explanatory comments; this could be done within two years, he estimated. The most remarkable aspect of his plan was the precision and clarity with which he was now able to approach the texts, analysing and classifying documents in such a way that it is clear that he could read substantial parts of them. It is equally clear that he had very limited and specialised interests when faced with the mass of texts, and his prejudices and views guided him in his evaluation of the significance of the different kinds of tablets. He explained that they cover a period of about two millennia and that 'under a mass of matter, sufficiently uninteresting, (such as religious ceremonial, benefactions to temples, legal contracts, and calculations relating to astrology and genethlialogy,) contain something of value'. His main interest, if not the only one, was in the historical texts, and in addition to them he proposed to bring texts which might serve as useful tools for the further interpretation of the historical documents: syllabaries and vocabularies, specimens of mathematical tables, astronomical formulae, calendars, and registers of observations, a selection of mythological tablets, 'the object being to show the names and attributes of the Gods and Goddesses worshipped by the early Semitic nations, and to explain the general system of the Pantheon'; passages from sculptures, obelisks and tablets which illustrate 'the wild sports of the Assyrians'; architectural descriptions, and 'a few other tablets may be noticed as deserving of early publication, such as those containing dynastic lists, descriptions of the seas, rivers, and mountains, and countries known to the Assyrians, classifications of birds and beasts, &c. &c. &c.' (Rawlinson 1855). Rawlinson had a clear view of his priorities.

In spite of the clear progress in the reading of the cuneiform texts, which such a list demonstrates, there were still scholars who completely rejected the decipherment and refused to accept the fundamental principles described by Hincks and Rawlinson. It was felt by many that the system was so complex that the script in practice would be unmanageable and that the lack of precision would make just about any reading possible. It was especially the principles of polyphony and homophony, the notion that each single sign could be read in many different ways, and that equally many signs could have the same readings, which created problems for the understanding. It was claimed that these ideas led to a situation where anything was acceptable, that every sequence of ten to fifteen signs could be read in so many different ways that it would be impossible to establish with certainty which one of them was the correct one. This critique could appear quite powerful for those who did not know how to actually read the script, but in practice the possibilities for confusion were really not such a serious problem. It was never formulated in a more witty and sharp way than in a small essay written by the Swedish playwright August Strindberg; he wrote his commentary around 1900, at

Figure 37.2 The old Rassam in his London otium, a disappointed and forgotten man. 'Having devoted his best years to maintaining British interests, Rassam spent the remainder of his long life – he died in 1910 – embittered and officially neglected' (Reade 1993: 60). Private collection. Reproduced by courtesy of Irving Finkel.

a time when he was quite alone with these points of view, but his words reflect quite closely the objections which were formulated fifty years earlier:

> Young people! Do not read Assyrian, for that is not a language, that is rubbish! Just take a look at this little sign!
>
> ▶———
>
> it looks like a finger pointing towards unsafe ice, or the public convenience, or the place *voi ch'entrate*! This little sign sounds first like this: *as, dil, til, dili, ina, ru, rum, salugub, simed, tal*!
>
> Do you believe in that?
>
> But it has other sound values and meanings! Look! aplu = son; Assud = Assur; edu = one; nadanu = to give.
>
> Do you believe in that?
>
> Or this:
>
> 𒐉
>
> which sounds: *dab, di, ti, dub, dug, dugn, ha, hi, sar, sur.*
>
> And means '4' or 'You' or 'which' or 'stand close' or Assur (everything means Assur) or sar tabu = be good, or tubbu = well or kusbu = great luxury.
>
> Is this possible?
>
> A young man swallows this raw! No doubt is possible, no contradiction, no absurdity, for the Professor has spoken!
>
> (Strindberg 1907–12)

Since no one in the 1850s found the time or had the inclination to write a book in English which presented a coherent account of the decipherment and an understandable explanation of the character and development of the script itself, a certain scepticism lingered on. It was dispelled in 1857, however, when the energetic Fox Talbot suggested to the Royal Academy that a test should be arranged. He handed over in a sealed envelope his own transliteration and translation of the large historical clay prism which had been found by Rassam at Kalah Shergat in 1853, and he asked that other leading experts should be invited to send in their versions. A comparison would make it plain whether it was in fact possible to read the texts in a convincing way. Rawlinson was invited to send in his interpretation, and he suggested that also Hincks and Oppert should be brought in; they all sent their renderings in sealed envelopes to the president of the society, Professor Wilson, and a committee was established to evaluate the results. The envelopes were opened on 25 May 1857, and it was quickly agreed that although the versions exhibited substantial differences, they were nevertheless close enough to warrant the conclusion that the cuneiform script could in fact be read. Rawlinson and Hincks were nearly identical in their readings; Talbot was an amateur and not really aware of the intricacies of the writing system, and Oppert's version deviated in certain ways from those of the others; one reason was that he had answered in English, a language he did not master, and it turned out that he had been using a slightly different copy. But the conclusion was unanimous and decisive: the cuneiform script was readable (Pallis 1956: 159–61).

Rawlinson's great publication project was realised with five large volumes, an edition which is still a classic in the field. He was the supervisor and left all the practical work to Norris, partly because he was now becoming deeply involved in politics. He entered a number of councils and committees that defined colonial policy, especially in regard to India, and in 1859 he received the appointment to the post of Ambassador at Tehran. This was clearly a dream come true for this man who had such strong views with respect to Persia and its role in the 'Great Game', the Anglo-Russian competition for power in Asia (Hopkirk 1994). However, he had hardly arrived at his new residence before he received a message from London informing him that the post as ambassador at Tehran had been transferred from the India Office to the Foreign Office, and this was intolerable to him; he felt that England's relations to a country such as Persia should be seen entirely within the context of Indian colonial policies, and he accordingly insisted on regarding himself as a colonial official, somewhat in the same way as the position he had held in Baghdad as Resident; he had no wish to become a diplomat and he felt that such a position would seriously curtail his ability to function at Tehran. He therefore resigned the post, and he sat in Tehran for a little less than a year until a new ambassador had been found and sent off.

Once back in London he was not terribly popular in the ministries, and he turned his attention towards the British Museum where the first volume in the new series appeared in 1861. The following year he married a young beauty of twenty-three, Louisa Seymour; he was fifty-two. From 1865–68 he was again member of Parliament, but he then resigned from his seat in order to re-enter the India Council. He was after all a sound man. His connections with the British Museum remained very close, and he also became a Trustee; his publication project developed into five volumes, and he was an active supervisor of both the publications and the excavations conducted by the Museum until his death in 1895 (see Figure 37.3).

Hincks never got away from Killyleagh. He was offered, and received, a yearly pension of £100 from the British government in 1854, but the most important honour and recognition came in May 1863 when he received the Prussian Order, 'for achievements in science and the arts', an honour which he thus shared with Rawlinson. He continued working but his contributions to the scholarly debate became more rare, and he died a forgotten man in 1866. However, in 1904 a bust of him was set up in the National Museum in Cairo as a somewhat belated recognition of his work in the decipherment of the Egyptian hieroglyphs. In 1933 a biography of Hincks was published in England, and the infamous Budge in a review of this modest volume had the nerve to write that he had not been 'a great scholar' (Davidson 1933; Budge 1934).

Layard had died in 1894, the year before Rawlinson, after a long and colourful career. Until 1869 he functioned with brief pauses as member of Parliament and gradually became a more effective and capable politician. In 1855 he had been one of the founders of a new Ottoman Bank, and as the chairman of the board he soon turned out to have a great talent for this kind of work, so from now on he was financially independent. In 1861 he again became Vice-Minister for Foreign Affairs, despite strong opposition from Queen Victoria. She regarded him as unsound and untrustworthy and could not forgive him for his attacks on the aristocratic system of privilege. In fact, he showed himself very able in this position, functioning for extended periods as the *de facto* leader of the ministry, especially when the 'real' minister withdrew to his manor house to hunt and party. He was thus in a central position in the conduct of English policy in the war between Denmark and Prussia in 1864, and when Hormuzd Rassam was sent to Abyssinia he controlled the affair from London.

He spent his own holidays in his beloved Italy and threw himself with great energy over the study of Italian art; he wrote a series of articles to English magazines on this topic, and as leader of the Arundel Society in London he was deeply engaged in the attempts to save and protect works of art which were threatened by destruction. Like Ruskin he took a special interest in the fate of Venice, which was threatened by restorations, by neglect and by pollution and rising waters. In 1868 Layard founded an industrial venture, the Murano Glassworks, which were designed to recreate the ancient tradition in Venice for glassblowing. His company started out with a contract to restore the Cathedral of St Mark. He also became a member of the board of the National Gallery, in London, where his not inconsiderable collection of paintings is preserved (Favaretto 1987). His last cabinet post was as Commissioner of Works and Buildings, in which capacity he had considerable influence on town planning in London and for the care of public buildings such as the new Parliament building at Westminster.

His relationship to cousin Charlotte deteriorated after 1855; her husband had then been dead a couple of years, and she decided to marry a certain Charles Schreiber, her son's teacher, who was fourteen years younger than herself. Layard did not regard this as a proper match and he may have suffered from jealousy, so his visits to Canford became rare in the following years. After five or six years these passions subsided, but new ones began to appear. He conducted an intense correspondence with Charlotte's youngest daughter, the very beautiful Blanche, and he began to visit again. In 1869, at the age of fifty-two, he proposed, but not to Blanche; instead he chose the slightly older Enid, Charlotte's eighth child, who was twenty-five. Although Charlotte was unhappy about it, they were married soon afterwards, and while they were travelling in Italy in October of that year, Layard was told that he was to be the next ambassador to Spain. He served here for eight years, and in 1877 he was transferred to Turkey where he took over the post Canning had held for so many years. The unpaid attaché returned as ambassador.

Cousin (and mother in law) Charlotte dedicated her life to the creation of an enormous collection of china, travelling around Europe in search of fine specimens during a period of fifteen years. The English part of her collection, some 2,000 pieces, is now in the Victoria & Albert Museum in London, whereas the Chinese part remains in the hands of the family. Her unique collection of cards and fans is in the British Museum. She was in fact the first great European private collector of china, and she kept up her interests as long as her health and her eyesight

Figure 37.3 Sir Henry Creswicke Rawlinson, baronet, F.R.S., at the age of 75, by Frank Holl. (From Rawlinson 1898: frontispiece)

Figure 37.4 Layard as an old man in his study in the house in Venice, by Ludwig Passini. Reproduced by courtesy of the National Portrait Gallery, London.

allowed. Her correspondence with Layard appears to have been removed by her daughter's censorship when she presented Layard's papers to the British Library.

Layard's work as Ambassador to Constantinople during seven years was based on the same views he had always maintained: the Ottoman Empire should be kept intact, but it had to reform drastically to become a European state. He had close connections with the Turkish elite and was a friend of the Sultan, and he had considerable influence. However, his old enemy Gladstone became prime minister in 1884 and immediately removed Layard from the post. He and Enid withdrew to a wonderful palazzo on the Grand Canal in Venice (see Figure 37.4). He became ill here in 1894, in some bitterness because of the treatment Hormuzd Rassam had been exposed to in England, and he was with difficulty brought back to London where he died in his house in Queen Anne Street at the beginning of July.

His house on the Grand Canal is now, by pure coincidence, the home of the Institute of Oriental Studies at the University of Venice, and I think back with some pride to an occasion a few years ago when I lectured on Assyrian matters here, in what had probably been Layard's study.

NOTES

———— •◆• ————

BL = British Library

1 Disraeli's alter ego wrote 'Time'.
2 Hughenden Papers, Bodleian Library, A/IV/F/1, dated 3 December 1831.
3 Hughenden Papers, Bodleian Library, A/IV/F/2, Sennar, July 1832.
4 Bergamini 1994: 71, claims that he became French consul in Egypt at the end of 1833, but it is uncertain what this is based on.
5 Hughenden Papers, Bodleian Library, A/IV/F/3, Lazaret de Marseille, 30 April 1834. Another letter from his hand at the lazaret is known; it was addressed to his friend G. Drovetti, the French consul at Alexandria and expressed his *ennui* in less explicit phrases; (Bergamini 1994: 73 with note 9).
6 Chicoricum bottae and Verbascum bottae.
7 I owe this reference to Dr Elisabeth Fontan of the Louvre.
8 For the later excavations of the mound see Thompson and Hutchinson 1929; Madhloom 1967; Madhloom 1968; Madhloom 1969; Russell 1991.
9 BL 58161, 5–6, dated Mosul, 1 June 1843.
10 BL 58161, 11–13, dated Constantinople, 3 July 1843.
11 BL 58161, 14–15, Mosul, 22 July 1843.
12 BL 58161, 14–15, Mosul, 22 July 1843.
13 BL 58161, 26–27, dated Mosul, 18 February 1845.
14 Among them the poet Walter Savage Landor, who impressed on the boy the need to learn Greek in order to write good English; later he composed an ode to Layard, entitled 'To Layard, Discoverer of Nineveh', originally published in 1853.
15 BL 39066; see the account of Thomsen's achievements in Jensen 1992.
16 BL 58149, 45–46, from Isfahan, dated 26 August 1840.
17 In Layard 1849 he discusses the characteristics of what he saw as the three basic races: Semitic, Indo-European and Mongolian, and sets out a scheme which is not racist but which reflects a curiously nineteenth-century attitude to race, one that seems not far from the preoccupations of the scholars who created the foundations for the short-lived science called 'Völkerpsychologie'. His aim was to characterise each 'race' and there does not seem to be any hierarchy involved in his analysis; the 'races' are different from each other, but not better or worse.
18 BL 58149, 60–61, Baghdad, 9 September 1841.

19 BL 58149, 67–68, from Cambridge, 26 November 1841.

20 BL 58154, 16–19, Baghdad, 19 January 1842.

21 BL 38975, 58–59, dated Büyükdere, 10 August 1842

22 BL 58154, 34–35, Pera Constantinople, 26 November 1842.

23 BL 38976, 231–233, dated 9 October 1845.

24 Chief interpreter, later Oriental Secretary at the Embassy; for his role as a calming influence on Canning see Waterfield 1963: 101. He later became Sir Henry Alison and an influential man in London.

25 BL 38976, 240–242, dated 12 November 1845.

26 BL 38976, 255–256, dated 26 November 1845.

27 BL 40637, dated 1 December 1845.

28 BL 58149, 211–212, Baghdad, 27 December 1845.

29 BL 38976, 294–295, dated 21 January 1846.

30 BL 40637, dated 1 December 1845.

31 BL 38976, 281–284, dated 27 December 1845.

32 BL 38976, letters to Canning, dated 24 January and 3 February.

33 BL 40637, letter dated 21 February 1846.

34 BL 40637, letter dated 6 April 1846.

35 BL 38976, 339–340, dated 15 April 1846.

36 BL 40637, dated 21 April 1846.

37 BL 58150, 9–10, from Nimroud, 21 April 1846.

38 BL 58161, 36–37, dated 12 August 1846.

39 BL 58161, 40–41, dated 5 October 1846.

40 BL 58150, 14–16, letter to his mother, dated 15 June 1846.

41 BL 38976, 355–358, letter from Canning, dated 6 May 1846.

42 BL 38976, 359–360, copy of the Viziral letter concerning excavations translated into French. The original letter dated 5 May 1846.

43 BL 38976, 363–364, dated 10 May 1846.

44 BL 58154, 159–165, dated 27 July 1846.

45 BL 38977, 25–27, dated 5 August 1846.

46 BL 38977, 25–27, dated 19 August 1846.

47 BL 58154, 167–169, Mosul, 29 September–5 October 1846.

48 BL 58150, 21–23, Mosul, 24 August 1846.

49 BL 38977, 54–59, dated 30 September 1846.

50 BL 58154, 176–178, dated 14 December 1846.

51 BL 39077, 14–17, dated 21 September 1846.

52 BL 38977, 119–121, dated 9 December 1846.

53 BL 38977, 104–105, dated November 1846.

54 *Athenæum*, 10 October 1846, pp. 1046–7.

55 BL 47658, 12–14, Nimroud, 1 January 1847.

56 BL 38977, 161–165, dated 20 January 1847.

57 BL 38976, 367–370, dated 13 May 1846.

58 BL 38976, 395–400, dated 24 June 1846.

59 BL 38977, 179–180, dated 3 February 1847.

60 BL 58150, 39–40, Nimroud, 28 January 1847.

61 BL 38977, 161–165, 20 January 1847.

62 BL 38977, 199–200, draft for a letter to Rawlinson, 24 February 1847.

63 BL 38977, 208–210, 17 March 1847.

64 BL 58161, 40–41, 5 October 1846.

65 BL 58161, 30–31, 20 May 1846.

66 BL 58150, 58–59, 14 June 1847.

67 BL 38977, 310–311, 23 June 1847.

68 BL 58150, 64–66, Cheltenham, 11 and 12 August 1847.

69 BL 58155, 13–14, Leghorn, 10 December 1847.

70 BL 58161, 55–56, undated, but undoubtedly from 1847.

71 Fontan 1994b: 14, writes: 'Flandin, déçu de ne pas avoir obtenu le poste de conservateur du musée assyrien du Louvre, se retira en Touraine'.

72 BL 58161, 44–45, 17 June (1847).

73 Hughenden Papers, Bodleian A/IV/F/5, Paris 17 January 1846.

74 Hughenden Papers, Bodleian A/IV/F/6, 'London 4th October 1847'.

75 BL 38978, 61–62, dated London, 27 March 1848.

76 BL 58161, 53–54, Paris, 20 May 1848.

77 BL 58161, 59–60, Jerusalem, 12 February 1849.

78 BL 39077, 29, 'At a Committee of the Trustees of the British Museum, 8th January, 1848'.

79 The official letter of appointment as attaché to Her Majesty's Embassy at Constantinople is dated 2 November 1847, and sent to Austen in London (BL 38977, 351–352). In a letter to Ross Layard wrote that he had been 'named to the Commission for the Settlement of the boundaries between Turkey and Persia, (still being attached to the Embassy) so that I shall probably be in Mosul again in 1848. I am ordered out in May' (BL 38977, 375–376, dated London, 31 December 1847).

80 BL 38977, 375–376, dated London, 31 December 1847.

81 *Literary Gazette* 1848, p. 59.

82 *Athenæum* 1848, p. 117.

83 *Athenæum* 1848, pp. 510, 1128, 1152.

84 BL 47658, 30–31, Cheltenham, 28 February 1848.

85 BL 38978, 61–62, dated London, 27 March 1848.

86 BL 38976, 281–284, from Alison, dated 27 December 1845.

87 BL 58161, 32–35, Botta's letter to Layard, dated Paris, 25 April 1846. See Mohl 1879: xxvii, for Max Müller's comments on the pricing of the volumes.

88 BL 47658, 30–31, Cheltenham, 28 February 1848.

89 BL 38977, 219–224, dated 31 March 1847.

90 BL 38976, 373–376, dated Florence, 24 May 1846.

91 BL 38976, dated 6 August 1845.

92 *Athenæum* 1847, pp. 650 and 706–7. The identity of the writer is shown by a letter from 11 September: 962.

93 *Athenæum* 1847, 7 August, p. 843.

94 BL 38977, 334–337, dated Bisitun, 20 September 1847.

95 Ibid.

96 BL 38977, 343–345, dated Baghdad, 13 October 1847.

97 *Literary Gazette*, 25 July 1846, p. 667, letter from Hincks with the title: 'Babylonian Antiquities. The great inscription of the East India Company.' In fact, he does not

specifically deal with the Old Persian system in this letter, but his remarks about Babylonian and the 'Median' system of writing (the second column) provide the essential clues.

98 BL 38977, 31–32, dated 2 September 1846.

99 BL 38977, 68–69, 14 October 1846.

100 *Literary Gazette*, 25 July 1846, p. 667, letter from Hincks. The definition of the linguistic category 'Semitic' was only about half a century old at this time. See Olender 1992: 11, who notes that one of the scholars responsible for this discovery, A.L. von Schlözer, 'explicitly proposed applying the formula "Semitic" to the languages of "Syrians, Babylonians, Hebrews, and Arabs"'.

101 BL 38976, 395–400, dated 24 June 1846.

102 *Literary Gazette*, 25 July 1846, p. 667.

103 BL 38977, 68–69, dated Camp Ctesiphon, 14 October 1846.

104 BL 38977, 192–194, dated 17 February 1847.

105 BL 38977, 219–224, dated 31 March 1847.

106 BL 38978, 53–54, dated 14 March 1848.

107 BL 38977, 343–345, dated Baghdad, 13 October 1847.

108 BL 38977, 334–337, dated Bisitun, 20 September 1847.

109 BL 38978, 23–26, dated 28 January 1848.

110 BL 38977, 334–337, dated Bisitun, 20 September 1847.

111 BL 38977, 119–121, dated Baghdad, 9 December 1846.

112 BL 38978, 17–20, from Hincks, dated Killyleagh, Co. Down, 22 January 1848.

113 W.A.A. Correspondence, New Series, vol. 8, 3326, from Layard to Birch, 7 July 1848.

114 Vaux moved his interest to the new field of Assyriology and a few years later wrote a large book on the Assyrians (Vaux 1855).

115 *Athenæum* 1849: pp. 45–7, 71–3, and 96–7; *Literary Gazette* 1849, four articles starting on pp. 5, 23, 38, and 58.

116 BL 58155, 151–154, dated 5 June 1849.

117 BL 38978, 63–66, dated 28 March 1848 (surely must be 1849!).

118 W.A.A. Correspondence vol. 8, 3198, undated memorandum, probably January 1849.

119 BL 38942, 1, letter to Sir Henry Ellis, from Constantinople, 20 August 1849.

120 BL 38979, 16–18, the official 'Memorandum for Mr Layard's Instruction' dated 14 July 1849.

121 BL 38979, 28–31, letter to Ross from Therapia, 24 August 1849.

122 BL 38979, 32–35, official memorandum from Canning, dated Therapia, 25 August 1849.

123 BL 38942, 2–4, letter to Canning from Mosul, dated 1 October 1849.

124 BL 38979, 46–49, from Hawkins, Flower Cottage, Godstone, 18 September 1849.

125 BL 39096 contains diary from August 1849–May 1850.

126 BL 47660 Rawlinson's diary from his journey from Baghdad to Europe in late 1849.

127 BL 38978, 63–66, dated 28 March 1848 (surely must be 1849!).

128 BL 38979, 1–4, Baghdad, 4 July 1849. He has received a copy of the plates for Layard's volume of inscriptions (Layard 1851) from Birch; in those pages he could find several texts from Tiglath-pilesar III, but they all surely came from Nimrud itself, from the much destroyed Central palace of this king.

129 BL 38979, 10–13, Baghdad, 18 July 1849.

130 BL 38979, 23–24, Baghdad, 1 August 1849.

131 BL 38979, 25–26, Baghdad, 15 August 1849.

132 BL 38979, 36–38, Baghdad, 29 August 1849.

133 BL 38979, 52–53, Baghdad, 26 September 1849.

134 BL 38979, 58–59, Baghdad, 10 October 1849.

135 BL 38979, 93–94, from Canning, Therapia, 28 November 1849.

136 BL 38979, 95–96, from Longworth, Therapia, 28 November 1849.

137 BL 38979, 86–87, Nipiris Hotel, 27 November 1849. In his diary he described Canning as 'a man of talent – but disfigured by many petitesses', BL 47660.

138 *Literary Gazette* 1849, p. 509.

139 BL 38979, 58–59. Hincks' Nebuchadnezzar reading was communicated in letters to the *Literary Gazette* in June and July 1846; in a letter dated 30 September 1846 (BL 38977, 54–59) Rawlinson wrote to Layard that he could now read the inscription on a brick from Babylon, giving the following translation: 'Nebuchadnezzar, the great king, the ruler of the land of the Chaldees, the son of Nabunassar the great king'.

140 BL 38979, 108–109, Athenæum Club, 28 December 1849.

141 BL 38979, 130–131, from Birch, 19 January 1850.

142 BL 38979, 142–143, from Ellis, 6 February 1850.

143 Rawlinson 1850b contains a revised version of the two lectures.

144 *Athenæum* 1850, pp. 234–6.

145 BL 38979, 155–156, from John Murray, 20 February 1850.

146 Letter in the *Literary Gazette*, p. 890, 17 October 1846, from W. Francis Ainsworth.

147 BL 38942, 19–20, to Birch, from Mosul, 16 March 1850.

148 BL 38979, 157–158, 39 St James's Street, 23 February 1850.

149 BL 38979, 173–174, 39 St James's Street, 27 March 1850.

150 BL 38979, 215–216, 39 St James's Street, 29 April 1850.

151 BL 38979, 283–284, Athenæum Club, 24 August 1850.

152 BL 38979, 404–405, 20 December 1850.

153 BL 38979, 401–403, from John Murray, 17 December 1850.

154 BL 38980, 7–8, from Birch, 17 January 1851.

155 BL 38979, 159–160, from Birch, 2 March 1850.

156 BL 38979, 173–174, 39 St James's Street, 27 March 1850.

157 BL 38979, 401–403, from John Murray, 17 December 1850.

158 BL 38979, 173–174, 39 St James's Street, 27 March 1850.

159 *Literary Gazette* 1849, p. 591: apparently the same lecture was given in June in Ireland on the Khorsabad Inscriptions (Hincks 1850).

160 *Athenæum* 1850 p. 555. A letter to Hincks from a certain Mr W.D. Cooley from 27 May 1850 indicates that he was the anonymous writer of the letter: 'I hope you have received a copy of the last *Athenaeum* which I ordered to be sent to you. It contains the long promised paragraph in vindication of your rights as a discoverer. . ..' (Davidson 1933: 147).

161 BL 38979, 283–284, Athenæum Club, 24 August 1850.

162 BL 38980, 27–28, from London, 24 February 1851.

163 BL 38980, 9–10, 24 January 1851.

164 *Athenæum* 1850, p. 1121.

165 BL 38979, 169–172, from Hawkins, 27 March 1850.

166 BL 38942, 31–32, to Canning, from Nimrud, 26 May 1850.

167 BL 38979, 411–412, from Canning to Palmerston, 18 December 1850.

168 BL 38979, 115–116, from John Murray, 1 January 1850.

169 BL 38979, 155–156, from John Murray, 20 February 1850.

170 BL 38942, 23, extract of letter to John Murray, dated Mosul, 13 March 1850.

171 BL 38979, 401–403, from John Murray, 17 December 1850.

172 BL 38977, 33–36, 2 September 1846.

173 BL 38979, 219–220, letter to Ross from Mosul, 13 May 1850.

174 BL 58156, 21–28, Mosul, 13 May 1850.

175 BL 58156, 38–46, Mosul, 10 June 1850 – to Layard's uncle.

176 BL 38941, 43–44, from Mosul, 24 June 1850, to Ross.

177 BL 38979, 289–290, to Ross from Mosul, 2 September 1850.

178 BL 38979, 207–208, from Matilda Rassam at Mosul, 16 April 1850.

179 BL 38942, 27–29, letter to Sir Henry Ellis, Mosul, 13 May 1850.

180 BL 38979, 237–240, from Capt. Felix Jones, Baghdad, 22 May 1850.

181 BL 38942, 37–38, to Sir Henry Ellis, dated 10 June 1850.

182 BL 38979, 207–208, from Matilda Rassam at Mosul, 16 April 1850.

183 The date is of course wrong, for in 1849 Layard was back in Constantinople.

184 BL 38942, 33–36, a very long report on 'the Government of the Arab tribes of the desert' addressed to Canning, dated 10 June 1850.

185 BL 38943, 1–3, to Sir Henry Ellis, from Mosul, 2 September 1850.

186 BL 38942, 45–51, to Canning, from Mosul, 2 September 1850.

187 BL 38943, 11–12, to Canning, dated Baghdad, 6 November 1850.

188 BL 38943, 11–12, to Canning, dated Baghdad, 6 November 1850.

189 BL 38943, 20–23, to Canning from Hillah, dated 13 January 1851.

190 BL 38981, 187–189, letter from Hormuzd Rassam to Layard, Mosul, 20 December 1852; the affair as seen from the French perspective is described in Pillet 1962: 30–2.

191 BL 38943, 24–26, to Canning, from Souk al Afaij, 29 January 1851.

192 BL 38980, 16–19, from Longworth at Constantinople, 6 February 1851.

193 BL 38943, 27, to Canning from Baghdad, 12 February 1851.

194 BL 38979, 404–405, 20 December 1850.

195 BL 38979, 401–403, from John Murray, 17 December 1850.

196 BL 38980, 20–21, a printed text entitled 'Mr. Layard's Researches in Assyria, Babylonia, &c'.

197 BL 38980, 27–28, from London, 24 February 1851.

198 BL 38943, 29–30, to Ellis from Mosul, 18 March 1851.

199 BL 38943, 31–32, to Canning, Mosul, 14 April 1851.

200 BL 38943, 35–36, to Mr Bell, Mosul, 21 April 1851.

201 BL 38943, 32, to Lynch from Nimrud, 17 April 1851.

202 BL 38943, 39, to Ellis, Alexandretta, 28 May 1851.

203 BL 38980, 243–244, copy of letter to Canning, 16 February 1852, from the Foreign Office.

204 BL 38980, 81, British Museum, 19 July 1851.

205 *Athenæum* 1851, p. 902.

206 *The Literary Gazette* 1849, p. 591.

207 BL 39981, 13–15, 10 April 1852.

208 BL 38948, 4–5, to B. Austen from Killyleagh, Co. Down, 3 October 1852.

209 BL 38981, 162, British Museum, 17 November 1852.

210 BL 38980, 3–4, from R. Stuart Poole, Hastings, Sussex, 13 January 1851.

211 BL 38980, 219–221, from Hormuzd, at Milton near Pembroke, 24 January 1852.

212 *Athenæum* 1852, p. 490.

213 BL 38980, 236–238, from Matilda Rassam, 14 February 1852.

214 BL 38981, 80–82, from Matilda Rassam, 5 July 1852.

215 BL 38981, 123–124, to Ross from the Athenæum Club, 13 September 1852.

216 BL 38981, 117–118, Baghdad, 5 September 1852.

217 BL 38981, 76–79, from Baghdad, 2 July 1852.

218 BL 38981, 117–118, Baghdad, 5 September 1852.

219 BL 38981, 200 Mosul, 20 December 1852, and BL 38981, 208–209, Mosul, 3 January 1853.

220 BL 38981, 262–264, Mosul, 28 February 1853.

221 BL 38981, 262–264, Mosul, 28 February 1853.

222 BL 38981, 281–283, Baghdad, 15 April 1853.

223 BL 38981, 286–288, Baghdad, 20 April 1853, from Rawlinson, and BL 38981, 293–295, Mosul, 25 April 1853, from Rassam.

224 BL 38982, 28–29, Nimroud, 18 July 1853.

225 Both the 'Broken Obelisk', as it is known, and the statue are from the reign of Ashur-bel-kala (1073–1056). For the text and references see Grayson 1991.

226 BL 38982, 63–65, Mosul, 15 August 1853.

227 BL 38982, 28–29, Nimroud, 18 July 1853. For the desire of the American missionaries to get a king, 'even old Sennacherib himself', see the correspondence cited in Stearns 1961: 12.

228 BL 38982, 63–65, Mosul, 15 August 1853.

229 BL 38982, 108–112, Mosul, 1 January 1854. 'Karkhana' is the term for a gang of workers.

230 BL 38982, 108–112, Mosul, 1 January 1854.

231 BL 38979, 180–182, from Aden, 10 October 1855, to Layard; the passages cited here are given as quotations from letters Hormuzd received from Rawlinson shortly before he began his dubious excavations in the northern half. Since he was sending these letters to Layard at the same time, there is no doubt that the quotes are correct.

232 BL 38982, 134–138, Mosul, 30 January 1854.

233 BL 38982, 134–138, Mosul, 30 January 1854.

234 BL 38983, 137–138, from The Albany, 7 April 1855.

235 BL 38983, 139–140, The Albany, 8 April 1855.

236 BL 38981, 286–288, Baghdad, 20 April 1853.

237 BL 38981, 299–302, Baghdad, 4 May 1853.

238 BL 38981, 299–302, Baghdad, 4 May 1853.

239 Copy in the papers of the Western Asiatic Department at the British Museum, letter from Rawlinson, dated British Residency, Baghdad, 24 May 1853. I owe my knowledge of this document to Dr Julian Reade.

240 BL 38982, 206–207, Killyleagh Co. Down, 6 May 1854.

241 W.A.A. Correspondence 1826–1867, New series, vol. 11, letter from Vaux to Rawlinson in Baghdad, dated 1 November 1854. Hincks' two notebooks are now in the British Library under the number BL 22097; vol. I is said to have been received at the BM

on 6 May 1854, II on 20 May; both are signed as received by Panizzi. 'By order of committee' they have been deposited in the department of MSS on 1 August 1857. The reference to Sir Henry Ellis's consternation and apparent unwillingness is surprising in view of the fact that he had himself told Rawlinson about the notebooks.

242 BL 38981, 299–302, Baghdad, 4 May 1853; 'Elchee' is a commonly used nickname for Canning.

243 BL 38948, 9–10, to S. Austen, from Constantinople, 25 April 1853.

244 I owe this reference to David Warburton.

245 BL 38982, 325–327, dated London, 24 October 1854.

246 For an exhaustive account of his archaeological activities here see Reade 1986b.

BIBLIOGRAPHY

—— •◆• ——

Abrams, M.H. (ed.) (1986). *The Norton Anthology of English Literature* (5th edn). New York: W.W. Norton & Company.

Ainsworth, W.F. (1888). *A Personal Narrative of the Euphrates Expedition*. London: Kegan Paul, Trench, & Co.

Albenda, P. (1986). *The Palace of Sargon King of Assyria*. Paris: Editions recherche sur les civilizations.

Andrae, W. (1977). *Das wiedererstandene Assur* (2nd edn). Munich: C.H. Beck.

André-Salvini, B. (1994). "Où sont-ils ces remparts de Ninive?" Les sources de connaissance de l'Assyrie.' In E. Fontan (ed.), *De Khorsabad à Paris. La découverte des Assyriens*: 22–44. Paris: Réunion des Musées Nationaux.

Anon. (1847). 'Layard's assyrische Ausgrabungen.' *Archäologische Zeitung, Neue Folge, Beilage* no. 4 (December 1847): 52–8.

Arnold, M. (1890). *Poetical Works*. London: Macmillan.

—— (1973 [1863]). 'The Bishop and the Philosopher'. In R.H. Super (ed.), *The Complete Prose Works of Matthew Arnold III, Lectures and Essays in Criticism*: 40–55. Ann Arbor: The University of Michigan Press.

Asmussen, J.P. (1992). 'Iransk filologi.' In P.J. Jensen and L. Grane (eds), *Københavns universitet 1479–1979* (vol. viii: 675–94). Copenhagen: G.E.C. Gad.

Barac, A. (1955). *A History of Yugoslav Literature*. Belgrade.

Barnett, R.D. (1967). 'Layard's Nimrud Bronzes and their Inscriptions.' *Eretz Israel*, 8: 1–7.

—— (1974). 'The Nimrud Bowls in the British Museum.' *Rivista di Studi Fenici*, 2: 11–33.

—— (1976). *Sculptures from the North Palace of Ashurbanipal*. London: British Museum Publications.

—— and Falkner, M. (1962). *The Sculptures of Assur-nasir-apli II (883–859 B.C.), Tiglath-pileser III (745–727 B.C.), Esarhaddon (681–669 B.C.) from the Central and South-West Palaces at Nimrud*. London: British Museum.

Bergamini, G. (1994). '"Spoliis Orientis onustus". Paul-Emile Botta et la découverte de la civilisation assyrienne.' In E. Fontan (ed.), *De Khorsabad à Paris. La découverte des Assyriens*, Paris: Réunion des Musées Nationaux.

Bessborough, the Earl of (ed.) (1950). *Lady Charlotte Guest. Extracts from her Journal 1833–1852*. London: John Murray.

Beyer, D. (1994). 'Les premières étapes de la découverte à Khorsabad.' In E. Fontan (ed.), *De Khorsabad à Paris. La découverte des Assyriens*: 46–59. Paris: Réunion des Musées Nationaux.

Blackie, J.S. (1866). *Homer and the 'Iliad'*, 7 vols. Edinburgh: Edmonston and Douglas.

Blake, R. (1982). *Disraeli's Grand Tour. Benjamin Disraeli and the Holy Land 1830–31*. New York: Oxford University Press.

Bohrer, F.N. (1989). 'Assyria as Art: A Perspective on the Early Reception of Ancient Near Eastern Artefacts.' *Culture & History*, 4: 7–33.

—— (1992). 'The Printed Orient: The Production of A.H. Layard's Earliest Works.' *Culture & History*, 11: 85–106.

Bonomi, J. (1852). *Nineveh and its Palaces. The discoveries of Botta and Layard, applied to the elucidation of Holy Writ*. London: Illustrated London Library.

Borger, R. (1975–8a). 'Dokumente zur Entzifferung der altpersischen Keilschrift durch H.C. Rawlinson.' *Persica*, 7: 1–5.

—— (1975–8b). 'Die Entzifferungsgeschichte der altpersischen Keilschrift nach Grotefend's ersten Erfolgen.' *Persica*, 7: 7–19.

Botta, P.-E. (1829). *De l'usage de fumer l'opium*. Docteur en médecine, Paris.

—— (1841). *Relation d'un voyage dans l'Yémen, entrepris en 1837 pour le Museum d'Histoire Naturelle de Paris*. Paris: Benjamin Duprat.

—— (1849). *Monument de Ninive découvert et décrit par M. P.E. Botta, mesuré et dessiné par M. E. Flandin. Ouvrage publié par ordre du gouvernement sous les auspices de M. le Ministre de l'Intérieur et sous la direction d'une commission de l'Institut*. Paris: Imprimerie nationale.

—— (1850). *M. Botta's Letters on the Discoveries at Nineveh. Translated from the French, by C.T.* London: Longman, Brown, Green, and Longmans.

—— (1952). *Observations on the Inhabitants of California, 1827–1828* (trans. John Francis Bricca). Los Angeles: Glen Dawson.

Brackman, A.C. (1980). *The Luck of Nineveh*. London: Methuen.

Brown, I.V. (1960). 'The Higher Criticism Comes to America, 1880–1900.' *Journal of the Presbyterian Historical Society*, 38 (no.4): 193–212.

Budge, E.A.W. (1925). *The Rise and Progress of Assyriology*. London: Martin Hopkinson & Co.

—— (1934). 'Review of Davidson 1933'. *Journal of the Royal Asiatic Society, 1934*: 597–9.

Burstein, S.M. (1978). 'The *babyloniaca* of berossus.' *Sources and Monographs on the Ancient Near East* vol. 1, fascicle 5. Malibu: Undena Publication.

Cathcart, K.J. (1994). 'Edward Hincks (1792–1866). A Biographical Essay.' In K.J. Cathcart (ed.), *The Edward Hincks Bicentenary Lectures*: 1–29. Dublin: University College Press.

—— and Donlon, P. (1983). 'Edward Hincks (1792–1866): A Bibliography of his Publications.' *Orientalia*, 52: 325–56.

Chadwick, O. (1966). *The Victorian Church. An Ecclesiastical History of England* vol. vii, part 1. London: Adam & Charles Black.

Chesney, L.-C. (1850). *The Expedition for the Survey of the Rivers Euphrates and Tigris, carried on by order of the British Government, in the years 1835, 1836, and 1837; preceded by geographical and historical notices of the regions situated between the rivers Nile and Indus*. (vols 1–4). London: Longman, Brown, Green, and Longmans.

Cooper, J.S. (1992). 'From Mosul to Manila: Early Approaches to Funding Ancient Near Eastern Studies Research in the United States.' *Culture & History*, 11: 133–164.

Curtis, J. (1976). 'Parthian gold from Nineveh.' *The British Museum Yearbook*, 1: 47–66.

—— (1988). 'Assyria as a Bronzeworking Centre in the Late Assyrian Period.' In J. Curtis (ed.), *Bronzeworking Centres of Western Asia c. 1000–539 B.C.*: 83–96. London: Kegan Paul.

Curtis, J.E. and Reade, J.E. (eds) (1995). *Art and Empire. Treasures from Assyria in the British Museum*. New York: The Metropolitan Museum of Art.

Daniels, P.T. (1994). 'Edward Hincks's Decipherment of Mesopotamian Cuneiform.' In K.J. Cathcart (ed.), *The Edward Hincks Bicentenary Lectures*: 30–57. Dublin: University College Press.

Davidson, E.F. (1933). *Edward Hincks. A Selection from his Correspondence with A Memoir*. London: Oxford University Press.

Desmond, A. and Moore, J. (1992). *Darwin*. London: Penguin.

Dickens, Charles (1882). *Letters*. London: Chapman and Hall.

Diodorus (1968). *Library of History* (trans. C.H. Oldfather). London: Heinemann.

Disraeli, B. (1832). *Contarini Fleming. A Psychological Auto-Biography*. London: John Murray.

Fallue, L. (1851). *Histoire du Château de Radepont et de l'abbaye de Fontaine-Guérard*. Rouen: Imprimerie de Alfred Péron.

Favaretto, I. (1987). 'La collezione Layard: storia, formazione e vicende.' In F.M. Fales and B.J. Hickey (eds), *Austen Henry Layard. Tra l'oriente e Venezia*, Rome: L'Erma di Bretschneider.

Ferguson, J. (1851). *The Palaces of Nineveh and Persepolis Restored*. London: John Murray.

—— (1845). 'Voyage archéologique à Ninive.' *Revue des Deux Mondes* (15 June): 1081–1106.

Flandin, E. (1853–76). *L'Orient*. Paris.

—— and Coste, P. (1843–54). *Voyage en Perse 1–5*. Paris: Imprimerie impériale.

Flaubert, G. (1910). *Notes de Voyages I*. Oeuvres complètes de Gustave Flaubert, ed. Louis Conard. Paris.

Fletcher, J.P. (1850). *Notes from Nineveh, and Travels in Mesopotamia, Assyria, and Syria*. London: Henry Colburn.

Fontan, E. (1994a). 'Félix Thomas (1815–75), l'architecte providentiel.' In E. Fontan (ed.), *De Khorsabad à Paris. La découverte des Assyriens*: 102–15. Paris: Réunion des Musées Nationaux.

—— (1994b). 'Introduction.' In E. Fontan (ed.), *De Khorsabad à Paris. La découverte des Assyriens*: 16–18. Paris: Réunion des Musées Nationaux.

—— (ed.) (1994c). *De Khorsabad à Paris. La découverte des Assyriens*. Paris: Réunion des Musées Nationaux.

Fresnel, F. (1853). 'Lettre de M. Fresnel à M. Mohl.' *Journal asiatique*, June and July 1853, 484–548; 5–78.

—— (1855). 'Extrait d'une lettre de M. Fresnel, datée de Hillah fin de Juin 1853.' *Journal asiatique*. 525–48.

Gadd, C.J. (1936). *The Stones of Assyria. The surviving remains of Assyrian sculpture their recovery and their original positions*. London: Chatto and Windus.

Ginzburg, C. (1988). 'Morelli, Freud, and Sherlock Holmes: Clues and Scientific Method.' In U. Eco and T.A. Sebeok (eds), *The Sign of Three. Dupin, Holmes, Peirce*: 81–118. Bloomington and Indianapolis: Indiana University Press.

Goldfrank, D.M. (1994). *The Origins of the Crimean War*. London: Longman.

374

Grayson, A.K. (1991). *Assyrian Rulers of the Early First Millennium BC* I *(1114–859 BC).* The Royal Inscriptions of Mesopotamia, Assyrian Periods vol. 2. Toronto: University of Toronto Press.

Grayson, D.K. (1983). *The Establishment of Human Antiquity.* New York: Academic Press.

Hansen, T. (1962). *Det lykkelige Arabien. En dansk ekspedition 1761–67.* Copenhagen: Gyldendal.

Harbottle, S. (1958). 'W.K. Loftus: An Archaeologist from Newcastle.' *Archaeologia Aeliana*: v, 1, 195–217.

Harrison, J.F.C. (1989). *Early Victorian Britain, 1832–51.* London: Fontana Press.

Herodotus (1954). *The Histories* (trans. Aubrey de Sélincourt). Harmondsworth: Penguin.

Herrmann, G. (1986). *Ivories from Room SW 37 Fort Shalmaneser.* London: British School of Archaeology in Iraq.

—— (1992). *The Small Collections from Fort Shalmaneser.* London: British School of Archaeology in Iraq.

Hibbert, C. (1985). *The Destruction of Lord Raglan. A Tragedy of the Crimean War 1854–55.* London: Penguin.

Hincks, E. (1846). 'On the First and Second Kinds of Persepolitan Writing.' *Transactions of the Royal Irish Academy*, xxi (Part i): 1–21.

—— (1847). 'Some passages of the life of king Darius, the son of Hystaspes, by himself.' *The Dublin University Magazine*, 29 (January to June 1847): 14–27.

—— (1850a). 'On the Language and Mode of Writing of the Ancient Assyrians.' *Report of the British Association for the Advancement of the Sciences*, 20: 140.

—— (1850b). 'On the Khorsabad Inscriptions.' *Transactions of the Royal Irish Academy*, xxii (Part ii): 1–72.

—— (1852). 'On the Assyrio-Babylonian Phonetic Characters.' *Transactions of the Royal Irish Academy*, xxii: 291–370.

—— (1854). *Report to the Trustees of the British Museum respecting certain cylinders and terra-cotta tablets, with cuneiform inscriptions.* London: British Museum.

Hobsbawm, E.J. (1988). *The Age of Revolution. Europe 1789–1848.* London: Cardinal.

—— (1989). *The Age of Capital 1848–1875.* London: Cardinal.

Hoffmann, C. (1988). *Juden und Judentum im Werk deutscher Althistoriker des 19. und 20. Jahrhunderts. Studies in Judaism in Modern Times.* Leiden: E.J. Brill.

Holthof, L. (ed.) (1899). *Heinrich Heines Sämtliche Werke.* Stuttgart und Leipzig: Deutsche Verlags-Anstalt.

Hopkirk, P. (1994). *The Great Game. The Struggle for Empire in Central Asia.* New York: Kodansha International.

Howard, M. (1961). *The Franco-Prussian War. The German Invasion of France, 1870–1871.* London: Rupert Hart-Davis.

Hunt, A.W. (1851). *Nineveh. A Prize Poem Recited in the Theatre, Oxford, July III. MDCCCLI.* Oxford: Macpherson.

Jenkins, I. (1992). *Archaeologists and Aesthetes.* London: British Museum Press.

Jensen, J. (1992). *Thomsens Museum. Historien om Nationalmuseet.* Copenhagen: Gyldendal.

Johnson, E. (1986). *Charles Dickens. His Tragedy and Triumph.* London: Penguin.

Kemp, W. (1990). *The Desire of My Eyes. The Life and Work of John Ruskin* (trans. Jan van Heurck). New York: The Noonday Press.

Landor, W. S. (1876). *Miscellaneous Poems.* London: Chapman and Hall.

Lane-Poole, S. (1888). *The Life of the Right Honourable Stratford Canning Viscount Stratford de Redcliffe.* London: Longmans, Green, and Co.

Layard, A.H. (1845). 'Discoveries at Nineveh.' *The Malta Times,* 21 January 1845: 2.

—— (1846). 'A Description of the Province of Khuzistan, Political conditions and divisions.' *Journal of the Royal Geographical Society:* xvi.

—— (1849). *Nineveh and its Remains: with an account of a visit to the Chaldæan Christians of Kurdistan, and the Yezidis, or devil-worshippers; and an enquiry into the manners and arts of the ancient Assyrians.* London: John Murray.

—— (1849–53). *The Monuments of Nineveh.* (vol. 1–2). London: John Murray.

—— (1851). *Inscriptions in the cuneiform character from Assyrian monuments.* London: Harrison and son.

—— (1852). *A Popular Account of Discoveries at Nineveh.* London: John Murray.

—— (1853). *Discoveries in the Ruins of Nineveh and Babylon; with travels in Armenia, Kurdistan and the desert: being the result of a second expedition undertaken for the Trustees of the British Museum.* London: John Murray.

—— (1855–8). 'Inaugural address of Austen Henry Layard, Esq., M.P. on his installation as Lord Rector of the Marischal College and University of Aberdeen. Thursday, 5th April, 1855,' *British Eloquence of the nineteenth century. Literary Addresses, delivered at various popular institutions,* third series. London and Glasgow: Richard Griffin and Company.

—— (1894). *Early Adventures in Persia, Susiana, and Babylonia. Including a residence among the Bakhtiyari and other wild tribes before the discovery of Nineveh.* London: John Murray.

—— (1903). *Autobiography and Letters from his childhood until his appointment as H.M. Ambassador at Madrid* (edited by the Hon. William N. Bruce, with a chapter on his parliamentary career by the Rt. Hon. Sir Arthur Otway ed.). London: John Murray.

Lee, J. (1976). *Dictionary of National Biography.* London.

Lloyd, S. (1955). *Foundations in the Dust. A Story of Mesopotamian Exploration.* Harmondsworth: Penguin.

Loftus, W.K. (1857). *Travels and Researches in Chaldea and Susiana.* London: James Nisbet and Co.

Longpérier, A.D. (1849). *Notice des monuments exposés dans la galerie d'antiquités assyriennes au Musée du Louvre.* Paris.

Loud, G. (1936) *Khorsabad I. Excavations in the Palace and at a City Gate.* vol. 38. Oriental Institute Publications, Chicago: Chicago University Press.

—— and C.B. Altman (1938). *Khorsabad II: The Citadel and the Town.* vol. 40. Oriental Institute Publications, Chicago: Chicago University Press.

Löwenstern, I. (1845). *Essai de déchiffrement de l'écriture assyrienne.* Paris.

—— (1847). *Exposé des éléments constitutifs du système de la troisième écriture cunéiforme de Persepolis.* Paris.

Madhloom, T. (1967). 'Excavations at Nineveh, 1965–67.' *Sumer,* 23: 76–9.

—— (1968). 'Nineveh, 1967–68 Campaign.' *Sumer,* 24: 45–51.

—— (1969). 'Nineveh, 1968–69 Campaign.' *Sumer,* 25: 44–9.

Mahmoud, A. and Kühne, H. (1993–94). 'Tall 'Agaga/Sadikanni. 1984–1990.' *Archiv für Orientforschung,* xl–xli: 215–20.

Mallowan, M. (1966). *Nimrud and Its Remains*. London: Collins.

—— and Davies, L.G. (1970). *Ivories in the Assyrian Style*. London: British School of Archaeology in Iraq.

—— and Herrmann, G. (1974). *Furniture from SW 7 Fort Shalmaneser*. London: British School of Archaeology in Iraq.

Markham, C.R. (1869). *A History of the Abyssinian Expedition. With a chapter containing an account of the mission and captivity of Mr Rassam and his companions, by Lieutenant W.F. Prideaux*. London: Macmillan.

McGovern, F.H. and McGovern, J.N. (1986). 'Paul Émile Botta.' *Biblical Archaeologist* (June 1986): 109–13.

Mitford, E.L. (1845). *An Appeal in Behalf of the Jewish Nation in Connection with British Policy in the Levant*. London: J. Hatchard and Son.

—— (1884). *A Land March from England to Ceylon Forty Years Ago*. London: W.H. Allen and Co.

Mohl, J. (1879). *Vingt-sept ans d'histoire des études orientales*. Paris.

—— (ed.) (1845). *Lettres de M. Botta sur ses découvertes a Khorsabad, près de Ninive*. Paris: Imprimerie royale.

Momigliano, A. (1975). *Alien Wisdom. The Limits of Hellenization*. Cambridge: Cambridge University Press.

Moorehead, A. (1983). *The Blue Nile*. London: Penguin.

Morelli, G. (1892). *Italian Painters* (trans. C.J. Ffoulkes). London: John Murray.

Morgan, K.O. (1984). *The Oxford Illustrated History of Britain, 1789–1983*. Oxford: Oxford University Press.

Münter, F. (1802). *Versuch über die keilförmigen Inschriften zu Persepolis*. Copenhagen.

Newman, J.P. (1876). *The Thrones and Palaces of Babylon and Nineveh*. New York: Harper and Bros.

Niebuhr, C. (1774–78). *Reisebeschreibung nach Arabien und den umliegenden Ländern*.

Njegosh, P. P. (1963). *Der Bergkranz*. Munich and Belgrade.

Nunn, A. (1988). *Die Wandmalerei und der glasierte Wandschmuck im alten Orient*. Handbuch der Orientalistik vol. 7.1.2.B.6. Leiden: E.J. Brill.

Oates, D. (1959). 'Fort Shalmaneser – an Interim Report.' *Iraq*, xxi: 98–129.

Olender, M. (1992). *The Languages of Paradise. Race, Religion, and Philology in the Nineteenth Century* (trans. Arthur Goldhammer). Cambridge, Mass.: Harvard University Press.

Oppert, J. (1859–63). *Expédition scientifique en Mésopotamie*. 2 vols, Paris: Imprimerie impériale.

Orchard, J.J. (1967). *Equestrian Bridle-Harness Ornaments*. Ivories from Nimrud vol. I: 2. London: British School of Archaeology in Iraq.

Pallis, S.A. (1956). *The Antiquity of Iraq. A Handbook of Assyriology*. Copenhagen: Ejnar Munksgaard.

Parpola, S. (1986). 'The Royal Archives of Nineveh.' In K.R. Veenhof (ed.), *Cuneiform Archives and Libraries*: 223–36. Leiden: Nederlands Historisch-Archaeologisch Instituut te Istanbul.

Pillet, M. (1918). *Khorsabad. Les découvertes de V. Place*. Paris: Ernest Leroux.

—— (1922). *L'expédition scientifique et artistique de Mésopotamie et de Médie 1851–1855*. Paris: Librairie Champion.

—— (1962). *Un pionnier de l'assyriologie. Victor Place.* Cahiers de la Société asiatique vol. xvi. Paris: Imprimerie nationale.

Place, V. (1867). *Ninive et l'Assyrie.* Paris: Imprimerie nationale.

Postgate, J.N. and Reade, J.E. (1976–80). 'Kalhu.' In D.O. Edzard (ed.), *Reallexikon der Assyriologie und Vorderasiatische Archäologie*: vol. 5, 303–23. Berlin: Walter de Gruyter.

Rasmussen, S.T. (1990). *Den Arabiske Rejse 1761–1767. En dansk ekspedition set i videnskabshistorisk perspektiv.* Copenhagen: Munksgaard.

Rassam, H. (1897). *Asshur and the Land of Nimrod, being an Account of the Discoveries Made in the Ancient Ruins of Nineveh, Asshur, Sepharvaim, Calah, Babylon, Borsippa, Cuthah, and Van, Including a Narrative of Different Journeys in Mesopotamia, Assyria, Asia Minor, and Koordistan.* New York: Eaton and Mains.

Rawlinson, G. (1898). *A Memoir of Major-General Sir Henry Creswicke Rawlinson.* London: Longmans, Green, and Co.

Rawlinson, H.C. (1839). 'Notes on a march from Zoháb, at the foot of Zagros, along the mountains to Khúzistán (Susiana), and from thence through the province of Luristan to Kermansháh, in the year 1836.' *Journal of the Royal Geographical Society*, ix: 26–116.

—— (1846–51). 'The Persian Cuneiform Inscription at Behistun, Deciphered and Translated; with a Memoir.' *Journal of the Royal Asiatic Society*, x, parts i–iii, xi, part i.

—— (1850a). *A Commentary on the Cuneiform Inscriptions of Babylonia and Assyria; including readings of the Inscription on the Nimrud Obelisk, and a brief notice of the ancient kings of Nineveh and Babylon.* London: John W. Parker.

—— (1850b). 'On the Inscriptions of Assyria and Babylonia.' *Journal of the Royal Asiatic Society*, xii: 401–83.

—— (1851). 'Memoir on the Babylonian and Assyrian Inscriptions.' *Journal of the Royal Asiatic Society*, XIV. Part I.

—— (1854). *Notes on the Early History of Babylonia.* London: John W. Parker & Son.

—— (1855). *Memorandum on the Publication of the Cuneiform Inscriptions.* London.

Reade, J.E. (1979a). 'Assyrian Architectural Decoration: Techniques and Subject-Matter.' *Baghdader Mitteilungen*, 10: 17–49.

—— (1979b). 'Narrative Composition in Assyrian Sculpture.' *Baghdader Mitteilungen*, 10, 52–110.

—— (1980). 'The Architectural Context of Assyrian Sculpture.' *Baghdader Mitteilungen*, 11: 75–87.

—— (1980). 'Space, Scale, and Significance in Assyrian Art.' *Baghdader Mitteilungen*, 11: 71–4.

—— (1983). *Assyrian Sculpture.* London: British Museum Press.

—— (1986a). 'Archaeology and the Kuyunjik Archives.' In K. R. Veenhof (ed.), *Cuneiform Archives and Libraries*: 213–22. Leiden: Nederlands Historisch-Archaeologisch Instituut te Istanbul.

—— (1986b). 'Introduction. Rassam's Babylonian Collection: The Excavations and the Archives.' In E. Leichty (ed.), *Catalogue of the Babylonian Tablets in the British Museum,*(vol. vi: Tablets from Sippar 1: xiii–xxxvi). London: British Museum Publications.

—— (1993) 'Hormuzd Rassam and his Discoveries.' *Iraq* lv: 39–62.

Rich, C.J. (1813). 'Memoir on the Ruins of Babylon.' *Fundgruben des Orients*, iii: 129–62, 197–200.

—— (1818). *Second Memoir on Babylon.* London.

—— (1836). *Narrative of a Residence in Koordistan, and on the Site of Ancient Nineveh* (edited by his widow). London: James Duncan.

Ross, J. (ed.) (1902). *Letters from the East by Henry James Ross, 1837–1857*. London: J.M. Dent & Co.

Rossetti, D.G. (1974). *Poems* (O. Doughty, ed.). London & New York: Everyman's Library.

Rufus, Q.C. (1984). *The History of Alexander* (trans. John Yardley). London: Penguin.

Russell, J.M. (1991). *Sennacherib's Palace without Rival at Nineveh*. Chicago: Chicago University Press.

Saggs, H.W.F. (ed.). (1970). *Nineveh and its Remains, by Henry Austen Layard, edited with an Introduction and Notes*. London: Routledge & Kegan Paul.

Schlözer, A.L.V. (1781). 'Von den Chaldäern.' *Repertorium für biblische und morgenländische Litteratur*: 8.

Schnapp, A. (1993). *La conquête du passé. Aux origines de l'archéologie*. Paris: Éditions Carré.

Searight, S. (1979). *The British in the Middle East* (revised edn). London: East-West Publications.

Seignobos, C. (1921). 'La révolution de 1848 – Le second Empire (1848–1859).' In E. Lavisse (ed.), *Histoire de France Contemporaine* (vol. 6). Paris: Librairie Hachette.

Sievernich, G. and Budde, H. (eds) (1989). *Europa und der Orient: 800–1900*. Berlin: Bertelsmann Lexikon Verlag.

Simpson, M.C.M. (1887). *Letters and Recollections of Julius and Mary Mohl*. London: Kegan Paul, Trench & Co.

Slatter, E. (1994). *Xanthus. Travels of Discovery in Turkey*. London: The Rubicon Press.

Spadijer, M. (1980). *Crna Gora*. Belgrade.

Stearns, J.B. (1961). *Reliefs from the Palace of Ashurnasirpal II*. Archiv für Orientforschung, Beiheft 15. Graz.

Stern, H.A. (1854). *Dawnings of Light in the East; with biblical, historical, and statistical notices of persons and places visited during a mission to the Jews, in Persia, Coordistan, and Mesopotamia*. London: Charles H. Purday.

Stolper, M.W. (1992). 'On Why and How.' *Culture & History*, 11: 13–22.

Strindberg, A. (1907–1912). *En blå bok*. Stockholm.

Thompson, R.C. and Hutchinson, R.W. (1929). *A Century of Exploration at Nineveh*. London: Luzac & Co.

Thomson, D. (1978). *England in the Nineteenth Century (1815–1914)*. The Pelican History of England, vol. 8. Harmondsworth: Pelican Books.

Trigger, B.G. (1989). *A History of Archaeological Thought*. Cambridge: Cambridge University Press.

Turner, F.M. (1981). *The Greek Heritage in Victorian Britain*. New Haven and London: Yale University Press.

Ussher, J. (1865). *A Journey from London to Persepolis; including wanderings in Daghestan, Georgia, Armenia, Kurdistan, Mesopotamia, and Persia*. London: Hurst and Blackett.

Ussishkin, D. (1982). *The Conquest of Lachish by Sennacherib*. Tel Aviv: Tel Aviv University Press.

Vaux, W.S.W. (1855). *Nineveh and Persepolis: An Historical Sketch of Ancient Assyria and Persia, with an Account of the Recent Researches in those Countries* (4th edn). London: Arthur Hall, Virtue & Co.

Volney, C.-F. (1822). *Les ruines, ou méditations sur les révolutions des empires* (10th edn). Paris: Bossange frères.

Ward, T.H. (1884). *Humphry Sandwith: A Memoir*. London: Cassell & Company.

Waterfield, G. (1963). *Layard of Nineveh*. London: John Murray.

Wescher, P. (1976). *Kunstraub unter Napoleon*. Berlin: Gebr. Mann.

Wilson, H.B. (1860). 'Séances Historiques de Genève. The National Church,' *Essays and Reviews*. London: John W. Parker.

Winter, I.J. (1981). 'Royal Rhetoric and the Development of Historical Narrative in Neo-Assyrian Reliefs.' *Studies in Visual Communication*, 7(2): 2–38.

—— (1983). 'The Program of the Throneroom of Assurnasirpal II.' In P.O. Harper and H. Pittman (eds), *Essays on Near Eastern Art and Archaeology in Honor of Charles Kyrle Wilkinson*. New York: The Metropolitan Museum of Art.

Wolf, F.A. (1795). *Prolegomena ad Homerum*. Halle.

Xenophon (1979). *The Persian Expedition* (trans. Rex Warner). Harmondsworth: Penguin.

INDEX

———— •◆• ————

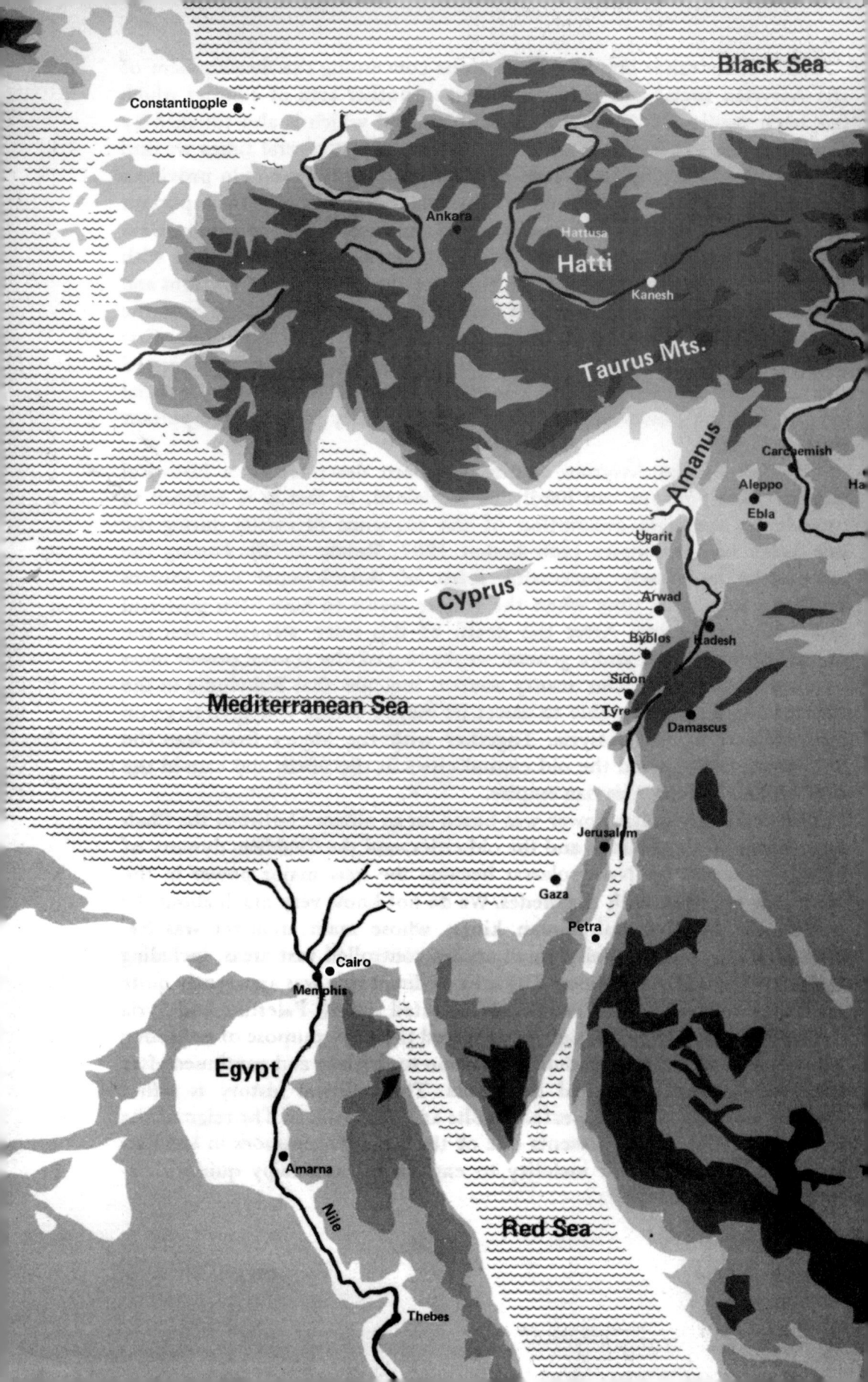